Budapest

"All you've got to do is decide to go
and the hardest part is over.

So go!"

TONY WHEELER, COFOUNDER – LONELY PLANET

THIS EDITION WRITTEN AND RESEARCHED BY

Steve Fallon,
Sally Schafer

Contents

(left) **Basilica of St Stephen p97** Hungary's most-important Catholic church.

....

(above) **City Park p145** Pest's green lung.

....

(right) **Széchenyi Baths p148** Hottest water in the city.

....

Welcome to Budapest

Straddling the Danube River, with the Buda Hills to the west and the Great Plain to the east, Budapest is a gem of a city.

The Human Touch

Budapest's beauty is not all God given; humankind has played a role in shaping this pretty face too. Architecturally, the city is a treasure trove, with enough baroque, neoclassical, Eclectic and Art Nouveau (or Secessionist) buildings to satisfy everyone. Overall, though, Budapest has a fin-de-siècle feel to it, for it was during the capital's 'golden age' in the late 19th century that most of what you see today was built.

The Past at Hand

They say the past is another country, but it's always been just around the corner in Budapest. Witness the bullet holes and shrapnel pockmarks on buildings from WWII and the 1956 Uprising. There are sad reminders like the poignant *Shoes on the Danube* memorial, but ones, too, of hope and reconciliation – like the 'sword' of the former secret-police building on Andrássy út now beaten into the 'ploughshare' that is the House of Terror, with both sides of the story told. And there's joy as much-loved concert halls and theatres are built and renovated, metro lines extended and busy streets repaved and pedestrianised.

Eat, Drink & Be Magyar

There's a lot more to Hungarian food than goulash, and it remains one of the most sophisticated styles of cooking in Europe. Magyars may exaggerate when they say that there are three essential world cuisines: French, Chinese and their own. But Budapest's reputation as a food capital dates largely from the late 19th and the first half of the 20th century and, despite a fallow period under communism, the city is once again commanding attention. So, too, are its excellent wines – from Villány's big-bodied reds and Somló's flinty whites to honey-gold sweet Tokaj.

In the Soak

The city is blessed with an abundance of hot springs. As a result, 'taking the waters' has been a Budapest experience since the time of the Romans. The choice of bathhouses is generous – you can choose among Turkish-era, Art Nouveau and modern establishments. Some people come seeking a cure for whatever ails them, but the majority are there for fun and relaxation – though we still maintain it's the world's best cure for what Hungarians call a *macskajaj* (cat's wail): a hangover.

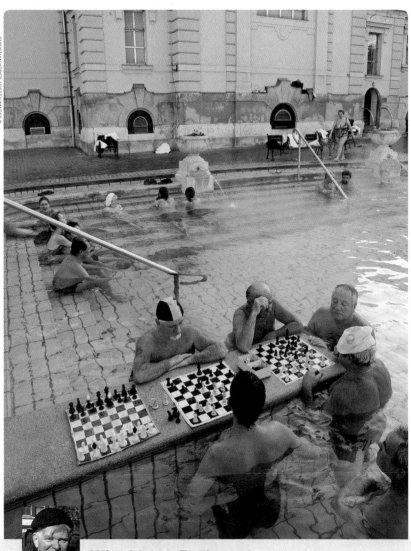

Why I Love Budapest

By Steve Fallon, Author

I love Budapest for all the right reasons – architecture (especially Art Nouveau), romance (particularly the views from the bridges) and sticky apricot jam – and some of the wrong ones, too – killer *pálinka* (fruit brandy), rickety trolleybuses and checking out bodies in the Turkish baths. When I first came to Budapest, I was bowled over by an often sad but confident city whose history seemed too complex to comprehend, by a beautiful but impenetrable language, and by a people I thought I'd never know. I stayed on to learn more about all three.

For more about our authors, see p256.

Top: Széchenyi Baths (p148)

Budapest's
Top 10

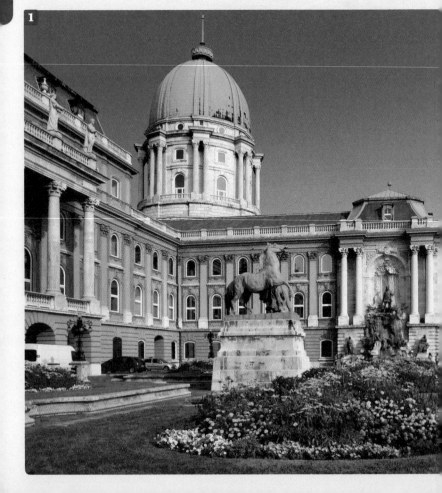

Royal Palace (p52)

1 Bombed and rebuilt at least half a dozen times since King Béla IV established a royal residence here in the mid-13th century, the Royal Palace has been home to kings and queens, occupiers like the Turks in the 16th and 17th centuries, and nondomiciled rulers like the Habsburg royalty. Today the Royal Palace contains two important museums, the national library and an abundance of statues and monuments. It is the focal point of Buda's Castle Hill and the city's most visited sight.

👁 *Castle District*

Thermal Baths & Spas (p29)

2 Budapest sits on a crazy quilt of almost 125 thermal springs, and 'taking the waters' is very much a part of everyday life here. Some baths date from Turkish times, others are Art Nouveau marvels and still others are spick-and-span modern establishments that boast all the mod cons. Which one you choose is a matter of taste and what exactly you're looking for – be it fun, a hangover cure or relief for something more serious. BELOW: GELLÉRT BATHS (P66)

🏃 *Thermal Baths & Spas*

JEAN-PIERRE LESCOURRET / GETTY IMAGES ©

The Danube & its Bridges (p110)

3 Budapest's dustless highway is ever present, neatly dividing the city into Buda and Pest and still serving as an important means of transport. The Danube bridges (all eight of them, not counting train bridges), at once landmarks and delightful vantage points over the river, are the stitches that have bound Buda and Pest together since well before the two were linked politically in 1873. The four bridges in the centre stand head and shoulders above the rest: Margaret Bridge, Széchenyi Chain Bridge, Elizabeth Bridge and Liberty Bridge.

⊙ *Margaret Island & Northern Pest, Castle District, Gellért Hill & Tabán*

Ruin Pubs & Garden Clubs (p37)

4 A visit to Budapest during the long, hot summer is not complete without an evening in one of the city's many so-called *kertek*, literally 'gardens' but in Budapest any outdoor spot that has been converted into an entertainment zone. These rough-and-ready venues, including courtyards, rooftops and *romkocsmák* ('pubs in a ruin') that rise phoenix-like from abandoned buildings, can change from year to year and are seasonal, but some of the more successful ones are now permanent and open year-round. LEFT: SZIMPLA KERT (P125)

🍷 *Drinking & Nightlife*

Parliament (p95)

5 If the Royal Palace atop Castle Hill is the focal point on the Buda side, Parliament is the centrepiece along the Danube in Pest. Stretching for some 268m along the river and counting a superlative number of rooms (690), courtyards (10) and gates (27), it is Hungary's largest building. Parliament is the seat of the unicameral National Assembly, but parts of it, including the awesome Domed Hall, which contains the iconic Crown of St Stephen, can be visited by guided tour.

⊙ *Parliament & Around*

Andrássy út & Heroes' Square (p120)

6 Andrássy út, an uber-elegant leafy boulevard stretching 2.5km, links Deák Ferenc tér to the south with City Park in the north and contains so much to see, do and enjoy that it has been given a place on Unesco's World Heritage list. Along the way are museums, cafes and architectural marvels, but perhaps its most important sight comes at the end. Heroes' Sq, the entrance to the park, is the nation's monument to its earliest ancestors and a memorial to its war dead. BELOW: HEROES' SQUARE (P149)

◉ *Erzsébetváros & the Jewish Quarter, City Park & Beyond*

Basilica of St Stephen (p97)

7 Budapest's largest and most important Christian house of worship is a gem of neoclassical architecture that took more than half a century to complete (largely due to the setback when its dome came crashing down in a storm). The dome can now be scaled, and there is a rich treasury of ecclesiastical objects. But the main reason for coming is to view (and perhaps venerate) Hungary's most sacred object: the holy right hand of its first king, St Stephen.

◉ *Parliament & Around*

8

Great Synagogue

(p117)

8 The largest Jewish temple in Europe, the Moorish-style Great Synagogue is one of Budapest's most eye-catching buildings. Built in 1859 for 3000 conservative faithful, the copper-domed structure is next to the Hungarian Jewish Museum and the haunting Holocaust Memorial Room. In the courtyard stands the Holocaust Memorial, a 'tree of life' designed by sculptor Imre Varga – its leaves bear the family names of many of the victims.

⊙ *Erzsébetváros & the Jewish Quarter*

Memento Park (p70)

9 Containing statues and other memorials from the Communist period, Memento Park can only be described as a cemetery of socialist mistakes, or a well-manicured trash heap of history. In southern Buda, it's home to about four dozen statues, busts and plaques of Lenin, Marx and home-grown henchman Béla Kun. Ogle the socialist-realist 'art' and try to imagine that some of the monstrosities were still being erected in the late 1980s and were in place until the early 1990s.

◉ *Gellért Hill & Tabán*

Buda Hills (p72)

10 They may be short on sights – though Béla Bartók's house, where he spent his final year in Hungary, is open to the public – but the Buda Hills are a very welcome respite from the hot, dusty city in the warmer months. Perhaps their biggest draws are their unusual forms of transport: a narrow-gauge cog railway dating from the late 19th century will get you up into the hills, a train run by children takes you across them and a chairlift will glide you back down to terra firma. ABOVE: BÉLA BARTÓK MEMORIAL HOUSE (P76)

◉ *Óbuda & Buda Hills*

What's New

M4 Metro Line Opens

We didn't think we'd live to see the day, but – sound the trumpets – the first section of Budapest's long-awaited M4 metro line linking Keleti train station in Pest with Kelenföld station in Buda has opened. And it's a cracker. First promised in 1998 with an opening date of 2003, the new line covers 7.5km and counts 10 stations (two of them transfers to lines M2 and M3). (p205)

Regulated Taxis

After decades of passengers' blood, sweat and/or tears, Budapest taxis are now fully regulated, with uniform flag fall (450Ft) and per-kilometre charges (280Ft). It's about time. (p206)

Liszt Academy

Liszt Academy (p118), the nation's foremost classical-music venue, an Art Nouveau jewel built in 1907, has emerged from a two-year, €45-million renovation shinier and prettier than ever before. So too the 1865 Pesti Vigadó (p84), almost as grand but acoustically challenged.

Bicycles for All

Following in the footsteps of Paris, London and, er, İzmir, Budapest has launched its own public bicycle-sharing scheme. Phase one of Bubi Bikes involves 1000 bicycles available from 75 docking station across the city. (p204)

Escape Games

Puzzle fans will adore the city's latest craze, where small groups lock themselves in themed spaces with just an hour to riddle their way to freedom.

Rácz Baths

Cross your fingers and hope to soak... By the time you read this the wonderful Turkish-era Rácz Baths may be open and operational after a very long spell closed. (p30)

Ferencváros Torna Club

Love 'em or hate 'em, the Fradi boys in green have taken ownership of a new purpose-built 23,000-seat stadium, Flórián Albert Stadium, a stone's throw from their former home. (p143)

Crazy Paving

Is there a street in Budapest not being dug up and pedestrianised these days? Do all the paving stones come in job lots? Some are looking pretty good, though (eg V Kossuth Lajos tér).

Up in Smoke

So what's with the profusion of porn shops with opaque windows and the number 18 circled in red? Nope, they're Nemzeti Dohány Boltek (National Tobacco Shops), part of the new (and controversial) state monopoly on tobacco sales from mid-2013.

Castle Bazaar

Once a pleasure park with shops that were later used as art studios, the so-called Castle Bazaar (Várbazár) and the royal gardens on the Danube bank side of Buda Castle have been rebuilt after decades of neglect. (p65)

For more recommendations and reviews, see **lonelyplanet. com/budapest**

Need to Know

For more information, see Survival Guide (p201)

Currency
Forint (Ft); some hotels quote in euros (€)

Language
Hungarian

Visas
Citizens of all European countries as well as Australia, Canada, Israel, Japan, New Zealand and the USA do not require visas for stays of up to 90 days.

Money
ATMs are everywhere, including the airport and train and bus stations. Visa, MasterCard and American Express widely accepted.

Mobile Phones
Most North American phones don't work here. Consider buying a rechargeable SIM chip to cut the cost of making local calls.

Time
Central European Time (GMT/UTC plus one hour)

Tourist Information
Budapest Info (Map p230; V Sütő utca 2; ⊘8am-8pm; ⓂM1/2/3 Deák Ferenc tér) is the main tourist office; there are smaller branches across the city.

Daily Costs
Budget:
Less than 15,000Ft
➡ Dorm bed: 2800–6000Ft
➡ Meal at self-service restaurant: 1500Ft
➡ Three-day transport pass: 4150Ft

Midrange:
15,000–30,000Ft
➡ Single/double private room: from 7000/9500Ft
➡ Two-course meal with drink: 3500–7500Ft
➡ Cocktail: from 1300Ft

Top End:
More than 30,000Ft
➡ Dinner for two with wine at good restaurant: from 12,500Ft
➡ Two-/three-course set lunch at gourmet restaurant: from 2500/3500Ft
➡ All-inclusive ticket at a spa: adult/child 5300/3100Ft
➡ Cover charge at a popular club: 2000–3500Ft

Advance Planning
Two months before Book your accommodation if you will be travelling in the high season and want to stay somewhere special. Take a look at the 'what's on' and English-language media websites.

One month before Reserve seats for a big-ticket concert, musical or dance performance. Book top-end restaurants now.

One week before Make sure your bookings are in order and you have all booking references.

Useful Websites
➡ **Budapest Sun Online** (www.budapestsun.com) Popular English-language site, with local news, interviews and features; now powered by Xpat Loop.

➡ **Caboodle** (www.caboodle. hu) Still Hungary's best English-language portal, with daily news, features, events and irreverent comment.

➡ **Budapest Info** (www. budapestinfo.hu) One of the better overall tourist websites.

➡ **We Love Budapest** (www. welovebudapest.com) Latest info on openings and places to eat, shop, drink and dance.

➡ **Lonely Planet** (www. lonelyplanet.com/budapest) Destination information, hotel bookings, traveller forum and more.

WHEN TO GO

Spring is glorious in
Budapest. Summer
is festival season.
Autumn is beautiful,
particularly in the
Buda Hills. In winter,
some attractions
curtail their hours.

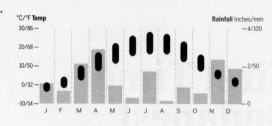

Arriving in Budapest

**Ferenc Liszt International
Airport** Minibuses, buses and
trains to central Budapest run
from 4am to midnight (350Ft
to 3200Ft); taxis cost from
6000Ft.

**Keleti, Nyugati and Déli train
stations** All three are on metro
lines of the same name and
night buses call when the metro
is closed.

**Stadion and Népliget bus sta-
tions** Both are on metro lines
(M2 and M3 respectively) and
are served by trams 1 and 1A.

For much more on
arrival, see p202

Getting Around

Travel passes valid for one
day to one month are valid
on all trams, buses, trolleybuses, HÉV suburban
trains (within city limits)
and metro lines.

➡ **Metro** The quickest but
least scenic way to get around.
Runs 4am to about 11.15pm.

➡ **Bus** Extensive network of
regular buses from around
4.15am to between 9pm and
11.30pm; from 11.30pm to just
after 4am a network of 40 night
buses (three digits beginning
with '9') kicks in.

➡ **Tram** Faster and more
pleasant for sightseeing than
buses; a network of 30 lines.

➡ **Trolleybus** Mostly useful to
and around City Park in Pest.

For much more on
getting around,
see p203

Sleeping

Hostels in Budapest range
from university residences
to very stylish modern af-
fairs; the latter usually offer
single and double rooms.
Private rooms can be good
value but are nowadays
rare; make sure they're centrally located. Hotels range
from very basic former
workers' hostels with shared
bathroom to five-star-plus
luxury accommodation.

Useful Websites

➡ **Discover Budapest** (www.
discoverbudapest.com) Tour
company that also books
accommodation.

➡ **Hungarian Tourism PLC**
(www.gotohungary.com) Top-
heavy with accommodation
choices in the capital.

➡ **Tourinform** (www.
tourinform.rackeve.hu) Wide
range of options.

➡ **Mellow Mood Group** (www.
mellowmood.hu) Chain with a
big variety of options.

➡ **Best Hotel Service** (www.
besthotelservice.hu) Good for
budget accommodation.

➡ **Hip Homes Hungary**
(www.hiphomeshungary.
com) Fabulous short-term
apartments.

For much more on
sleeping, see p163

First Time Budapest

For more information, see Survival Guide (p201)

Checklist

➡ Check the validity of your passport.

➡ Make necessary bookings (for sights, accommodation and/or travel).

➡ Check your airline's baggage restrictions.

➡ Inform your credit/debit card company you're going abroad.

➡ Arrange travel insurance.

➡ Check to see if you can use your mobile (cell) phone.

What to Pack

➡ Phrasebook

➡ Money belt

➡ Mobile-phone charger

➡ Adaptor plug

➡ Small kettle or coil immersion heater for hot drinks

➡ Hat/cap for sun

➡ Swimsuit and towel

➡ Thongs/flip-flops

➡ Umbrella

➡ Padlock

➡ Torch (flashlight)

➡ Pocketknife

➡ Clothespins/pegs

Top Tips for Your Trip

➡ Bring good walking shoes and be prepared to hoof it – this is a city best seen from ground level.

➡ Buy a public-transport travel pass (p204), which will save you both money and time.

➡ Set lunches at fine restaurants cost a fraction of set menus at night; eat by day and snack by night.

What to Wear

In general, Hungarian dress is very casual; many people attend classical-music concerts and even the opera in jeans. Men needn't bother bringing a tie, as it will be seldom – if ever – used. There are no particular items of clothing to re-member, apart from bringing an umbrella in late spring and autumn, and a warm hat (everyone wears them) in winter. A swimsuit for use in the mixed-sex thermal spas and pools is a good idea, as are plastic sandals or thongs (flip-flops). The summer fashions and beachwear are daringly brief, even by Western standards.

Be Forewarned

➡ Do not even think of riding 'black' (without paying a fare) on public transport – you will be caught and severely fined.

➡ Scams involving attractive young women, gullible guys, expensive drinks in nightclubs and a frog-marching to the nearest ATM by gorillas-in-residence have been common in Budapest for almost two decades now. Guys, please, if it seems too good to be true, it is. Trust us.

➡ Avoid at all costs taxis with no company name on the door and only a removable taxi light box on the roof; these are just guys with cars and likely to rip you off.

Money

Credit and debit cards can be used almost everywhere and there is usually no minimum-purchase requirement. Visa and MasterCard are the most popular options; American Express is less frequently accepted. ATMs are everywhere, but be warned that those at branches of OTP, the national savings bank, dispense 20,000Ft notes, which can be hard to break.
For more information, see p209.

Taxes & Refunds

ÁFA, a value-added tax of up to 27%, covers the purchase of all new goods in Hungary. It's usually included in the price quoted, but not always, so check. Non-EU residents can claim refunds for ÁFA paid. For more, see p210.

Tipping

Hungarians are very tip conscious. The way you tip in restaurants here is unusual: you never leave the money on the table – that is considered rude – but instead you tell the waiter how much you're paying in total. If the bill is 3600Ft, you're paying with a 5000Ft note and you think the waiter deserves a gratuity of about 10%, first ask if service is included (some places now add it to the bill automatically). If it is not, tell the waiter you're paying 4000Ft or that you want 1000Ft back.

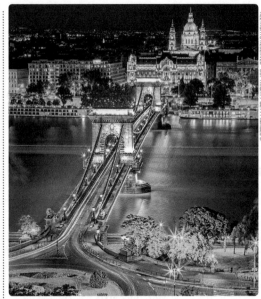

Pest at night, as seen from Buda Hills

Etiquette

Hungarians are usually extremely polite in their social interactions, and the language can be very courtly – even when doing business with the butcher or having one's hair cut.

➡ **Greetings** An older man will often kiss a woman's hand, and young people's standard greeting to their elders is *Csókolom* ('I kiss it' – 'it' being the hand, of course). People of all ages, even close friends, shake hands when meeting up.

➡ **Asking for help** Say *legyen szíves* ('be so kind as') to attract attention; say *bocsánat* ('sorry') to apologise.

➡ **Eating and drinking** If you're invited to someone's home, bring a bunch of flowers or a bottle of good local wine.

➡ **Name days** As much as their birthday, Hungarians celebrate their name day, which is usually the Catholic feast day of their patron saint (all Hungarian calendars list them). Flowers, sweets or a bottle of wine are the usual gifts.

Language

Hungarians like to boast that their language ranks with Japanese and Arabic as among the world's most difficult to master. Hungarian is very difficult to learn well. However, this should not put you off attempting a few phrases.

Though things are changing, the majority of Hungarians tend to speak only Hungarian. Even when they do have a smattering of a foreign language, they might be hesitant to speak it. If you attempt a few words in Hungarian (Magyar), they will be impressed and be extremely encouraging. For more, see p212.

Top Itineraries

Day One

Castle District (p50)

 Spend your first morning in Budapest on Castle Hill, taking in the views from the **Royal Palace** and establishing the lay of the land. There are museums aplenty up here, but don't be greedy: you only have time for one. We recommend either the **Hungarian National Gallery** for fine art or the renovated **Museum Castle** (part of the Budapest History Museum) for a painless introduction to the city's long and tortuous past.

> **Lunch** Have a quick bite at the upbeat self-service Vár Bistro (p58).

Castle District (p50)

In the afternoon ride the **Sikló** (funicular) down to **Clark Ádám tér** and, depending on the day of the week and your sex, make your way up Fő utca to the **Király Baths** for a relaxing soak.

> **Dinner** Superb Csalogány 26 (p61) is around the corner from the baths.

Castle District (p50)

Depending on your mood, check to see what's on in the way of *táncház* (folk music and dance) at the **Marczibányi tér Cultural Centre** just north of Széll Kálmán tér or head for stylish **Oscar American Bar** south of the square for cocktails and canned music.

Day Two

Erzsébetváros & the Jewish Quarter (p115)

 On your second day, cross the Danube and see Pest at its very finest by walking up leafy **Andrássy út**, which will take you past unmissable sights such as the **House of Terror** and **Heroes' Square**, architectural gems like the **Hungarian State Opera House** and **New Theatre**, and wonderful cafes including **Művész Kávéház** and **Alexandra Book Cafe**.

> **Lunch** Menza (p124) has an excellent-value weekday set lunch.

City Park & Beyond (p145)

As you approach City Park, decide whether you want an afternoon of culture or leisure (or both). Heroes' Sq is flanked by the **Museum of Fine Arts** and the **Palace of Art**, both with excellent exhibitions, and City Park contains the **Budapest Zoo**, the **Capital Circus**, the newly renamed **Holnemvolt Park** ('Once Upon a Time' Park) of amusement rides and the wonderful **Széchenyi Baths**.

> **Dinner** Robinson (p151) by the lake is a wonderful choice.

City Park & Beyond (p145)

You might have drinks in the park at **Kertem** or boogie the night (and most of the morning) away at the open-air **Dürer Kert**. But if there happens to be a big-name act in town they'll be at the nearby **László Papp Budapest Sportaréna**.

Hungarian State Opera House (p130)

Torah scrolls, Great Synagogue (p117)

Day Three

Parliament & Around (p93)

 On day three it's time to see a few of Budapest's big-ticket attractions. In the morning concentrate on the two icons of Hungarian nationhood and the places that house them: the Crown of St Stephen in **Parliament** and the saint-king's mortal remains in the **Basilica of St Stephen**. To get from one to the other cut through **Szabadság tér** and have a glance at the last remaining Soviet memorial in the city.

> **Lunch** Kisharang (p99) is an excellent choice for Hungarian soul food.

Erzsébetváros & the Jewish Quarter (p115)

 In the afternoon concentrate on the Jewish Quarter – what people still call the Ghetto here. The easiest way to see the most important sights is to follow the Erzsébetváros and the Jewish Quarter neighbourhood walk, but make sure you leave ample time to have a good look inside the **Great Synagogue** and the **Hungarian Jewish Museum** and have a slice of something sweet at the **Fröhlich Cukrászda** kosher cake shop.

> **Dinner** The Spinoza Café (p123) is a convivial place for an evening meal.

Erzsébetváros & the Jewish Quarter (p115)

There might be *klezmer* (traditional Jewish music) on at the **Spinoza Café**, then move on to the wealth of *kertek* (outdoor 'garden clubs') within easy striking distance along Kazinczy utca: **Kőleves Kert**, **Ellátó Kert**, or the granddaddy of them all, **Szimpla Kert**.

Day Four

Óbuda & Buda Hills (p72)

 On your last day have a look at what the west side of the Danube used to be like by strolling through **Óbuda** and learning how Buda, Óbuda and Pest all came together. Again, the choice of museums and attractions is legion, but the **Vasarely Museum** and its hallucinogenic works never fail to please and the nearby **Hungarian Museum of Trade & Tourism** is a positive delight. Alternatively, **Aquincum** is just a short HÉV ride away.

> **Lunch** The fish soup at Új Sípos Halászkert (p78) goes down a treat.

Óbuda & Buda Hills (p72)

In the afternoon head south for **Margaret Bridge**. Just up the hill to the west is **Gül Baba's Tomb**, the only Muslim place of pilgrimage in northern Europe. Spend the rest of the afternoon pampering yourself at the **Lukács Baths**.

> **Dinner** Fióka (p79) is a fine and intimate eatery just west of Széll Kálmán tér.

Margaret Island & Northern Pest (p108)

 Cross over Margaret Bridge to Margaret Island and **Holdudvar** bar-club, an excellent place to both cool down and kick up your heels. It's open till the wee hours, so there's no hurry.

If You Like...

Classical Music

Liszt Academy The recently renovated interior of Budapest's most important classical-music venue is worth a look even if you're not attending a performance. (p129)

Palace of Arts The two concert halls at this palatial arts centre by the Danube seating 1700 and 450 people both have near-perfect acoustics. (p142)

Matthias Church Some of the best organ recitals can be heard in the city's many churches, including this landmark one atop Castle Hill. (p58)

Franz Liszt Memorial Museum Situated in the Old Music Academy; the great composer lived here until his death in 1886. Weekend concerts too. (p121)

Béla Bartók Memorial House This lovely house in the Buda Hills where Bartók resided until emigrating to the US in 1940 is a temple to the great composer, his life and work. (p76)

Rózsavölgyi és Társa An excellent and very central classical-music shop, with CDs and sheet music. (p92)

Art Nouveau

Royal Postal Savings Bank This extravaganza of floral mosaics, folk motifs and ceramic figures is one of Budapest's best Secessionist buildings. (p98)

Bedő House A stunning Art Nouveau apartment block that contains a museum over three floors dedicated to Hungarian Secessionist applied arts. (p98)

Matthias Church (p58)

Museum of Applied Arts
Purpose-built in 1896, the museum is faced and roofed in Zsolnay ceramic tiles, with 'Mogul-style' turrets, domes and ornamental figures. (p138)

Párisi udvar Under renovation at the time of writing, this splendid arcade (1909) in the Belváros contains many influences, including elements of architect Ödön Lechner's own eclectic style. (p83)

City Park Art Nouveau Buildings Two of the most extravagant Art Nouveau (Secessionist) buildings are near the park: the National Institute for the Blind and Ödön Lechner's Institute of Geology. (p150)

Traditional Coffee Houses

New York Café The city's most extravagant cafe dates from 1894; it has been turned into an opulent hang-out for tourists and the haves of Pest. (p127)

Művész Kávéház Still homey and down-to-earth after all these years (since 1898!), the 'Artist Coffeehouse' is the best cafe in town for people watching. (p129)

Gerbeaud Budapest's most fashionable cafe is also its most expensive, but you get what you pay for: the cakes here are sublime. (p87)

Ruszwurm Cukrászda The city's oldest cafe (1827) and also its tiniest is a positive delight – if you can manage to get inside the door. (p62)

Centrál Kávéház The *grande dame* of traditional cafes, dating back to 1887, has reclaimed her title as the place to sit and look intellectual in Pest. (p87)

Jewish Heritage

Synagogues There are three synagogues in what many still call the Ghetto of Erzsébetváros: the Great Synagogue, the Orthodox Synagogue and the Rumbach Sebestyén Utca Synagogue; visit the first two. (p117 & p118)

Hungarian Jewish Museum Rich collection of Judaica dating back to the 3rd century AD, along with a harrowing exhibit devoted to the Hungarian Holocaust. (p117)

Ghetto Wall A 30m fragment of the original ghetto wall can now be seen at the back of a courtyard at VI Király utca 15. (p119)

Spinoza Café If you want to hear live *klezmer* (traditional Jewish music), this is one of the best places to go. (p123)

Fröhlich Cukrászda This time-warp kosher cake shop and cafe makes and sells old Jewish sweets like *flódni* (three-layer cake with apple, walnut and poppy-seed fillings). (p125)

Folk Culture

Ethnography Museum The sprawling museum opposite Parliament is the best place in Budapest to see and appreciate work by the finest folk artists in Hungary. (p98)

Hungarian Open-Air Ethnographical Museum Many of the objects on view in the Ethnography Museum are in use at this huge outdoor museum in Szentendre, an easy day trip from Budapest. (p156)

Táncház One of the best ways to appreciate living traditions, hear music and see folk dancing is at a traditional 'dance house', held regularly at venues around town.

Holló Atelier Among the finest folk-craft shops in town, Holló makes and sells traditional Hungarian items with a contemporary look. (p90)

XD Design&Souvenir Fantastic new shop showcasing everything from the embroidery of the Matyó people to modern design. (p90)

Communist Heritage

Memento Park Nothing beats this historical trash heap in south Buda for recalling the bad old days. (p70)

Pántlika This time-warp cafe in City Park is housed in a Communist-era kiosk dating back to the 1970s. (p151)

Museum of Military History This sword-rattling place has a facsimile of the electrified fence that once separated Hungary from Austria. (p56)

Bambi Presszó Bambi still has all the hallmarks of the socialist past, including linoleum on the floor and Naugahyde on the seats. (p62)

Kerepesi Cemetery The good and not-so-great buried here include János Kádár; this is also the site of the monumental Workers' Movement Pantheon for party honchos. (p137)

For more top Budapest spots, see the following:
➡ Thermal Baths & Spas (p29)
➡ Eating (p32)
➡ Drinking & Nightlife (p37)
➡ Entertainment (p41)
➡ Shopping (p44)

Month by Month

January

Budapest looks lovely in a winter gown, with bright blue skies, a light dusting of snow on church spires, perhaps ice floes in the Danube and ice skating in City Park.

New Year's Day Concert

This event (www.hungaria koncert.hu), usually held in the Duna Palota, ushers in the New Year and is the favourite of local glitterati.

February

By now winter has hung on a bit too long and the days are cold, short and bleak. Some museums and tourist attractions sharply curtail their hours.

VinCE Budapest

The primary focus of this three-day event (www.vincebudapest.hu), held at the Corinthia Hotel Budapest, is wine (*vin*) in Central Europe (CE), with over 100 wineries from Hungary and neighbouring countries offering tastings.

March

An excellent month to visit. With the start of the city's red-letter event – the annual Budapest Spring Festival – both music and spring are in the air.

Budapest Spring Festival

The capital's largest and most important cultural event (www.festivalcity.hu) has more than 200 events over two weeks in late March and early April at some 60 venues across town.

National Dance House Festival

Hungary's biggest *táncház* (www.tanchaztalalkozo.hu) is held over two days in very late March at the Palace of Arts and other venues across town.

April

Full spring is just glorious in Budapest: it looks and feels like the season in e.e. cummings' poem 'in Just': 'spring – when the world is puddle-wonderful'.

Budapest Dance Festival

This annual 10-day festival (www.budapestdancefestival.hu), held at the National Dance Theatre in the Castle District to coincide with International Dance Day (29 April), features an array of styles from ballet and contemporary to folk.

May

The selection of fresh vegetables and fruit isn't great in winter, but in spring the bounty begins.

Budapest Pálinka Festival

The Budapest Pálinka Festival (www.budapestipalinkafesztival.hu/home), held in Erzsébet tér, is a four-day gastronomic event where visitors can taste over 300 types of Hungarian fruit brandy.

June

Late spring is wonderful, but June can be pretty wet, especially early in the month. And beware the start of the holiday crowds.

📸 Museum Night

Dozens of Budapest museums of all shapes and sizes mark the summer solstice by reopening their doors at 6pm and not closing them till the wee hours, sometimes as late as 2am (www.muzej.hu).

July

School's out for the summer. So now you're competing with not only foreign visitors but local ones too.

📸 Budapest Pride

This week-long gay, lesbian, bisexual and transgender film and cultural festival (http://budapestpride.hu) culminates in the annual Pride Parade, usually held on the first Saturday in July.

☆ Formula 1 Hungarian Grand Prix

Hungary's premier sporting event (www.hungaroring.hu) is held in late July at the Hungaroring in Mogyoród, 24km northeast of Budapest.

August

Once called the 'cucumber-growing month' because that was about the only thing happening, August is now festival month.

📸 Sziget Festival

Now one of the biggest and most popular music festivals (www.szigetfestival.com) in the world, the 'Island' festival is held in mid-August on Budapest's Óbuda (Hajógyár) Island.

📸 Jewish Summer Festival

This unique 10-day festival (www.zsidonyarifesztival.hu) starting at the end of August showcases Jewish culture through music and theatre performances, exhibitions, gastronomy and films, with many events taking place at Pest's Great Synagogue.

September

September brings summer to a close and the crowds back from their holidays. It's a good time to visit as there's still a lot going on, wine is starting to flow and peak season has ended.

🍷 Budapest International Wine Festival

Hungary's foremost winemakers introduce their vintages to festival-goers (www.aborfesztival.hu) in mid-September in the Castle District.

October

Though the days are getting shorter and everyone is back into their routines, autumn is beautiful, particularly in the Buda Hills.

🏃 Budapest International Marathon

Eastern Europe's most celebrated foot race (www.budapestmarathon.com) goes along the Danube and across its bridges in mid-October.

November

The month kicks off with a public holiday – All Saints' Day on 1 November. After that, though, the winter season begins, with many museums and other tourist attractions around the country sharply curtailing their hours or closing altogether.

🔒 Christmas Markets

Each year, from late November to the end of December, Christmas markets sprout up in several venues across Budapest, with the largest in Vörösmarty tér (www.festivalcity.hu).

December

The build-up to Christmas intensifies as December wears on, and the arrival of decorations, trees and coloured lights is a welcome and very festive sight.

📸 New Year Gala & Ball

The calendar's most coveted ticket is this gala concert and ball (www.opera.hu), held at the Hungarian State Opera House on the last day of the year.

With Kids

Budapest abounds in places that will delight children, and there is always a special child's entry rate (and often a family one as well) to paying attractions. Visits to many areas of the city can be designed around a rest stop or picnic – at City Park, say, or on Margaret Island.

Pedal car, Margaret Island (p108)

INGOLF POMPE / GETTY IMAGES ©

Come Rain or Shine

Raining cats and dogs? Our select committee of under-10s chose the relocated Palace of Wonders (p70), the Széchenyi Baths (p148) and the Hungarian Natural History Museum (p137) as their favourite wet-weather venues.

Too hot to trot (or do much else)? They tell us to head for the playground on Margaret Island, the nearby Palatinus Strand (p111) or the cool underground corridors of the Buda Castle Labyrinth (p57).

Hands-On Learning

The Hungarian Natural History Museum (p137) has a lot of hands-on activities on offer, including a stunning Dinosaur Garden and a new interactive exhibit on Hungary's natural world called the *Variety of Life*. The Palace of Wonders (p70) was custom-made for hands-on learning, and the Transportation Museum (p150) also has a lot of show-and-tell explanations from enthusiastic attendants. The granddaddy of museums for kids, though, is the Hungarian Railway History Park (p111), with vintage locomotives to clamber about, and carriages and trains to 'drive' via a high-tech simulator. It closes in winter, though.

Culture

Not many museums here or anywhere are suitable for the very young, but the Museum of Fine Arts (p147) has an excellent program in which kids are allowed to handle original Egyptian artefacts and create their own master works of art. The Hungarian Agricultural Museum (p150) has all kinds of stuffed animals (for real) and mock-ups of traditional ways of life like hunting and fishing. The Vasarely Museum (p75) might be adult-themed, but the wacky art – which seems to move about the canvas of its own accord – will surprise and please kids of all ages. The revamped Aquincum Museum (p74) has lots of great interactive exhibits including virtual duelling with a gladiator.

Thermal Baths & Pools

Both the Széchenyi Baths (p148) and the Gellért Baths (p66) are huge and have an abundance of indoor and outdoor pools. Gellért's outdoor pool has a wave machine, Széchenyi's has a whirlpool. Palatinus Strand (p111) and Dagály (p111) have vast lawns for lounging and playing around on a summer's day.

Aquaworld (p111) in northern Pest, a favourite with kids of all ages, is a bit far out of the city but easily reached by free shuttle bus and public transport. Some of the slides reach five storeys in height (kids have to be 150cm tall to use these), and there's a baby-swimming program available.

Live Entertainment

The Capital Circus (p152), Europe's only permanent big top, is often booked out by school groups at matinees, but there are almost always seats in the evening. Most kids will be transfixed by the marionette and other shows at the Budapest Puppet Theatre (p130), even if they don't speak Hungarian.

Táncház (a folk music and dance evening), whether they participate or just watch, is always a big hit with kids. Most of the children's ones have instructors, with folk musicians playing the tunes. The best are the children's programs at the Budavár Cultural Centre (p63) and the Municipal Cultural House (p71) in Buda.

Public Transport

Kids love transport and the city's many unusual forms of conveyance will delight. The Cog Railway (p77) and Children's Railway (p77) in the Buda Hills and the Sikló (p51) funicular climbing up to Castle Hill are particular favourites. But even the mainstays of getting around town – the trams, trolleybuses and little M1 metro that are so commonplace to young Budapesters – will be a lot of fun for kids who rarely (if ever) board such forms of public transport.

NEED TO KNOW

➨ An ever-growing number of hotels in Budapest offer babysitting services, but try to book at least six hours beforehand.

➨ Most car-rental firms have children's safety seats for hire at a nominal cost, but book them in advance.

➨ High chairs and cots (cribs) are standard equipment in many restaurants and hotels, but numbers can be limited; request them when booking.

Parks & Playgrounds

The Budapest Zoo (p149) and the adjoining Holnemvolt Park (p149) of amusement rides at the northern end of City Park is an excellent place to while away the afternoon and early evening.

Great playgrounds include ones on XIII Margaret Island, about 50m northeast of the fountain at the southern end; on III Óbuda (Hajógyári) Island, about 200m along the main road (take the HÉV to the island's footbridge); and in XIII Szent István Park. Smaller playgrounds are located at V Hild tér, VII Hunyadi tér and VII Almássy tér.

Eating

Most restaurants won't have a set children's menu but will split the adult portion. When they do they're usually priced around 1200Ft. Budapest's traditional cafes and *cukrászdák* (cake shops) will satisfy a sweet tooth of any size, but for a really special occasion treat the little rascals to the all-you-can-eat dessert bar at the **Budapest Marriott Hotel** (Map p238; ☑1-737 7377; www.marriott.com; Apáczai Csere János utca 4). Just 2200Ft gets you as many cakes as they can manage from noon to 10pm daily. A cafe made for kids is Briós (p113) in Újlipótváros.

Like a Local

It's not difficult to live like a local in Budapest. The natives are friendly, the food is excellent and the wine's even better. And there are lots of things here that everyone everywhere likes: hot mineral baths, sweet cakes and diamonds-and-rust flea markets.

Eating Like a Local

Learn to like meat. Hungarians are big carnivores, and 'meat-stuffed meat' is actually a dish here. For stick-to-the-ribs fare on the hoof try Belvárosi Disznótoros (p84), a butcher-caterer who satisfies the ravenous daily. Still all the rage are retro-style *étkezdék,* diner-like eateries that serve traditional Hungarian favourites and comfort food like *főzelék* (vegetables fried or boiled and then mixed into a roux with milk). The most local of these are Kádár (p121) in Erzsébetváros in Pest and Toldi Konyhája (p61) in Buda's Víziváros. The best place for traditional fish soup is Horgásztanya Vendéglő (p61).

Drinking Like a Local

Budapesters love their wine and take it seriously, but in summer spritzers of red or white wine and mineral water are consumed in large quantities. Knowing the hierarchy and the art of mixing a spritzer to taste is important and will definitely win you the distinction of 'honorary local'. A *kisfröccs* (small spritzer) is 10cL wine and the same amount of soda water; *a nagyfröccs* (big spritzer) doubles the quantity of wine. A *hosszúlépés* (long step) is 10cL of wine and 20cL of water, while a *házmester* (janitor) trebles the amount of wine. Any bar in town will serve you these, but don't expect one at a *borozó,* a traditional 'wine bar' (usually a dive) where liquid plonk (rotgut) is doled out by metal ladle.

Entertaining Like a Local

No self-respecting Budapester ever clubs indoors in the warm summer months; that's what *kertek* (outdoor garden clubs) and rough-and-ready *romkocsmák* (ruin pubs) are for.

As for more high-brow entertainment, while the Ferenc Liszt Music Academy (p129) and Palace of Arts (p142) are incomparable for their acoustics and talent, many Budapesters prefer to hear music in smaller, more intimate venues such as the Óbuda Society (p80) or organ recitals in one of the city's many fine churches such as St Michael's Inner Town Church (p41).

If you want to see Budapest down and dirty on the playing field, attend a Ferencváros Football Club match at the new €40-million Flórián Albert Stadium (p143).

Shopping Like a Local

The Nagycsarnok (p143) is a great place to shop, but don't expect to see peasant women fresh in from the countryside selling snowdrops in spring or homemade tomato juice in summer. For that sort of thing head for the Rákóczi tér market (p143) – but never on a Sunday (or a Monday for that matter) – or even the covered Lehel Market (p112) in Újlipótváros.

Locals almost never go to the Ecseri Piac (p142), the largest flea market in Central Europe, during the week but head out as early as they can make it on Saturday morning to see what treasures are coming in from the countryside or being flogged by amateurs.

Boat Trips & City Tours

If you can't be bothered making your own way around Budapest or don't have the time, a guided tour can be a great way to learn the lay of the land.

Boat Tours

A slew of companies offer cruises on the Danube that include taped commentary in a multitude of languages and (usually) a free drink.

Mahart PassNave (Map p238; ☑1-484 4013; www.mahartpassnave.hu; V Belgrád rakpart, Vigadó tér Pier; adult/student/child 2990/2490/1490Ft; ☉10am-9pm late Mar-late Oct, to 10pm Jul & Aug; ☐2) One-hour trip between Margaret and Rákóczi Bridges departs hourly.

Legenda (Map p238; ☑1-266 4190; www. legenda.hu; V Vigadó tér, pier 7; adult/student/child day 3900/3500/2400Ft, night 5500/4400/2750Ft; ☐2) Similar deal in 30 languages has between five and six daily departures but only in winter.

River Ride (Map p244; ☑1-332 2555; www. riverride.com; V Széchenyi István tér 7-8; adult/child 7500/5000Ft; ☐2) Amphibious bus takes you on a two-hour heart-stopping tour of Budapest by road *and* river; live commentary (English and German).

Bus Tours

Hugely popular are hop-on, hop-off bus tours that allow you to board and alight as you please for a selected length of time.

Program Centrum (Map p238; ☑1-317 7767; www.programcentrum.hu; V Erzsébet tér 9-11, Le Meridien Hotel; adult/12-18yr/child 6000/4800/3000Ft; Ⓜ M1/2/3 Deák Ferenc tér, ☐47, 49) Valid on two bus routes (one taped in 24 languages, one live commentary in English and German) and a one-hour river cruise for 48 hours.

Giraffe Hop On Hop Off City Tour (Map p244; ☑1-374 7050; www.citytour.hu; VI Andrássy út 2; adult/student 5000/4500Ft; ☉10am-7.30pm Mar-Oct; Ⓜ M1/2/3 Deák Ferenc tér) Tours of the city in 20 languages.

Cityrama (Map p244; ☑1-302 4382; www. cityrama.hu; V Báthory utca 22; adult/concession 6500/5500Ft; ☐15, Ⓜ M3 Arany János utca) If you prefer to stay on the bus, this operator offers three-hour city tours, with several photo stops and live commentary in five languages.

STUART WESTMORLAND / GETTY IMAGES ©

nube River (p157)

Cycling Tours

Most bike-hire companies offer tours for around 5000Ft per person, but itineraries often depend on the whim of the group leader.

Yellow Zebra Bikes (Map p244; 1-269 3843; www.yellowzebrabikes.com; VI Lázár utca 16 ; 1hr/half-day/full-day hire from 600/3000/3700Ft; 9am-8.30pm Apr-Oct, 10am-7pm Nov-Mar; M1 Opera) This outfit runs cycling tours (adult/student/child 6500/6000/3000Ft) of the city that take in Heroes' Sq, City Park, central Pest and Castle Hill in around four hours. Tours, which include the bike, depart from in front of the Discover Budapest office behind the Opera House, at 11am daily from April to October, with an additional departure at 5pm in July and August. In November and March they depart at 11am on Friday, Saturday and Sunday only.

Budapest Segway Tours (Map p244; 1-269 3843; www.yellowzebrabikes.com; VI Lázár utca 16; per person €65-80; 9.30am & 3pm year-round, plus 6pm Apr-Oct only; M1 Opera) Yellow Zebra also offers two- to three-hour tours on Segways (two-wheeled, electric-powered conveyances). Tours follow an abbreviated version of the bike tour's Pest route and depart from the Discover Budapest office at 9.30am and 3pm daily. There's an evening tour at 6pm from April to October only. You must book at least a day ahead for these tours.

NEIGHBOURHOOD WALKS & LOCAL LIFE

➡ Neighbourhood Walk: Boutique Browsing in the Belváros (p85)

➡ Neighbourhood Walk: Erzsébetváros & the Jewish Quarter (p119)

➡ Neighbourhood Walk: Touring the Buda Hills (p77)

➡ Local Life: A Night Out in Erzsébetváros (p128)

➡ Neighbourhood Walk: Castle Hill (p60)

Walking Tours

Free Budapest Tours (Map p238; 06 20 534 5819; www.freebudapesttours.eu; V Deák Ferenc tér; free; 10.30am & 2.30pm) Innovative and professional walking tours organised by an outfit whose name is as descriptive as it is, er, pedestrian; the guides work for tips only, so dig deep into your pockets. A 2½-hour tour of both Pest and Buda leaves from V Deák Ferenc tér (opposite Le Meridien Hotel) daily at 10.30am and the 1½-hour tour of Pest from the same place at 2.30pm. See the website for details on private tours.

Absolute Walking Tours (Map p244; 1-269 3843; www.absolutetours.com; VI Lázár utca 16; adult/student/child 7500/7000/5000Ft; 10am; M1 Opera) A three-hour guided walk through City Park, central Pest and Castle Hill run by the people behind Yellow Zebra Bikes. Tours depart daily at 10am year-round from the Discover Budapest office behind the Opera House. It also has specialist tours, including the popular 3½-hour Hammer & Sickle Tour (adult/student 13,500/13,000Ft) of Budapest's Communist past.

Hungária Koncert (1-317 1377; www. ticket.info.hu; tours from 3900Ft) Focusing on Budapest's Jewish heritage, a 1½- to two-hour tour leaves at 10am Monday to Friday, again at 2pm Monday to Thursday, and at 11am Sunday from May to October. The tour includes a visit to the Great Synagogue, the Jewish Museum and the Holocaust Cemetery for 3900Ft. The Grand Tour (an hour longer) adds the Orthodox Synagogue, a ghetto walking tour and a kosher snack for 9400/8900Ft per adult/student. Tickets are available from locations throughout the city, including the Duna Palota (p105).

Paul Street Tours (06 20 933 5240; www. paulstreettours.com; per hour €25-30) This company offers very personal walking tours covering the Castle District (about two hours), less-explored areas of Pest, such as the Jewish Quarter and Andrássy út (two to three hours), the Little Ring Rd, the parks and gardens of Budapest, and shopping, with lots of anecdotal information on architecture and social history, especially life in and around the *udvar* (courtyards) of fin-de-siècle Pest. Tours are available by appointment year-round in English or Hungarian.

WILL SANDERS / LONELY PLANET ©

Széchenyi Baths (p148)

Thermal Baths & Spas

Budapest lies on the geological fault separating the Buda Hills from the pancake-flat Great Plain, and more than 30,000 cu metres of warm to scalding (21°C to 76°C) mineral water gush forth daily from some 123 thermal and more than 400 mineral springs. As a result, the city is a major spa centre and 'taking the waters' at one of the city's many spas or combination spa–swimming pool complexes is a real Budapest experience.

History of a Spa City

Remains of two sets of baths found at Aquincum indicate that the Romans took advantage of Budapest's thermal waters almost two millennia ago. But it wasn't until the Turkish occupation of the 16th and 17th centuries that bathing became an integral part of Budapest life. In the late 18th century, Habsburg empress Maria Theresa ordered that Budapest's mineral waters be 'analysed and recorded in a list at the expense of the Treasury'. By the 1930s Budapest had become a fashionable spa resort.

As a result, the choice of bathhouses today is legion. Some date from Turkish times, others are Art Nouveau marvels, and still others are spick-and-span modern establishments. The most recent arrival, the **Veli Bej Baths** (p80) in Buda, is a modernised 16th-century spa. Also, with Hungarians such keen swimmers, it's not surprising that Budapest boasts dozens of pools. They're always excellent places to get in a few laps (if indoor), cool off on a hot summer's day (if outdoor) or watch all the posers strut their stuff.

NEED TO KNOW

Opening Hours

Opening times and whether men or women or everybody is welcome depend on the day of the week. Many baths now open at night at the weekend.

Costs

Admission charges start at 2400Ft; in theory this allows you to stay for two hours on weekdays and 1½ hours at weekends, though this rule is seldom enforced.

Useful Websites

Budapest Spas and Hot Springs (www. spasbudapest.com) Excellent and up-to-date source of information.

Points to Ponder

➡ Fewer and fewer baths have male- and female-only days, so pack a bathing suit or be prepared to rent one (1000Ft).

➡ Though some of the baths look a little rough around the edges, they are clean and the water is changed regularly. However, you might consider taking along a pair of plastic sandals or flip-flops.

➡ Flip-flops are also useful at some of the pools (eg Palatinus Strand), where the abundant concrete reaches scorching point in hot weather.

Healing Waters

Of course, not everyone goes to the baths for fun and relaxation. The warm, mineral-rich waters are also meant to relieve a number of specific complaints, ranging from arthritis and pains in the joints and muscles, to poor blood circulation and post-traumatic stress. And they are a miracle cure – we can vouch for this – for that most unpleasant affliction: the dreaded hangover.

What's Inside

The layout of most of Budapest's baths follows a similar pattern: a series of indoor thermal pools, where temperatures range from warm to hot, with steam rooms, saunas, ice-cold plunge pools and rooms for massage. Some have outdoor pools with fountains, wave machines and whirlpools.

Most baths offer a full range of serious medical treatments plus more indulgent services such as massage (3500/4700Ft for 20/30 minutes) and pedicure (3200Ft). Specify what you want when buying your ticket.

Depending on the time and day, a few baths can be for men or women only. There are usually mixed days and nowadays many baths – including the Széchenyi, Gellért and Király Baths – are always for men and women together. On single-sex days or in same-sex sections, men are usually handed drawstring loincloths and women apron-like garments to wear, though the use of bathing suits is on the increase even on single-sex days. You must wear a bathing suit on mixed-sex days; these are available for hire (1000Ft) if you don't have your own. Many pools require the use of a bathing cap, so bring your own or wear the disposable one provided or sold for about 200Ft. Most pools also rent towels (700Ft).

Getting In & Out

The procedure for getting out of your street clothes and into the water requires some explanation. All baths and pools have cabins or lockers. In most of the baths nowadays you are given an electronic bracelet that directs you to, and then opens, your locker or cabin. Ask for assistance if you can't work it out. Others – the Gellért Baths springs to mind – still employ the old, more personal method. Find an empty locker or cabin yourself, and after getting changed in (or beside) it, seek out an attendant, who will lock it for you and hand you a numbered tag to tie on your swimming costume or 'apron'. Please note: in order to prevent theft should you lose or misplace the tag, the number is not the same as the one on the locker, so commit the locker number to memory.

Choosing a Bathing Experience

Which bath you decide to visit is really a matter of choice, but certainly consider one of our four favourites – make that five favourites if the **Rácz Baths** (Map p236; ☎1-266 0606; www.budapestbaths.net/racz-bath; I Hadnagy utca 8-10; ☐178, ☐18) has reopened by the time you visit:

Rudas Baths These renovated baths are the most Turkish of all in Budapest, built in 1566, with an octagonal pool, domed cupola with coloured glass and eight massive pillars. They're mostly men-only during the week but turn into a real zoo on mixed weekend nights. (p71)

Thermal Baths & Spas

Gellért Baths Soaking in these Art Nouveau baths, now open to both men and women at all times, has been likened to taking a bath in a cathedral. The indoor swimming pools are the most beautiful in the city. (p66)

Széchenyi Baths The gigantic 'wedding-cake' building in City Park houses the Széchenyi Baths, which are unusual for three reasons: their immensity (some 15 thermal baths and three outdoor swimming pools); the bright, clean atmosphere; and the high temperature of the water (up to 38℃). (p148)

Veli Bej Baths This venerable (1575) Turkish bath in Buda has got a new lease of life after having been forgotten for centuries. (p80)

Other baths also have their special features. The waters of the **Lukács Baths** (p80) are meant to cure just about everything from spinal deformation and vertebral dislocation (ouch!) to calcium deficiency. The four small Turkish pools at **Király Baths** (p63),

while begging for renovation, are the real McCoy and date back to 1565. The facilities at the **Danubius Health Spa Margitsziget** (p110) on Margaret Island are soulless but modern and the choice of special treatments (lymph drainage, anyone?) is enviable.

As for pools, well, again it depends on what you have in mind. If you're serious about doing laps and keeping fit, visit the pools at **Alfréd Hajós** (p111) on Margaret Island or **Császár-Komjádi** (p80) in Óbuda. If you're just after a day of sunbathing with the occasional dip, consider the **Palatinus Strand** (p111) on Margaret Island or the **Dagály** (p111) complex north of Újlipótváros.

Pörkölt (stew)

 # Eating

The dining scene in Budapest has undergone a sea change in recent years. Hungarian food has 'lightened up', offering the same wonderfully earthy and spicy tastes but in less calorific dishes. A number of vegetarian (or partially meatless) restaurants have opened, and the choice of eateries with cuisines other than Magyar is greater than ever before.

Wining & Dining in Budapest

Many midrange and top-end eateries are concentrating on wine as never before, and they are excellent places to try some of Hungary's superb vintages. It won't be long before you discover some of Hungarian cuisine's 'matches made in heaven': sweet Tokaji Aszú with goose liver; ruby-red Kékfrankos with *pörkölt* (goulash); bone-dry white Furmint with fish.

A wide choice of ethnic food – from Middle Eastern and Greek to Indian and Chinese has become almost the norm in Budapest. And the fast food of choice in the capital is no longer cheap-and-cheerful *lángos* (deep-fried dough with various toppings, usually cheese and sour cream), but kebabs and felafel.

Hungarian Specialities
BREAD & PASTA

Hungarians say they 'eat bread with bread', and leftover *kenyér* (bread) is always used to thicken soups and stews. Uniquely Magyar are the flour-based *galuska* (dumplings) and *tarhonya* (barley-shaped egg pasta) served with *pörkölt* and *csirke paprikás* (chicken cooked with sour cream and paprika).

SOUPS & STEWS

A Hungarian meal always starts with *leves* (soup). This is usually something relatively light like *gombaleves* (mushroom soup) or *húsgombócleves* (tiny liver dumplings in bouillon). A more substantial soup is *bableves,* a thick bean soup usually made with meat. Another favourite is *halászlé* (fisherman's soup), a rich soup of fish stock, poached carp or catfish, tomatoes, green peppers and paprika.

Gulyás (or *gulyásleves*) is a thick beef soup cooked with onions, cubed potatoes and paprika and generally eaten as a main course. *Pörkölt* (stew), is closer to what foreigners call goulash.

VEGETABLE DISHES

Fresh salad is often called *vitamin saláta* here; everything else is *savanyúság* (sours) that can be anything from mildly sour-sweet cucumbers to pickled peppers to very acidic sauerkraut. All go well with heavy meat dishes.

The traditional way of preparing *zöldség* (vegetables) is in *főzelék,* Hungary's unique 'twice-cooked' vegetable dish: peas, green beans, lentils, marrow or cabbage are fried or boiled and then mixed into a roux with milk. This dish is sometimes topped with a few slices of meat and enjoyed at lunch.

PATISSERIES & CAKE SHOPS

Hungarians love sweets, and desserts taken at lunch or dinner include *Somlói galuska* (sponge cake with chocolate and whipped cream) and *Gundel palacsinta* (flambéed pancake with chocolate and nuts).

How to Eat Like a Local

WHEN TO EAT

For the most part Hungarians are not big eaters of *reggeli* (breakfast), preferring a cup of tea or coffee with a plain bread roll at the kitchen table or on the way to work. *Ebéd* (lunch), eaten at around 1pm, is traditionally the main meal in the countryside and can consist of two or even three courses, but this is no longer the case for working people in the cities and towns. *Vacsora* (dinner or supper) is less substantial when eaten at home: often just sliced meats, cheese and some pickled vegetables.

PLAN YOUR TRIP EATING

NEED TO KNOW

Price Ranges

The following price indicators represent the cost of a two-course meal with drink for one person:

€	under 3500Ft
€€	3500Ft to 7500Ft
€€€	over 7500Ft

Opening Hours

➡ Most restaurants are open from 10am or 11am to 11pm or midnight.

➡ Arrive by 9pm or 10pm (at the latest) to ensure being seated and served.

Reservations

➡ It is advisable to book tables at mid-range to top-end restaurants, especially at the weekend.

Etiquette

➡ People in Budapest tend to meet their friends and entertain outside their homes at cafes and restaurants.

➡ If you are invited to a local person's home, bring a bunch of flowers or a bottle of good local wine.

➡ Hungarians don't clink glasses when drinking beer – wine is fine – because that's how the Habsburgs celebrated the defeat of Lajos Kossuth in the 1848–49 War of Independence.

➡ For information on tipping, see p209.

WHERE TO EAT

An *étterem* is a restaurant with a large selection of dishes, sometimes including international options. A *vendéglő* (or *kisvendéglő*) is smaller and is supposed to serve inexpensive regional dishes or 'home cooking', but the name is now 'cute' enough for a lot of large places to use it. An *étkezde* or *kifőzde* is something like a diner, smaller and cheaper than a *kisvendéglő* and often with seating at a counter. The overused term *csárda* originally signified a country inn with a rustic atmosphere, Gypsy music and hearty local dishes; now any place that puts dried peppers and a couple of painted plates on the wall is one. Most restaurants offer an excellent-value *menü* (set menu) of two or three courses at lunch, but make sure to book ahead at top-shelf places.

PAPRIKA: HUNGARY'S RED GOLD

Paprika, the *piros arany* ('red gold') so essential in Hungarian cuisine, is cultivated primarily around the cities of Szeged and Kalocsa on Hungary's Great Plain. Between 8000 and 10,000 tonnes of the spice are produced annually, over half of which is exported. Hungarians each consume about 500g of the red stuff – richer in vitamin C than citrus fruits – every year. Not only is paprika used when preparing dishes but it also appears on restaurant tables as a condiment beside the salt and pepper shakers.

There are many types of fresh or dried paprika available in Budapest markets and shops, including the rose, apple and royal varieties. But as a ground spice it is most commonly sold as *csípős* (hot) or *erős* (strong) paprika and *édes* (sweet) paprika.

A *bisztró* is a much cheaper sit-down place that is often *önkiszolgáló* (self-service). A *büfé* (snack bar) is cheaper still and has a very limited menu. Food stalls, known as *Lacikonyha* (literally 'Larry's kitchen') or *pecsenyesütő* (roast ovens), can be found near markets, parks or train stations. At these you eat while standing at counters.

A *kávéház* (coffee house; cafe) is the best place to get something hot or nonalcoholic and cold. An *eszpresszó,* along with being a type of coffee, is essentially a coffee house too, but it usually also sells alcoholic drinks and light snacks.

VEGETARIAN & VEGAN

Outside the city's few vegetarian restaurants you'll have to make do with what's on the regular menu or shop for ingredients in the markets. The selection of fresh vegetables and fruit is not great in the dead of winter, but come spring a cycle of bounty begins.

In regular restaurants vegetarians can usually order any number of types of *főzelék* as well as *rántott gombafejek* (fried mushroom caps) and pasta and noodle dishes with cheese, such as *túrós csusza* and *sztrapacska*. Other vegetarian dishes include *gombaleves* (mushroom soup), *gyümölcsleves* (fruit soup) in season, *rántott sajt* (fried cheese) and *sajtos kenyér* (sliced bread with soft cheese). *Bableves* (bean soup) usually contains meat. *Palacsinták* (pancakes) may be savoury and made with *sajt* (cheese) or *gomba* (mushrooms), or sweet and prepared with *dió* (nuts) or *mák* (poppy seeds).

Eating by Neighbourhood

➡ **Castle District** It's relatively expensive and touristy on Castle Hill, but serious restaurants have recently arrived on the scene. (p58)

➡ **Gellért Hill & Tabán** A substantial choice of assorted eateries in the shadow of Buda Castle and along the Danube. (p69)

➡ **Óbuda & Buda Hills** Some eateries in Óbuda date so far back they appear in literary works; the Buda Hills are known for outdoor restaurants and barbecues. (p76)

➡ **Belváros** The choice is good but prices are not always right in what is expense-account territory; head north or south for better deals. (p84)

➡ **Parliament & Around** Some fine eateries catering to all budgets around the basilica and Central European University. (p99)

➡ **Margaret Island & Northern Pest** Limited on the island, but well-heeled Újlipótváros has excellent restaurants and cafes. (p112)

➡ **Erzsébetváros & the Jewish Quarter** This area has the largest choice of cuisine – from French and South Slav to Jewish/kosher. (p121)

➡ **Southern Pest** IX Ráday utca is Restaurant Central in this neighbourhood. (p139)

➡ **City Park & Beyond** Splurge territory – be it at fancy Gundel or lakeside Robinson. (p150)

COOKING COURSES

Cooking courses are thin on the ground in Budapest. The best-known cookery school dealing with foreigners is **Chefparade** (Map p242; ☑06 20 316 1876, 1-210 6042; www.chefparade.hu; IX Páva utca 13; Ⓜ M3 Ferenc körút) in Ferencváros. Course dates vary – consult the website – but they usually run from 10am to 1pm and include visiting a market and preparing a four-course lunch (€69 per person, €129 for two). Courses at other times and of a longer duration can be organised in advance. There's a **Chefparade branch** (Map p234; ☑1-210 6042; II Bécsi út 27; ⊗8am-6pm Mon-Thu, to 4pm Fri; ☐17) in Óbuda.

MENU DECODER

Menus are often translated into German and English, with mixed degrees of success. The following sample menu is far from complete, but it gives a good idea of what to expect. *Készételek* are ready-made dishes that are kept warm or just heated up, while *frissensültek* are made to order and thus take longer. Other words you might encounter are *halak* or *halételek* (fish dishes), *szárnyasok* (poultry) and *sajtok* (cheeses).

Előételek (Appetisers)

Hortobágyi palacsinta Meat-filled pancake with paprika sauce

libamáj pástétom Goose-liver pâté

rántott gombafejek Breaded and fried mushroom caps

Levesek (Soups)

csontleves Consommé/bouillon (usually beef)

Jókai bableves Bean soup with meat

meggyleves Cold sour-cherry soup (seasonal)

tyúkhúsleves Chicken soup with carrot, kohlrabi, parsley and celery root

Saláták (Salads)

cékla saláta Pickled beetroot salad

ecetes almapaprika Pickled small round peppers

uborka saláta Lightly pickled cucumber salad

vegyes saláta Mixed salad (usually of pickles)

vitamin saláta Fresh salad

Köretek (Side Dishes)

rizi-bizi Rice with peas

sült hasábburgonya Chips (French fries)

Készételek (Ready-Made Dishes)

csirke paprikás Chicken cooked with sour cream and paprika

(marha/borjú) pörkölt (Beef/veal) stew

töltött káposzta/paprika Stuffed cabbage/peppers

Frissensültek (Dishes Made to Order)

Bécsiszelet Wiener schnitzel

Brassói aprópecsenye Braised pork 'Braşov-style'

cigánypecsenye Roast pork 'Gypsy-style'

csülök Smoked pork knuckle

hagymás rostélyos Beef sirloin fried with onions

rántott pulykamell Breaded and fried turkey breast

sült libacomb Roast goose leg

Édességek (Desserts)

Dobos torta Multilayered 'Dobos' chocolate and cream cake with a caramelised brown-sugar top

Gundel palacsinta 'Gundel' flambéed pancake with chocolate and nuts

rétes Strudel

Somlói galuska 'Somló-style' sponge cake with chocolate and whipped cream

Lonely Planet's Top Choices

Borkonyha The 'Wine Kitchen' is currently our favourite in Pest, Michelin accolades notwithstanding. (p101)

Kisbuda Gyöngye *Fin-de-siècle* atmosphere in an antique-cluttered Óbuda eatery. (p79)

Kispiac Hole-in-the-wall retro-style eatery near Parliament with seriously Hungarian dishes. (p100)

Múzeum Still going strong a quarter into its second century, this old-world place combines excellent service and top-notch cooking. (p140)

Klassz Unusual for a wine restaurant, both the vintages *and* the food are top-class. (p124)

Rosenstein Upmarket Jewish (but not kosher) and Hungarian cuisine near the Keleti train station. (p140)

Best by Budget

€

Halkakas Fresh, simple and good-value fish dishes. (p86)

Culinaris Something for all tastes at a gourmet food shop. (p99)

Ring Cafe One of the best places in town for a burger. (p124)

Vár Bistro Cheap and cheerful Hungarian fast food in the Castle District. (p58)

€€

Déryné Former coffee house turns to fine bistro dining. (p61)

Pesti Disznó Hungarian soul food with an excellent wine list. (p102)

Zeller Bistro Cellar restaurant with wonderful Hungarian home cooking. (p123)

Macesz Huszár Hungarian-Jewish classics, done to perfection. (p123)

Café Kör Favourite casual restaurant still going strong. (p101)

€€€

Csalogány 26 *Haute cuisine à la hongroise* in the heart of Buda. (p61)

Bock Bisztró Elegant and traditional Hungarian with a great wine selection. (p80)

Nobu Impeccable sushi in modernist surrounds. (p86)

Laci Konyha Boutique and very eclectic eatery in northern Pest. (p113)

Best by Cuisine

ASIAN

Seoul House Authentic Korean with decades of experience. (p61)

Fuji Japán Everyone's favourite Japanese restaurant in the Buda Hills. (p80)

Parázs Presszó Excellent Thai with a loyal following. (p103)

FISH & SEAFOOD

Horgásztanya Vendéglő Reliable Hungarian fish dishes by the Danube. (p61)

Új Sípos Halászkert The place to try one of many Hungarian fish soups. (p78)

bigfish Super-fresh fish and shellfish. (p124)

HUNGARIAN (TRADITIONAL)

Kádár Lunch-only *étkezde* on an atmospheric square. (p121)

Toldi Konyhája Very traditional Hungarian eatery in Buda. (p61)

Fülemüle Hungarian favourites in an old-fashioned dining room. (p140)

HUNGARIAN (MODERN)

Mák Inventive Hungarian dishes from a daily-changing blackboard. (p101)

21 Magyar Vendéglő Fine Hungarian dining in the Castle District. (p59)

Aranyszarvas Game dishes and more in the shadow of the castle. (p69)

ITALIAN

Da Mario Our new favourite Italian for superb pasta dishes and wood-fire pizzas. (p100)

Trattoria Toscana Pizza, pasta and antipasto with river views. (p86)

Fausto's Classy two-part restaurant with a great wine list. (p123)

VEGETARIAN

Édeni Vegán Strictly vegan place serves veggie platters and ragouts. (p59)

Napfényes Ízek Out-of-the-way cellar restaurant that's a must for vegans. (p123)

Govinda Budapest's first meatless eatery has excellent fixed menus. (p100)

Best Places to Eat Like a Local

Kisharang (p99) The *étkezde* of choice among Budapest cognoscenti.

Pozsonyi Kisvendéglő Retro-style resto serves stick-to-the-ribs favourites. (p112)

Fortuna Önkiszolgáló The place where local people grab a quick lunch in the castle. (p59)

Nagyi Palacsintázója A student favourite with a shopping list of sweet and savoury pancakes. (p59)

Földes Józsi Konyhája Rustic little place with a good range of *főzelék* dishes. (p79)

Cafe, Liszt Ferenc tér

![glass icon] Drinking & Nightlife

In recent years Budapest has justifiably gained a reputation as one of Europe's top nightlife destinations. Alongside its age-old cafe culture, it offers a magical blend of unique drinking holes, fantastic wine, home-grown fire waters and emerging craft beers, all served up with a warm Hungarian welcome and a wonderful sense of fun.

Pubs & Bars

Drinking establishments in the city run the gamut from quirky pubs and bohemian bars to much more refined wine and cocktail bars.

If you want to sample the local beer (most commonly Dreher, Kőbányai and Arany Ászok) head for a *söröző*, a 'pub' with draught beer *(csapolt sör)* served in a *pohár* (0.3L) or *korsó* (0.4L or 0.5L). Many pubs and bars now also serve a range of the nation's craft beers from microbreweries across the country.

Hungary makes some excellent wines too, many unknown outside its borders. The most distinctive reds come from Villány and Szekszárd in Southern Transdanubia and the best dry whites are produced around Lake Balaton and in Somló. The red Bikavér (Bull's Blood) from Eger and the honey-sweet white Tokaj wines are much better known abroad, however. For more on wine, see p198.

A *borozó* is a traditional establishment (usually a dive) serving wine; a *pince* (or *bor pince*) is the same thing but in a cellar. Modern wine bars are the new black. Many

NEED TO KNOW

Opening Hours

➡ Cafes: 8am or 9am to anywhere from 6pm to 1am

➡ Bars: 11am to midnight Sunday to Thursday, to between 2am and 4am Friday and Saturday

➡ Clubs: anywhere from between 8pm and 11pm to between 3am and dawn

Print & Online Resources

➡ Useful freebies include **Budapest Funzine** (www.funzine.hu) and **PestiEst** (www.pestiest.hu).

➡ **welovebudapest.com** has great up-to-date bar and club reviews.

➡ **Where Budapest** (www.wherebudapest.hu) has a printed monthly pull-out specifically on nightlife, as well as extensive listings online.

➡ ruinpubs.com is a good resource for these one-off Budapest bars.

Costs

➡ *Korsó* (0.5L) of Dreher beer in pub or cafe: 450Ft to 900Ft

➡ Cheap/good bottle of wine (75cL) in supermarket: 700/2500Ft

➡ Cup of coffee in cafe: 300Ft to 750Ft

➡ Glass of wine: from 550Ft

➡ Cocktail: from 1000Ft

➡ Club cover charge (if any): 300Ft to 3500Ft

What to Wear

The city takes a very relaxed attitude to dress – in almost all bars and clubs jeans and trainers are perfectly acceptable. In ultra-swish venues you may be expected to go a bit more smart-casual.

serve wine by the deci (decilitre, 0.1L) so you can sample a wide range of vintages. And, just in case, they usually serve light dishes (cheese, sliced meats, salads etc) as a blotter. Another very popular way of drinking wine is to water it down with soda to make a drink known as *fröccs* (spritzer); these come in a variety of sizes with ratios of wine to water altered to your taste.

Don't leave Hungary without trying its two most famous spirits. *Pálinka*, a strong brandy or eau-de-vie distilled from a variety of fruits (most commonly from apricots or plums), kicks like a mule and is served in most bars, some of which carry an enormous range. You'll also come to recognise Unicum and its unique medicinal-looking bottle. It's a bitter aperitif that has been around since 1790 and is now available in three different versions. If you acquire a taste for it, head to the Zwack Unicum Heritage Visitors' Centre (p138) in Southern Pest.

Garden Clubs & Ruin Pubs

During the long and often very hot summers, so-called *kertek* (literally 'gardens', but in Budapest any outdoor spot that has been converted into an entertainment zone) empty out even the most popular indoor bars and clubs. These vary enormously, from permanent bars with an attached garden, and clubs with similar outdoor sections, to totally alfresco spaces, only frequented in good weather.

Ruin pubs (*romkocsmák*) began to appear in the city from the early 2000s, when entrepreneurial free thinkers took over abandoned buildings and turned them into pop-up bars. At first a very word-of-mouth scene, the ruin bars' popularity grew exponentially and many have transformed from ramshackle, temporary sites full of flea-market furniture to more slick, year-round fixtures with covered areas to protect patrons from the winter elements.

Many garden clubs and ruin pubs have DJs, live music or jam sessions. Table football, ping-pong, pool and other pub games are frequently a fixture, and a number of places offer street food; some also host escape games.

Clubs

The line between garden clubs, ruin bars, live-music venues and clubs here is a blurry one, with many places morphing from bar to club and hosting DJs and a dance floor without charging an entrance fee. Where there is a cover charge, the amount will vary on the event or DJ; it can be as low as 300Ft or go to around 3500Ft. Clubs in the city run from small underground caverns playing quality house and techno, and more mainstream complexes offering a variety of rooms and styles, to vast outdoor spaces that mimic summer music festivals. There are even club nights in the city's famous thermal baths.

Drinking & Nightlife by Neighbourhood

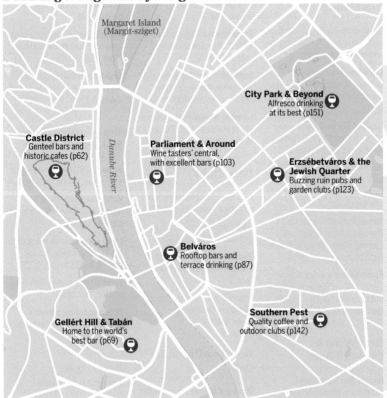

Margaret Island
(Margit-sziget)

City Park & Beyond
Alfresco drinking
at its best (p151)

Castle District
Genteel bars and
historic cafes (p62)

Danube River

Parliament & Around
Wine tasters' central,
with excellent bars (p103)

**Erzsébetváros & the
Jewish Quarter**
Buzzing ruin pubs and
garden clubs (p123)

Belváros
Rooftop bars and
terrace drinking (p87)

Gellért Hill & Tabán
Home to the world's
best bar (p69)

Southern Pest
Quality coffee and
outdoor clubs (p142)

Some indoor clubs are forced to shut up shop during the summer months, when everyone prefers to party outside. All venues usually stay open till dawn.

Cafes & Teahouses

Cafes have long been an integral part of Budapest's social life. A *kávéház* is literally a 'coffee house' (ie cafe). An *eszpresszó,* along with being a type of coffee, is essentially a coffee house too (also called *presszó*), but it usually also sells alcoholic drinks and light snacks. A *cukrászda* serves cakes, pastries and ice cream as well as hot and cold drinks.

Old-style cafes, some of which date back as much as a century and a half, abound in Budapest and some of them are classic examples of their type, with ornate fin-de-siècle decor. Generally, these cafes are frequented by older folk and tourists. Younger

Budapesters prefer the new breed of coffee house, of which there are a growing number, roasting their own blends and importing specific beans to ensure the quality of their cappuccinos and flat whites.

You'll also find teahouses across the city. In general, black or 'English' is not so popular (and never served with milk), though you'll always be able to choose from a wide range of herbal teas and fruit tisanes.

Lonely Planet's Top Choices

Corvintető Rooftop dance floor with a view right across the city and quality DJs. (p141)

Csendes Társ Lovely little outdoor terrace on the edge of one of the city's prettiest parks. (p87)

Szatyor Bár és Galéria Funky bar with street art and Hadik Kávéház as annexe. (p69)

Ruszwurm Cukrászda Dating back to the early 19th century, this is the oldest traditional cafe in town. (p62)

Bambi Presszó Bambi hasn't changed a bit in almost half a century, which seems to please just about everyone. (p62)

Kiadó Kocsma A nice alternative to the 'Tér' just across the road, the 'For Sale' is a chilled spot for a pint. (p104)

Best Wine & Cocktail Bars

Boutiq' Bar High-quality cocktails in a fantastic speakeasy setting. (p125)

Doblo Romantic brick-lined bar with a huge variety of Hungarian wine. (p124)

Oscar American Bar Film decor and cool cocktails below the castle. (p62)

DiVino Borbár The place to taste your way though Hungary's wine regions. (p103)

Spiccproject Stylish wine bar with some well-received blotter on the side. (p62)

Best Bars & Pubs

Kisüzem Relaxed backstreet find in the heart of the nightlife district. (p125)

Csendes Quirkily decorated cafe-bar with DJs and great snacks. (p87)

Fröccsterasz Alfresco fun with wine spritzers in an old bus terminal. (p87)

Suttogó Piano Bar Romantic and camp, this piano bar is always a laugh. (p105)

Lánchíd Söröző Friendly retro bar at the Buda end of Chain Bridge. (p62)

Best Clubs

A38 Watertight watering hole voted the world's best. (p205)

GMK Cool cavern with an excellent sound system. (p125)

Budapest Park Huge outdoor club and live-music venue. (p141)

Ötkert Chichi champagne bar with some excellent dance floors. (p103)

Best Traditional Cafes

Művész Kávéház People-watch with the Hungarian State Opera House as backdrop. (p129)

Gerbeaud Dating back to 1858 and still serving impeccable cakes and coffee. (p87)

Alexandra Book Cafe Glamour, glitz and Károly Lotz frescoes at the back of a bookshop. (p129)

Szalai Cukrászda Forget the decor – go for the memorable cherry strudel. (p104)

Best Modern Cafes & Teahouses

Lumen Arty cafe-bar with great own-roasted coffee and live music. (p141)

Tamp & Pull Trendy spot with delicious treats and brilliant brews. (p141)

Mozaik Calm oasis with a huge variety of teas above bustling Király utca. (p125)

Espresso Embassy Probably the best cafe in town for coffee lovers. (p104)

Best Garden Clubs & Ruin Bars

Instant Multilevel venue with a bar for every taste. (p104)

Holdudvar Something for everyone at this most outdoor of garden clubs. (p113)

Lokàl Ruin pub with swing dancing, fancy-dressing, escape-gaming and tattooing. (p124)

Élesztő High-quality craft beer, and lots of it. (p141)

Pótkulcs Almost a garden club, with a variety of live acts. (p104)

Best Gay & Lesbian Venues

Score Club The (only) place to do just that in Buda. (p62)

Mystery Bar Club Friendly neighbourhood gay bar with cool decor. (p103)

Club AlterEgo Still the city's premier gay club (and don't you forget it).(p104)

Action Bar Basement bar with a weekly strip show. (p90)

CoXx Men's Bar Three bars and a whole world of cruising. (p125)

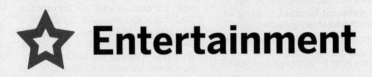

Entertainment

For a city its size, Budapest has a huge choice of things to do and places to go after dark – from opera and folk dancing to live jazz and films screened in palatial cinemas. It's usually not difficult getting tickets or getting in; the hard part is deciding what to do and where to go.

Music

CLASSICAL & OPERA

Apart from the city's main concert halls, including the Ferenc Liszt Music Academy (p129), the Palace of Arts (p142) and the Hungarian State Opera House (p130), many museums and other venues feature chamber music. They include, in Pest, the Old Music Academy, where the Franz Liszt Memorial Museum (p121) is housed; **Magyar Rádió Marble Hall** (Magyar Rádió Márványterme; Map p242; ☏1-328 7878; www.radio.hu; VIII Pollack Mihály tér 8; ⊡47, 49); the Hungarian Academy of Sciences (p98); the Duna Palota (p105) and the newly renovated Pesti Vigadó (p90). 'Second-tier' venues in Buda include the Béla Bartók Memorial House (p76), the Music History Museum (p56) and the Millennium Theatre (p58).

Organ recitals are best heard in the city's churches, including Matthias Church (p58) and the Church of St Anne (p57) in Buda, and, in Pest, the Basilica of St Stephen (p97), the Inner Town Parish Church and **St Michael's Inner Town Church** (Belvárosi Szent Mihály Templom; Map p238; www.szentmihalytemplom.hu; V Váci utca 47/b; ⓂM3 Ferenciek tere).

ROCK, POP & JAZZ

A number of bars and pubs feature live pop or rock music throughout the week. Top venues include Gödör (p130), Trafó (p142) and Akvárium Klub (p90) in Pest and A38 (p205) in Buda. For jazz, nothing beats the recently relocated Budapest Jazz Club (p113), though the Budapest Music Center (p143) is also recommended. Columbus Club, on a boat moored in the Danube, also has jazz.

FOLK & TRADITIONAL

Authentic *táncház* (literally 'dance house', but really folk-music workshops) are held at various locations throughout the week (though frequently in summer). Times and venues often change; consult the publications listed on the next page and expect to pay between 600Ft and 1000Ft. Useful, too, are the websites of the **Dance House Guild** (www.tanchaz.hu) and **Folkrádió** (www.folkradio.hu). Among other types of traditional music is *klezmer* (Jewish folk music); one of the best bands, **Sabbathsong Klezmer Band** (www.sabbathsong.hu), plays regularly at the Spinoza Café (p123) in Pest.

Dance

CLASSICAL & MODERN

The **Hungarian National Ballet** (Magyar Nemzeti Balett; www.opera.hu) is based at the Hungarian State Opera House, though visiting ballet companies often perform at the National Dance Theatre (p63). The premier venue for modern dance is the MU Színház (p71).

FOLK

Two of Hungary's best-known folk-dance troupes, the Hungarian State Folk Ensemble (Magyar Állami Népi Együttes) and the Hungária Orchestra & Folk Ensemble (Hungária Zenekar és Népi Együttes), perform on

NEED TO KNOW

Print & Online Resources

➜ Useful freebies for popular listings include **Budapest Funzine** (www.funzine.hu) and **PestiEst** (www.pestiest.hu).

➜ Another giveaway, **Where Budapest** (www.wherebudapest.hu), is more mainstream but has listings and reviews too.

➜ The **Koncert Kalendárium** (www.muzsikalendarium.hu) website has more serious offerings: classical concerts, opera, dance and the like.

Buying Tickets

You can book almost anything online from the following sites:

➜ **Jegymester** (www.jegymester.hu)

➜ **Kulturinfo** (www.kulturinfo.hu)

➜ **Ticket Express** (www.eventtim.hu)

➜ **Ticket Pro** (www.ticketpro.hu)

selected evenings from May to October. For bookings, contact **Hungária Koncert** (☑1-317 1377; www.ticket.info.hu).

Theatre & Film

It's unlikely you'll brave a play in the Hungarian language, but the József Katona Theatre (p90) is the place to go if you do. Budapest's most celebrated English-language improvisational theatre company is **Scallabouche** (☑06 20 541 5833; www.scallabouche.com).

Many cinemas in Budapest screen English-language films with Hungarian subtitles. Consult the listings in the freebie *Budapest Funzine* or *PestiEst* to find out where and when these showings are on.

Be aware, though, that many foreign films are also dubbed into Hungarian, usually indicated in listings with the words *magyarul beszélő* or simply 'mb'. Films that have been given Hungarian subtitles *(feliratos),* rather than being dubbed, will retain their original soundtrack.

Spectator Sport

The most popular spectator sports are football and water polo, although motor racing (especially during the Formula 1 Hungarian Grand Prix) and horse racing – both trotting and flat racing – at Kincsem Park (p152) also have their fans.

FOOTBALL

Once on top of the heap of European football – the national team's victory over England both at Wembley (6-3) in 1953 and at home (7-1) the following year are still talked about as if the winning goals were scored yesterday – Hungary has failed to qualify for any major tournament since 1986. The national team plays at Ferenc Puskás Stadium (p153).

Although it is not one of the five premier-league football teams in Budapest, no club has dominated football here over the years like Ferencvárosi Torna Club (FTC), which plays at the newly built Flórián Albert Stadium (p143) in Pest. For match schedules check the **Hungarian Football** (www.hungarianfootball.com) website.

WATER POLO

Hungary has won the European Championships in water polo a dozen times since 1926, the World Championships three times (most recently in 2013) and taken nine gold medals at the Olympic Games, so it's worth catching a professional or amateur game of this exciting seven-a-side sport. The **Hungarian Water Polo Association** (☑info 1-412 0041; www.waterpolo.hu) is based at the Alfréd Hajós swimming complex (p111) on Margaret Island.

Activities

The best place for canoeing and kayaking in Budapest is on the Danube from the Buda side at Rómaifürdő. To get there, take the HÉV suburban line to the Rómaifürdő stop and walk east towards the river. Rent kayaks or canoes from the **Béke Rowing Club** (Béke Evezős Klub; ☑06 20 338 4563, 1-388 9303; www.hajotarolas.com; III Római part 53 ; canoe per day for 2/4 people 2600/3200Ft, kayak for 1/2 people 1600/2600Ft; ⊙8am-8pm Jun-Aug, to 7pm May & Sep, to 5pm Apr & Oct; ⓂHÉV to Rómaifürdő stop) or the **Óbuda Sport Club** (ÓSE; ☑1-240 3353; www.ose.hu; III Rozgonyi Piroska utca 28; canoes & kayaks per day from 2500Ft; ⊙8am-6pm May-Sep, 10am-4pm Oct-Apr; ⓂHÉV to Rómaifürdő stop), both about 5km north of the Árpád Bridge.

If you'd prefer to get down and dirty, head for the hills and visit one of Buda's underground caverns (p78): Mátyáshegy Cave, Pálvölgy Cave or Szemlőhegy Cave.

Lonely Planet's Top Choices

Ferenc Liszt Music Academy Budapest's premier venue for classical concerts is not just a place to go to hear music but an opportunity to ogle the wonderful decorative Zsolnay porcelain and frescoes as well. (p129)

Palace of Arts The city's most up-to-date cultural venue with two concert halls and near-perfect acoustics. (p142)

Hungarian State Opera House Small but perfectly formed home to both the state opera company and the Hungarian National Ballet. (p130)

Trafó House of Contemporary Arts A mixture of music, theatre and especially the cream of the crop of dance in southern Pest. (p142)

Budapest Operetta Campy fun for the whole family on Nagymező utca, Budapest's Broadway or West End. (p105)

Uránia National Cinema Art Deco/neo-Moorish extravaganza – a palatial place to see any type of film. (p142)

Best for Táncház

Fonó Buda Music House Probably the best place in town to hear and see *táncház* (folk music and dance). (p71)

Municipal Cultural House Your chance to hear the incomparable Muzsikás. (p71)

Aranytíz Cultural Centre (p106) Hosts the wonderful Kalamajka Táncház on Saturday.

Marczibányi tér Cultural Centre Magyar, Slovakian and Moldavian dance and music. (p63)

Budavár Cultural Centre Wonderful line-up of kids' programs beneath the castle. (p63)

Best for Jazz & Blues

Budapest Jazz Club Reliable music venue still swings in its new location. (p113)

Jedermann Relaxed Ráday utca hang-out for jazz and great grills. (p143)

Budapest Music Center Sleek, modern venue with concert hall, jazz club and restaurant. (p143)

Nothin' but the Blues As it says on the tin, there's just blues at this basement bar. (p143)

Best for Live Music

Spinoza Café An excellent place to see *klezmer* (Jewish folk music) concerts. (p123)

Akvárium Klub In an old bus terminal, two large halls serve up a quality line-up of live acts. (p90)

Gödör Great gigs in the midst of banging Erzsébetváros. (p130)

Ladó Café Folk, jazz, opera and tango in a restaurant setting. (p130)

Best for Sport

Flórián Albert Stadium See the Fradi boys play in this recently rebuilt stadium. (p143)

Hungaroring Stages Hungary's prime sporting event, the Formula 1 Grand Prix. (p152)

Kincsem Park Year-round equine trotting and meetings. (p152)

Alfréd Hajós Sports Pools Home to Hungary's Olympic swimming and water-polo teams. (p111)

Best for Dance

National Dance Theatre Magnet for virtually every dance troupe in town. (p63)

MU Színház Nerve centre for modern dance in Budapest. (p71)

Hungarian State Opera House Neo-Renaissance opera house dating back to 1884. (p130)

Best for Film

Örökmozgó Foreign classics in their original languages. (p130)

Művész Art Mozi Mostly (but not only) artsy and cult films. (p105)

Puskin Art Mozi A healthy mix of art-house and popular releases. (p90)

Uránia National Cinema Tarted-up film palace with an excellent cafe. (p142)

Best for Theatre

József Katona Theatre Public theatre hosting some of the best troupes in the country. (p90)

National Theatre Classic plays in an Electic building right on the Danube. (p143)

Budapest Puppet Theatre Certain to entertain if you have little 'uns in tow. (p130)

# Shopping

Budapest is a fantastic city for shopping, whether you're in the market for traditional folk craft with a twist, cutting-edge designer goods, the latest in flash headgear or honey-sweet dessert wine. Traditional markets stand side by side with mammoth shopping malls, and old-style umbrella makers can still be found next to avant-garde fashion boutiques.

Specialities & Souvenirs

Traditional items with a Hungarian branding – called Hungarica here – include folk embroidery and ceramics, pottery, wall hangings, painted wooden toys and boxes, dolls, all types of basketry, and porcelain (especially that from Herend and Zsolnay). Feather or goose-down pillows and duvets (comforters) are of exceptionally high quality.

Foodstuffs that are expensive or difficult to buy elsewhere – goose liver (both fresh and potted), dried mushrooms, jam (especially the apricot variety), prepared meats like Pick salami, the many types of paprika – make nice gifts (as long as you're allowed to take them into your country). Some of Hungary's 'boutique' wines also make excellent gifts: a bottle of six-*puttonyos* (the sweetest) Tokaji Aszú dessert wine always goes down a treat. Fruit brandy *(pálinka)* is a stronger option.

Books and CDs are affordable, and there's an excellent selection, especially of folk and classical music.

Markets & Malls

Some people consider a visit to one of Budapest's flea markets – the celebrated Ecseri Piac (p142) or the smaller City Park (p153) one – a highlight, not just as a place to indulge their consumer vices but as the consummate Budapest experience.

In the mid-1990s Budapest began to go mall crazy, and at last count the city had upwards of two dozen in the centre of town and on the fringes. However, 'mall' may not properly describe what the Hungarians call *bevásárló és szórakoztató központ* (shopping and amusement centres); here you'll find everything from designer salons, traditional shops and dry cleaners to food courts, casinos, cinemas and clubs. It's a place to spend the entire day, much as you would just about anywhere in the globalised world of the third millennium. Don't bother, we say.

Instead visit one of the city's 20 large food markets, most of them in Pest. The vast majority are closed on Sunday, and Monday is always very quiet, with only a few stalls open. The Nagycsarnok (p143) is a good introduction but can get crammed with tourists in season. Instead, check out the Rákóczi tér market (p143) or the covered market at Lehel tér (p112) in Újlipótváros.

Shopping Streets

Some streets or areas in Budapest specialise in certain goods or products.

Antiques: V Falk Miksa utca in Pest and II Frankel Leó út in Buda.

Antiquarian & secondhand books: V Múzeum körút in Pest.

Boutiques & souvenirs: V Váci utca in Pest.

International fashion brands: V Deák Ferenc utca (aka Fashion St) in Pest.

Local designer goods & fashion: VI Király utca in Pest.

Lonely Planet's Top Choices

BÁV Check out any branch of this pawn and secondhand shop chain if you can't make it to the flea markets. (p106)

XD Design&Souvenir Excellent choice for 'Made in Hungary' traditional gifts as well as some cracking newly designed items. (p90)

Mézes Kuckó Still the very best place in town for nut-and-honey cookies. (p114)

Herend Village Pottery Big, bold and colourful platters make a lovely change from traditional Herend porcelain. (p63)

Billerbeck The place to buy an all-goose-down duvet (comforter) or set of pillows. (p131)

Bomo Art The finest paper and paper goods are sold here, including leather-bound notebooks, photo albums and address books. (p90)

Best for Hungarica

Holló Atelier Attractive folk art all handmade on site. (p90)

Herend Finest Hungarian porcelain is the ultimate gift or souvenir. (p63)

Intuita Two shops full of contemporary crafts on Váci utca. (p92)

Memories of Hungary Museum-quality souvenirs a step from the basilica. (p106)

Best for Food & Drink

Bortársaság The first port of call for buying wine. (p63)

Magyar Pálinka Háza Shelves and shelves of all kinds of *pálinka* (fruit brandy). (p143)

Nagycsarnok Huge market hall selling everything from fruit and veg to paprika and goose liver. (p143)

Rózsavölgyi Csokoládé Artisan chocolate bars and bonbons, beautifully packaged. (p90)

Hecserli All manner of Hungarian goodies, and coffee and sandwiches too. (p91)

Best for Fashion & Clothing

Romani Design Extravagant Roma fashion and accessories with a modern twist. (p106)

Valeria Fazekas Beautiful designer millinery. (p92)

Retrock Vintage superstore with Hungarian streetwear designs. (p131)

Vass Shoes Classic footwear – cobbled for you or ready to wear. (p91)

Manier Luxury home-grown ready-to-wear and designer streetwear. (p107)

Best for Books

Bestsellers Budapest's most complete English-language bookshop; helpful staff. (p106)

Szőnyi Antikváriuma Printed treasures to read or frame. (p106)

Írók Boltja The 'Writers' Bookshop' – pick up Hungarian authors in translation here. (p131)

Massolit New and secondhand in an atmospheric old shop with a little garden. (p130)

Book Station No one does secondhand books like these guys. (p114)

Explore Budapest

BUDAPEST'S TOP SIGHTS

Neighbourhoods at a Glance

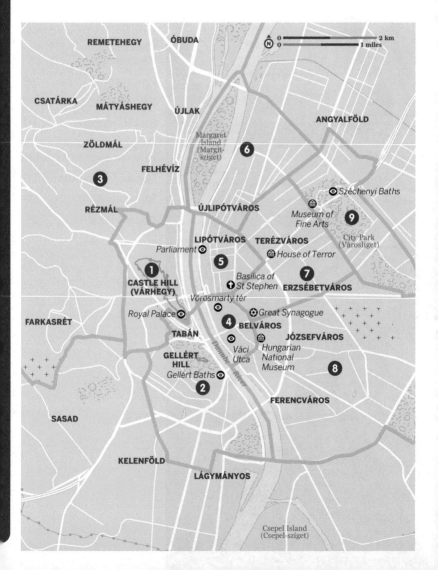

❶ Castle District (p50)

The Castle District encompasses Castle Hill (Várhegy) – nerve centre of Budapest's history and packed with many of the capital's most important museums and other attractions – as well as ground-level Víziváros (Watertown). What the latter lacks in sights it makes up for in excellent restaurants, many of them around Széll Kálmán tér, a major transport hub and the centre of urban Buda.

❷ Gellért Hill & Tabán (p64)

Standing atop Gellért Hill and proclaiming freedom throughout the city is the lovely Liberty Monument, Budapest's most visible statue. She looks down on the Tabán, a leafy neighbourhood originally settled by the Serbs, and a great many students; the Budapest University of Technology and Economics (BME) is here.

❸ Óbuda & Buda Hills (p72)

Óbuda is the oldest part of Buda and retains a lost-in-the-past village feel; here you'll find excellent museums, the remains of the Roman settlement of Aquincum and some legendary eateries. The Buda Hills are a breath of fresh air and offer forms of transport that will delight kids of all ages.

❹ Belváros (p81)

The 'Inner Town' is just that – the centre of Pest's universe, especially when it comes to tourism. This is where you'll find Váci utca, with its luxury shops, restaurants and bars, and Vörösmarty tér, home to the city's most celebrated *cukrászda* (cake shop) and one of its two Michelin-starred restaurants. The centre is Deák Ferenc tér, where metro lines M1, M2 and M3 (but not M4) converge.

❺ Parliament & Around (p93)

Bordering the Belváros to the north is Lipótváros (Leopold Town), with the landmark Parliament facing the Danube to the west and the equally iconic Basilica of St Stephen to the east. In this guide we've included part of Terézváros (Teresa Town), named in honour of Empress Maria Theresa, as well. Budapest's Broadway or West End is that district's Nagymező utca.

❻ Margaret Island & Northern Pest (p108)

Lovely Margaret Island is neither Buda nor Pest, but its shaded walkways, large swimming complexes, thermal spa and gardens offer refuge to the denizens of both sides of the river. Northern Pest in this section means Újlipótváros (New Leopold Town). Vaguely reminiscent of New York's Upper West Side, it has tree-lined streets, antique shops, boutiques and lovely cafes.

❼ Erzsébetváros & the Jewish Quarter (p115)

You'll probably be spending the bulk of your time in this neighbourhood, which takes in Erzsébetváros (Elizabeth Town) and most of Terézváros, including well- and high-heeled Andrássy út, the long, dramatic and *très chic* boulevard that slices through Terézváros. Here you'll find a large percentage of Budapest's accommodation, restaurants serving everything from Chinese to Serbian, and Pest's hottest and coolest nightspots.

❽ Southern Pest (p134)

The colourful districts of Józsefváros (Joseph Town) and Ferencváros (Francis, or Franz, Town) – no prizes for guessing which Habsburg emperors these were named after – are traditionally working class and full of students. It's a lot of fun wandering the backstreets, peeping into courtyards and small, often traditional, shops.

❾ City Park & Beyond (p145)

City Park, at the northern end of epic Andrássy út, is the largest park in Budapest but a lot more than just a pretty face. Its main entrance, Heroes' Sq, is ringed by important museums and significant monuments. The streets on the fringes of the park are paradise for fans of Art Nouveau and Secessionist architecture.

Castle District

CASTLE HILL | VÍZIVÁROS

Neighbourhood Top Five

1 Comprehending Budapest's long and often convoluted story by visiting the revamped **Castle Museum** (p54) and then viewing many of the events captured forever by some of the nation's greatest artists at the **Hungarian National Gallery** (p52).

2 Enjoying views of the Danube, Gellért Hill and Pest from the landmark **Fishermen's Bastion** (p56).

3 Reliving the WWII siege of Budapest by descending into the **Hospital in the Rock** (p57) deep below Buda Castle.

4 Savouring a *Dobos torta* (a multilayered chocolate-and-cream cake with a caramelised brown-sugar top) at the famous **Ruszwurm Cukrászda** (p62).

5 Soaking the travel-weary blues away at the **Király Baths** (p63), another legacy of the Turkish occupation.

For more detail of this area, see Map p230 ➡

Explore: Castle District

Castle Hill (Várhegy), also called the Castle Quarter (Várnegyed), is a 1km-long limestone plateau towering above the Danube. The premier sight in the capital and high on Unesco's World Heritage list, it contains Budapest's most important medieval monuments and museums.

The walled area consists of two distinct parts: the Old Town to the north, where commoners lived in the Middle Ages (the present-day owners of the coveted burgher houses are anything but 'common'); and the Royal Palace, the original site of the castle built in the 13th century, now housing important sights, to the south.

There are many ways to reach Castle Hill, but the most fun is to board the **Sikló** (I Szent György tér; ☉7.30am-10pm; one way/return adult 1000/1700Ft, child 650/1100Ft), a funicular railway built in 1870 that ascends from Clark Ádám tér at the western end of Chain Bridge to Szent György tér near the Royal Palace.

Víziváros (Watertown) is the narrow area between the Danube and Castle Hill that widens as it approaches Óbuda to the north and Rózsadomb (Rose Hill) to the northwest, spreading as far west as Széll Kálmán tér, Buda's most important transport hub. In the Middle Ages those involved in trades, crafts and fishing lived here. Many of the district's churches were used as mosques under the Turks, who also built bathhouses here, including the Király Baths.

Local Life

→ **Eating** Locals working on Castle Hill avoid the tourists by eating at the self-service Fortuna Önkiszolgáló (p59).

→ **Sights** Be one of a crowd of maybe two and catch the low-key but ceremonial changing of the guard at Sándor Palace (p60) hourly between 9am and 6pm.

→ **Entertainment** Try to catch something – anything – at the renovated Jenő Hubay Music Hall (p63).

Getting There & Away

→**Bus** I Clark Ádám tér or V Deák Ferenc tér in Pest for 16 to I Dísz tér on Castle Hill; I Fő utca for 86 to Óbuda and south Buda.

→**Funicular** I Clark Ádám tér for Sikló to I Szent György tér on Castle Hill.

→**HÉV** Batthyány tér.

→**Metro** M2 Batthyány tér and Széll Kálmán tér.

→**Tram** II Vidra utca for 17 to Óbuda; I Batthyány tér for 19 to I Szent Gellért tér and south Buda; 4 and 6 to Pest (Big Ring Rd).

Lonely Planet's Top Tip

A real 'insider's' way to get to and from Castle Hill is from I Dózsa tér (bus 16 from Pest), where you'll find a **lift** (200Ft; ☉6am-7pm Mon, to 8.30pm Tue-Sat, 9am-6.30pm Sun) that will whisk you up to the Lion Court and National Széchenyi Library. Glass cases in the hallway where the lift starts and ends are filled with archaeological finds from the Royal Palace.

✕ Best Places to Eat

→ Csalogány 26 (p61)
→ Atakám (p61)
→ Déryné (p61)
→ Horgásztanya Vendéglő (p61)
→ Artigiana Gelati (p61)

For reviews, see p58➡

⚲ Best Places to Drink

→ Ruszwurm Cukrászda (p62)
→ Oscar American Bar (p62)
→ Lánchíd Söröző (p62)
→ Score Club (p62)

For reviews, see p62➡

🔒 Best Places to Shop

→ Mester Porta (p63)
→ Bortársaság (p63)
→ Herend Village Pottery (p63)

For reviews, see p63➡

TOP SIGHT
ROYAL PALACE

The enormous Royal Palace has been razed and rebuilt at least six times over the past seven centuries. Béla IV established a residence here in the mid-13th century and subsequent kings added to it. The palace was levelled in the battle to rout the Turks in 1686; the Habsburgs rebuilt it but spent very little time here. Today the palace contains two important museums, the national library and an abundance of statues and monuments.

There are two entrances. The first is via the **Habsburg Steps** and through an ornamental gateway dating from 1903. The other way in is via **Corvinus Gate**, with its big black raven symbolising King Matthias Corvinus. Either is good for the museums.

Hungarian National Gallery

The **Hungarian National Gallery** (Nemzeti Galéria; ☏1-201 9082; www.mng.hu; I Szent György tér 2, Buildings A-D; adult/concession 1400/700Ft; audioguide 800Ft; ⏰10am-6pm Tue-Sun; 🚌16, 16A, 116) is an overwhelming collection spread across four floors that traces Hungarian art from the 11th century to the present day. The largest collections include medieval and Renaissance stonework, Gothic wooden sculptures and panel paintings, late Gothic winged altars and late Renaissance and baroque art. The museum also has an important collection of Hungarian paintings and sculpture from the 19th and 20th centuries.

The museum was formed in 1957 from a collection started in the mid-19th century that was previously exhibited at the Museum of Fine Arts and the Hungarian National Museum, and moved to this site in 1975. The permanent collection is, for the most part, exhibited in Buildings B, C and D, with A and the 3rd floor of all four buildings usually reserved for temporary exhibits. The lapidarium on the ground floor with medieval

DON'T MISS...

➡ Late Gothic altarpieces

➡ Csontváry's works

➡ Rippl-Rónai's *Father and Uncle Piacsek Drinking Red Wine*

➡ Gothic statues and heads

➡ Renaissance door frame

PRACTICALITIES

➡ Királyi Palota

➡ Map p230

➡ I Szent György tér

and Renaissance stone carvings may be closed for renovations.

Gothic Works

The winged altarpieces in the so-called **Great Throne Room** on the 1st floor of Building D date from the 15th and early 16th centuries and form one of the greatest collections of late Gothic painting in the world. The almost modern *Visitation* (1506) by Master MS is both lyrical and intimate, but keep an eye open for the monumental Annunciation Altarpiece (1510–20) and the intense, almost Renaissance face of John the Baptist in a series of four paintings (1490) of scenes from his life.

Renaissance & Baroque Works

The finest 18th-century baroque painters in Hungary were actually Austrians, including Franz Anton Maulbertsch (1724–96; *Death of St Joseph*) and his contemporary István Dorfmeister (1725–97; *Christ on the Cross*). Other greats of the period with more of a Magyar pedigree include Jakob Bogdány (1660–1724), whose *Two Macaws, a Cockatoo and a Jay, with Fruit* is a veritable Garden of Eden, and Ádám Mányoki (1673–1757), court painter to Ferenc Rákóczi II. You'll find their works in the galleries adjoining the Great Throne Room on the 1st floor.

Nineteenth-Century Works

Move into Building C for examples of the saccharine National Romantic School of heroic paintings, whose most prolific exponents were Bertalan Székely (1835–1910; *Women of Eger*) and Gyula Benczúr (1844–1920; *Recapture of Buda Castle, The Baptism of Vajk*). This style of painting gave way to the realism of Mihály Munkácsy (1844–1900), the 'painter of the Great Plain' *(Storm in the Puszta)* and of intense religious subjects *(Golgotha, Christ Before Pilate)*, whose works are in Building B. Here too are works by Pál Szinyei Merse (1845–1920), the country's foremost Impressionist painter *(Picnic in May, The Skylark)*.

Twentieth-Century Works & Beyond

The greatest painters working in the late 19th and early 20th centuries were Tivadar Kosztka Csontváry (1853–1919), who has been compared to Van Gogh, and József Rippl-Rónai (1861–1927), the key exponent of Secessionist painting in Hungary. Among the latter's greatest works (Building C, 2nd floor) are *Father and Uncle Piacsek Drinking Red Wine* and *Woman with Bird Cage*. Don't overlook the harrowing depictions of war and the dispossessed by WWI artist László Mednyánszky (1852–1919; *In Serbia, Soldiers Resting*) and the colourful,

TIVADAR KOSZTKA CSONTVÁRY

Many critics consider Tivadar Kosztka Csontváry – a symbolist artist whose tragic life is sometimes compared with that of his contemporary, Vincent van Gogh – to be Hungary's greatest painter. Csontváry produced his major works in just half a dozen years starting in 1903 when he was 50. His efforts met with praise at his first exhibition in 1907 in Paris, but critics panned his work at a showing in Budapest the following year. He died penniless just after WWI. View his works, including *Ruins of the Greek Theatre at Taormina* (1905) and *Pilgrimage to the Cedars of Lebanon* (1907), on the 1st floor of the Hungarian National Gallery's Building C.

The Gothic statues found in the outer bailey of the Royal Palace in 1974 are a treasure trove for social historians. They total almost 80 and portray both commoners and aristocrats of both sexes. They are invaluable tools in the research of medieval dress, hairstyles and personal effects.

HUNGARIAN NATIONAL GALLERY

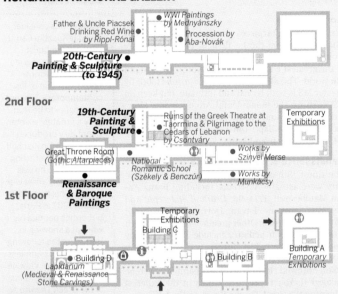

2nd Floor

- 20th-Century Painting & Sculpture (to 1945)
- Father & Uncle Piacsek Drinking Red Wine by Rippl-Rónai
- WWI Paintings by Mednyánszky
- Procession by Aba-Novák

1st Floor

- 19th-Century Painting & Sculpture
- Ruins of the Greek Theatre at Taormina & Pilgrimage to the Cedars of Lebanon by Csontváry
- Temporary Exhibitions
- Great Throne Room (Gothic Altarpieces)
- National Romantic School (Székely & Benczúr)
- Works by Szinyei Merse
- Renaissance & Baroque Paintings
- Works by Munkácsy

Ground Floor

- Temporary Exhibitions Building C
- Building D
- Lapidarium (Medieval & Renaissance Stone Carvings)
- Building B
- Building A Temporary Exhibitions

upbeat paintings of carnivals and celebrations by Vilmos Aba-Novák (1894–1941; *Procession, The Fair at Csikszereda*). On the 3rd floor in Building C, you'll find the impressive new *Shifts*, the totally revamped permanent exhibition of Hungarian art since WWII.

Castle Museum

The **Castle Museum** (Vármúzeum; ☎1-487 8800; www.btm.hu; I Szent György tér 2, Bldg E; adult/concession 1800/900Ft; ☺10am-6pm Tue-Sun Feb-Oct, to 4pm Nov-Mar; ☒16, 16A, 116, ☒19, 41), part of the multi-branched Budapest History Museum, explores the city's 2000-year history over three floors. Restored palace rooms dating from the 15th century can be entered from the basement, where there are three vaulted halls, one with a magnificent Renaissance door frame in red marble bearing the seal of Queen Beatrice and tiles with a raven and a ring (the seal of her husband, King Matthias Corvinus), leading to the Gothic and Renaissance Halls, the Royal Cellar and the vaulted Tower Chapel (1320) dedicated to St Stephen.

On the ground floor, exhibits showcase Budapest during the Middle Ages, with dozens of important Gothic statues, heads and fragments of courtiers, squires and saints discovered during excavations in 1974. There are also artefacts recovered from a well in 1999 that date back to the Middle Ages, notably a 14th-century tapestry of the Hungarian coat of arms with the fleur-de-lis of King Charles Robert's House of Anjou. A wonderful new exhibit on the 1st floor called *1000 Years of a Capital* traces the history of Budapest from the arrival of the Magyars and the Turkish occupation to modern times in 10 multimedia sections, taking an interesting and very intelligent look at housing, ethnic diversity, religion and other such issues over the centuries. The excellent audioguide is 1200Ft.

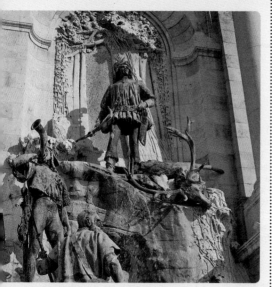

Matthias Fountain

To the east of the Habsburg Steps entrance to the palace is a bronze statue from 1905 of the **Turul**, a hawk-like totemic bird that had supposedly impregnated Emese, the grandmother of Árpád, the chief military commander who led the Magyar tribes into the Carpathian Basin in about AD 895. To the southeast, just in front of Building C, stands a statue of **Eugene of Savoy**, the Habsburg prince who wiped out the last Turkish army in Hungary at the Battle of Zenta in 1697. Designed by József Róna 200 years later, it is considered to be the finest equestrian statue in Budapest. In the middle of the square on the other side of the building is a statue by György Vastagh of a **Hortobágyi csikós**, a Hungarian cowboy in full regalia breaking a mighty *bábolna* steed.

National Széchenyi Library

The **National Széchenyi Library** (Országos Széchenyi Könyvtár; ☎1-224 3700; www.oszk.hu; I Szent György tér 4-6, Bldg F; ☉9am-8pm, stacks to 7pm Tue-Sat; ☑16) contains codices and manuscripts, a large collection of foreign newspapers and a copy of everything published in Hungary or the Hungarian language. It was founded in 1802 by Count Ferenc Széchenyi, father of the heroic István, who endowed it with 15,000 books and 2000 manuscripts. This library allows **members** (adult/student annual 6500/3500Ft, per six months 3500/2000Ft, daily per person 1200Ft) to do research, peruse the general stacks and read the rather hefty collection of foreign newspapers and magazines.

Matthias Fountain

Facing the Royal Palace's large courtyard to the northwest is the Romantic-style Matthias Fountain (Mátyás kút), portraying the young king Matthias Corvinus in hunting garb. To the right below him is Szép Ilona (Beautiful Helen). The middle one of the king's three dogs was blown up during the war; canine-loving Hungarians quickly had an exact copy made.

Ilona, the girl featured prominently in the Matthias Fountain, is the protagonist of a Romantic ballad by poet Mihály Vörösmarty: she fell in love with a dashing 'hunter' – King Matthias – and, upon learning his true identity and feeling unworthy, died of a broken heart.

⦿ SIGHTS

⦿ Castle Hill

ROYAL PALACE   PALACE

See p52.

SZÉCHENYI CHAIN BRIDGE   BRIDGE

Map p230 (Széchenyi lánchíd; 🚊16) This twin-towered span is the oldest and arguably the most beautiful bridge over the Danube. It is named in honour of its initiator, István Széchenyi, but was built by a Scotsman named Adam Clark. When it opened in 1849, Széchenyi Chain Bridge was unique for two reasons: it was the first permanent dry link between Buda and Pest, and the aristocracy, previously exempt from all taxation, had to pay the toll.

FISHERMEN'S BASTION   MONUMENT

Map p230 (Halászbástya; I Szentháromság tér; adult/concession 700/500Ft; ⊙9am-11pm mid-Mar–mid-Oct; 🚊16, 16A, 116) Built as a viewing platform in 1905 by Frigyes Schulek, the architect behind Matthias Church, the bastion is a neo-Gothic masquerade that looks medieval and offers among the best views in Budapest. The bastion's name was taken from the medieval guild of fishermen responsible for defending this stretch of the castle wall.

MUSEUM OF MILITARY HISTORY   MUSEUM

Map p230 (Hadtörténeti Múzeum; ☎1-325 1600; www.militaria.hu; I Tóth Árpád sétány 40; adult/child 1100/550Ft; ⊙10am-6pm Tue-Sun Apr-Sep, to 4pm Tue-Sun Oct-Mar; 🚊16, 16A, 116) Loaded with weaponry dating from before the Turkish conquest, this museum also does a good job with uniforms, medals, flags and battle-themed fine art. Exhibits focus particularly on the 1848–49 War of Independence and the Hungarian Royal Army under the command of Admiral Miklós Horthy (1918–43).

MAGDALENE TOWER   RUIN

Map p230 (Magdolona toronye; I Kapisztrán tér; 🚊16, 16A, 116) The big steeple on the south side of Kapisztrán tér, opposite the Museum of Military History and visible for kilometres to the west of Castle Hill, is the reconstructed spire of an 18th-century church. The church, once reserved for Hungarian speakers in this district, was used as a mosque during the Turkish occupation and was destroyed in a 1944 air raid.

GOLDEN EAGLE PHARMACY   MUSEUM

Map p230 (Arany Sas Patika; ☎1-375 9772; www.semmelweis.museum.hu; I Tárnok utca 18; adult/concession 500/250Ft; ⊙10.30am-8pm Tue-Sun mid-Mar–Oct, to 6pm Nov–mid-Mar; 🚊16, 16A, 116) Just north of Dísz tér on the site of Budapest's first pharmacy (1681), this branch of the Semmelweis Museum of Medical History in Tabán contains an unusual mixture of displays, including a mock-up of an alchemist's laboratory with dried bats and tiny crocodiles in jars, and a small 'spice rack' used by 17th-century travellers for their daily fixes of curative herbs.

HOUSE OF HUNGARIAN WINES   WINE CELLAR

Map p230 (Magyar Borok Háza; ☎1-201 3057; www.budavaribor.hu; I Szentháromság tér 6; tastings of 4/6 wines from 3500/4500Ft; ⊙noon-8pm; 🚊16, 16A, 116) This wine centre opposite the Hilton offers a crash course in Hungarian viticulture, with hundreds of wines from Hungary's six main regions to try. Be careful, though; 'crash' may soon become the operative word.

MEDIEVAL JEWISH PRAYER HOUSE   JEWISH

Map p230 (Középkori Zsidó Imaház; www.btm.hu; I Táncsics Mihály utca 26; adult/child 800/400Ft; ⊙10am-5pm Tue-Sun May-Oct, to 4pm Wed-Sun Nov-Apr; 🚊16, 16A, 116) With sections dating from the late 14th century, this tiny, ancient house of worship contains items linked to the Jewish community of Buda, as well as Gothic stone carvings and tombstones.

MUSIC HISTORY MUSEUM   MUSEUM

Map p230 (Zenetörténeti Múzeum; ☎1-214 6770; www.zti.hu; I Táncsics Mihály utca 7; adult/child 600/300Ft; ⊙10am-4pm Tue-Sun; 🚊16, 16A, 116) Housed in an 18th-century palace with a lovely courtyard, this wonderful little museum traces the development of music in Hungary from the 18th century to the present day. There are rooms devoted to the work of Béla Bartók, Franz Liszt and Joseph Haydn, with lots of instruments and original scores and manuscripts.

TELEPHONY MUSEUM   MUSEUM

Map p230 (Telefónia Múzeum; ☎1-201 8857; www.postamuzeum.hu; I Úri utca 49 & Országház utca 30; adult/child 500/250Ft; ⊙10am-4pm Tue-Sun; 🚊16, 16A, 116) This museum documents the history of the telephone in Hungary since 1881, when the world's first switchboard – a Rotary 7A1, still working and the centrepiece of the exhibition – was set up in Budapest. Other exhibits pay tribute to Tivadar Puskás, a Hungarian

TOP SIGHT
CASTLE HILL CAVES

Below Castle Hill is a 28km-long network of caves formed by thermal springs. The caves were used for military purposes during the Turkish occupation, as air-raid shelters during WWII, and as a secret military installation during the Cold War. Two sections can be visited.

The **Buda Castle Labyrinth** (Budavári Labirintus; ☎1-212 0207; www.labirintusbudapest.hu; I Úri utca 9 & Lovas út 4/a; adult/under 12yr/senior & student 2000/600/1500Ft; ☺10am-7pm) is a 1200m-long system 16m under the Castle District that explores how the caves have been used since prehistoric times in five separate labyrinths encompassing 10 halls and galleries. It's good fun and a relief from the heat on a hot day, but it can get scary if you lose your way or after 6pm when you tour in the dark with lanterns.

Far more instructive is the excellent **Hospital in the Rock** (Sziklakórház; ☎06 70 701 0101; www.sziklakorhaz.eu/en; I Lovas út 4/c; adult/6-25yr & senior 3600/1800Ft; ☺10am-8pm), used extensively during WWII and again during the 1956 Uprising. It contains original medical equipment, graffiti and 200 wax figures. The guided hour-long tour includes a walk through a Cold War nuclear bunker.

DON'T MISS...

➡ Prehistoric labyrinth

➡ WWII hospital equipment

➡ Cold War nuclear bunker

PRACTICALITIES

➡ Map p230

➡ 🚌16, 16A, 116

---

associate of Thomas Edison, and cover the latter's fleeting visit to Budapest in 1891. Enter from Országház utca 30 at the weekend.

◉ Víziváros

CLARK ÁDÁM TÉR　　　　　　　SQUARE
Map p230 (Adam Clark Square; 🚌16, 86) Víziváros begins at this square named after the 19th-century Scottish engineer who supervised the building of the Széchenyi Chain Bridge and who designed the all-important *alagút* (tunnel) under Castle Hill, which took just eight months to carve out of the limestone in 1853. What looks like an elongated concrete doughnut hidden in the bushes to the south is the **0km stone**. All Hungarian roads to and from the capital are measured from this spot.

FŐ UTCA　　　　　　　　　　STREET
Map p230 (🚌86) Fő utca is the arrow-straight 'Main St' running from Clark Ádám tér through Víziváros; not surprisingly, it dates from Roman times. At the former **Capuchin church** (I Fő utca 30-32; 🚌86, 🚌19, 41) you can see the remains of an Islamic-style ogee-arched door and window on the southern side; it was used as a mosque during the Turkish occupation. Around the corner is the seal of King Matthias Corvinus – a raven with a ring in its beak – and a little square called Corvin tér. Here you'll find the delightful Lajos Fountain (Lajos kútja) dating from 1904.

BATTHYÁNY TÉR　　　　　　　SQUARE
Map p230 (Ⓜ️M2 Batthyány tér, 🚌19, 41) The centre of Víziváros, Batthyány tér is the best place to take pictures of the photogenic Parliament building across the Danube. On the southern side is the 18th-century baroque **Church of St Anne**, with one of the most eye-catching interiors of any baroque church in Budapest, including a magnificent late 18th-century pulpit and organ.

NAGY IMRE TÉR　　　　　　　SQUARE
Map p230 (🚌86, Ⓜ️M2 Batthyány tér) Nagy Imre tér is home to the former **Military Court of Justice** (II Fő utca 70-78) on its northern side. Imre Nagy and others were tried and sentenced to death here in 1958 for their role in the 1956 Uprising. It was also the site of the notorious **Fő utca prison**, where many other victims of the

TOP SIGHT
MATTHIAS CHURCH

Parts of Castle Hill's landmark church date back 500 years, notably the carvings above the southern entrance (Mary Portal). But basically the Matthias Church – so named because King Matthias Corvinus married Beatrice here in 1474 – is a neo-Gothic creation designed by architect Frigyes Schulek in 1896.

The church has a delicate spire and a colourful Zsolnay-tiled roof, which massive works in the last decade restored to its 19th-century glory. The interior houses remarkable stained-glass windows, frescoes and wall decorations by Romantic painters Károly Lotz and Bertalan Székely. Organ concerts take place on certain evenings (usually Friday and Saturday at 8pm), continuing a tradition dating from 1867 when Franz Liszt's *Hungarian Coronation Mass* was first played here for the coronation of Franz Joseph and Elizabeth.

Steps in the southwestern corner lead up to the **Royal Oratory** and the small **Matthias Church Collection of Ecclesiastical Art** (Mátyás-templom Egyházművészeti Gyűteménye), included in the admission fee, which exhibit ornate monstrances, reliquaries, chalices, lamps and censers as well as replicas of the Crown of St Stephen and other items of coronation regalia.

DON'T MISS...

➡ Zsolnay-tiled roof
➡ Mary Portal
➡ Frescoes
➡ Ecclesiastical art

PRACTICALITIES

➡ Mátyás Templom
➡ Map p230
➡ ☎1-355 5657
➡ www.matyas-templom.hu
➡ I Szentháromság tér 2
➡ adult/concession 1000/700Ft
➡ ◷9am-5pm Mon-Sat, 1-5pm Sun
➡ 🚌16, 16A, 116

Communist regime were incarcerated and tortured.

FOUNDRY MUSEUM MUSEUM
Map p230 (Öntödei Múzeum; ☎1-201 4370; www.omm.hu; II Bem József utca 20; adult/child 800/400Ft; ◷9am-5pm Tue-Sun Apr-Oct; 🚌86, 🚋4, 6) This museum – a lot more interesting than it sounds – is housed in the Ganz Machine Works foundry that was in use until the 1960s, and the massive ladles and cranes still stand, anxiously awaiting employment. Alas, time and progress have frozen them still. Have a look at the church a short distance to the east across pedestrianised Ganz utca: it's the 1760 Greek Catholic **Chapel of St Florian** (Szent Flórián kápolna; Map p230; II Fő utca 88) dedicated to the patron saint of firefighters.

MILLENNIUM PARK OUTDOORS
Map p230 (Millenáris Park; ☎1-336 4000; www.millenaris.hu; II Kis Rókus utca 16-20; ◷6am-1am; 🚼; MM2 Széll Kálmán tér, 🚋4, 6) Millennium Park is an attractive landscaped complex comprising fountains, ponds, little bridges, a theatre, a playground and a gallery containing the **Invisible Exhibition**

(Lathatatlan Kiállítás; ☎06 20 771 4236; www.lathatatlan.hu; adult/student Mon-Fri 1700/1400Ft, Sat & Sun 1990/1700Ft; ◷10am-8pm Sat-Thu, to 11pm Fri), a unique interactive 1½-hour 'tour' of a half-dozen settings (crossing the road, taking a bus) in total darkness, led by a blind or partially sighted person. The idea is to help participants understand what life is like without the one sense that provides us with the most information. Also here is the **Millennium Theatre**. You can also enter the park from Fény utca 20-22 and Lövőház utca 37.

EATING

✕ Castle Hill

VÁR BISTRO HUNGARIAN $
Map p230 (☎06 30 237 0039; www.facebook.com/pages/Vár-Bistro/301382759927362; I Dísz tér 8; mains 1500-2400Ft; ◷8am-9pm; 🚌16, 16A, 116) This cheap and very cheerful self-service restaurant straddles the Royal Palace and the Old Town and is a good choice if you're

looking for something fast and low priced. Salads are 650Ft to 990Ft and there's a two-course fixed 'tourist' menu for 1250Ft.

BUDAVÁRI RÉTESVÁR   HUNGARIAN $

Map p230 (Strudel Castle; ☑06 70 314 2559; www.budavariretesvar.hu; I Balta köz 4; strudel 299Ft, menu 990Ft; ⊘8am-7pm; ☐16, 16A, 116) Strudel in all its permutations – from cherry and apple to dill with cheese and cabbage – is available at this hole-in-the wall dispensary in a narrow alley of the Castle District.

FORTUNA ÖNKISZOLGÁLÓ   HUNGARIAN $

Map p230 (Fortune Self-Service Restaurant; ☑1-375 2401; I Fortuna utca 4; mains 700-1200Ft; ⊘11.30am-2.30pm Mon-Fri; ☐16, 16A, 116) You'll find cheap and quick weekday lunches in a place you'd least expect it – on Castle Hill – at this very basic but clean and cheerful self-service restaurant. Reach it via the stairs on the left side as you enter the Fortuna Passage – and note the *sedile* (medieval stone niche) to the right as you go in.

VÁR: A SPEIZ   INTERNATIONAL $$$

Map p230 (Castle: The Pantry; ☑1-488 7416; www.varaspeiz.hu; I Hess András tér 6; mains 2800-4300Ft; ⊘noon-midnight; ☐16, 16A, 116) Michelin may have taken its 'bib' away, but we still love this romantic bistro and its perennial warm welcome. Vár: A Speiz takes its food very seriously indeed and the five-course tasting menu (9800Ft) is memorable. It's just opposite the Hilton Budapest.

RIVALDA   INTERNATIONAL $$$

Map p230 (☑1-489 0235; www.rivalda.net; I Színház utca 5-9; mains 3100-5600Ft; ⊘11.30am-11.30pm; ☐16, 16A, 116) An international cafe-restaurant in a former convent next to the National Dance Theatre, Rivalda has a thespian theme, a delightful garden courtyard and excellent service. The menu changes frequently, and the wine list is among the best. There's a four-course set menu for 13,200/8550Ft with/without wine.

CAFÉ PIERROT   INTERNATIONAL $$$

Map p230 (☑1-375 6971; www.pierrot.hu; I Fortuna utca 14; mains 3840-7640Ft; ⊘11am-midnight; ☐16, 16A, 116) This very stylish and long-established cafe-bar-restaurant is housed in what was a bakery in the Middle Ages. The decor is, well, clownish, and there's live piano music nightly and delightful garden seating in the warmer months.

21 MAGYAR VENDÉGLŐ   HUNGARIAN $$$

Map p230 (☑1-202 2113; www.21restaurant.hu; I Fortuna utca 21; mains 3460-5360Ft; ⊘11am-midnight; ☐16, 16A, 116) This new place with a less-than-inspiring name (at least you get the address and the cuisine in one go) has some wonderfully innovative modern takes on traditional Hungarian. There's super old/new decor and friendly service, and it bottles its very own wine.

✖ Víziváros

ILDIKÓ KONYHÁJA   HUNGARIAN $

Map p230 (Ildikó's Kitchen; ☑1-201 4772; www.ildiko-konyhaja.hu; I Fő utca 8; dishes 590-1650Ft; ⊘11.30am-10pm; ☐86) This spick-and-span new *étkezde* (canteen that serves simple dishes) has all the traditional Hungarian favourites at rock-bottom prices just below the Castle District.

ÉDENI VEGÁN   VEGETARIAN $

Map p230 (☑60 20 337 7575; www.edenivegan.hu; I Iskola utca 31; mains 650-1190Ft; ⊘8am-9pm Mon-Thu, 8am-7pm Fri, 11am-7pm Sun; ☑; ☐86) Located in an early 19th-century townhouse just below Castle Hill, this self-service place offers stodgy but healthy vegetarian and vegan platters and ragouts without a single no-no (fat, preservatives, MSG, white sugar etc).

À TABLE   BAKERY $

Map p230 (www.atable.hu; II Retek utca 6; ⊘7am-7pm Mon-Fri, 7am-6pm Sat, 8am-6pm Sun; ⓂM2 Széll Kálmán tér, ☐4, 6) Branch of a new bakery chain that has taken Budapest to its heart (and stomach) with excellent pastries, Danishes and savoury snacks.

DURAN   SANDWICHES $

Map p230 (www.duran.hu; II Retek utca 18; sandwiches 210-470Ft; ⊘8am-6pm Mon-Fri, to 2pm Sat; ⓂM2 Széll Kálmán tér) Just behind the Mammut shopping mall in Buda, this place with its small but perfectly formed open-face sandwiches offers an alternative to the fast-food places in the mall.

NAGYI PALACSINTÁZÓJA   HUNGARIAN $

Map p230 (Granny's Palacsinta Place; www.nagyi-pali.hu; I Hattyú utca 16; pancakes 190-680Ft; set menus 1090-1190Ft; ⊘24hr; ☑; ⓂM2 Széll Kálmán tér) This small eatery serves Hungarian pancakes – both savoury and sweet – round the clock and is always packed. There

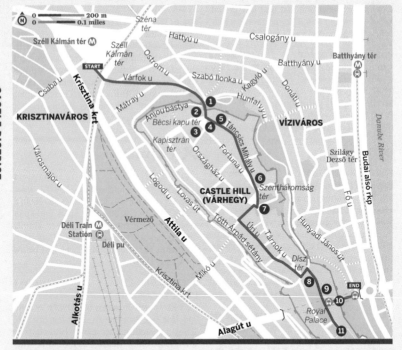

🏃 Neighbourhood Walk
Castle Hill

START II SZÉLL KÁLMÁN TÉR
END II CLARK ÁDÁM TÉR
LENGTH 1.2KM; TWO HOURS

Walk up Várfok utca from Széll Kálmán tér to **①Vienna Gate**, the medieval entrance to the Old Town. The large building to the west with the superbly coloured majolica-tiled roof contains the **②National Archives** (Országos Levéltár; 1920). To the west of Bécsi kapu tér (Vienna Gate Sq) – a weekend market in the Middle Ages – is an attractive group of **③burgher houses**.

Narrow **④Táncsics Mihály utca** is full of little houses painted in lively hues and adorned with statues. In many courtyard entrances you'll see *sedilia* (13th-century stone niches perhaps used as merchant stalls). Further along the road to the southeast at Táncsics Mihály utca 9 is the **⑤former prison** where the leader of the 1848–49 War of Independence, Lajos Kossuth, was held from 1837 to 1840.

The architecturally controversial **⑥Hilton Budapest** incorporating parts of a medieval Dominican church and a baroque Jesuit college, is further south. To the southeast, in the centre of **⑦I Szentháromság tér**, is a replica statue of the Holy Trinity (Szentháromság szobor), a 'plague pillar' erected by grateful (and healthy) Buda citizens in the early 18th century.

Walking along Úri utca south to Dísz tér you'll come face to face with the bombed-out **⑧former Ministry of Defence**, a casualty of WWII, and NATO's supposed nuclear target for Budapest during the Cold War. It's getting a long-overdue renovation.

Further south on the left is the restored **⑨Sándor Palace** (Sándor palota), now housing the offices of the president of the republic. A rather low-key guard change takes place in front hourly between 9am and 6pm.

Just south of the upper station of the **⑩Sikló** (funicular), which descends to I Clark Ádám tér, are the **⑪Habsburg Steps**, a 1903 ornamental gateway leading to the Royal Palace.

are other branches with the same prices and hours, including one on **Batthyány tér** (Map p230; I Batthyány tér 5; M M2 Batthyány tér).

TOLDI KONYHÁJA   HUNGARIAN $
Map p230 (✆1-214 3867; I Batthyány utca 14; mains 1100-1690Ft; ⏰11am-4pm Mon-Fri; ✍; ⛁39, M M2 Batthyány tér) This little eatery west of Fő utca is the place to come if you're in search of Hungarian comfort food at lunchtime on weekdays. Unusually for this kind of place, 'Toldi's Kitchen' offers about a half-dozen *real* vegetarian dishes (1200Ft to 1490Ft).

ARTIGIANA GELATI   GELATERIA $
Map p230 (✆1-212 2439; www.etterem.hu/8581; XII Csaba utca 8; per scoop 350Ft; ⏰11am-8pm Tue-Sun; M M2 Széll Kálmán tér) We're told by readers that this place sells the best shop-made ice cream and sorbet in Buda, with flavours such as fig, pomegranate, Sacher-torte and gorgonzola-walnut.

MARXIM   PIZZA $
Map p230 (✆1-316 0231; www.marximpub.hu; II Kis Rókus utca 23; pizza 890-1590Ft, pasta 1190-1290Ft; ⏰noon-1am Mon-Thu, to 2am Fri & Sat, 6pm-1am Sun; M M2 Széll Kálmán tér, ⛁4, 6) This odd place is a hang-out for teens, who have added a layer of their own graffiti to the Communist memorabilia and kitsch – a joke that's now more than two decades old.

DÉRYNÉ   BISTRO $$
Map p230 (✆1-225 1407; www.bistroderyne.com; I Krisztina tér 3; mains 1780-4950Ft; ⏰7.30am-midnight Mon-Thu, to 1am Fri, 9am-1am Sat, to midnight Sun; ⛁16, 105, 178, ⛁18) What was until not too long ago a traditional cafe near the entrance to the *alagút* tunnel established the year WWI broke out has metamorphosed into a beautiful bistro with excellent breakfasts (890Ft to 2450Ft) and more substantial meals throughout the day.

ATAKÁM   FRENCH $$
Map p230 (✆1-781 4129; www.atakam.hu; I Iskola utca 29; mains 2900-6500Ft; ⏰10am-11pm; ⛁86) This low-key restaurant in a residential Buda neighbourhood just below the Castle District serves Provençal-style French food with a Hungarian twist. The fresh pasta dishes are usually excellent.

HORGÁSZTANYA VENDÉGLŐ   FISH $$
Map p230 (Fisherfarm Restaurant; ✆1-212 3780; www.horgasztanyavendeglo.hu; II Fő utca 20; mains 1550-2990Ft; ⏰noon-midnight; ⛁86) A classic fish restaurant by the Danube where soup is served in bowls, pots or kettles, and your carp, catfish or trout might be prepared Baja-, Tisza- or more spicy Szeged-style.

SEOUL HOUSE   KOREAN $$
Map p230 (✆1-201 7452; I Fő utca 8; dishes 2700-6000Ft; ⏰noon-11pm Mon-Sat; ⛁86) This place serves pretty authentic Korean food, from barbecue grills (from 4000Ft) and *bibimbap* (rice served in a sizzling pot topped with thinly sliced beef and cooked with preserved vegetables, then bound by a raw egg and flavoured with chilli-laced soy paste; 2800Ft) to *kimchi* (pickled spicy cabbage) dishes.

MEZZO MUSIC
RESTAURANT   INTERNATIONAL $$
Map p230 (✆1-356 3565; www.mezzorestaurant.hu; XII Maros utca 28; mains 2800-4200Ft; ⏰8am-midnight Mon-Fri, noon-midnight Sat, noon-10pm Sun; ⛁128, M M2 Széll Kálmán tér) A glamorous bistro between Széll Kálmán tér and Déli train station, Mezzo has upmarket international and Hungarian dishes – and jazz from 7.30pm Monday to Saturday.

CARNE DI HALL   STEAK $$
Map p230 (✆06 30 446 9004; www.carnedihall.eu; I Bem rakpart 20; mains 2790-4690Ft; ⏰noon-midnight; ⛁39, M M2 Batthyány tér) Not just a steakhouse but very meaty indeed in a nation of uber-carnivores, Carne di Hall also dabbles in venison and goose liver. It's in a cellar with outside seating facing the Danube. A two-/three-course lunch is 1290/1490Ft.

MONGOLIAN BARBECUE   ASIAN $$
Map p230 (✆1-356 6363; www.mongolianbbq.hu; XII Márvány utca 19/a; buffet before/after 5pm & weekends 3890/4990Ft; ⏰noon-5pm & 6-11pm; ⛁105, ⛁61) Just south of Széll Kálmán tér, this is one of those all-you-can-eat Asian(ish) places where you choose the raw ingredients and legions of cooks stir-fry it for you.

★CSALOGÁNY 26   INTERNATIONAL $$$
Map p230 (✆1-201 7892; www.csalogany26.hu; I Csalogány utca 26; mains 3600-5000Ft; ⏰noon-3pm & 7-10pm Tue-Sat; ⛁11, 39) Judged by Hungary's most respected food guide to be the best restaurant in town, this intimate place with the unimaginative name and spartan decor turns its creativity to its superb food. A three-course set lunch is a budget-pleasing 2500Ft. Four-/eight-course tasting menus are 8000/12,000Ft.

KACSA
HUNGARIAN $$$

Map p230 (☑1-201 9992; www.kacsavendeglo. hu; II Fő utca 75; mains 3800-5600Ft; ⊘noon-midnight; ⊠86) The 'Duck' is the place to go, well, 'quackers', though you need not restrict yourself to the eight dishes with a bill (4400Ft to 5500Ft); it does a couple of things prepared from Hungarian grey-horned cattle, for example. Set lunch is a snip at 3500Ft.

PAVILLON DE PARIS
FRENCH $$$

Map p230 (☑1-225 0174; www.pavillondeparis. hu; II Fő utca 20-22; mains 3500-6000Ft; ⊘noon-midnight Tue-Sat; ⊠86) A regular haunt of staff from the French Institute across the road, the Pavillon is housed in a wonderful old townhouse abutting an ancient castle wall. The food is Central Casting French (snails, frogs' legs etc) but substantial.

ZÓNA
INTERNATIONAL $$$

Map p230 (☑06 30 422 5981; www.zonabudapest.com; I Lánchíd utca 7-9; mains 3700-6500Ft; ⊘noon-3pm & 6.30-10.30pm Tue-Sat; ⊠86) Where the beautiful set eat and sup, Zóna is as much an architectural triumph as a foodie magnet. We love the idea of wild carp in a red shrimp and lobster sauce (6500Ft), but those turnips on the side leave us cold.

🍸 DRINKING & NIGHTLIFE

🍷 Castle Hill

★ RUSZWURM CUKRÁSZDA
CAFE

Map p230 (☑1-375 5284; www.ruszwurm.hu; I Szentháromság utca 7; ⊘10am-7pm Mon-Fri, to 6pm Sat & Sun; ⊠6, 6A, 116) This diminutive cafe dating from 1827 is the perfect place for coffee and cakes (380Ft to 580Ft) in the Castle District, though it can get pretty crowded. Indeed, in high season it's almost always impossible to get a seat.

OSCAR AMERICAN BAR
BAR

Map p230 (☑06 20 214 2525; www.oscarbar.hu; I Ostrom utca 14; ⊘5pm-2am Mon-Thu, to 4am Fri & Sat; ⓂM2 Széll Kálmán tér) The decor is cinema inspired (film memorabilia on the wood-panelled walls, leather directors chairs) and the beautiful crowd often act like they're on camera. Not to worry: the potent cocktails (1350Ft to 1750Ft) go down a treat. There's music most nights.

🍷 Víziváros

LÁNCHÍD SÖRÖZŐ
BAR

Map p230 (Chain Bridge Pub; ☑1-214 3144; www. lanchidsorozo.hu; I Fő utca 4; ⊘10am-midnight; ⊠16, 86, ⊠19, 41) As its name implies, this pub near the Chain Bridge head has a wonderful retro Magyar feel to it, with old movie posters and advertisements on the walls and red-checked cloths on the tables.

★ BAMBI PRESSZÓ
CAFE

Map p230 (☑1-213 3171; www.facebook.com/bambieszpresszo; II Frankel Leó út 2-4; ⊘7am-10pm Mon-Fri, 9am-10pm Sat & Sun; ⊠86) The words 'Bambi' and 'modern' do not make comfortable bedfellows; nothing about this place has changed since the 1960s. And that's just the way the crowd here likes it.

AUGUSZT CUKRÁSZDA
CAFE

Map p230 (☑1-316 3817; www.auguszt1870.hu; II Fény utca 8; cakes 260-640Ft; ⊘10am-6pm Mon-Fri, from 10am Sat; ⓂM2 Széll Kálmán tér) Tucked away behind the Fény utca market and Mammut shopping mall complex, this is the original Auguszt and only sells its own shop-made cakes, pastries and biscuits. Seating is on the 1st floor.

SPICCPROJECT
WINE BAR

Map p230 (☑06 70 313 3257; www.facebook. com/spiccproject; I Krisztina tér 3; ⊘11.30am-1am Tue-Fri, 5pm-1am Sat; ⊠16, 105, 178, ⊠18) Essentially a wine bar, this place also does food, usually lighter things and one-plate specials like duck rillettes (580Ft) and fish and chips (2480Ft).

ANGELIKA KÁVÉHÁZ
CAFE

Map p230 (☑1-225 1653; www.angelikacafe.hu; I Batthyány tér 7; cakes 490-750Ft; ⊘9am-11pm; ⓂM2 Batthyány tér) Attached to an 18th-century church, Angelika is now as much a restaurant as a cafe with a raised outside terrace. The more substantial dishes are just so-so; come here for the cakes and the views across the square to the Danube and Parliament.

SCORE CLUB
GAY

Map p230 (☑06 20 341 4577; www.scoreclub.hu; II Tölgyfa utca 1-3; cover 1500-2000Ft; ⊘10pm-6am Sat, one Fri per month; ⊠4, 6) We don't know whether the name is a threat or a promise, but Buda's only gay bar at the moment is a magnet for a slightly older crowd. A welcome arrival.

⭐ ENTERTAINMENT

BUDAVÁR CULTURAL CENTRE   MUSIC
Map p230 (Budavári Művelődési Háza; ☑1-201 0324; www.bem6.hu; Bem rakpart 6; programs 800-1000Ft; 🚊86, 🚋19, 41) This cultural centre just below Buda Castle has frequent programs for children and adults, including the excellent Sebő Klub és Táncház at 7pm on the first Saturday of every month and the Regejáró Misztrál Folk Music Club at the same time on the last Sunday.

MARCZIBÁNYI TÉR
CULTURAL CENTRE   MUSIC
Map p230 (Marczibányi téri Művelődési Központ; ☑1-212 2820; www.marczi.hu; II Marczibányi tér 5/a; performances 500-2000Ft; ⊘from 8pm Wed; 🚊4, 6) This venue has Hungarian, Moldavian and Slovakian dance and music by Guzsalyas every Thursday at 7pm and táncház (folk music and dance) every second Sunday at 1pm.

BUDA CONCERT HALL   DANCE
Map p230 (Budai Vigadó; ☑1-225 6049; www.hagyomanyokhaza.hu; I Corvin tér 8; performances 3600-6200Ft; 🚊86, 🚋19, 41) The 30 artistes of the Hungarian State Folk Ensemble (Magyar Állami Népi Együttes) perform at this venue, also known as the Hagyományok Háza (House of Traditions) at 8pm on Tuesday and Thursday from June to October, with occasional performances at other times during the rest of the year.

NATIONAL DANCE THEATRE   DANCE
Map p230 (Nemzeti Táncszínház; ☑1-201 4407, box office 1-375 8649; www.nemzetitancszinhaz.hu; I Színház utca 1-3; tickets 750-5000Ft; ⊘box office 10am-6pm Mon-Thu, to 5pm Fri; 🚌16, 16A, 116) The National Dance Theatre on Castle Hill hosts at some point every troupe in the city, including the national ballet company and the **Budapest Dance Theatre** (www.budapestdancetheatre.hu), one of the most exciting contemporary troupes in the city.

JENŐ HUBAY MUSIC HALL   CONCERT VENUE
Map p230 (☑1-457 8080; www.hubayzeneterem.hu; I Bem rakpart 11; tickets 2800Ft; 🚊86, 🚋19) The renovated 19th-century music hall now serves as a small concert venue and theatre. It's a wonderfully intimate place to hear a concert as there are only 70 seats. Check website for dates.

🛍 SHOPPING

HEREND   PORCELAIN
Map p230 (☑1-225 1051; www.herend.com; I Szentháromság utca 5, Castle Hill; ⊘10am-6pm Mon-Fri, to 4pm Sat & Sun; 🚌16, 16A, 116) For both contemporary and traditional fine porcelain, there is no other place to go but Herend, Hungary's answer to Wedgwood. Among the most popular motifs produced by the company is the Victoria pattern of butterflies and wildflowers designed for the British queen during the mid-19th century. Closes at 2pm on weekends from November to March.

MESTER PORTA   MUSIC
Map p230 (☑06 20 232 5614; www.facebook.com/mesterporta.galeria; I Corvin tér 7, Víziváros; ⊘10am-6pm Mon-Fri; 🚊86, 🚋19) This wonderful shop has CDs and DVDs of Hungarian and other folk music as well as musical instruments, scores, books and now even folk costumes.

BORTÁRSASÁG   WINE
Map p230 (☑1-212 0262; www.bortarsasag.hu; I Batthyány utca 59; ⊘10am-7pm Mon-Fri, to 6pm Sat; Ⓜ M2 Széll Kálmán tér, 🚊4, 6) Once known as the Budapest Wine Society, this place has 10 retail outlets in the capital with an exceptional selection of Hungarian wines. No one knows Hungarian wines like these guys do.

HEREND VILLAGE POTTERY   CERAMICS
Map p230 (☑1-356 7899; www.herendimajolika.hu; II Bem rakpart 37; ⊘9am-5pm Tue-Fri, to noon Sat; Ⓜ M2 Batthyány tér, 🚋19, 41) An alternative to delicate Herend porcelain is the hard-wearing Herend pottery and dishes sold here, decorated with bold and colourful fruit and flower patterns.

🏃 SPORTS & ACTIVITIES

KIRÁLY BATHS   BATHHOUSE
Map p230 (Király Gyógyfürdő; ☑1-202 3688; www.spasbudapest.com; II Fő utca 84; daily ticket incl cabin 2400Ft; ⊘9am-9pm; 🚊86, 🚋4, 6) The four pools here, with water temperatures of between 26°C and 40°C, are genuine Turkish baths erected in 1570 and have a wonderful skylit central dome (though the place is begging for a renovation). The Király is now open to both men and women every day of operation, so pack a swimsuit.

Gellért Hill & Tabán

Neighbourhood Top Five

1 Taking in the incomparable views of Castle Hill, the Danube and Pest from the **Liberty Monument** (p67).

2 Soaking in the Art Nouveau **Gellért Baths** (p66) – an experience that has been likened to taking a bath in a cathedral.

3 Reliving history at the **former Swedish Embassy** (p68) from where Raoul Wallenberg and others rescued thousands of Hungarian Jews from deportation and death.

4 Having the not-so-distant past surprise you by visiting **Memento Park** (p70), a 'cemetery' of

Communist monuments that has to be seen to be believed.

5 Making the short and easy journey to the **Palace of Wonders** (p70) in Nagytétény, one of the most popular attractions for kids in Budapest.

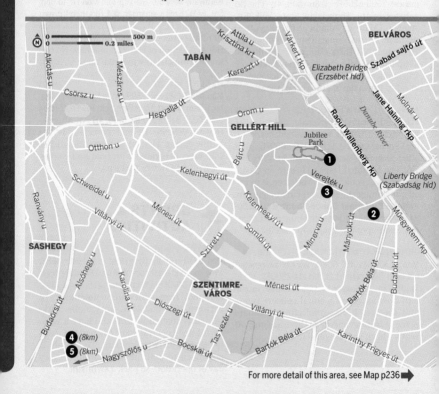

For more detail of this area, see Map p236 ➡

Explore: Gellért Hill & Tabán

Gellért Hill (Gellért-hegy) is a 235m-high rocky hill southeast of Castle Hill. Crowned with a fortress (of sorts) and the spectacular Liberty Monument, it is Budapest's unofficial symbol. You can't beat the views of the Royal Palace or the Danube and its fine bridges from Gellért Hill, and Jubilee Park on the south side is an ideal spot for a picnic.

The Tabán, the leafy area between Gellért and Castle Hills, and stretching northwest towards Déli train station, is associated with the Serbs, who settled here after fleeing from the Ottoman Turks in the early 18th century. Plaques on I Döbrentei utca mark the water level of the Danube during devastating floods in 1775 and again in 1838 that hit the area particularly hard.

The Tabán later became known for its restaurants and wine gardens, but all that remains of them is a lovely little renovated building with a fountain designed by Miklós Ybl in 1878, known as the **Castle Garden Palace** (Várkert Palota; Map p236; ☎1-212 1936; I Ybl Miklós tér 9), which was once a pump house for Castle Hill. The steps and archways across the road are part of the renovated **Castle Bazaar** (Várbazár) pleasure park built in 1883.

Local Life

➡ **Views** If you walk west for a few minutes along Citadella sétány north of the Citadella itself, you'll come to a lookout with one of the best vantage points in Budapest.

➡ **Táncház** For some excellent *táncház* (folk music and dance) programs, head for the Municipal Cultural House (p71).

➡ **Architecture** Not just a great place to soak away your cares and aches, the Rudas Baths (p71) boasts some of the best Turkish architecture in Hungary.

Getting There & Away

➡ **Bus** XI Szent Gellért tér can be reached from V Ferenciek tere in Pest on bus 7, and from points in Óbuda or south Buda on bus 86. Bus 27 runs almost to the top of Gellért Hill from XI Móricz Zsigmond körtér.

➡ **Metro** The new M4 metro line, with stations at XI Gellért tér and XI Móricz Zsigmond körtér, now makes this neighbourhood even more accessible by public transport.

➡ **Tram** XI Szent Gellért tér is linked to Déli station by tram 18, and to I Batthyány tér by tram 19. Trams 47 and 49 cross over to Pest and follow the Little Ring Rd from the same place. Trams 18 and 47 run south along XI Fehérvári út – useful for several entertainment venues mentioned in this chapter.

Lonely Planet's Top Tip

A handful of thermal spas in this district make good use of the hot springs gushing from deep below, including the Gellért, the Rudas and (still holding our breath) the Rácz, which closed for renovation in 2002 and is still awaiting resurrection. If you don't like getting wet or you don't have the time, do what locals do and try a 'drinking cure' by visiting the **Pump Room** (Ivócsarnok; Map p236; I Erzsébet hid; ☉11am-6pm Mon, Wed & Fri, 7am-2pm Tue & Thu), which is just below the western end of Elizabeth Bridge. A half-litre/litre of the hot, smelly water, which is meant to cure whatever ails you, is just 40/70Ft. Bring your own container.

Best Places to Eat

➡ Aranyszarvas (p69)
➡ Hemingway (p69)
➡ Marcello (p69)

For reviews, see p69 ➡

Best Places to Drink

➡ Szatyor Bár és Galéria (p69)
➡ A38 (p69)
➡ Tranzit Art Café (p69)

For reviews, see p69 ➡

Best Places to Relax

➡ Gellért Baths (p66)
➡ Rudas Baths (p71)

For reviews, see p71 ➡

TOP SIGHT
GELLÉRT BATHS

Soaking in the thermal waters of the Art Nouveau Gellért Baths, open to both men and women in mixed areas (thus a bathing suit is required at all times), has been compared to bathing in a cathedral. The eight thermal pools range in temperature from 26°C to 38°C, and the water – high in calcium, magnesium and hydrogen carbonate – is said to be good for joint pains, arthritis and blood circulation.

The springs here were favoured by the Turks as they were hotter than the others in Buda. In the 17th century the site was named Sárosfürdő (Mud Bath) after the fine silt that was pushed up with the spring water and settled at the bottom of the pools. The Gellért Baths as we know them today opened in 1918; they were expanded in 1927 with an outdoor wave bath and in 1934 with an indoor effervescent whirlpool.

In most other baths nowadays you are given an electronic bracelet that directs you to and then opens your locker or cabin. The Gellért is still doing it the old way: you find a free locker or cabin yourself and – after you get changed in (or beside) it – you call the attendant, who will lock it for you and hand you a numbered tag. Make sure you remember your locker number; in a bid to prevent thefts the number on the tag is not the same as the one on the locker.

The swimming pools at the Gellért are also mixed. The indoor ones, open year-round, are the most beautiful in Budapest; the outdoor wave pool (open May to September) has lovely landscaped gardens.

DON'T MISS...

➡ Art Nouveau mosaics and statues
➡ Glass-domed main indoor swimming pool
➡ Outdoor wave pool (in season)

PRACTICALITIES

➡ Gellért Gyógyfürdő
➡ Map p236
➡ ☎1-466 6166
➡ www.gellertbath.hu
➡ XI Kelenhegyi út 4, Danubius Hotel Gellért
➡ weekdays/weekends with locker 4900/5100Ft, cabin 5300/5500Ft
➡ ⊘6am-8pm
➡ ☐7, 86, Ⓜ M4 Szent Gellért tér, ☐18, 19, 47, 49

TOP SIGHT
CITADELLA & LIBERTY MONUMENT

The **Citadella** atop Gellért Hill is a fortress that never saw a battle. Built by the Habsburgs after the 1848–49 War of Independence to defend the city from further insurrection, by the time it was ready two years later the political climate had changed and the Citadella was obsolete. Today the fortress contains some big guns and dusty displays in the central courtyard, the **1944 Bunker Waxworks** (1944 Bunkér Panoptikum) inside a bunker used during WWII, and a hotel-hostel. Just east of the Citadella is the **Liberty Monument** (Szabadság szobor), the lovely lady with a palm frond in her outstretched arms, proclaiming freedom throughout the city from atop Gellért Hill. Standing 14m high, she was erected in 1947 in tribute to the Soviet soldiers who died liberating Budapest in 1945. But the names of the fallen, once spelled out in Cyrillic letters on the plinth, and the statues of the soldiers themselves were removed in 1992.

To reach the Citadella take the stairs leading up behind the St Gellért Monument or, from the Cave Church, follow XI Verejték utca (Perspiration St) through the park. Bus 27 runs almost to the top of Gellért Hill from XI Móricz Zsigmond körtér, which is served by the new metro line M4.

DON'T MISS...

➡ Liberty Monument
➡ Citadella (from outside)
➡ The views from both

PRACTICALITIES

➡ Map p236
➡ www.citadella.hu
➡ ☉24hr

GELLÉRT HILL & TABÁN SIGHTS

◉ SIGHTS

CAVE CHURCH
CHURCH

Map p236 (Sziklatemplom; ☎06 20 775 2472; www.sziklatemplom.hu; XI Szent Gellért rakpart 1/a; adult/child 500/400Ft; ☉9.30am-7.30pm Mon-Sat; ⓜM4 Szent Gellért tér, ◻47, 49, 18, 19) This chapel is on a small hill directly north of the landmark Art Nouveau Danubius Hotel Gellért. The chapel was built into a cave in 1926 and was the seat of the Pauline order in Hungary until 1951, when the priests were arrested and imprisoned by the Communists and the cave sealed off. It was reopened and reconsecrated in 1992. Behind the chapel is a monastery with neo-Gothic turrets that are visible from Liberty Bridge.

Mass is said daily at 8.30am, 5pm and 8pm, with an additional service at 11am on Sunday.

SEMMELWEIS MUSEUM OF MEDICAL HISTORY
MUSEUM

Map p236 (Semmelweis Orvostörténeti Múzeum; ☎1-201 1577, 1-375 3533; www.semmelweis.museum.hu; I Apród utca 1-3; adult/child 700/350Ft; ☉10.30am-6pm Tue-Sun mid-Mar–Oct, to 4pm Tue-Sun Nov–mid-Mar; ◻86, ◻19) This quirky (and sometimes grisly) museum traces the history of medicine from Graeco-Roman times through medical tools, instruments and photographs; yet another antique pharmacy also makes an appearance. Featured are the life and works of Ignác Semmelweis (1818–65), the 'saviour of mothers', who discovered the cause of puerperal (childbirth) fever. He was born here.

ELIZABETH BRIDGE
BRIDGE

Map p236 (Erzsébet híd; ◻7, 86, ◻19) A gleaming white (though rather generic-looking) suspension bridge dating from 1964, Elizabeth Bridge enjoys a special place in the hearts of many Budapesters, as it was the first newly designed bridge to reopen after WWII (the original span, erected in 1903, was too badly damaged in the war to rebuild). Boasting a higher arch than the other bridges spanning the Danube, it offers dramatic views of both Castle and Gellért Hills and, of course, the river.

LIBERTY BRIDGE
BRIDGE

Map p236 (Szabadság híd; ⓜM4 Szent Gellért tér, ◻47, 49) Opened in time for the Millenary Exhibition in 1896, Liberty Bridge

RAOUL WALLENBERG, HERO FOR ALL TIMES

The **former Swedish Embassy** (Map p236; XI Minerva utca 3a/b; ⊠27) on Gellért Hill bears a plaque attesting to the heroism of Raoul Wallenberg (1912–47), a Swedish diplomat and businessman who, together with his colleagues Carl-Ivan Danielsson (1880–1963) and Per Anger (1913–2002), rescued as many as 35,000 Hungarian Jews during WWII.

Wallenberg began working in 1936 for a trading firm whose owner was a Hungarian Jew. In July 1944 the Swedish Foreign Ministry, at the request of Jewish and refugee organisations in the US, sent the 32-year-old Swede on a rescue mission to Budapest as an attaché to the embassy there. By that time almost half a million Jews in Hungary had been sent to Nazi death camps in Germany and Poland.

Wallenberg immediately began issuing Swedish safe-conduct passes (called 'Wallenberg passports') from the Swedish embassy in Budapest. He also set up a series of 'safe houses' flying the flag of Sweden and other neutral countries where Jews could seek asylum. He even followed German 'death marches' and deportation trains, distributing food and clothing and actually pulling some 500 people off the cars along the way.

When the Soviet army entered Budapest in January 1945, Wallenberg went to report to the authorities but in the wartime confusion was arrested for espionage and sent to Moscow. In the early 1950s, responding to reports that Wallenberg had been seen alive in a labour camp, the Soviet Union announced that he had in fact died of a heart attack two years after the war ended. Many believe Wallenberg was executed by the Soviets, who suspected him of spying for the USA.

Wallenberg was made an honorary citizen of the city of Budapest in 2003. Other foreigners associated with helping Hungarian Jews in Budapest include Carl Lutz (1885–1975), a Swiss consul who has a memorial devoted to him on VII Dob utca in Pest, and Jane Haining (1897–1944), a Budapest-based Scottish missionary who died in Auschwitz. In 2010 the city of Budapest named a section of the Pesti alsó rakpart along the Danube in Pest in her honour.

To reach the former Swedish Embassy from the Cave Church follow the small path, Verejték utca (Perspiration St) and a walkway named after Dezső Szabó, a controversial writer killed in the last days of WWII. You'll pass a funny bust of this large and rather angry-looking man along the way as you ascend through what were once vineyards and are now the well-kept lawns and gardens of Jubilee Park (Jubileum park). Another route to follow from Gellért tér is along Kelenhegyi út. At No 12–14 is the interesting Art Nouveau Studio Building (1903), which has enormous rooms with high ceilings that were once used to construct huge socialist-realist monuments. Continue up Kelenhegyi út and turn north on Minerva utca. The short flight of steps rejoins Verejték utca.

has a fin-de-siècle cantilevered span. Each post of the bridge, which was originally named after Habsburg emperor Franz Joseph, is topped by a mythical *turul* bird ready to take flight. It was rebuilt in the same style immediately after WWII.

ST GELLÉRT MONUMENT   STATUE

Map p236 (⊠86, ⊠18, 19) Looking down on Elizabeth Bridge from Gellért Hill is a large and quite theatrical monument to St Gellért, an Italian missionary invited to Hungary by King Stephen to convert the natives. The monument marks the spot where, according to legend, pagan Magyars, resisting the new faith, hurled the bishop to his death in a spiked barrel in 1046.

QUEEN ELIZABETH STATUE   STATUE

Map p236 (I Döbrentei tér; ⊠19, 41) To the northwest of Elizabeth Bridge is a statue of Elizabeth, Habsburg empress and Hungarian queen. Consort to Franz Joseph, 'Sissi' was much loved by the Magyars because, among other things, she learned to speak Hungarian. She was assassinated by an Italian anarchist in Geneva in 1898 with a sharpened needle file. What a brute.

EATING

Second only to eating atop Castle Hill is dining below looking up at the Royal Palace. The Tabán, an area once known for its jolly outdoor cafes and wine gardens – Budapest's answer to Montmartre – still has some wonderful places in which to eat and drink, as does the area south of Gellért Hill.

MARCELLO   ITALIAN $
Map p236 (☏1-466 6231; www.marcelloetterem.hu; XI Bartók Béla út 40; mains 1250-3980Ft; ☺noon-10pmMon-Sat; 🚌6) A perennial favourite with students from the nearby university since it opened more than two decades ago, this family-owned operation just down the road from XI Szent Gellért tér offers reliable Italian fare at affordable prices. The pizzas (1300Ft to 1800Ft) are good value, as is the salad bar, and the lasagne (1390Ft) is still legendary in these parts.

CSERPES TEJIVÓ   CAFE $
Map p236 (www.cserpestejivo.hu; Allee Shopping Centre, off Kőrösy József utca; sandwiches & salads 480-780Ft, menus 670-920Ft; ☺7.30am-11pm Mon-Sat, 9am-8pm Sun; Ⓜ M4 Móricz Zsigmond körtér, 🚌6) This modern version of the traditional Hungarian *tejivó* (milkbar) is sponsored by the country's No 1 producer of dairy products so it's just got to be good. One of three branches, this one is in the flash new Allee Shopping Centre near XI Móricz Zsigmond körtér.

DAIKICHI   JAPANESE $$
(☏1-225 3965; I Mészáros utca 64; mains 2200-6500Ft, set menus 3200-4800Ft; ☺noon-10pm; 🚌8,112,178) Everyone's favourite little Japanese eatery, in a nondescript area on the Buda side, this minuscule restaurant (with additional seating below) serves up decent soba noodles and seafood and pork dishes.

HEMINGWAY   INTERNATIONAL $$
Map p236 (☏1-381 0522; www.hemingway-etterem.hu; XI Kosztolányi Dezső tér 2; mains 2590-3600Ft; ☺noon-midnight Mon-Sat, to 4pm Sun; 🚌19, 47, 49) This very stylish eatery, in a fabulous location in a small park overlooking Feneketlen-tó (Bottomless Lake) in south Buda, has a varied and ever-changing menu and a wonderful terrace. There are lots of pasta dishes (1500Ft to 2490Ft) should you want something easy, and Sunday brunch

(3990Ft, with unlimited drinks 5190Ft) is a crowd pleaser.

★ARANYSZARVAS   HUNGARIAN $$$
Map p236 (☏1-375 6451; www.aranyszarvas.hu; I Szarvas tér 1; mains 3200-3800Ft; ☺noon-11pm; 🚌86) Set in an 18th-century inn literally down the steps from the southern end of Castle Hill, the 'Golden Stag' serves up some very meaty and unusual dishes (try the saddle of boar with celeriac and sage or the duck breast with bok choy). The covered outside terrace is a delight in summer, and the views upward of the Royal Palace are sublime.

DRINKING & NIGHTLIFE

★A38   BAR, CLUB
Map p236 (A38 Ship; ☏1-464 3940; www.a38.hu; XI Pázmány Péter sétány 3-11; ☺11am-4pm, terraces 4pm-4am Tue-Sat; 🚌906, 🚋4, 6) Moored on the Buda side just south of Petőfi Bridge, the 'A38 Ship' is a decommissioned Ukrainian stone hauler from 1968 that has been recycled as a major live-music venue. It's so cool that Lonely Planet readers online voted it the best bar in the world. Surprised us too. The ship's hold rocks throughout the year.

★SZATYOR BÁR ÉS GALÉRIA   BAR
Map p236 (Carrier Bag Bar & Gallery; ☏1-279 0290; www.szatyorbar.com; XIII Bartók Béla út 36-38; ☺noon-1am Mon-Fri, 2pm-1am Sat & Sun; Ⓜ M4 Móricz Zsigmond körtér, 🚌18, 19, 47, 49) Sharing the same building as the Hadik Kávéház cafe (p70) and separated by just a door, the Szatyor is the funkier of the twins, with cocktails, street art on the walls and a Lada driven by the poet Endre Ady. Cool or what?

TRANZIT ART CAFÉ   CAFE
Map p236 (☏1-209 3070; www.tranzitcafe.com; XI Bukarest utca & Ulászló utca; ☺9am-11pm Mon-Fri, 10am-10pm Sat; 🚌7, 🚋19, 49) As chilled a place to drink and nosh as you'll find in south Buda, the Tranzit made its home in a small disused bus station, put art on the walls and filled the leafy courtyard with hammocks and comfy sofas. Breakfast and sandwiches are available, and two-course lunches (including a veggie one) can be had for 1200Ft during the week.

WORTH A DETOUR

SOUTH BUDA SIGHTS

Memento Park

Home to more than 40 statues, busts and plaques of Lenin, Marx, Béla Kun and others whose likenesses have ended up on trash heaps elsewhere in the former socialist world, **Memento Park** (⌨1-424 7500; www.mementopark.hu; XXII Balatoni út 16; adult/student 1500/1000Ft; ⊘10am-dusk), 10km southwest of the city centre, is truly a mind-blowing place to visit. Ogle the socialist realism and try to imagine that at least four of these relics were erected as recently as the late 1980s; a few of them, including a memorial of Béla Kun in a crowd by fence-sitting sculptor Imre Varga, were still in place when one of us moved to Budapest in early 1992. Also here are the replicated remains of Stalin's boots (all that was left after a crowd pulled the enormous statue down from its plinth on XIV Dózsa György út during the 1956 Uprising). An exhibition centre in an old barracks has displays on the events of 1956 and the changes since 1989, and a documentary film with rare footage of secret agents collecting information on 'subversives'.

To reach this socialist Disneyland, take the M4 to Kelenföld train station and then bus 101 or 150 (25 minutes, every 20 to 30 minutes) to Budatétény vasútállomás (Camponia) and the park. An easier – though more expensive – way to go is via the direct **park bus** (Map p238; adult/child return incl park admission 4900/3500Ft; ⊘11am daily Apr-Oct, Sat-Mon Nov-Mar), which departs from in front of Le Meridien Budapest hotel on V Deák Ferenc tér.

Nagytétény Castle Museum

Housed in a baroque mansion in deepest south Buda, the **Nagytétény Castle Museum** (Nagytétényi Kastélymúzeum; ⌨1-207 0005; www.nagytetenyi.hu; XXII Kastélypark utca 9-11; adult/child 800/400Ft; ⊘10am-6pm Tue-Sun Apr-Dec, to 4pm Fri-Sun Jan & Feb, to 6pm Thu-Sun Mar; ⎗33 from XI Móricz Zsigmond körtér in south Buda), a branch of the Museum of Applied Arts, traces the development of European furniture – from Gothic (1450) to Biedermeier (1850) styles – with some 300 items on display in more than two dozen rooms.

Palace of Wonders

Subtitled the Centre of Scientific Wonder, the **Palace of Wonders** (Csodák Palotája; ⌨06 30 210 5569; www.csopa.hu; Campona Shopping Mall, II Nagytétényi út 37-43; adult/student & child 2200/1700Ft; ⊘10am-8pm; ⎗; ⎗33 from XI Móricz Zsigmond körtér in south Buda) is a playhouse for children of all ages, with 'smart' toys and puzzles, most with a scientific bent, and lots of interactive stuff, such as a 'wind tunnel', 'velvet harp' and 'fakir bed'.

Tropicarium

The vast aquarium complex **Tropicarium** (⌨1-424 3053; www.tropicarium.hu; Campona Shopping Mall, XXII Nagytétényi út 37-45; adult/child/senior & student 2300/1600/1900Ft; ⊘10am-8pm; ⎗33 from XI Móricz Zsigmond körtér in south Buda) is apparently the largest in central Europe. The place prides itself on its local specimens – 'fish species of the Hungarian fauna' – though there's an 11m-long shark aquarium containing all manner of the beasties. Feeding time is between 3pm and 4pm on Thursday.

KISRABLÓ PUB   PUB

Map p236 (⌨1-209 1588; www.kisrablopub.hu; XI Zenta utca 3; ⊘11am-2am; ⎗M4 Móricz Zsigmond körtér, ⎗18, 19, 47, 49) Close to the Budapest University of Technology and Economics (BME), the 'Little Pirate' is, not surprisingly, very popular with students. But don't be misled – it's an attractive and well-run

place with decent food available, including cheap set lunches at 990Ft.

HADIK KÁVÉHÁZ   CAFE

Map p236 (⌨1-279 0291; www.hadikkavehaz.com; XIII Bartók Béla út 36; ⊘9am-11pm; ⎗M4 Móricz Zsigmond körtér, ⎗18, 19, 47, 49) This place has brought history back to Bartók Béla út. The Hadik is a revived olde-worlde cafe that pulled in the punters for almost four decades before being shut down in 1949. It's now back, as relaxed and atmospheric as ever. Excellent daily lunch menu for 990Ft.

CAFÉ PONYVAREGÉNY   CAFE
Map p236 (☏06 30 920 2470; www.cafeponyvaregeny.hu; XI Bercsényi utca 5; ☺10am-midnight Mon-Sat, 2-10pm Sun; Ⓜ M4 Móricz Zsigmond körtér, 🚌18, 19, 47, 49) The 'Pulp Fiction' is a quirky little place that has a loyal following despite all the new competition in this part of south Buda and the fact that it's clearly not as friendly as it once was. The old books and fringed lampshades are a nice touch, though, and the coffee (660Ft to 700Ft) is excellent.

SZAMOS CUKRÁSZDA   CAFE
Map p236 (☏1-209 9088; www.szamosmarcipan.hu; XI Váli utca 3, Allee Shopping Centre; cakes 220-640Ft; ☺10am-9pm Mon-Sat, to 7pm Sun; Ⓜ M4 Móricz Zsigmond körtér, 🚌6) The shop that introduced Hungary to marzipan and opened an outlet on every high street in the land has now started up its own line of attractive cake shops, including this one in south Buda's Allee Shopping Centre.

ZÖLD PARDON   BAR
Map p242 (☏1-279 1880; www.zp.hu; XI Neumann János utca 2; ☺4pm-5am Mon-Fri, 11am-5am Sat, 11am-6am Sun; 🚌103) What bills itself as the 'world's longest summer festival' is a rocker's paradise in south Buda just west of Rákóczi Bridge. The place counts nine bars as well as a *pálinkaház* serving Hungarian fruit-flavoured brandies.

ROMKERT   CLUB
Map p236 (☏06 30 540 6991; www.rudasromkert.hu; I Döbrentei tér 9; ☺11am-5am Apr-Sep; 🚌18, 19) Tucked away beside the Rudas Baths with its Ottoman domes in full view, the seasonal 'Ruin Garden' attracts a younger crowd with its large dance area, DJs and themed nights.

☆ ENTERTAINMENT

MUNICIPAL CULTURAL HOUSE   MUSIC
(Fővárosi Művelődési Háza, FMH; ☏1-203 3868; www.fmhnet.hu; XI Fehérvári út 47; ☺box office 3-7pm Mon, 3-6pm Tue, 1-6pm Wed & Thu, 4-6pm

Fri; 🚌18, 41) There's folk music and dance at what is also called the Folklore Theatre (Folklór Színház) on alternate Mondays, Fridays and Saturdays (see the website) at 7pm. A children's dance house hosted by the incomparable folk group Muzsikás runs every Tuesday from 5pm to 7pm.

FONÓ BUDA MUSIC HOUSE   MUSIC
(☏1-206 5300; www.fono.hu; XI Sztregova utca 3; ☺box office 9am-5pm Mon-Fri; 🚌18, 41) This venue has *táncház* programs several times a week (especially on Wednesday) at 8pm, as well as concerts by big-name bands (mostly playing world music) throughout the month; it's one of the best venues in town for this sort of thing. Consult the website for more details.

MU SZÍNHÁZ   DANCE
Map p236 (☏1-209 4014; www.mu.hu; XI Kőrösy József utca 17; ☺box office 10am-6pm Mon-Fri; 🚌4) Virtually everyone involved in the Hungarian dance scene got their start at this landmark place in south Buda, where excellent modern-dance performances can still be enjoyed.

🏃 SPORTS & ACTIVITIES

GELLÉRT BATHS   BATHHOUSE
See p66.

RUDAS BATHS   BATHHOUSE
Map p236 (Rudas Gyógyfürdő; ☏1-356 1322; www.spasbudapest.com; I Döbrentei tér 9; with cabin weekdays/weekends 3000/3300Ft, morning/night ticket 2300/3700Ft; ☺men 6am-8pm Mon & Wed-Fri, women 6am-8pm Tue, mixed 10pm-4am Fri, 6am-8pm & 10pm-4am Sat & Sun; 🚌7, 86, 🚌18, 19) Built in 1566, these renovated baths are the most Turkish of all in Budapest, with an octagonal pool, domed cupola with coloured glass and massive columns. It's a real zoo on mixed weekend nights, when bathing costumes are compulsory. You can enter the lovely **swimming pool** (with locker weekday/weekend 2000/23000Ft; ☺6am-8pm daily, 10pm-4am Fri & Sat) separately if you're more interested in swimming than soaking.

Óbuda & Buda Hills

ÓBUDA | BUDA HILLS

Neighbourhood Top Five

1 Touring the Buda Hills by three of the most unusual conveyances you're likely to encounter: the **Cog Railway** (p77) up into the hills, the unique **Children's Railway** (p77) through them, and the **Chairlift** (p77) down.

2 Walking backwards in time by strolling through the fabulously upgraded Roman-era **Aquincum** (p74).

3 Exploring the world beneath you by visiting any or all of the Buda Hills' trio of caves: **Mátyáshegy** (p78), **Pálvölgy** (p78) or **Szemlőhegy** (p78).

4 Spacing out while viewing the truly mind-blowing works of op art at the **Vasarely Museum** (p75).

5 Enjoying Bartók's music in the very place of its birth: the **Béla Bartók Memorial House** (p76).

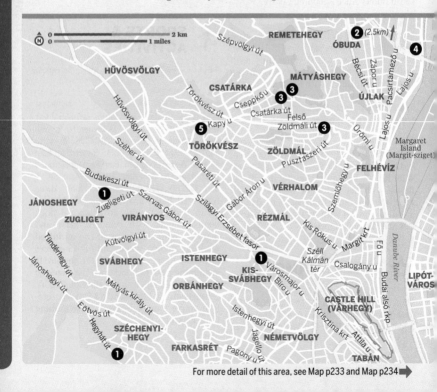

For more detail of this area, see Map p233 and Map p234 ➡

Explore: Óbuda & Buda Hills

Ó means 'ancient' in Hungarian, so no prizes for guessing that Óbuda is the oldest part of Buda. The Romans established Aquincum, a military garrison and civilian town, north of here at the end of the 1st century AD, and it became the seat of the Roman province of Pannonia Inferior in AD 106. When the Magyars arrived, they named it Buda, which became Óbuda when the Royal Palace was built on Castle Hill and turned into the real centre.

Most visitors en route to Szentendre on the Danube Bend are put off by what they see of Óbuda from the highway or the HÉV suburban train. But behind all the prefabricated housing blocks and the flyover are some of the most important Roman ruins in Hungary, plus museums and small, quiet neighbourhoods that recall fin-de-siècle Óbuda.

Contiguous with Óbuda to the west is the start of the Buda Hills (Budai-hegység), with 'peaks' exceeding 500m, a comprehensive system of trails and some unusual modes of public transport. The hills are the city's lung and playground – a welcome respite from hot, dusty Pest in summer. Apart from the Béla Bartók Memorial House, there are few sights here as such, though you might want to explore one of the hills' caves.

Local Life

➡ **Sleeping** If you take your morning swim seriously, stay at Hotel Császár (p167), where some of the rooms look onto the Olympic-size pools of the Császár-Komjádi swimming complex.

➡ **Classical Music** One of the most intimate spots to hear a concert is the Óbuda Society (p80) venue.

➡ **Museum** Visit Béla Bartók Memorial House (p76) for 'free' by attending one of the frequent concerts.

Getting There & Away

➡**Bus** Bus 86 links XI Szent Gellért tér and other points in south Buda with III Flórián tér in Óbuda. Buses 34 and 106 go to Aquincum from III Szentlélek tér in Óbuda. Bus 291 links the Chairlift's lower terminus on XII Zugligeti út with II Szilágyi Erzsébet fasor and Nyugati train station.

➡**Trams** Trams 1 and 1A run along the Outer Ring Rd (eg XIII Róbert Károl körút) from City Park in Pest to Árpád Bridge east of III Flórián tér in Óbuda. Trams 59 and 61 run from II Széll Kálmán tér to the Cog Railway's lower terminus. Tram 17 links II Margit körút with III Bécsi út.

➡**HÉV** Árpád híd stop serves Óbuda; the Aquincum stop is handy for the Roman ruins.

Lonely Planet's Top Tip

You can reach Óbuda and Aquincum by bus, or take tram 17 to Óbuda, but the fastest and easiest way is to hop on the HÉV suburban train from Batthyány tér or Margit híd in Buda. Be aware that tickets are *always* checked by a conductor on the HÉV.

✖ Best Places to Eat

➡ Kisbuda Gyöngye (p79)

➡ Fuji Japán (p80)

➡ Fióka (p79)

➡ Náncsi Néni (p79)

For reviews, see p76➡

◉ Best Museums & Galleries

➡ Aquincum Museum (p74)

➡ Hungarian Museum of Trade & Tourism (p75)

➡ Vasarely Museum (p75)

➡ Béla Bartók Memorial House (p76)

For reviews, see p75➡

⚲ Best for Taking the Plunge

➡ Lukács Baths (p80)

➡ Veli Bej Baths (p80)

➡ Császár-Komjádi Pools (p80)

For reviews, see p80➡

ÓBUDA & BUDA HILLS

TOP SIGHT
AQUINCUM

Aquincum, the most complete Roman civilian town in Hungary and now both an enclosed museum and open-air archaeological park, had paved streets and sumptuous single-storey houses with courtyards, fountains and mosaic floors, as well as sophisticated drainage and heating systems. Not all that is apparent today as you walk among the ruins, but you can see its outlines as well as those of the big public baths, the *macellum* (market), an early Christian church and a temple dedicated to the god Mithra, the chief deity of a religion that once rivalled Christianity.

The newly built **Aquincum Museum** (Aquincumi Múzeum), on the southwestern edge of what remains of the Roman civilian settlement, puts the ruins in perspective, with a vast collection of coins and wall paintings and some tremendous virtual games such as battling with a gladiator in the basement. Look out for the replica of a 3rd-century portable organ called a hydra, the mock-up of a Roman bath, the road map of the Roman Empire *(Tabula Peutingeriana)* and the wonderful **Painter's House**, a re-created Roman dwelling. Most of the big sculptures and stone sarcophagi are outside in the park to the north or in the lapidary in the old museum building. Across Szentendrei út to the northwest and close to the HÉV stop is the **Roman Civilian Amphitheatre** (Római polgári amfiteátrum), about half the size of the amphitheatre reserved for the garrisons and seating 3000. Lions were kept in the small cubicles while slain gladiators were carried through the 'Gate of Death' to the west.

DON'T MISS...

➡ Aquincum's main thoroughfare

➡ Painter's House

➡ Virtual games

➡ Hydra (portable organ)

➡ *Tabula Peutingeriana* (Roman road map)

PRACTICALITIES

➡ ☑1-250 1650

➡ www.aquincum.hu

➡ III Szentendre út 133-135

➡ adult/student & senior 1600/800Ft, archaeological park only 1000/500Ft

➡ ⊘museum 10am-6pm Tue-Sun Apr-Oct, to 4pm Nov-Mar, park 9am-6pm Tue-Sun Apr-Oct

➡ ⊠34, 106, ℝHÉV to Aquincum

SIGHTS

⦿ Óbuda

AQUINCUM MUSEUM
MUSEUM

See p74.

VASARELY MUSEUM
GALLERY

Map p234 (⌂1-388 7551; www.vasarely.hu; III Szentlélek tér 6; adult/child 800/400Ft; ⊙10am-5.30pm Tue-Sun; ⌷86, ⌷HÉV to Árpád híd) Installed in the imposing Zichy Mansion (Zichy kastély) built in 1757, this museum contains the works of Victor Vasarely (or Vásárhelyi Győző as he was known before he emigrated to Paris in 1930), the late 'father of op art'. The works, especially *Keek* and *Ibadan-Pos,* are excellent and fun to watch as they 'swell' and 'move' around the canvas.

IMRE VARGA COLLECTION
GALLERY

Map p234 (Varga Imre Gyűjtemény; ⌂1-250-0274; www.budapestgaleria.hu; III Laktanya utca 7; adult/child 800/400Ft; ⊙10am-6pm Tue-Sun Apr-Oct, to 4pm Tue-Sun Nov-Mar; ⌷86) This collection includes sculptures, statues, medals and drawings by Imre Varga (b 1923), one of Hungary's foremost sculptors. Like others before him, notably Zsigmond Kisfaludi Strobl, Varga seems to have sat on both sides of the fence politically for decades – sculpting Béla Kun and Lenin as dexterously as he did St Stephen, Béla Bartók and even Imre Nagy. But his work always remains fresh and is never derivative. Note the fine bust of Winston Churchill (2003) near the entrance. A very short distance to the southwest of the museum you'll see a group of outdoor sculptures by Varga. They portray four rather worried-looking women holding umbrellas in the middle of the street.

AQUINCUM BY NUMBERS

➡ Size: 2.7 sq km
➡ Population: 50,000
➡ Amphitheatres: 2
➡ Baths: 9
➡ Forums: 2
➡ Wall length: 1.5km
➡ Aqueducts: 5
➡ Bridges: 2

KISCELL MUSEUM
MUSEUM

Map p234 (Kiscelli Múzeum; ⌂1-388 7817; www.btmfk.iif.hu; III Kiscelli utca 108; adult/student & senior 1000/500Ft; ⊙10am-6pm Tue-Sun Apr-Oct, to 4pm Tue-Sun Nov-Mar; ⌷160, 165, ⌷17) Housed in an 18th-century monastery, this museum contains two excellent sections. In the **Contemporary City History Collection** (Újkori Várostörténeti Gyűjtemény) you'll find a complete 19th-century apothecary brought from Kálvin tér; a wonderful assembly of ancient signboards advertising shops and other trades; and rooms dressed in Empire, Biedermeier and Art Nouveau furniture and bric-a-brac. The **Municipal Picture Gallery** (Fővárosi Képtár), with its impressive collection of works by József Rippl-Rónai, Lajos Tihanyi, István Csók and Béla Czóbel, is upstairs.

ROMAN MILITARY AMPHITHEATRE
ARCHAEOLOGICAL SITE

Map p234 (Római Katonai Amfiteátrum; III Pacsirtamező utca; ⌷86, ⌷HÉV to Tímár utca) Built in the 2nd century for the Roman garrisons, this amphitheatre, about 800m south of Flórián tér, could accommodate 6000 spectators. The rest of the military camp extended north to Flórián tér. Archaeology and classical-history buffs taking bus 86 to Flórián tér should get off at III Nagyszombat utca.

ÓBUDA MUSEUM
MUSEUM

Map p234 (Óbudai Múzeum; ⌂1-250 1020; www.obudaimuzeum.hu; III Fő tér 1; adult/child 800/400Ft; ⊙10am-6pm Tue-Sun; ⌷86) Anchor tenant of the Zichy Mansion, where you'll also find the Vasarely Museum, but with its own entrance on Fő tér, this museum contains a motley assortment of exhibits related to Óbuda's past through three distinct periods: medieval, industrial and present-day. Highlights include a 19th-century farmhouse kitchen from Békásmegyer, the output of master cooper Simon Tóbiás, and a vintage 1970s apartment interior.

★ HUNGARIAN MUSEUM OF TRADE & TOURISM
MUSEUM

Map p234 (Magyar Kereskedelmi és Vendéglátó-ipari Múzeum; ⌂1-375 6249; www.mkvm.hu; III Korona tér 1; adult/child 800/400Ft; ⊙10am-6pm Tue-Sun; ⌷86, ⌷HÉV to Tímár utca) One of our favourite small museums in Budapest, this unusual one looks at the catering and hospitality trade, with restaurant items, tableware, advertising posters, packaging and original shop signs. Go upstairs for an intimate look at the lives of various tradespeople – from bakers and publicans to launderers. The lovely cafe is lit by antique lamps. A gem.

FRANKEL LEÓ ÚT STREET

Map p230 (Frankel Leó út; 🚌86, 🚊17) At Bem József tér, Fő utca, the busy main drag in Víziváros, becomes Frankel Leó út, a quiet, tree-lined street with two spas at its southern end: the very serious Lukács Baths and the newly opened Veli Bej Baths (both p80). A short distance north and tucked away in an apartment block is the **Újlak Synagogue** (Újlaki zsinagóga; II Frankel Leó út 49 & Árpád fejedelem útja 70; 🚊17), built in 1888 on the site of an older prayer house and still in use.

About 2km to the northeast and beside the landmark Aquincum Hotel is the much larger **Óbuda Synagogue** (Óbudai zsinagóga; 🕿1-268 0183; http://obudaizsinagoga.zsido.com; III Lajos utca 163; 🚌86), built in 1821. For many years it housed Hungarian TV (MTV) sound studios, but it's now functioning at least part-time as a *súl* (Jewish prayer house). Phone ahead to visit the interior.

GÜL BABA'S TOMB ISLAMIC

Map p234 (Gül Baba türbéje; 🕿1-237 4400; www.museum.hu/budapest/gulbabaturbe; II Türbe tér 1; ⊙10am-6pm; 🚌4, 6, 17) **FREE** This reconstructed tomb contains the mortal remains of Gül Baba, an Ottoman dervish who took part in the capture of Buda in 1541 and is known in Hungary as the 'Father of Roses'. The tomb and mosque are a pilgrimage place for Muslims, especially from Turkey, and you must remove your shoes before entering. From Török utca, which runs parallel to Frankel Leó út, walk up steep Gül Baba utca to the set of steps just past No 16.

You can also get here from Mecset utca, which runs north from Margit utca.

⊙ Buda Hills

For information on touring the Buda Hills, see opposite page. For details on caving in the area, see p78.

BÉLA BARTÓK MEMORIAL HOUSE MUSEUM

Map p233 (Bartók Béla Emlékház; 🕿1-394 2100; www.bartokmuseum.hu; II Csalán út 29; adult/senior & student 1200/600Ft; ⊙10am-5pm Tue-Sun; 🚌5, 29, 🚌61) North of Szilágyi Erzsébet fasor, this house (1924) is where the great composer resided from 1932 until 1940,

when he emigrated to the US. The visit is by guided tour and includes seeing the old Edison recorder (complete with wax cylinders) that Bartók used to record Hungarian folk music in Transylvania, as well as his beloved hand-carved dining-room furniture and even half a cigarette he smoked! Chamber-music concerts take place here throughout the year; see the website for details.

EATING

Some of the little neighbourhood eateries of Óbuda are so long established they make cameo appearances in Hungarian literature. Few of the restaurants in the Buda Hills are posh, but some are so popular they've become legends in their own lunchtime.

✗ Óbuda

PASTRAMI INTERNATIONAL $

Map p234 (🕿1-430 1731; www.pastrami.hu; III Lajos utca 93-99; mains 1800-4700Ft; ⊙8am-11pm; 🚌86, 🚊17, 🚇HÉV to Tímár utca) A sort-of attempt at a New York–style deli in a loft-like building in Óbuda's Újlak district, this place does indeed serve its namesake in its many guises, including the celebrated Reuben sandwich (1700Ft). But come here too for breakfast, more complicated mains, and *caponata*, their out-of-this-word sweet-and-sour Sicilian relish.

VAPIANO ITALIAN $

Map p234 (🕿1-336 0610; www.vapiano.hu; II Bécsi út 33-35; pizza & pasta 1390-2390Ft; ⊙8am-11pm Mon-Thu, to midnight Fri, 11am-midnight Sat, to 11pm Sun; 🚗; 🚊17) This branch of the popular pizza and pasta bar is a welcome addition to Óbuda's dining scene and convenient to everything.

NAGYI PALACSINTÁZÓJA HUNGARIAN $

(www.nagyipali.hu; III Szentendrei út 131; pancakes 190-680Ft, set menus 1090-1190Ft; ⊙24hr; 🚇HÉV to Aquincum) This branch of 'Granny's Palacsinta Place', the popular pancake chain, is hard by the Aquincum Museum and open round the clock.

GASZTRÓ HÚS-HENTESÁRU HUNGARIAN $

Map p234 (🕿1-212 4159; II Margit körút 2; dishes from 300Ft; ⊙7am-6pm Mon, 6am-7pm Tue-Fri, 6am-1pm Sat; 🚌4, 6) Opposite the first stop

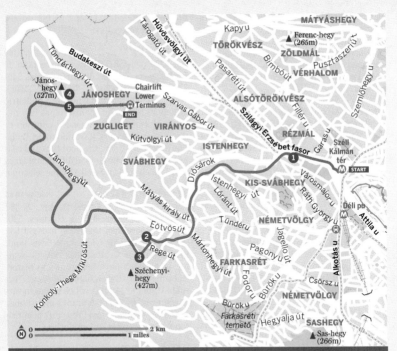

Neighbourhood Walk
Touring the Buda Hills

START SZÉLL KÁLMÁN TÉR METRO STATION
END CHAIRLIFT LOWER TERMINUS
LENGTH ABOUT THREE HOURS

With all the unusual transport options, getting to and from the Buda Hills is half the fun. From Széll Kálmán tér metro station on the M2 line in Buda, walk westward along Szilágyi Erzsébet fasor for 10 minutes (or take tram 59 or 61 for two stops) to the circular Hotel Budapest at II Szilágyi Erzsébet fasor 47. Directly opposite the hotel is the lower terminus of the ❶ **Cog Railway** (www.bkv.hu; admission 1 BKV ticket or 350Ft; ⊙5am-11pm). Built in 1874, the Cog climbs for 3.7km in 15 minutes three or four times an hour to Széchenyi-hegy (427m).

There you can stop for a picnic in the attractive park south of the old-time station, visit the station's tiny ❷ **museum** (admission 50Ft) or board the unique narrow-gauge ❸ **Children's Railway** (www.gyermekvasut. hu; ⊙closed Mon Sep-Apr; adult/child 1 section 600/300Ft, entire line 700/350Ft), two minutes to the south on Hegyhát út opposite

Rege út. The railway, with eight stops, was built in 1951 by *Pioneers* (socialist Scouts) and is now staffed entirely by schoolchildren aged 10 to 14 (the engineer excluded). The little train chugs along for 11km, terminating at Hűvösvölgy 45 minutes later. Departure times vary widely depending on the day of the week and the season; consult the website.

There are walks fanning out from any of the stops along the Children's Railway line or you can return to Széll Kálmán tér on tram 61 from Hűvösvölgy. A more interesting way down, however, is to get off at János-hegy, the fourth stop and the highest point (527m) in the hills. From atop the 23.5m-tall ❹ **Elizabeth Lookout** (Erzsébet kilátó), with 101 steps, you can see the Tatra Mountains in Slovakia on a clear day. About 700m to the east of the tower is the ❺ **Chairlift** (www.bkv.hu; ⊙10am-7pm May-Aug, to 6pm Apr & Sep, to 5pm Mar & Oct, to 3.30pm Nov-Feb; adult/child 900/600Ft), which will take you 1040m down at 4km/h to Zugligeti út. From here bus 291 will take you to Szilágyi Erzsébet fasor.

of trams 4 and 6 on the Buda (west) side of Margaret Bridge, this place with the unappetising name of 'Gastro Meat and Butcher Products' is a traditional butcher shop also serving cooked sausages and roast chicken to be eaten in situ or taken away.

DAUBNER CUKRÁSZDA
BAKERY $

Map p234 (⏰1-335 2253; www.daubnercukraszda.hu; II Szépvölgyi út 50; cakes 290-490Ft; ⊙9am-7pm; ⏸65) It may seem quite a journey for your *Sachertorte* (chocolate cake) and you can only stand and nibble here, but Daubner gets rave reviews from locals and expats alike as the best shop for cakes in Buda.

CODE 7
INTERNATIONAL $$

Map p234 (⏰1-707 7777; www.code7.hu; III Perc utca 6; mains 1890-3790Ft; ⊙9am-11pm Mon-Fri, noon-11pm Sat; ⏸86) Stylish loft-like restaurant in the heart of Óbuda serves up excellent burgers and steaks amid industrial decor. Good breakfasts (890Ft) and two-/three-course lunches for just 1290/1590Ft.

KÉHLI VENDÉGLŐ
HUNGARIAN $$

Map p234 (⏰1-368 0613; www.kehli.hu; III Mókus utca 22; mains 1990-4990Ft; ⊙noon-midnight; ⏸86) Self-consciously rustic, Kéhli has some of the best traditional Hungarian food in town. One of Hungary's best-loved writers, the novelist Gyula Krúdy (1878–1933), who lived in nearby Dugovics Titusz tér, moonlighted as a restaurant critic and enjoyed Kéhli's *forró velőscsont pirítóssal* (bone marrow on toast; 990Ft) so much

that he included it in one of his novels. There's live music too.

PATA NEGRA
SPANISH $$

Map p234 (⏰1-438 3227; www.patanegra.hu; III Frankel Leó út 51; tapas 380-1150Ft, plates 840-2200Ft; ⊙11am-midnight; ⏸17) The 'Black Foot' (a kind of Spanish ham, not a podiatric affliction) is a lovely Spanish tapas bar and restaurant and a much-needed addition to this desert district of gastronomy in Buda. The decor is fine, and the floor tiles and ceiling fans help create a mood *à la valenciana*. Good cheese and an excellent wine selection.

ÚJ SÍPOS HALÁSZKERT
HUNGARIAN $$

Map p234 (New Piper Fisher's Garden; ⏰1-388 8745; www.ujsipos.hu; III Fő tér 6; mains 1590-3690Ft; ⊙noon-11pm Mon-Fri, to midnight Sat; ⏸; ⏸86) This old-style eatery faces (and, in the warmer weather, has outside seating in) Óbuda's most beautiful and historical square. Try the signature *halászlé* (fish soup; 1190Ft to 2490Ft), which comes in various guises. As the restaurant's motto says: *Halászlében verhetetlen* (You can't beat fish soup). Good vegetarian options too.

ITALIAN FUSION
ITALIAN $$

Map p234 (⏰1-333 5656; www.symbolbudapest.hu; III Bécsi út 56; pasta 2280-3980Ft, mains 1980-5480Ft; ⊙11.30am-midnight; ⏸; ⏸17) Part of Óbuda's ambitious Symbol complex of five bars and restaurants built in and around a late 18th-century townhouse, this eatery serves relatively reasonably priced 'Italian fusion' (meaning they Magyarise

---

CAVES UNDER THE BUDA HILLS

Budapest is sitting on an underground system of up to 200 caves, and two in the Buda Hills can be visited on walk-through guided tours. Most of the hostels also offer adventurous 2½- to three-hour caving excursions of both **Mátyáshegy Cave** (Mátyáshegyi-barlang; ☑06 20 356 4406, 06 20 928 4969; www.barlangaszat.hu; II Szépvölgyi út; adult/child 5000/4000Ft; ⊙tours 4.30pm Mon, Wed & Fri; ⏸65 from Kolosy tér in Óbuda) and **Pálvölgy Cave** (Pálvölgyi-barlang; ☑1-325 9505; www.palvolgyi.atw.hu; II Szépvölgyi út 162/a; adult/child 1300/1000Ft; ⊙10am-4pm Tue-Sun; ⏸65), at 29km the longest in Hungary. The system was discovered in 1904 and is noted for both its stalactites and its bats. Be advised that part of the route involves climbing a ladder and about 120 steps, so it may not be suitable for the elderly or young children. The temperature is a constant 8°C, so wear a jacket or jumper. Much shorter tours of just Pálvölgy lasting 45 minutes depart several times a day; see the website for times.

A much easier visit is to the beautiful **Szemlőhegy Cave** (Szemlőhegyi-barlang; Map p234; ☑1-325 6001; www.szemlohegyi.atw.hu; II Pusztaszeri út 35; adult/child 1150/900Ft; ⊙10am-4pm Wed-Mon; ⏸29) about 1km southeast of Pálvölgy and Mátyáshegy Caves. The temperature at Szemlőhegy is 12°C and the cave has stalactites, stalagmites and weird grapelike formations. The tour lasts 35 to 45 minutes.

the pasta) as well as simpler fare like wood-fired pizza (1380Ft to 2380Ft). There's live music and a good kids' menu.

OKUYAMA NO SUSHI
JAPANESE $$
Map p234 (⌖1-250 8256; www.okuyamanosushi.uw.hu; III Kolosy tér 5-6, basement; sushi 2200-5000Ft, mains 1500-3500Ft; ⊙1-10pm Tue-Sun; ⌖86, ⌖17) This tiny hole-in-the-wall restaurant in the basement of a mini shopping mall in Óbuda serves some of the best Japanese food in town. There's a special daily menu of five dishes for 4500Ft.

FÖLDES JÓZSI KONYHÁJA
HUNGARIAN $$
Map p234 (www.foldesjozsikonyhaja.hu; Frankel Leó út 30-34; mains 1900-2400Ft; ⊙11.30-3.30pm Mon, to 10pm Tue-Sat, noon-3.30pm Sun; ⌖4,6,17) This rustic little place just opposite the Lukács Baths was established by former hotel chef Joe Earthy – hey, that's what his name means! – a few years back and still serves excellent Hungarian home-style dishes including a good range of *főzelék* (vegetables in a roux; 690Ft to 750Ft).

MAHARAJA
INDIAN $$
Map p234 (⌖1-250 7544; www.maharaja.hu; III Bécsi út 89-91; mains 2190-3990Ft; ⊙noon-11pm; ⌖86, ⌖17) This Óbuda institution was the first Indian restaurant to open in Budapest. It specialises in Northern Indian dishes, especially tandoori (2290Ft to 2490Ft). It's never been the best subcontinental eatery in town, but makes decent samosas.

WASABI
JAPANESE $$
Map p234 (⌖1-430 1056; www.wasabi.hu; III Szépvölgyi út 15; lunch/dinner 4990/5900Ft; ⊙11am-11pm; ⌖86, ⌖17) This sushi restaurant with a central conveyor belt has more than 60 items to choose from and the decor is dark, minimalist and very cool. The all-you-can-eat deal will keep the ravenous satisfied.

★KISBUDA GYÖNGYE
HUNGARIAN $$$
Map p234 (⌖1-368 6402; www.remiz.hu; III Kenyeres utca 34; mains 2780-4980Ft; ⊙noon-3pm & 7-10pm Tue-Sat; ⌖160, 260, ⌖17) Operating since the 1970s, this traditional yet very elegant Hungarian restaurant has an antique-cluttered dining room and attentive service, and manages to create a fin-de-siècle atmosphere. Try the excellent goose-liver speciality plate with a glass of Tokaj (3980Ft), or a less complicated dish like roast duck with apples (2980Ft), which is still out of this world.

✗ Buda Hills

★FIÓKA
HUNGARIAN $$
Map p233 (⌖1-426 5555; www.fiokaetterem.hu; XII Városmajor utca 75; mains 2400-3600Ft; ⊙11am-midnight Wed-Sun) This newish bistro and wine bar gets the nod from the cognoscenti, who rave about the Hungarian duck and pork dishes and the great selection of wines from not just Hungary but the whole Carpathian Basin. It's in a one-time office building near the foot of tiny Kissváb Hil.

NÁNCSI NÉNI
HUNGARIAN $$
(Auntie Nancy; ⌖1-397 2742; www.nancsineni.hu; II Ördögárok út 80; mains 2180-3250Ft; ⊙noon-11pm Mon-Fri, 9am-11pm Sat & Sun; ⌖61, then bus 157) Auntie Náncsi (Hungarian for any loopy old lady) is a favourite with locals and expats alike, and she's very much of sound mind. Located up in Hűvösvölgy, the restaurant specialises in game in autumn and winter. In summer it's the lighter fare – lots of stuff cooked with grapes and morello cherries – and garden seating that attracts.

SZÉP ILONA
HUNGARIAN $$
Map p233 (⌖1-275 1392; www.szepilonavendeglo.hu; II Budakeszi út 1-3; mains 1600-3600Ft; ⊙noon-11pm; ⌖61) This recently tarted up Buda Hills spot is still the place to come for hearty indigenous fare at modest prices. The name refers to the 'Beautiful Helen' in the ballad by poet Mihály Vörösmarty: she falls in love with a dashing 'hunter', who turns out to be the young King Matthias Corvinus. Alas...

REMÍZ
HUNGARIAN $$
Map p233 (⌖1-275 1396; www.remiz.hu; II Budakeszi út 5; mains 1680-4150Ft; ⊙noon-11pm; ⌖61) Next to a tram depot *(remíz)* in the Buda Hills, this veritable institution remains popular for its reliable food (try the grilled dishes, especially the ribs; 2780Ft to 3780Ft), competitive prices and verdant garden terrace. Portions are huge, service flawless.

MUGHAL SHAHI
PAKISTANI $$
(⌖1-202 4488; www.pakistani-etterem.hu; XII Városmajor utca 57; mains 1600-3000Ft; ⊙11.30am-10.30pm; ⌖128) Authentic and reasonably priced Pakistani fare on the way up to the Buda Hills (of all places). Pakistani dishes usually pack more of a punch than their Indian equivalents: hotter, spicier and somewhat more salty.

FUJI JAPÁN
JAPANESE $$$

Map p233 (☎1-325 7111; www.fujirestaurant.hu; II Csatárka út 54; mains 2100-7200Ft; ☺noon-11pm; ☐29) Above Rózsadomb in posh district II, Fuji is a long way to go for sushi and sashimi and hot mains like sukiyaki. But this is the most authentic Japanese game in town, judging from the repeat clientele who nip in regularly for noodles and more. Set weekday lunch is just 1990Ft.

BOCK BISZTRÓ
BISTRO $$$

Map p233 (☎1-376 6044; www.bockbisztro.hu; XII Szarvas Gábor utca 8; mains 3200-4100Ft; ☺noon-11pm Tue-Sun; ☐156, ☐61) Bock's sister bistro in Erzsébetváros may have lost its Michelin recommendation recently, but there's no stopping this almost luxurious place in the Buda Hills catering to the well-heeled denizens of district XII. The tapas (from 1200Ft) are particularly good.

🍷 DRINKING & NIGHTLIFE

PUSKÁS PANCHO SPORTS PUB
PUB

Map p234 (☎1-333 5656; www.symbolbudapest.hu; III Bécsi út 56; ☺7.30am-midnight Mon-Fri, from 11.30am Sat & Sun; ☐86, ☐17) In Óbuda's sprawling Symbol entertainment complex, this popular sports pub is named after Ferenc Puskás (1927–2006), Hungary's greatest football player, who emigrated to Spain after the 1956 Uprising and played for Real Madrid. Ferenc in Hungarian and Pancho in Spanish are the same name: Frank. See the statue of him outside III Bécsi út 61.

CALGARY ANTIK BÁR
BAR

Map p234 (☎1-316 9087; www.etterem.hu/669; II Frankel Leó utca 24; ☺4pm-4am; ☐4,6) Teensy bar just over Margaret Bridge hides an Aladdin's cave, filled to bursting with antiques and a host of loyal regulars who stay up all night playing cards, drinking and gossiping with owner Viky Szabó, model turned junk-shop proprietor.

⭐ ENTERTAINMENT

ÓBUDA SOCIETY
CONCERT VENUE

Map p234 (Óbudai Társaskör; ☎1-250 0288; www.obudaitarsaskor.hu; III Kis Korona utca 7; tickets 800-3500Ft; ☐86, ☐HÉV to Tímár utca) This very intimate venue in Óbuda takes its music

seriously and hosts recitals and some chamber orchestras. Highly recommended.

SHOPPING

BÁV
ANTIQUES

Map p234 (☎1-315 0417; www.bav.hu; II Frankel Leó utca 13 & II Margit körút 4; ☺10am-6pm Mon-Fri, to 2pm Sat; ☐4, 6) This branch of BÁV is good for jewellery, lamps and fine porcelain.

SPORTS & ACTIVITIES

⭐ VELI BEJ BATHS
BATHHOUSE

Map p234 (Veli Bej Fürdője; ☎06 30 996 7255, 1-438 8641; www.irgalmas.hu/veli-bej-furdo; II Árpád fejedelem útja 7 & Frankel Leó út 54; 6am-noon 2240Ft, 3-7pm 2800Ft, after 7pm 2000Ft; ☺6am-noon & 3-9pm; ☐86, ☐4, 6, 17) One of the oldest (1575) and most beautiful Ottoman-era baths in Budapest has now come back to life after a complete renovation in 2011 with the help of archaeologists and art historians. The central cupola is surrounded by four smaller domed buildings, creating a total of five thermal pools. The water, pumped in at 38°C through original clay pipes, is high in sodium, potassium and calcium and good for joint ailments, chronic arthritis and calcium deficiency.

LUKÁCS BATHS
BATHHOUSE

Map p234 (Lukács Gyógyfürdő; ☎1-326 1695; www.spasbudapest.com; II Frankel Leó út 25-29; with locker/cabin weekdays 3000/3400Ft, weekends 3100/3500Ft; ☺6am-9pm; ☐86, ☐4, 6, 17) Housed in a sprawling 19th-century complex, these baths are popular with spa aficionados. The thermal baths (temperatures 24°C to 40°C) are always mixed and a bathing suit is required. The use of the three swimming pools is included in the admission fee.

CSÁSZÁR-KOMJÁDI POOLS
SWIMMING

Map p234 (☎1-212 2750; www.mnsk.hu; II Árpád fejedelem útja 8; adult/child 1800/1100Ft; ☺6am-7pm; ☐86, ☐17) This swimming complex, which includes two 50m pools and a 25m one, is used by serious swimmers and fitness freaks – so don't come here for fun and games.

Belváros

Neighbourhood Top Five

1 Strolling up **Váci utca** (p83), the nerve centre of Budapest tourism, and taking in all that that entails: unusual architecture, some fine shops, and crowds of people.

2 Savouring a cup of something warm and a slice of something sweet at **Gerbeaud** (p87), Buda-pest's finest *cukrászda* (cake shop).

3 Climbing the grand staircase at **Pesti Vigadó** (p84), enjoying the views from the terrace and then watching a classical concert in its sumptuous hall.

4 Having a moonlit drink and surveying the city from the roof of **Tip Top Bar** (p87).

5 Starting in Egyetem tér and spending a morning browsing the multitude of **independent boutiques** (p90) dotted all over the neighbourhood.

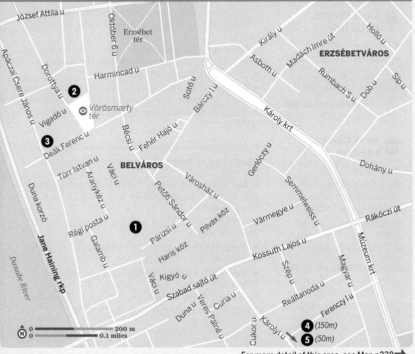

For more detail of this area, see Map p238➡

Lonely Planet's Top Tip

A lovely way to see the Belváros from a different angle altogether is to hop on one of the BKV passenger ferries that make stops all along the Danube. Board at IX Boráros tér, from where the ferry crosses to the opposite bank and then returns to Pest; get back on dry land at V Petőfi tér, or stay on for stops up to Margaret Island and beyond.

✖ Best Places to Eat

➡ Kárpátia (p86)

➡ Gerlóczy (p86)

➡ Halkakas (p86)

➡ Gepárd És Űrhajó (p86)

For reviews, see p84 ➡

🍷 Best Places to Drink

➡ Gerbeaud (p87)

➡ Csendes Társ (p87)

➡ Csendes (p87)

➡ Centrál Kávéház (p87)

For reviews, see p87 ➡

🛍 Best Places to Shop

➡ Bomo Art (p90)

➡ XD Design&Souvenir (p90)

➡ Holló Atelier (p90)

➡ Rózsavölgyi Csokoládé (p90)

➡ Rododendron (p91)

For reviews, see p90 ➡

Explore: Belváros

The Belváros ('Inner Town') is the very heart of Pest and contains the most valuable commercial real estate in the city. The area north of busy Ferenciek tere is full of flashy boutiques and well-frequented bars and restaurants; you'll usually hear more German, Italian, Spanish and English spoken here than Hungarian. The neighbourhood to the south was once rather studenty, quieter and much more local; now much of it is reserved for pedestrians, and there's no shortage of trendy shops and cafes, along with the usual souvenir shops and boutiques.

The Belváros contains four important 'centres': V Deák Ferenc tér is a busy square in the northeast corner, where three metro lines (M1/2/3) converge, also accessible by trams 47 and 49; touristy V Vörösmarty tér is on the M1 metro at the northern end of V Váci utca; V Ferenciek tere, on metro M3, divides the Inner Town at Szabad sajtó út; and V Egyetem tér (University Sq) is a five-minute walk south along V Károlyi utca from Ferenciek tere and 250m northwest of Kálvin tér on the M3 and M4 metro along leafy V Kecskeméti utca.

Local Life

➡ **Lunch** Chow down with the locals at Belvárosi Disznótoros (p84) on huge portions of all kinds of sausages, meat and fish, eaten standing up at outside benches.

➡ **Hang-out** Take a moment to relax, read a book or let your kids have a run around at the neighbourhood's secret garden, Károlyi kert (p86).

➡ **Fröccs** Join the throngs of locals who start the night as the sun goes down drinking spritzers in Erzsébet tér, before tripping over to see who's on at Akvárium Klub (p90).

Getting There & Away

➡ **Bus** V Ferenciek tere for 7 or 7E to Buda or points east in Pest; V Egyetem tér for 15 or 115 to IX Boráros tér and northern Pest.

➡ **Ferry** Petőfi tér pier for ferries to IX Boráros tér and Margaret Island.

➡ **Metro** M3 Ferenciek tere, M1 Vörösmarty tér, M1/2/3 Deák Ferenc tér, M3/4 Kálvin tér.

➡ **Tram** Little Ring Rd (Károly körút and Múzeum körút) for 47 or 49 from V Deák Ferenc tér to Liberty Bridge and points in south Buda; Belgrád rakpart for the 2 to V Szent István körút or southern Pest.

TOP SIGHT
VÁCI UTCA & VÖRÖSMARTY TÉR

Váci utca is the capital's premier shopping street, crammed with chain stores, touristy restaurants and a smattering of shops and notable buildings worth seeking out. It was the total length of Pest in the Middle Ages.

A good place to start is at the **Párisi Udvar** (V Ferenciek tere 5), built in 1909. It was under renovation at the time of writing, but if you can, get a glimpse of the interior and its ornately decorated ceiling. Váci utca is immediately to the west.

Head first to the **Philanthia flower and gift shop** (V Váci utca 9; 🚇2), which has an original (and very rare) Art Nouveau interior from 1906. **Thonet House** (V Váci utca 11/a; 🚇2) is a masterpiece built by Ödön Lechner in 1890 and to the west, at Régi Posta utca 13, there's a **relief** of an old postal coach by the ceramicist Margit Kovács of Szentendre.

Just off the top of Váci utca in Kristóf tér is the little **Fishergirl Fountain**, dating from the 19th century and complete with a ship's wheel that actually turns. A short distance to the northwest is the sumptuous **Bank Palace** (Bank Palota; V Deák Ferenc utca 5), built in 1915 and once the home of the Budapest Stock Exchange. It has been converted into a shopping gallery called **Váci 1** (www.vaci1.hu).

Váci utca empties into **Vörösmarty tér**, a large square of smart shops, galleries, cafes and an artist or two, who will draw your portrait or caricature. In the centre is a **statue of Mihály Vörösmarty**, the 19th-century poet after whom the square is named. At the northern end is **Gerbeaud** (p87), Budapest's fanciest and most famous cafe and cake shop.

A pleasant way to return to Ferenciek tere is along the **Duna korzó**, the riverside 'Danube Promenade' between Chain and Elizabeth Bridges.

DON'T MISS...

➡ Párisi Udvar
➡ Philanthia
➡ Gerbeaud
➡ Bank Palace

PRACTICALITIES

➡ Map p238
➡ 🚋7, Ⓜ M1 Vörösmarty tér, M3 Ferenciek tere, 🚋2

 SIGHTS

VÁCI UTCA STREET
See p83.

VÖRÖSMARTY TÉR SQUARE
See p83.

UNDERGROUND RAILWAY MUSEUM MUSEUM
Map p238 (Földalatti Vasúti Múzeum; www.bkv.
hu; Deák Ferenc tér metro station; adult/child
350/280Ft; ⊙10am-5pm Tue-Sun; ⓂM1/2/3
Deák Ferenc tér) In the pedestrian subway beneath V Deák Ferenc tér, next to the main ticket window, the small Underground Railway Museum traces the development of the capital's underground lines. Much emphasis is put on the little yellow metro (M1), Continental Europe's first underground railway, which opened for the millenary celebrations in 1896. The museum is housed in a stretch of tunnel and station, and atmospherically houses wonderfully restored carriages.

PESTI VIGADÓ NOTABLE BUILDING
Map p238 (www.pestivigado.hu; V Vigadó tér 1;
adult/senior 2000/1200Ft, temporary exhibitions 2500Ft; ⊙10am-7.30pm; ⓂM1 Vörösmarty tér, 🚊2) Pesti Vigadó, the Romantic-style concert hall built in 1864 but badly damaged during WWII, faces the river to the west of Vörösmarty tér. Reopened in 2014 after a 10-year closure and reconstruction, the building has been fully restored to its former grandeur. Additional space has been set aside for temporary exhibitions and there's now a fantastic terrace affording expansive views over the Danube. It's a fantastic place to catch a classical concert in glamorous surrounds.

Start your visit in the ground-floor gallery space, before ascending the magnificent stone staircase for a peek into the 2nd-floor concert hall. A lift will whisk you to the 5th- and 6th-floor exhibition rooms and from the 6th you can step out onto the *panorámaterasz* (terrace) to take in the views.

INNER TOWN PARISH CHURCH CHURCH
Map p238 (Belvárosi plébániatemplom; www.
belvarosiplebania.hu; V Március 15 tér 2; ⊙9am-7pm; 🚊2) On the eastern side of Március 15 tér, a Romanesque church was first built in the 12th century within a Roman fortress. You can still see bits and pieces of the fort, **Contra Aquincum**, protected under Plexi-

glas on the square. The present church was rebuilt in the 14th century and again in the 18th century, and you can easily spot Gothic, Renaissance, baroque and even Turkish – eg the *mihrab* (prayer niche) in the eastern wall – elements.

The best times to visit the church (if you want to avoid services) are between 10am and 3pm and 3pm and 5.30pm Wednesday to Saturday.

PETŐFI MUSEUM OF LITERATURE MUSEUM
Map p238 (Petőfi Irodalmi Múzeum; www.pim.
hu; V Károlyi utca 16; adult/child 600/300Ft,
plus temporary exhibitions 200/100Ft; ⊙10am-6pm Tue-Sun; 🚊15, 115, ⓂM3/4 Kálvin tér) Just north of Egyetem tér and housed in the sumptuous neoclassical **Károly Palace** (Károlyi Palota), dating from 1840, this museum is devoted to Sándor Petőfi and has great examples of period furniture and dress. Temporary exhibitions explore other Hungarian poets such as Endre Ady, Mór Jókai and Attila József. Also here is a centre for contemporary literature, a library, a concert/lecture hall and a terrace restaurant in the courtyard.

EGYETEM TÉR SQUARE
Map p238 (University Square; ⓂM3/4 Kálvin tér) Recently repaved and boasting new lighting, seating, water features and shade sails, 'University Sq' takes its name from the branch of the prestigious **Loránd Eötvös Science University** (ELTE; V Egyetem tér 1-3) located here. Attached to the main university building to the west is the lovely baroque 1742 **University Church** (Egyetemi templom; ☎1-318 0555; V Papnövelde utca 5-7; ⊙7am-7pm). Over the altar is a copy of the Black Madonna of Częstochowa so revered in Poland. The building north of the square with the multicoloured dome is the **University Library** (Egyetemi könyvtár; V Ferenciek tere 10).

 EATING

BELVÁROSI DISZNÓTOROS HUNGARIAN $
Map p238 (V Károlyi utca 17; dishes 400-1400Ft;
⊙7am-8pm Mon-Fri, to 3pm Sat; 🚊15, 115,
ⓂM3/4 Kálvin tér) If your level of hunger could be described as ravenous, visit this butcher-caterer (a *disznótor* is where the animal is turned into sausages and other comestibles) that does every type of Hungarian meat dish known to humankind,

BELVÁROS

Neighbourhood Walk
Boutique Browsing in the Belváros

START KÁLVIN TÉR METRO
END ASTORIA METRO
LENGTH 2.5KM; THREE HOURS

From Kálvin tér metro, head up Keckeméti utca to recently revamped Egyetem tér, a pleasant place to linger for a coffee. Just around the corner from Café Alibi, ❶ **Rózsavölgyi Csokoládé** (p90) sells beautifully packaged artisan chocolate. For more home-grown Hungarian goodies, retrace your steps and turn left down Szerb utca, where ❷ **Hecserli** (p91) is bursting with jams, honey, cooked meats and home-made syrups. Continue to the end of Szerb utca and turn right onto pedestrianised Váci utca, the city's main shopping strip. Easily missed here is the Hungarian designer ❸ **Valeria Fazekas** (p92), who creates wonderful and unusual headgear. Just around the corner, ❹ **Kamchatka Design** (p91) showcases more interesting, locally produced fashion. For a hipper selection of pieces, take a left up Veres Pálné utca,

where ❺ **Wonderlab** (p91) brings together numerous up-and-coming designers.

A short stroll north brings you to Ferenciek tere. Cross Kossuth Lajos utca and rejoin Váci utca before taking a right into Haris köz. Here you'll find two great institutions of Budapest commerce – the glove- and shoemakers ❻ **Balogh Kesztyű Üzlet** (p91) and ❼ **Vass Shoes** (p91). On the opposite side of the street, ❽ **Nami** (p91) has cute toys offering a modern take on handmade Hungarian craft. Backtrack to Váci utca and continue north to the gorgeous paper craft at ❾ **Bomo Art** (p90) on Régi Posta utca. At the end of this street take a right, and check out the modern Hungarian designs at ❿ **Magma** (p91). A left down Pilvax köz will bring you on to Vitkovics Mihály utca, where ⓫ **Garden Studio** (p91) has yet more excellent local fashion, and ⓬ **Holló Atelier** (p90) beautifully handcrafted Hungarica. At the end of the street, ⓭ **Rododendron** (p91) is great for quirky gifts, and in tiny Röser udvar, you'll find ⓮ **Kontakt** (p87), for a well-deserved coffee.

LOCAL KNOWLEDGE

KÁROLYI KERT

A glorious place to take a breather, flora-filled Károlyi kert is the garden built for the Károly Palace (housing the Petőfi Museum of Literature, p84). Frequented by locals, many with families – it has a lovely playground – the garden is a riot of colourful flower beds in the summer months, and there are plenty of shady benches. Csendes Társ is an atmospheric spot for a sundowner or snack, with a little terrace of tables crowded round the park's pretty, wrought-iron entrance gate.

and whose name could be loosely translated as 'Inner Town Feast'. Take away or eat standing up at the counters inside and out.

HALKAKAS
FISH $

Map p238 (✑06 30 226 0638; www.halkakas.hu; V Veres Pálné utca 33; mains 1300-1600Ft; ⊙noon-10pm Mon-Sat; 🛜; ⓜM4 Fővám tér) Charming corner restaurant on a quiet street close to Váci utca that throws back its doors on sunny days, when diners spill onto the pavement outside. Fresh, simple and great-value fish dishes are served from the kitchen directly behind the service counter on mismatched plates to happy punters.

GERLÓCZY
BISTRO $$

Map p238 (✑1-501 4000; www.gerloczy.hu; V Gerlóczy utca 1; mains 2900-4900Ft; ⊙7am-11pm; 🛜; ⓜM2 Astoria, ⓖ47, 49) The expanded terrace of this wonderful retro-style cafe looks out onto one of Pest's most attractive little squares and serves excellent breakfasts (700Ft to 1800Ft), light meals and home-baked bread, as well as full meals. Live music (jazz) nightly.

GEPÁRD ÉS ŰRHAJÓ
HUNGARIAN $$

Map p238 (✑06 70 329 7815; www.gepardesurhajo.com; V Belgrád rakpart 18; mains 2550-4900Ft; ⊙noon-midnight; 🛜; ⓜM3 Ferenciek tere, ⓖ2) It's difficult not to love the 'Cheetah and Rocket', for four reasons: the name, the excellent Hungarian wine (these guys stock more than 100 vintages), the food and the fabulous river views. In inspired takes on Hungarian dishes such as lamb knuckle or beef cheeks, the meats are cooked to perfection and the weekly specials are based on seasonal ingredients.

CAFÉ ALIBI
INTERNATIONAL $$

Map p238 (✑1-317 4209; www.cafealibi.hu; V Egyetem tér 4; mains 1890-3590Ft; ⊙8am-11pm; 🛜; ⓜM3/4 Kálvin tér) We usually come to this cafe-restaurant with a great terrace in the heart of university-land for late breakfast (till noon weekdays, till 4pm Saturday and Sunday) with coffee roasted in-house, plus snacks (1490Ft to 2790Ft) or an excellent-value set lunch (1090Ft).

BORSSÓ BISTRO
HUNGARIAN, FRENCH $$

Map p238 (✑1-789 0975; www.borsso.hu; V Királyi pál utca 14; mains 2900-5900Ft; ⊙noon-11pm Wed-Sun, from 6pm Tue; 🛜; ⓜM3/4 Kálvin tér) Cosy, classy and welcoming corner restaurant set over two levels, with dark-wood furniture and romantic candlelight come evening. There's clear attention to detail in the French-influenced Hungarian dishes as well as other touches, such as the homemade bread and courteous service.

TRATTORIA TOSCANA
ITALIAN $$

Map p238 (✑1-327 0045; www.toscana.hu; V Belgrád rakpart 13; mains 2990-5990Ft; ⊙noon-midnight; 🛜✏; ⓖ15, 115, ⓖ2) Hard by the Danube, this trattoria serves rustic and very authentic Italian and Tuscan food, including *pasta e fagioli* (a hearty soup of beans and pasta) and a wonderful Tuscan farmer's platter of prepared meats. The pizza and pasta dishes are excellent too, as is the antipasto buffet.

★KÁRPÁTIA
HUNGARIAN $$$

Map p238 (✑1-317 3596; www.karpatia.hu; V Ferenciek tere 7-8; mains 2500-7900Ft; ⊙11am-11pm Mon-Sat, from 5pm Sun; 🛜✏; ⓜM3 Ferenciek tere) A palace of fin-de-siècle design dating from 1877 that has to be seen to be believed, the 'Carpathia' serves almost modern Hungarian and Transylvanian specialities in both a palatial restaurant in the back and a less-expensive *söröző* (brasserie); there's also a lovely covered garden terrace. This is one place to hear authentic *csárdás* (Gypsy-style folk music), played from 6pm to 11pm.

NOBU
JAPANESE $$$

Map p238 (✑1-429 4242; www.noburestaurants.com/budapest; V Erzsébet tér 7-8, Kempinski Hotel Corvinus; sashimi per piece 1100-3800Ft, mains 2900-9900Ft; ⊙noon-3.30pm & 6-11.45pm; 🛜; ⓜM1 Vörösmarty tér) Budapest knew it had arrived when it got a branch of a favourite canteen of the London glitterati. As elsewhere, Nobu is minimalist in decor, anonymously efficient in service, and out of this world when it comes to exquisitely prepared and presented sushi and sashimi.

ONYX
HUNGARIAN $$$

Map p238 (☑06 30 508 0622; www.onyxrestaurant.hu; V Vörösmarty tér 7-8; tasting menus from 25,500Ft, mains 8500-9500Ft; ☉noon-2.30pm Tue-Fri, 6.30-11pm Tue-Sat; 🛜; Ⓜ M1 Vörösmarty tér) This Michelin-starred eatery adjacent to (and owned by) Gerbeaud has taken it upon its own lofty shoulders to modernise Hungarian cuisine, and its six-course 'Hungarian Evolution' tasting menu (25,500Ft) suggests it's well on its way to achieving that goal. The decor is a little too bejewelled for us, though.

🍷⚓ DRINKING & NIGHTLIFE

GERBEAUD
CAFE

Map p238 (☑1-429 9001; www.gerbeaud. hu; V Vörösmarty tér 7; ☉9am-9pm; 🛜; Ⓜ M1 Vörösmarty tér) Founded on the northern side of Pest's busiest square in 1858, Gerbeaud has been the most fashionable meeting place for the city's elite since 1870. Along with exquisitely prepared cakes and pastries (from 1950Ft), it serves continental/full breakfast (1490/2890Ft) and sandwiches (1950Ft to 4950Ft). A visit here is mandatory.

TIP TOP BAR
BAR

Map p238 (☑06 70 333 2113; www.facebook. com/pages/Tip-Top-Bar/386238754823394; V Királyi pál utca 4; ☉4-11pm Apr-Sep; Ⓜ M3/4 Kálvin tér) The spiral staircase to the 5th floor may be a bit of a hike, but reaching this rooftop alfresco bar and relaxing with views out over Egyetem tér and beyond is more than worth the effort. Call ahead if the weather's bad or you want to secure a table.

★CSENDES TÁRS
CAFE

Map p238 (www.facebook.com/csendestars; Magyar utca 18; ☉10am-midnight; Ⓜ M2 Astoria, 🚌4, 6) Just around the corner from the original Csende, in fair weather this little cafe sets up a terrace around the gates of peaceful Károlyi kert and serves coffee, wine and light meals to a carefree crowd. The adjoining takeaway provides top-quality snack food – tortillas, ciabattas and *tramezzini* (Italian sandwiches) – as well as ice cream; perfect for a sunny day.

FRÖCCSTERASZ
BAR

Map p238 (www.facebook.com/froccsterasz; V Erzsébet tér 13; ☉noon-4am; Ⓜ M1/2/3 Deák Ferenc tér) In what was once a bus terminal, this hugely popular open-air bar heaves in summer, when crowds flock here to drink *fröccs* (wine spritzer), meet friends and catch up beneath fairy-lit trees. The handy graphic menu provides a language-proof way to know what to order.

CSENDES
CAFE, BAR

Map p238 (www.facebook.com/csendesvintagebar; V Ferenczy István utca 5; ☉10am-2am Mon-Fri, from 2pm Sat, 2pm-midnight Sun; 🛜; Ⓜ M2 Astoria) A quirky cafe just off the Little Ring Rd with junkyard chic decorating the walls and floor space, the 'Quietly' is just that until the regular DJ arrives and cranks up the volume. There's great food available from Csendes Társ around the corner and a vintage-clothing store out back (open 5pm to 8pm Monday to Friday).

CENTRÁL KÁVÉHÁZ
CAFE

Map p238 (www.centralkavehaz.hu; V Károlyi utca 9; ☉8am-11pm; 🛜; Ⓜ M3 Ferenciek tere) This *grande dame* of a traditional cafe dates back to 1887. Awash with leather and dark wood inside, it's also a great spot for pavement people-watching. It serves meals as well as breakfast until 11.45am (2090Ft to 2690Ft) and cakes and pastries (400Ft to 850Ft).

KONTAKT
CAFE

Map p238 (www.facebook.com/kontaktstore; Károly körút 22, Röser udvar; ☉8am-6pm; 🛜; Ⓜ M2 Astoria) Design-led decor, excellent locally roasted coffee and delicious breakfasts make this little cafe, down a tiny pedestrian passage, a great place to pause. It serves sandwiches, cakes and fantastic home-roasted muesli.

1000 TEA
TEAHOUSE

Map p238 (☑1-337 8217; www.1000tea.hu; V Váci utca 65; ☉noon-9pm Mon-Thu, to 10pm Fri & Sat; 🛜; 🚌15, 115, 🚋2) In a small courtyard off lower Váci utca, this is the place if you want to sip a soothing blend made by tea-serious staff and relax in a Japanese-style tearoom. You can also sit in the bamboo-filled courtyard. There's a shop here too.

Budapest's Coffee Houses

My Cafe, My Castle

Cafe life has a long and colourful history in Budapest. The Turks introduced what the Magyars nicknamed *fekete leves* (black soup) to Hungary in the early 16th century, and the coffee house was an essential part of the social scene here long before it had even made an appearance in, say, Vienna or Paris. In the final decades of the Austro-Hungarian Empire, Budapest counted 600 cafes.

Budapest cafes of the 19th century were a lot more than just places to drink coffee. They embodied the progressive ideal that people of all classes could mingle under one roof, and acted as an incubator for Magyar culture and politics. Combining the neighbourliness of a local pub, the bonhomie of a gentlemen's club and the intellectual activity of an open university, coffee houses were places to relax, gamble, work, network, do business and debate. As the writer Dezső Kosztolányi put it in his essay *Budapest, City of Cafés: 'Az én kávéházam, az én váram'* (My cafe is my castle).

Different cafes catered to different groups. Actors preferred the Pannónia, artists the Café Japán and businessmen the Orczy, while cartoonists frequented the Lánchíd and stockbrokers the Lloyd. But the two most important cafes in terms of the city's cultural life were the still extant New York and Centrál.

The literary New York Café (1891) hosted virtually every Hungarian writer of note at one time or another. Indeed, the playwright Ferenc Molnár famously threw the key into the Danube the night the cafe opened so that it would never close. And it remained open round the

1. Central Kávéház (p87) **2.** New York Café (p127) **3.** Pastries, St Stephen's Day

clock 365 days a year for decades. The Centrál Kávéház attracted the same literary crowd, and two influential literary journals – *Nyugat* (West) and *A Hét* (The Week) – were edited here.

But the depression of the 1930s, the disruption of WWII and the dreary days of Communism conspired against grand old cafes in favour of the cheap (and seldom cheerful) *eszpresszó* (coffee shop). By 1989 and the return of the Republic of Hungary only about a dozen remained.

Nowadays, though, you're more likely to find young Budapesters drinking a beer or a glass of wine at one of the new modern cafes. The cafe is, in fact, very much alive in Budapest. It's just reinvented itself.

WHAT TO ORDER WHERE

Hungarians drink a huge amount of coffee (*kávé*) generally as a single black (*fekete*), a double (*dupla*) or with milk (*tejes kávé*). Most cafes now serve some variation of cappuccino and latte. Decaffeinated coffee is *koffeinmentes kávé*.

Pastries such as *Dobos torta* (a layered chocolate and cream cake with a caramelised-brown-sugar top) and the wonderful *rétes* (strudel), filled with poppy seeds, cherry preserves or *túró* (curd or cottage cheese), are usually eaten not as desserts but mid-afternoon in one of Budapest's ubiquitous *kávézók* (cafes) or *cukrászdák* (cake shops), including our favourites: **Ruszwurm Cukrászda** (p62) and **Auguszt Cukrászda** (p62) in Buda and **Művész Kávéház** (p129) in Pest.

ACTION BAR GAY

Map p238 (📱1-266 9148; www.action.gay.hu; V Magyar utca 42; admission 1000Ft; ⏰9pm-4am; Ⓜ M3/4 Kálvin tér) Action is where to head if you want just that (though there's a strip show at 1am on Friday, which may distract). Take the usual precautions and don't forget to write home. Men only. Entrance fee includes a drink.

FEKETE CAFE

Map p238 (www.feketekv.hu; V Múzeum körút 5; ⏰7.30am-6.30pm Mon-Fri, 9am-7pm Sat; 📞; Ⓜ M2 Astoria) Squeeze into this minute coffee shop (there's just a bar to perch at and tables on busy Múzeum körút in fine weather), where you can sample well-poured, Budapest-roasted Casino Mocca or London's Alchemy coffee in cool, monochrome surrounds.

HABROLÓ GAY

Map p238 (www.habrolo.hu; V Szép utca 1; ⏰11am-late; Ⓜ M3 Ferenciek tere) This welcoming neighbourhood gay bar on 'Beautiful St' (could it be anywhere else?) is a cafe with a tiny lounge space upstairs and a small stage.

 ## ENTERTAINMENT

PESTI VIGADÓ CONCERT VENUE

Map p238 (www.vigado.hu; V Vigadó tér 1; ⏰box office 10am-7.30pm; Ⓜ M1 Vörösmarty tér, 🚋2) Pesti Vigadó, the Romantic-style concert hall built in 1864 and reopened in 2014 after a 10-year closure and reconstruction, hosts classical concerts in opulent surrounds.

AKVÁRIUM KLUB LIVE MUSIC

Map p238 (📱06 30 860 3368; www.akvariumklub.hu; V Erzsébet tér; ⏰ticket office 9am-8pm or end of show Mon-Sat, to 6pm Sun; 📞; Ⓜ M1/2/3 Deák Ferenc tér) In the old bays below Erzsébet tér, where once buses used to drop off and pick up passengers, you'll now find Akvárium Klub, delivering a varied program of Hungarian and international live music, from indie, jazz, world and pop to electronica and beyond. The main hall has capacity for 1500, the small for 700. There are also regular club nights here, and a bar and bistro. A carpet of drinkers layers the surrounding steps in warm weather.

JÓZSEF KATONA THEATRE THEATRE

Map p238 (Katona József Színház; 📱1-266 5200; www.katonajozsefszinhaz.hu; V Petőfi Sándor utca 6; tickets 1200-3900Ft; ⏰box office 11am-7pm Mon-Fri, from 3pm Sat & Sun; Ⓜ M3 Ferenciek tere) The József Katona Theatre is the best known theatre in Hungary and a public enterprise supported mainly by the city of Budapest. Its studio theatre, Kamra, hosts some of the best troupes in the country.

PUSKIN ART MOZI CINEMA

Map p238 (📱1-459 5050; puskinmozi.hu; V Kossuth Lajos utca 18; 🚋7, Ⓜ M2 Astoria) The long-established 'Pushkin Art Cinema' screens a healthy mix of art-house and popular releases.

🛍 SHOPPING

★ BOMO ART ARTS & CRAFTS

Map p238 (www.bomoart.hu; V Régi Posta utca 14; ⏰10am-6.30pm Mon-Fri, to 2pm Sat; Ⓜ M3 Ferenciek tere) This tiny shop just off Váci utca sells some of the finest paper and paper goods in Budapest, including leather-bound notebooks, photo albums and address books.

★ XD DESIGN&SOUVENIR HANDICRAFTS

Map p238 (www.facebook.com/pages/XD-DesignSouvenir/1434242860124002; V Régi Posta utca 7-9; ⏰10am-6pm; 🚋2) A great place to seek out a modern take on traditional Hungarian handicrafts, XD Design&Souvenir showcases the work of a number of innovative enterprises. Matyó Design is preserving the art of embroidery with intricate hand-stitched designs, and Folqa produces a line of wooden figurines humorously depicting the many faces of the nation. Great prints, fashion pieces and jewellery also on offer.

HOLLÓ ATELIER HANDICRAFTS

Map p238 (V Vitkovics Mihály utca 12; ⏰10am-6pm Mon-Fri, to 2pm Sat; Ⓜ M2 Astoria) Holló Atelier has attractive folk art with a modern look and remains our favourite place to shop for gifts and gewgaws. Everything – from ceramics and woodwork to Christmas decorations – is handmade on site.

RÓZSAVÖLGYI CSOKOLÁDÉ CHOCOLATE

Map p238 (www.rozsavolgyi.com; V Királyi Pál utca 6; ⏰10.30am-6.30pm Mon-Fri, noon-6pm

Sat; Ⓜ M3/4 Kálvin tér) Tiny, low-lit boutique selling delicious and artfully packaged, award-winning bean-to-bar chocolate as well as a range of handmade bonbons.

RODODENDRON ARTS & CRAFTS, GIFTS

Map p238 (www.rododendron.hu; V Semmelweis utca 19; ⊙10am-7pm Mon-Fri, to 4pm Sat; Ⓜ M2 Astoria) This delightful shop presents the work of numerous local designers, with everything from jewellery and cuddly toys to handbags and a range of beautiful and quirky prints on offer.

BALOGH KESZTYŰ ÜZLET GLOVES

Map p238 (V Haris köz 2; ⊙11am-6pm Mon-Thu, to 5pm Fri, to 1pm Sat; Ⓜ M3 Ferenciek tere) If he can have a pair of bespoke shoes from Vass Shoes, why can't she have a pair of custom-made gloves lined with cashmere? You'll get them here at the 'Balogh Gloves Shop' – and there's any number of materials to choose from for men too, including shearling-lined leather gloves.

VASS SHOES SHOES

Map p238 (www.vass-cipo.hu; V Haris köz 2; ⊙10am-6pm Mon-Fri, to 2pm Sat; Ⓜ M3 Ferenciek tere) A traditional shoemaker that stocks ready-to-wear and cobbles to order, Vass has a reputation that goes back to 1896, and some people travel to Hungary just to have their footwear made here. A second, larger **branch** (Map p238; V Haris köz 6; ⊙10am-6pm Mon-Fri, to 2pm Sat; Ⓜ M3 Ferenciek tere) is just up the street.

NANUSHKA FASHION

Map p238 (www.nanushka.hu; V Deák Ferenc utca 17; ⊙10am-8pm Mon-Sat, to 6pm Sun; Ⓜ M1/2/3 Deák Ferenc tér) Flagship store of Budapest-born designer Nanushka (aka Sandra Sandor), whose inspired retail space, with log floor and all-white canvas drapes sets off the cutting-edge and covetable designs inside.

HECSERLI FOOD

Map p238 (www.hecserli.hu; V Szerb utca 15; ⊙10am-7pm Mon-Fri, to 4pm Sat; Ⓜ M3/4 Kálvin tér) A world of Hungarian cuisine awaits in Hecserli, where helpful staff wax lyrical about the freshly pressed, potted, homemade and home-grown products. Ham, salami, cheese, syrups, tea and fresh bread, as well as sandwiches and coffee, are available.

MAGMA HOMEWARES

Map p238 (www.magma.hu; V Petőfi Sándor utca 11; ⊙10am-7pm Mon-Fri, to 3pm Sat; Ⓜ M3 Ferenciek tere) This showroom in the heart of the Inner Town focuses on Hungarian design and designers exclusively – with everything from glassware, porcelain and toys to textiles and furniture.

NAMI CHILDREN

Map p238 (www.namibudapest.hu; V Haris Köz 3; ⊙10am-6pm Mon-Sat; Ⓜ M3 Ferenciek tere) Wonderfully quirky handmade soft toys for kids in funky colours. Clothes too.

WONDERLAB CLOTHING, ACCESSORIES

Map p238 (www.facebook.com/wonderLABconcept; V Veres Pálné utca 3; ⊙noon-8pm Tue-Sat; 🚇2) Hip and very wearable fashion by a collection of Hungarian designers who've clubbed together to get retail space, and are often on hand to discuss their work. Interesting pieces, as well as handbags and other accessories.

GARDEN STUDIO FASHION, CHILDREN

Map p238 (www.thegardenstudio.hu; V Vitkovics Mihály utca 5-7; ⊙10am-7pm Mon-Fri, to 2pm Sat; Ⓜ M2 Astoria) Choice garments hang artfully in this trendy whitewashed space, which stocks up-and-coming Hungarian designs. At the back you'll find Small Garden, offering toys, books and designer clothes for little 'uns.

KAMCHATKA DESIGN CLOTHING

Map p238 (www.kamchatka.hu; V Nyári Pál utca 7; ⊙noon-6pm Mon-Fri, 10am-2pm Sat; Ⓜ M3 Ferenciek tere, 🚇2) Stylish, casual women's wear, locally designed and made by Márta Schulteisz. Some lovely accessories, too.

BÁV ANTIQUES

Map p238 (www.bav.hu; V Bécsi utca 1-3; Ⓜ M1/2/3 Deák Ferenc tér) This branch of the BÁV chain is good for knick-knacks, porcelain, glassware, carpets and artwork.

MÚZEUM ANTIKVÁRIUM BOOKS

Map p238 (www.muzeumantikvarium.hu; V Múzeum körút 35; ⊙10am-6pm Mon-Fri, to 2pm Sat; Ⓜ M3/4 Kálvin tér) Just opposite the Hungarian National Museum, this well-stocked bookshop has both used and antique volumes in a Babel of languages, including English. It's our favourite of the many bookshops on this street.

VALERIA FAZEKAS
CLOTHING, HATS

Map p238 (www.valeriafazekas.com; V Váci utca 50; ⊙10am-6pm Mon-Fri, to 4pm Sat; Ⓜ M3 Ferenciek tere) Are they hats or is it art? We'll say both. Some of the limited headgear in a wide range of colours and fabrics on offer in this small gem of a boutique are out of this world (or at least on their way there). Artist-designer Fazekas also does silk scarves and stylish tops.

RÓZSAVÖLGYI ÉS TÁRSA
MUSIC

Map p238 (www.rozsavolgyi.hu; V Szervita tér 5; ⊙10am-10pm Mon-Sat; Ⓜ M1/2/3 Deák Ferenc tér) Housed in Béla Latja's Rózsavölgyi House, a wonderful example of early modernist architecture, this is a great choice for CDs and DVDs of traditional folk and classical music, with a good selection of sheet music. Also sells concert tickets and hosts performances in its upstairs cafe.

CADEAU
CHOCOLATE

Map p238 (www.cadeaubonbon.hu; V Veres Pálné utca 8; ⊙10am-6pm Mon-Fri; Ⓜ M3 Ferenciek tere) 'Death by chocolate' has arrived in Budapest by way of Gyula, a city in Hungary's southeast where the delectable handmade bonbons sold here are made and served at the celebrated Százéves Cukrászda (Century Cake Shop). Also serves delicious ice cream (220Ft a scoop).

LE PARFUM CROISETTE
PERFUME

Map p238 (www.leparfum.hu; V Deák Ferenc utca 18; ⊙10am-7pm Mon-Fri, to 5pm Sat & Sun; Ⓜ M1/2/3 Deák Ferenc tér) Hungary's only *parfumeur*, Zsolt Zólyomi, creates scents at his atelier-shop as well as selling perfume from around the globe. Zólyomi, who fore-

sees a renaissance in the once great Hungarian perfume industry, holds perfume-making workshops here too.

FOLKART KÉZMŰVÉSHÁZ
HANDICRAFTS, SOUVENIRS

Map p238 (www.folkartkezmuveshaz.hu; V Régi Posta utca 12; ⊙10am-6pm Mon-Fri, to 3pm Sat & Sun; Ⓜ M3 Ferenciek tere) This is a large shop where everything Magyar (and all of it made here) is available, from embroidered waistcoats and tablecloths to painted eggs and plates. The staff are helpful.

SZAMOS MARCIPÁN
MARZIPAN

Map p238 (www.szamosmarcipan.hu; V Párizsi utca 3; ⊙10am-7pm; Ⓜ M3 Ferenciek tere) 'Many Kinds of Marzipan' sells just that – in every shape and size imaginable. Its ice cream (250Ft per scoop) rates among the best in town – another major draw.

MONO FASHION
FASHION

Map p238 (www.facebook.com/monofashionbp; V Kossuth Lajos utca 20; ⊙11am-8pm Mon-Fri, 10am-6pm Sat; Ⓜ M2 Astoria, ⊠47, 49) Swish shop stocking the work of local clothes designers as well as its own brand, NUBU.

INTUITA
ARTS & CRAFTS

Map p238 (www.intuitashop.com; V Váci utca 67; ⊙10am-6pm Mon-Fri, 10am-4pm Sat; Ⓜ M4 Fővám tér, ⊠2) You're not about to find painted eggs and *pálinka* (fruit brandy) here, but it's chock-a-block with contemporary crafted items such as jewellery, ceramics and notebooks. The **branch** (Map p238; V Váci utca 61) several doors away keeps the same hours but concentrates on clothing and accessories.

Parliament & Around

LIPÓTVÁROS | TERÉZVÁROS (WEST)

Neighbourhood Top Five

1 Entering the hallowed halls of **Parliament** (p95), arguably the most iconic of all Budapest's buildings, and making your way to the Crown of St Stephen, symbol of the Hungarian nation for more than 1100 years.

2 Visiting the **Basilica of St Stephen** (p97) and Hungary's most revered religious relic, the Holy Right (hand) of St Stephen.

3 Carousing in and around Nagymező utca, Budapest's own 'Broadway' and home to a plethora of wild and crazy clubs, including **Instant** (p104).

4 Ogling the sinuous curves and asymmetrical forms of the **Royal Postal Savings Bank** (p98), one of Budapest's many incomparable Art Nouveau buildings.

5 Eating at one of the little eateries called *étkezde*, such as **Kisharang** (p99), that serve Hungarian soul food.

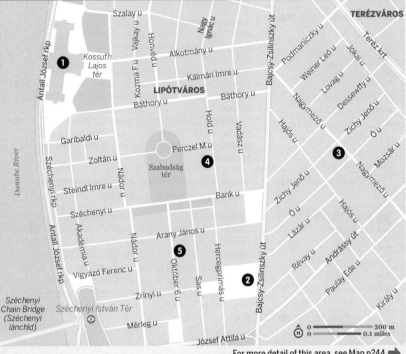

For more detail of this area, see Map p244 ➡

Lonely Planet's Top Tip

One of our favourite places to while away part or all of a Saturday morning is along V Falk Miksa utca, which is lined with antique and curio shops. Start at the northern end with BÁV (p106) to get an idea of what your average householder might be getting rid of during spring cleaning and move south on to the various other shops, ending up at the largest of them all: Pintér Antik (p106).

✖ Best Places to Eat

➡ Borkonyha (p101)
➡ Pesti Disznó (p102)
➡ Da Mario (p100)
➡ Kispiac (p100)
➡ Café Kör (p101)
➡ Mák (p101)

For reviews, see p99 ➡

🍷 Best Places to Drink

➡ Instant (p104)
➡ DiVino Borbár (p103)
➡ Pótkulcs (p104)
➡ Club AlterEgo (p104)
➡ Morrison's 2 (p103)
➡ Teaház a Vörös Oroszlánhoz (p105)

For reviews, see p103 ➡

🔒 Best Places to Shop

➡ BÁV (p106)
➡ Bestsellers (p106)
➡ Memories of Hungary (p106)
➡ Pintér Antik (p106)

For reviews, see p106 ➡

Explore: Parliament & Around

North of the Belváros, the district called Lipótváros (Leopold Town) is full of offices, government ministries and 19th-century apartment blocks. It's an easy and fun neighbourhood to explore on foot, and its defining squares are V Széchenyi István tér (sometimes still called Roosevelt tér) facing the river; V Szabadság tér, with the only Soviet memorial left in the city; and V Kossuth Lajos tér, fronted by Parliament. Come to this neighbourhood for exceptional architecture, two of the city's most important sights (Parliament and the Basilica of St Stephen), some excellent restaurants and cafés and, especially around the Central European University, some very great bars.

The neighbourhood on either side of Teréz körút – Terézváros (Theresa Town) – which was named in honour of Maria Theresa and carries on from Szent István körút as the Big Ring Rd after Nyugati train station, is where to head after dark. More compact than Erzsébetváros and not quite as raucous (and perhaps more attractive for those reasons), Terézváros has no shortage of lively watering holes and raving clubs. Here you'll also find VI Nagymező utca, lined with theatres and music halls, and home to the city's largest and most active gay club.

Local Life

➡ **Entertainment** Everyone goes to the Hungarian State Opera House; dare to be different and take in a very glitzy production at the Budapest Operetta (p105).
➡ **Museum** The Ethnography Museum (p98) will take you on a colourful tour of the folk-art heritage and traditions across Hungary – without you even leaving Budapest.
➡ **Eating** If you want to try authentic Hungarian sausage and salami but don't feel up to eating at food stalls, head for the Pick Ház (p100) outlet near Parliament.

Getting There & Away

➡**Bus** V Szabadság tér for 15 to IX Boráros tér and northern Pest; V Deák Ferenc tér for 16 to Castle Hill and 105 to Buda.
➡**Metro** M2 Kossuth Lajos tér, M3 Arany János utca and M1, M2 and M3 Deák Ferenc tér.
➡**Tram** Antall József rakpart (formerly Pesti alsó rakpart) for 2 to V Szent István körút or south Pest; V Szent István körút for 4 or 6 to Buda or Big Ring Rd in Pest.

TOP SIGHT
PARLIAMENT

Hungary's largest building, Parliament stretches for some 268m along the Danube in Pest from Kossuth Lajor tér. The choice of location was not made by chance. As a counterweight to the Royal Palace rising high on Buda Hill on the opposite side of the river, the placement was meant to signify that the nation's future lay with popular democracy and not royal prerogative.

Architecture

Designed by Imre Steindl in 1885 and completed just weeks before his death in 1902, this iconic structure is thought to have been inspired by London's rebuilt Palace of Westminster, which had opened in 1860. The building is a blend of many architectural styles (neo-Gothic, neo-Romanesque, neobaroque). Sculptures of the great and the good – kings, princes and historical figures – gaze out onto the river from the western facade, while the main door, the **Lion Gate**, is off recently renovated V Kossuth Lajos tér. Unfortunately, what was spent on the design wasn't matched in the building materials. The ornate structure was surfaced with a porous form of limestone that does not resist pollution very well. Due to its extensive surface and detailed stonework, the building is under constant renovation.

Interior

The interior contains just short of 700 sumptuously decorated rooms, but you'll only get to see a handful on a guided tour of the North Wing. Through the Lion Gate you ascend the sweeping 96-step **main staircase**, with frescoes by Károly Lotz and stained glass by Miksa Róth. This leads to the 16-sided, 66m-high **Domed Hall** where the **Crown of St Stephen**,

---

DON'T MISS...

➡ Crown of St Stephen
➡ Domed Hall
➡ Main staircase
➡ Royal Sceptre
➡ Congress Hall

PRACTICALITIES

➡ Országház
➡ Map p244
➡ ☎1-441 4904, 1-441 4415
➡ www.parlament.hu
➡ V Kossuth Lajos tér 1-3
➡ adult/student & EU citizen 4000/2000Ft
➡ ⊙ticket office 8-11am Mon, to 4pm Tue-Sun Nov-Mar, 8am-6pm Mon-Fri, to 4pm Sat & Sun Apr-Oct
➡ Ⓜ M2 Kossuth Lajos tér

PARLIAMENT BY NUMBERS

➡ Rooms: 691 (including 200 offices)

➡ Roof area: 1.8 hectares

➡ Gates: 27

➡ Courtyards: 10

➡ Staircases: 29

➡ Lifts: 13

➡ Light bulbs: 8730

➡ Clocks: 108

➡ Statues outside/inside: 90/152

➡ Decorative gold: 40kg

You can join a tour in any of eight languages; the English-language ones are at 10am, noon, 1pm, 2pm and 3pm daily. To avoid disappointment, book ahead in person or online through Jegymester (www.jegymester.hu). The tour takes about 45 minutes. Note that tours of Parliament are not conducted when the National Assembly is in session.

the nation's most important national icon, is on display, along with the 15th-century ceremonial sword, the orb (1301) and the oldest object among the coronation regalia: the 10th-century Persian-made **sceptre**, with a large crystal head depicting a lion. The guards here change hourly between 8am and 7pm. You'll also see one of the **vaulted lobbies**, where political discussions take place, and the 400-seat **Congress Hall**, where the House of Lords of the one-time bicameral assembly sat until 1944. It is almost identical to the National Assembly Hall, where parliamentary sessions are held, in the South Wing.

Crown of St Stephen

Legend tells us that it was Asztrik, the first abbot of the Benedictine monastery at Pannonhalma in western Hungary, who presented a crown to Stephen as a gift from Pope Sylvester II around AD 1000, thus legitimising the new king's rule and assuring his loyalty to Rome over Constantinople. It's a nice story but has nothing to do with the object on display in the Domed Hall. The two-part crown here, with its characteristic bent cross, pendants hanging on either side and enamelled plaques of the Apostles, dates from the 12th century. Its provenance notwithstanding, the Crown of St Stephen has become the very symbol of the Hungarian nation. The crown has disappeared several times over the centuries – purloined or otherwise – only to later reappear. It was damaged when placed in its carrying case in the 17th century, giving it a slightly skewed look. More recently, in 1945, Hungarian fascists fleeing ahead of the Soviet army took the crown to Austria. Eventually it fell into the hands of the US army, which transferred it to Fort Knox in Kentucky. In January 1978 the crown was returned to Hungary with great ceremony – and relief. Because legal judgments had always been handed down 'in the name of St Stephen's Crown' it was considered a living symbol and thus to have been 'kidnapped'!

Government

Hungary's constitution provides for a parliamentary system of government. The unicameral assembly sits in the National Assembly Hall in the South Wing from February to June and from September to December. A change in the electoral laws in late 2012 reduced the number of members to 199 (from 386); they are now chosen for four years on a one-round system. Of the total, 106 MPs enter parliament by individual constituency elections and 93 on the basis of party lists. The prime minister is head of government. The president, the head of state, is elected by the house for five years.

TOP SIGHT
BASILICA OF ST STEPHEN

The Basilica of St Stephen is the most important Catholic church in all of Hungary, if for no other reason than that it contains the nation's most revered relic: the mummified right hand of the church's patron. The church is also the Budapest seat of the shared Metropolitan Archdiocese of Esztergom-Budapest.

The neoclassical cathedral, the largest in Hungary, is in the form of a Greek cross and can accommodate 8000 worshippers. It was originally designed by József Hild, and though work began in 1851 the structure was not completed until 1905. Much of the interruption had to do with the fiasco in 1868 when the dome collapsed during a storm. The building then had to be demolished and rebuilt from the ground up by Hild's successor, Miklós Ybl. It underwent a 20-year renovation from 1983 to 2003.

The facade of the basilica is anchored by two large **bell towers**, one of which contains a bell weighing 9.25 tonnes, a replacement for one looted by the Germans during WWII. Behind the towers is the 96m-high **dome** (adult/child 500/400Ft; ⊙10am-5.30pm Apr-Jun, to 6.30pm Jul-Sep, to 4.30pm Oct-Mar), with statues of the four Evangelists filling its niches. The top of the dome can be reached by two lifts and 40 steps (302 steps if you want to walk) and offers one of the best views in the city.

The basilica's interior is rather dark and gloomy, Károly Lotz's golden **mosaics** on the inside of the dome notwithstanding. Noteworthy items include Alajos Stróbl's statue of the king-saint on the main altar and Gyula Benczúr's painting of St Stephen dedicating Hungary to the Virgin Mary, to the right of the main altar.

Behind the altar and to the left is the basilica's major drawcard: the **Holy Right Chapel** (Szent Jobb kápolna; ⊙9am-4.30pm Mon-Sat, from 1pm Sun Apr-Sep, 10am-4pm Mon-Sat, from 1pm Sun Oct-Mar). It contains the Holy Right (also known as the Holy Dexter), the mummified right hand of St Stephen and an object of great devotion. It was restored to Hungary by Habsburg empress Maria Theresa in 1771 after it was discovered in a monastery in Bosnia. Like the Crown of St Stephen, it was snatched after WWII but was soon returned home. Put a 200Ft coin in the slot to illuminate the hand for closer inspection. (Look at it from the right-hand side to see its knuckles.)

To the right as you enter the basilica is a small lift that will bring you to the 2nd-floor **treasury** (kincstár; adult/child 400/300Ft; ⊙10am-5.30pm Apr-Jun, to 6.30pm Jul-Sep, to 4.30pm Oct-Mar) of ecclesiastical objects, including censers, chalices, ciboria and vestments. Don't miss the Art Deco double monstrance (1938). Otherwise, the treasury is a veritable shine to Cardinal Mindszenty, including his clothing, devotional objects and death mask.

English-language guided tours of the basilica (2000/1500Ft with/without dome visit) usually depart at 9.30am, 11am, 2pm and 3.30pm on weekdays and at 9.30am and 11am on Saturday, but phone or check the website to confirm. Organ concerts are held here at 8pm, usually on Thursday and Friday.

DON'T MISS...

→ Holy Right
→ Views from the dome
→ Treasury
→ Dome interior mosaics

PRACTICALITIES

→ Szent István Bazilika
→ Map p244
→ ☎06 30 703 6599
→ www.basilica.hu
→ V Szent István tér
→ requested donation 200Ft
→ ⊙9am-5pm Apr-Sep, 10am-4pm Oct-Mar
→ Ⓜ M2 Arany János utca

◉ SIGHTS

◉ Lipótváros

PARLIAMENT   HISTORIC BUILDING
See p95.

BASILICA OF ST STEPHEN   CHURCH
See p97.

ETHNOGRAPHY MUSEUM   MUSEUM
Map p244 (Néprajzi Múzeum; ☑1-473 2401; www.neprajz.hu; V Kossuth Lajos tér 12; adult/concession 1000/500Ft, combined ticket for all exhibitions 1400/700Ft; ☺10am-6pm Tue-Sun; ⓂM2 Kossuth Lajos tér) Visitors are offered an easy introduction to traditional Hungarian life at this sprawling museum opposite Parliament with thousands of displays in a dozen rooms on the 1st floor. The mockups of peasant houses from the Őrség and Sárköz regions of Western and Southern Transdanubia are well done, and there are some priceless objects, which are examined through institutions, beliefs and stages of life.

On the ground floor, most of the excellent temporary exhibitions deal with other peoples of Europe and further afield: Africa, Asia, Oceania and the Americas. The building itself was designed in 1893 by Alajos Hauszmann to house the Supreme Court; note the ceiling fresco in the lobby of Justice by Károly Lotz.

SZÉCHENYI ISTVÁN TÉR   PLAZA
Map p244 (☐16, 105, ☐2) Named Roosevelt tér in 1947 after the long-serving (1933–45) American president, this square has now been renamed to honour the statesmen and developer of Chain Bridge, which it faces. The square offers among the best views of Castle Hill in Pest.

On the southern end of Széchenyi István tér is a **statue of Ferenc Deák**, the Hun-

garian minister largely responsible for the Compromise of 1867, which brought about the Dual Monarchy of Austria and Hungary.

The statue on the western side is of an Austrian and a Hungarian child holding hands in peaceful bliss. The Magyar kid's hair is tousled and he is naked; the *osztrák* is demurely covered by a bit of the patrician's robe and his hair is neatly coiffed.

The Art Nouveau building with the gold tiles to the east is **Gresham Palace**, built by an English insurance company in 1907. It now houses the sumptuous **Four Seasons Gresham Palace Hotel** (p170). The **Hungarian Academy of Sciences** (Magyar Tudományos Akadémia), founded by Count István Széchenyi, is at the northern end of the square.

BEDŐ HOUSE   NOTABLE BUILDING
Map p244 (Bedő-ház; ☑1-269 4622; www.magyarszecessziohaza.hu; V Honvéd utca 3; adult/student & child 1500/1000Ft; ☺10am-5pm Tue-Sat; ⓂM2 Kossuth Lajos tér) Just around the corner from Kossuth Lajos tér is this stunning Art Nouveau apartment block (1903) designed by Emil Vidor. Now a shrine to Hungarian Secessionist interiors, its three levels are crammed with furniture, porcelain, ironwork, paintings and objets d'art. The lovely Secessio Café (p104) is on the ground floor.

IMRE NAGY STATUE   STATUE
Map p244 (V Vértanúk tere; ⓂM2 Kossuth Lajos tér) Southeast of V Kossuth Lajos tér is an unusual statue of Imre Nagy standing in the centre of a small footbridge. Nagy was the reformist Communist prime minister executed in 1958 for his role in the uprising two years earlier.

SZABADSÁG TÉR   SQUARE
Map p244 (Liberty Square; ☐15) 'Liberty Sq', one of the largest in Budapest, is a few minutes' walk northeast of Széchenyi István tér. As you enter you'll pass a delightful

---

SECESSIONIST ARCHITECTURAL GEMS

Southeast of Szabadság tér are two of the most beautiful buildings in Pest. The former **Royal Postal Savings Bank** (Map p244; V Hold utca 4; ☐15) is a Secessionist extravaganza of colourful tiles and folk motifs built by Ödön Lechner in 1901. It is now part of the **National Bank of Hungary** (Magyar Nemzeti Bank; Map p244; V Szabadság tér 9; ☐15) next door, which has terracotta reliefs that illustrate trade and commerce through history: Arab camel traders, African rug merchants, Chinese tea salesmen – and the inevitable solicitor witnessing contracts.

fountain that works on optical sensors and turns off and on as you approach or back away from it. In the centre of the square is a **Soviet army memorial**, the last of its type still standing in the city.

On the eastern side is the fortress-like US Embassy, now cut off from the square by high metal fencing and concrete blocks. It was here that Cardinal József Mindszenty sought refuge after the 1956 Uprising and stayed for 15 years until departing for Vienna in 1971. The embassy backs onto Hold utca (Moon St), which, until 1990, was named Rosenberg házaspár utca (Rosenberg Couple St) after the American husband and wife Julius and Ethel Rosenberg who were executed as Soviet spies in the US in 1953.

A controversial statue of Miklós Horthy, Hungary's intra-war leader called a hero by the right wing but reviled as a fascist dictator by many others, was unveiled in front of the **Homecoming Presbyterian Church** (Hazatérés Református Templom) in the square's southwest corner in late 2013.

SHOES ON THE DANUBE   MONUMENT

Map p244 (V Antall József rakpart; 🚊2) Along the banks of the river between Széchenyi István tér and Parliament is a monument to Hungarian Jews shot and thrown into the Danube by members of the fascist Arrow Cross Party in 1944. Entitled *Shoes on the Danube* (Cipők a Dunaparton) by sculptor Gyula Pauer and film director Can Togay, it's a simple but poignant display of 60 pairs of old-style boots and shoes in cast iron, tossed higgledy-piggledy on the bank of the river.

⊙ Terézváros (West)

NYUGATI TRAIN STATION   HISTORIC BUILDING

Map p244 (Nyugati pályaudvar; VI Teréz körút 55-57; 🅼M3 Nyugati pályaudvar) The large iron-and-glass structure on Nyugati tér is the 'Western' train station, built in 1877 by the Paris-based Eiffel Company. In the early 1970s a train crashed through the enormous glass screen on the main facade when its brakes failed; it came to rest at the tram line. The old dining hall on the south side now houses one of the world's most elegant McDonald's. The mammoth **West End City Centre** (www.westend.hu; ⊙8am-11pm) shopping mall is just north.

✖ EATING

Lipótváros is a happy hunting ground for fine eating, especially around the area of the basilica and the Central European University. Terézváros within the Big Ring Rd is really where you head for after-dark fun and games, especially around Nagymező utca, but there is no shortage of eateries, including a few late-night venues.

✖ Lipótváros

KISHARANG   HUNGARIAN $

Map p244 (📞1-269 3861; www.kisharang.hu; V Október 6 utca 17; mains 590-2350Ft; ⊙11.30am-9pm; 🚊15) Centrally located 'Little Bell' is an *étkezde* (canteen serving simple Hungarian dishes) that's top of the list with students and staff of the nearby Central European University. The daily specials are something to look forward to and the retro decor is fun. *Főzelék* (480Ft to 650Ft), the traditional Hungarian way of preparing vegetables, is always a good bet here.

The daily menu is 950Ft.

CULINARIS   INTERNATIONAL $

Map p244 (📞1-345 0777; www.culinaris.hu; XIII Balassi Bálint utca 7; mains 1590-2490Ft; ⊙8am-3pm Mon-Sat, 10am-3pm Sun; 🚊2) Is it a restaurant? A cafe? A gourmet food shop? Apparently all three and we love it for its welcoming colours and chaotic selection (Madras-style chicken, Moroccan lamb pita, duck quesadilla etc) but not its bankers' hours. Still, the store stays open till 8pm (6pm on Sunday), so self-catering is an option.

MOMOTARO METÉLT   NOODLES $

Map p244 (📞1-269 3802; www.momotaroramen.com; V Széchenyi utca 16; noodles & dumplings 600-1800Ft, mains 1860-4750Ft; ⊙11am-10.30pm Tue-Sun; 🌶; 🚊15, 🚌2) This is a favourite pit stop for noodles – especially the soup variety – and dumplings when *pálinka* (fruit brandy), Unicum and other lubricants have been a-flowin' the night before. It's also good for more substantial dishes.

GASTRONOMIA POMO D'ORO   ITALIAN $

Map p244 (📞1-374 0288; www.pomodorobudapest.com; V Arany János utca 9; dishes 1490-2490Ft; ⊙9am-10pm Mon-Sat; 🚊15, 🚌2) Next door to a much more extravagant trattoria bearing the same name, this Italian delicatessen-caterer has a little dining area on the 1st floor where you can choose from a small selection of dishes or sample cheese and prepared meats by the 100g measure (480Ft to 1800Ft). Sandwiches are 1490Ft to 1940Ft.

PICK HÁZ
HUNGARIAN $

Map p244 (☑1-331 7783; V Kossuth Lajos tér 9; sandwiches & salads from 225Ft, mains 415-800Ft; ⊗6am-7pm Mon-Thu, to 6pm Fri; ⓂM2 Kossuth Lajos tér) Next to the Kossuth Lajos tér metro station, this self-service eatery sits above the famous salami manufacturer's central showroom opposite the Parliament building. It's convenient for lunch if you're visiting Parliament or any of the sights in the area. The set menu is 870Ft.

HUMMUS BAR
MIDDLE EASTERN $

Map p244 (☑1-354 0108; www.hummusbar.hu; V Október 6 utca 19; dishes 800-1890Ft; ⊗11.30am-11pm; ☑; ◻15) If you're looking for an easy vegetarian dish on the run, this is the place to go for mashed chickpeas blended with sesame-seed paste, oil and lemon juice. Enjoy it au naturel (we mean the hummus) on pita or in a dish with accompaniments such as mushrooms or felafel. Not all dishes are vegetarian – though many are.

DURAN
SANDWICHES $

Map p244 (☑1-332 9348; www.duran.hu; V Október 6 utca 15; sandwiches 200-390Ft; ⊗8am-5pm Mon-Fri, to 1pm Sat; ◻15) This branch of the popular sandwich bar is by the Central European University and always rammed with penny-pinching students.

PADTHAI WOKBAR
THAI $

Map p244 (☑1-784 5079; www.padthaiwokbar. com; Október 6 utca 4; dishes 1180-1280FT; ⊗11am-11pm; ◻15, ◻2) Thai eatery on two levels offers a base of rice or noodles (990Ft) with accompanying toppings (190Ft to 290Ft) and sauces free of charge. Popular with students of the Central European University who like the rough communal wooden tables and the too-clever-by-half aphorisms etched into the glass walls.

ROOSEVELT ÉTTEREM
HUNGARIAN $

Map p244 (☑06 30 460 6476;www.facebook. com/roosevelttetterem; V Széchenyi István tér 7-8; mains around 2500Ft; ⊗8am-5pm Mon-Fri; ◻15, ◻2) This brightly coloured caf that *used* to be on Roosevelt tér is a modern take

on a Hungarian *önkiszolgáló* (self-service restaurant) where, along with light meals available throughout the day, main dishes are sold by weight (275Ft per 100g).

GOVINDA
VEGETARIAN $

Map p244 (☑1-473 1310; www.govinda.hu; V Vigyázó Ferenc utca 4; dishes 190-990Ft; ⊗11.30am-9pm Mon-Fri, from noon Sat; ☑; ◻15, ◻2) This basement restaurant northeast of the Chain Bridge serves wholesome salads, soups and desserts as well as daily set-menu plates for 990/1890/2990Ft for one/two/three courses.

SZERÁJ
KEBAB $

Map p244 (☑1-311 6690; XIII Szent István körút 13; mains 450-1500Ft; ⊗9am-4am; ◻4, 6) A very inexpensive self-service Turkish place good for *lahmacun* (Turkish 'pizza', 650Ft), felafel (1100Ft) and kebabs (from 1300Ft), with up to a dozen varieties on offer. It heaves after midnight, so whoever you were cruising in the pub or on the dance floor probably got here before you did.

FRUCCOLA
SANDWICHES $

Map p244 (☑1-327 7896; www.fruccola.hu; V Arany János utca 32; breakfast 720-1290Ft, sandwiches 400-830Ft; ⊗7am-7pm Mon-Fri; ⓂM3 Arany János utca, ◻72, 73) Alive and well and bursting with flavour, what bills itself as a 'fast casual restaurant' pulls in the punters with its excellent baguettes, self-build salads and fresh vegetable and fruit juices.

★DA MARIO
ITALIAN $$

Map p244 (☑1-301 0967; www.damario.hu; V Vécsey utca 3; mains 2000-5500Ft; ⊗11am-midnight; ◻15, ⓂM2 Kossuth Lajos tér) Owned and operated by three Italian *ragazzi* (lads) from southern Italy, Da Mario (yes, he's one of them) can't put a foot wrong in our book. While the cold platters, soups and meat and fish mains all look good, we stick to the house-made pasta dishes (2000Ft to 3500Ft) and pizzas (1250Ft to 3000FT) from the wood-burning stove.

★KISPIAC
HUNGARIAN $$

Map p244 (☑1-269 4231; www.kispiac.eu; V Hold utca 13; mains 1950-3500Ft; ⊗noon-10pm Mon-Sat; ⓂM3 Arany János utca) This recent arrival is a hole-in-the-wall retro-style restaurant next to the Hold utca market serving *seriously* Hungarian things like stuffed *csülök* (pig's trotter – and way better than it sounds), roast *malac* (piglet) and an infinite variety of *savanyúság* (sour pickled vegetables). Thoroughly enjoyable and you might not eat again for a week.

KASHMIR
INDIAN $$

Map p244 (☎1-354 1806; www.kashmiretterem. hu; V Arany János utca 13; mains 1890-2990Ft; ◷noon-4pm & 6-11pm Tue-Sun; ☷; ⓂM3 Arany János utca) Our favourite subcontinental in Pest, this places serves the cuisine of its namesake, which is always a bit sweeter than other Indian food, as well as a variety of tandoori cooked meats. There are about 20 vegetarian choices and a weekday buffet lunch for 1390Ft.

CAFÉ KÖR
INTERNATIONAL $$

Map p244 (☎1-311 0053; www.cafekor.com; V Sas utca 17; mains 1980-4690Ft; ◷10am-10pm Mon-Sat; ☷15, ⓂM3 Arany János) Just behind the Basilica of St Stephen, the 'Circle Café' is a long-standing favourite for lunch or dinner but a great place for a light meal at any time, including breakfast (150Ft to 790Ft), which is served till noon. Service is welcoming and helpful.

IGUANA
MEXICAN $$

Map p244 (☎1-331 4352; www.iguana.hu; V Zoltán utca 16; mains 1860-4890Ft; ◷11.30am-11pm Mon-Fri, to midnight Sat & Sun; ☷; ☷15, ⓂM2 Kossuth Lajos tér) Iguana serves decent enough Mexican food, but it's hard to say whether the pull is the enchilada and burrito combination *platos,* the fajitas or the frenetic and boozy 'we-party-every-night' atmosphere. Busy bar. Two-course lunch for just 1490Ft.

SALAAM BOMBAY
INDIAN $$

Map p244 (☎1-411 1252; www.salaambombay.hu; V Mérleg utca 6; mains 1690-3100Ft; ◷noon-3pm & 6-11pm; ☷; ☷15, ☷2) If you're hankering for a fix of authentic Indian curry or tandoori in a bright, upbeat environment, look no further than this attractive eatery just east of Széchenyi István tér. Don't believe us? Even staff from the Indian embassy are said to come here regularly. A large choice of vegetarian dishes (950Ft to 1990Ft) is also available.

ELSŐ PESTI RÉTESHÁZ
HUNGARIAN $$

Map p244 (☎1-428 0135; www.reteshaz.com; V Október 6 utca 22; mains 2990-5990Ft; ◷9am-11pm; ☷15) It may be a bit overdone, with 'olde-worlde' counters, painted plates stuck on the walls and old letters and curios embedded in Plexiglas washbasins, but the 'First Strudel House of Pest' is just the place to taste this Hungarian stretched and filled pastry (from 370Ft), with or without a full meal preceding it.

Fillings include apple, cheese, poppy seed or sour cherry. Breakfast (from 1290Ft) is served till noon.

★BORKONYHA
HUNGARIAN $$$

Map p238 (Wine Kitchen; ☎1-266 0835; www. borkonyha.hu; V Sas utca 3; mains 3750-7150Ft; ◷noon-midnight Mon-Sat; ☷15, ⓂM1 Bajcsy-Zsilinszky út) The third restaurant in Budapest to receive a Michelin star well and truly deserves the honour. When we last visited – before said honour was bestowed – we were overwhelmed by the food, the astonishing selection of fine Hungarian wine (200 types, four dozen by the glass) and the warm and knowledgeable service.

Chef Ákos Sárközi's approach to Hungarian cuisine is contemporary and the menu changes every week or two. Go for the signature foie gras appetiser wrapped in strudel pastry and a glass of sweet Tokaj wine. If *mangalica* (a special type of Hungarian pork) is on the menu, try it with a glass of dry Furmint.

MÁK
INTERNATIONAL $$$

Map p244 (☎06 30 723 9383; www.makbistro. hu; V Vigyázó Ferenc utca 4; mains 2700-6200Ft; ◷noon-3pm & 6-11pm Tue-Sat; ☷15, ☷2) Still one of our favourite restaurants in Lipótváros, the 'Poppy' serves inventive international dishes that lean in the direction of Hungary from a chalkboard menu that changes daily. Casual surrounds and seamless service with good advice on wine. At lunch two/three courses from the menu are a budget-enhancing 2800/3500Ft.

LACIPECSENYE
HUNGARIAN $$$

Map p244 (☎06 70 370 7474; www.lacipecsenye. eu; V Sas utca 11; mains 3780-5940Ft; ◷noon-midnight; ☷15, ⓂM1 Bajcsy-Zsilinszky út) Inside this minimalist-chic bistro next to the basilica, the changing daily mains on black slate are brought to you by trendy young staff in 'Who the **** is Laci?' T-shirts. Dishes are mostly for the carnivorously inclined, and some are truly inspired, such as calamari stuffed with meat and anything with duck liver. You can order à la carte or in sharing 'sets' (three/four/five dishes for 6740/8100/9450Ft). Two/three-course lunch is 2450/2950Ft.

LOCAL KNOWLEDGE

ROZI VÁCZI: MATYÓ MAVEN

Rozi Váczi is cofounder of Matyó Design, a fashion company that has pulled the traditional craft of embroidery into the 21st century by using it to brighten up everyday articles of clothing.

OK, so is embroidery the next big thing?

What has become trendy nowadays in this world of mass production is to own something others do not. And a craft like this one is in fact self-perpetuating as no two items are ever the same.

So we defer to your expertise… How do you tell the difference between _kézimunka_ (needlework, literally 'hand work') and the machine-made stuff?

Turn it over and you'll see the imperfections; a handmade item is never perfect. Also the thread is a little thicker in needlework. There are considerable differences both visually and intellectually between the two. For a start, machine work takes five minutes, handmade five hours.

Why is Hungary so much richer in folk traditions than its European neighbours?

Hungarians have held onto their culture and traditions during all of the historical hardships in order to maintain a sense of origin and national continuity. Nowadays traditions are a tool for cultural revival and just possibly a national awakening.

Is there any place in particular in Budapest where you can feel Hungary's folk past most intensively?

Well, there used to be old Transylvanian ladies selling flowers at the entrances to the metro stations. Oh and there's _táncház_ (folk music and dance evenings). But I suppose it's the Ethnography Museum (p98).

Do you have any recommendations as to where to find the best example of folk art?

There's the monthly WAMP (www.wamp.hu) market, of course. Best shops include XD Design&Souvenir (p90) in the Belváros and Memories of Hungary (p106) near the basilica.

TIGRIS HUNGARIAN $$$

Map p244 (☑1-317 3715; www.tigrisrestaurant.hu; V Mérleg utca 10; mains 3800-7800Ft; ☺noon-midnight Mon-Sat; 🚊15, 🚎2) What at first appears to be no more than an upbeat modern Hungarian restaurant, with its wooden tables covered in white linen tablecloths and antique-looking cupboards, is a very serious Michelin-rated restaurant with links to the Gere family of wine fame.

Expect faultless service, a sommelier who will take you on a giddy tour of Hungary's major wine regions, and as many variations on goose liver as you can imagine.

✗ Terézváros (West)

NAPOS OLDAL VEGETARIAN $

Map p244 (☑1-354 0048; www.naposoldal.com; VI Jókai utca 7; dishes 780-840Ft; set meals 910-1300Ft; ☺10am-8pm Mon-Fri, to 2pm Sat; MM1 Oktogon, 🚎4, 6) This tiny cafe-restaurant in-side a health-food shop on the 'Sunny Side' of the street serves fresh salads, pastries and soups.

BUTTERFLY ICE CREAM $

Map p244 (☑1-311-3648; www.butterflyfagyizo.hu; VI Teréz körút 20; ☺10am-7pm; MM1 Oktogon) This place – and not the pastry shop next door – is where to head for Pest's best ice cream (190Ft per scoop), as you'll be able to deduce from the queues. In winter, let them eat cakes (210Ft to 560Ft).

★PESTI DISZNÓ HUNGARIAN $$

Map p244 (☑1-951 4061; www.pestidiszno.hu; VI Nagymező utca 19; mains 1490-2890Ft; ☺11am-midnight Sun-Wed, to 1am Thu-Sat; MM1 Oktogon) Punters would be forgiven for thinking that the 'Pest Pig' was all about pork. In fact, of the dozen main courses half are poultry, fish or vegetarian. It's a wonderful space, loft-like almost, with high tables and charming, informed service. The wine card is very, very good and most wines are available by the glass, too.

CAFÉ BOUCHON   FRENCH $$
Map p244 (☎1-353 4094; www.cafebouchon. hu; VI Zichy Jenő utca 33; mains 2980-4980Ft; ⊙11am-11pm Mon-Sat; ⋈M3 Arany János utca, 🚊70, 78) A little bit pricey for what and where it is, but *Ooo la la, c'est si bon!* A family-run *bouchon* (small restaurant) with an Art Nouveau–style interior, this place serves provincial French food stirred with a little Hungarian inspiration and the occasional Italian stray (eg osso bucco) making an appearance. Warm welcome.

MOST KORTÁRS BISZTRÓ   INTERNATIONAL $$
Map p244 (Now Contemporary Bisto; ☎06 70 248 3322; www.facebook.com/mostbisztro/info; VI Zichy Jenő utca 17; mains 1450-2200Ft; ⊙10am-2am Sun & Mon, to 3am Tue, to 4am Wed, to 5am Thu-Sat; ⋈M3 Arany János utca) This place with the mouthful of a name is a restaurant-bistro-cafe-bar that clearly wants to be everything to everyone. And it almost succeeds. There is a small bar, a stage and a roof terrace, a large indoor dining room with communal tables and a big garden. Food is a mixed bag (burgers and Indian dishes, anyone?). We mostly come for the brunch menu (1690Ft), though, available from 10am to 4pm on Saturday and Sunday.

PARÁZS PRESSZÓ   THAI $$
Map p244 (☎1-950 3770; www.parazspresszo. com; VI Jókai utca 8; mains 1950-2750Ft; ⊙11am-midnight Mon-Fri, from noon Sat & Sun; ⋈M1 Oktogon, 🚊4, 6) This *presszó* (coffee shop) serving Thai food just off the Big Ring Rd has all the favourites – from *tom yum gung* (850Ft) to the full range of green, red, Penang and Massaman curries. It boasts a very loyal following.

MARQUIS DE SALADE   INTERNATIONAL $$
Map p244 (☎06 30 223 3520; www.facebook. com/restaurant.MarquisdeSalade; VI Hajós utca 43; mains 2800-4800Ft; ⊙11am-midnight; ☎; ⋈M3 Arany János utca, 🚊72, 73) This basement restaurant is a strange hybrid of a place, with dishes from Russia and Azerbaijan as well as Hungary. There are lots of quality vegetarian choices. And, by the way, it's not just about *salade* (though there are more than a dozen to choose from).

🍷 DRINKING & NIGHTLIFE

🍷 Lipótváros

⭐DIVINO BORBÁR   WINE BAR
Map p244 (☎06 70 935 3980; www.divino borbar.hu; V Szent István tér 3; ⊙4pm-midnight Sun-Wed, to 2am Thu-Sat; ⋈M1 Bajcsy-Zsilinszky út) Central and always heaving, DiVino is Budapest's most popular wine bar and the crowds spilling out into the square in front of the basilica will immediately tell you that. Choose from 120 types of wine produced by some 30 winemakers under the age of 35 at the bar, but be careful: those 0.1L glasses (650Ft to 2800Ft) go down quickly. Glass deposit is 500Ft.

MORRISON'S 2   CLUB
Map p244 (☎1-374 3329; www.morrisons.hu; V Szent István körút 11; ⊙5pm-4am; 🚊4, 6) Far and away Budapest's biggest party venue, this cavernous club attracts a younger crowd with its five dance floors and half-dozen bars (including one in a covered courtyard and one with table football). Great DJs.

INNIO   WINE BAR
Map p244 (☎06 70 311 1010; www.innio.hu; V Október 6 utca 9; ⊙8am-midnight Sun-Wed, to 2am Thu-Sat; ☎; 🚊15, ⋈M1/2/3 Deák Tér) On weekends, you have to jostle Budapest's bold and beautiful just to get some elbow room inside this trendy wine bar. Perch on a stool and sup Hungarian wine to a pounding electronica soundtrack, try *pálinka* or else drop by on a weekday for a quiet lunch – this place does some imaginative salads and fusion mains too.

MYSTERY BAR CLUB   GAY
Map p244 (☎1- 312 1436; www.mysterybar.hu; V Nagysándor József utca 3; ⊙5pm-4am Sun-Thu, to 6am Sat; ☎; ⋈M3 Arany János utca) Our favourite (err, actually, just about the only) neighbourhood gay bar in Budapest has super-cool decor and friendly staff.

ÖTKERT   CLUB
Map p244 (☎06 70 330 8652; www.otkert.hu; V Zrínyi utca 4; ⊙4pm-5am; 🚊15, 🚊2) It's not really a 'garden club', though the 'Five Garden' ('five' as in district V) does pretend to be that. This rather chichi champagne bar

(glass/bottle from 850/2800Ft) has great drinking and dancing spaces, including a cool central courtyard.

TERV ESZPRESSZÓ
BAR

Map p244 (☑1-269 3132; V Nádor utca 19; ⊙9am-midnight Mon-Fri, to 11pm Sat, 10am-11pm Sun; ▣15, Ⓜ M3 Arany János utca) 'Plan' (as in the Communist five-year variety) is a retro-style cafe-bar on two levels decorated with photographs of Hungarian athletes, politicians, actors and so on from the 1950s and '60s. Unlike a lot of such places, the theme doesn't get old in a half-hour. It's slightly off the beaten track and never rammed.

ESPRESSO EMBASSY
CAFE

Map p244 (☑06 30 864 9530; www.espressoembassy.hu; V Arany János utca 15; ⊙7:30am-7pm Mon-Fri, 8am-7pm Sat; Ⓜ M3 Arany János utca) Some people say that this upbeat cafe just south of Szabadság tér has the best espressos, flat whites, cappuccinos and lattes in town.

FARGER KÁVÉ
CAFE

Map p244 (☑06 20 237 7825; www.farger.hu; V Zoltán utca 18; ⊙7am-9pm Mon-Fri, 9am-6pm Sat & Sun; Ⓜ M2 Kossuth Lajos tér) This modern cafe is among the leafiest in Pest thanks to an ingenious 'urban gardening' plan and has first-rate views of Szabadság tér from the window seats and terrace. Gotta love the mug collection in the window and the two-course lunch for 990Ft.

CAFÉ MONTMARTRE
CAFE, LIVE MUSIC

Map p244 (☑06 20 490 8780; www.facebook.com/CafeMontmartreBudapest; V Zrínyi utca 18; ⊙9am-1am; Ⓜ M3 Arany János utca, Ⓜ15) This very unpretentious cafe–art gallery in full splendid view of the Basilica of St Stephen is always fun, especially on the nights when there is live music (Latino, folk, rock and/or jazz). The welcome here is always warm.

SECESSIO CAFÉ
CAFE

Map p244 (☑1-269 0540; www.secessio-cafe.hu; V Honvéd utca 3; ⊙9am-7pm Mon-Fri, 10am-6pm Sat; Ⓜ M2 Kossuth Lajos tér) This small but comfortable cafe on the ground floor of delightful Bedő House is tailor-made for fans of the Secessionist style. The cakes (280Ft to 470Ft) are fine, but the homemade food products like jams and so on are out of this world.

SZALAI CUKRÁSZDA
CAFE

Map p244 (☑1-269 3210; www.szalaicukraszda.hu; V Balassi Bálint utca 7; ⊙9am-7pm Wed-Mon; ▣2) This humble cake shop in Lipótváros just north of Parliament and dating back to 1917 probably has the best cherry strudel (380Ft) in the capital. It does apple and *túrós* (cheese curd) ones too.

OPTICA
CLUB

Map p244 (☑06 30 998 7735; www.facebook.com/Opticaclub; V Szent István körút 11; ⊙10pm-6am; ▣4, 6) This very flash, very chichi bar and club next to Morrison's 2 opened in late 2013 and is already attracting Budapest's *beau monde* (think Russian oligarchs, porn stars, the odd lost school teacher). Don't go near the place if you're allergic to strobe lights.

🍸 Terézváros (West)

★INSTANT
CLUB

Map p244 (☑06 30 830 8747; www.instant.co.hu; VI Nagymező utca 38; ⊙4pm-6am Sun-Thu, to 11am Fri & Sat; Ⓜ M1 Opera) We still love this 'ruin bar' on Pest's most vibrant nightlife strip and so do all our friends. It has six bars on three levels with underground DJs and dance parties. Always heaving.

CLUB ALTEREGO
GAY

Map p244 (☑06 70 345 4302; www.alteregoclub.hu; VI Dessewffy utca 33; ⊙10pm-6am Fri & Sat; ▣4, 6) Still Budapest's premier gay club, AlterEgo has the chicest (think attitude) crowd and the best dance music on offer.

PÓTKULCS
BAR

Map p244 (☑1-269 1050; www.potkulcs.hu; VI Csengery utca 65/b; ⊙5pm-1.30am Sun-Wed, to 2.30am Thu-Sat; Ⓜ M3 Nyugati pályaudvar) The 'Spare Key' is a fine little drinking venue with a varied menu of live music most evenings and occasional *táncház* (Hungarian music and dance). The small central courtyard is a wonderful place to chill out in summer.

★KIADÓ KOCSMA
PUB

Map p244 (☑1-331 1955; www.facebook.com/kiadokocsma; VI Jókai tér 3; ⊙10am-1am Mon-Fri, 11am-1am Sat & Sun; Ⓜ M1 Oktogon) The 'Pub for Rent' is a great place for a swift pint and a quick bite (sandwiches 870Ft to 1570Ft, salads 1590Ft) just a stone's throw – and light years – away from flashy VI Liszt Fer-

PHOTOGRAPHY ON SHOW

Two superb galleries just doors away from one another in the city's theatre district have put Budapest at the forefront of the showing of photography both as art and as testimonial. The more established of the pair, the **House of Hungarian Photographers** (Magyar Fotográfusok Háza; Map p244; ☑1-473 2666; www.maimano.hu; VI Nagymező utca 20; adult/student 1500/700Ft; ◷2-7pm Mon-Fri, 11am-7pm Sat & Sun; Ⓜ︎M1 Opera, ◰70, 78), an extraordinary venue with top-class photography exhibitions, is in Mai Manó Ház, which was built in 1894 as a photo studio and is worth a visit in itself. There's a great cafe here open daily from 8am to 1am, too. The newer **Capa Contemporary Photography Center** (Map p250; ☑06 30 729 9711; www.capacenter. hu; VI Nagymező utca 8; adult/concession 1500/800Ft; ◷11am-7pm ; Ⓜ︎M1 Opera, ◰70, 78), named after the Hungarian-born photographer and Magnum cofounder Robert Capa (born Endre Friedmann; 1913–54) and housed in a renovated cultural centre dating back 100 years, seeks to show the best in contemporary visual arts through changing exhibitions.

enc tér. Breakfast is on till noon and there's a bargain set lunch for 900Ft.

BORDÓ BISZTRÓ
WINE BAR

Map p250 (☑06 70 359 8777; www.facebook.com/bordobisztro; VI Nagymező utca 3; ◷10am-midnight Sun-Tue, to 1am Wed & Thu, to 2am Fri & Sat; Ⓜ︎M1 Opera) This bistro at the southern end of Budapest's Broadway takes wine (and itself) very seriously indeed. About the only thing funny about this place is its cheesy name – a clumsy pun on Bordeaux and *bor* ('wine' in Hungarian). The food – Thai-Vietnamese fusion – is an afterthought.

TEAHÁZ A VÖRÖS OROSZLÁNHOZ
TEAHOUSE

Map p244 (☑1-269 0579; www.vorosoroszlanteahaz.hu; VI Jókai tér 8; ◷1-11pm Mon-Sat, from 3pm Sun; Ⓜ︎M1 Oktogon) This serene place with quite a mouthful of a name (it means 'Teahouse at the Sign of the Red Lion') just north of Liszt Ferenc tér is quite serious about its teas (680Ft to 1190Ft). It's on two levels.

BALLETT CIPŐ
CAFE

Map p244 (☑1-269 3114; www.balettcipo.hu; VI Hajós utca 14; ◷10am-midnight Mon-Fri, from noon Sat, noon-11pm Sun; Ⓜ︎M1 Opera) The pretty little 'Ballet Slipper' in the theatre district – just behind the Hungarian State Opera House – is a delightful place to stop for a rest and refreshment or to have a snack or light meal (dishes 950Ft to 1800Ft).

SUTTOGÓ PIANO BAR
BAR

Map p244 (☑06 20 455 73 29; www.suttogopianobar.hu; VI Hajós utca 27; ◷7pm-5am Tue-Sat; Ⓜ︎M1 Oktogon) Camp as a caravan park – agreed – but we always have fun at this ro-

mantic spot near the Opera House. Music starts nightly around 10pm. Cocktails are especially good (if a titch pricey) and you won't lack for nibbles.

☆ ENTERTAINMENT

DUNA PALOTA
LIVE MUSIC

Map p244 (☑1-235 5500; www.dunapalota.hu; V Zrínyi utca 5; tickets 3600-6200Ft; ◰15, 115) The elaborate 'Danube Palace' is diagonally opposite the main Central European University building. It hosts any number of cultural performances, from light classical-music concerts to folk dance by the Hungária Orchestra & Folk Ensemble, at 7pm throughout the week for the most part from June to October.

MŰVÉSZ ART MOZI
CINEMA

Map p244 (☑1-459 5050; www.artmozi.hu; VI Teréz körút 30; Ⓜ︎M1 Oktogon, ◰4, 6) The 'Artist Art Cinema' shows, appropriately enough, art and cult films, but not exclusively so.

BUDAPEST OPERETTA
OPERA

Map p244 (Budapesti Operettszínház; ☑1-312 4866; www.operettszinhaz.hu; VI Nagymező utca 17; tickets 1000-8000Ft; ◷box office 10am-7pm Mon-Fri, 1-7pm Sat & Sun; Ⓜ︎M1 Opera) This theatre presents operettas, which are always a riot, especially campy ones like *The Gypsy Princess* by Imre Kálmán or Ferenc Lehár's *The Merry Widow,* with their over-the-top staging and costumes. Think baroque Gilbert and Sullivan – and then some. There's an interesting bronze statue of Kálmán outside the main entrance.

ARANYTÍZ CULTURAL CENTRE
TRADITIONAL MUSIC

Map p244 (Aranytíz Művelődési Központ; ☑1-354 3400; www.aranytiz.hu; ⓥ Arany János utca 10; ⓞbox office 2-9pm Mon & Wed, 9am-3pm Sat; ◪15) At this cultural centre in Lipótváros, the wonderful Kalamajka Táncház has programs from 7pm on Saturday that run till about midnight. Bring the kids in earlier (about 5pm) for a children's version.

SHOPPING

★ BESTSELLERS
BOOKS

Map p244 (☑1-312 1295; www.bestsellers.hu; ⓥ Október 6 utca 11; ⓞ9am-6.30pm Mon-Fri, 10am-5pm Sat, 10am-4pm Sun; ⓜM1/2/3 Deák Ferenc tér) Our favourite English-language bookshop in town, with fiction, travel guides and lots of Hungarica, as well as a large selection of newspapers and magazines overseen by master bookseller Tony Láng. Helpful staff are at hand to advise and recommend.

MEMORIES OF HUNGARY
HANDICRAFTS

Map p244 (☑1-780 5844; www.memoriesofhungary.hu; ⓥ Hercegprímás utca 8; ⓞ10am-10pm; ⓜM1 Bajcsy-Zsilinszky út) One of our favourite places to buy souvenirs and gifts, this place has (mostly genuinely) Hungarian handicrafts as well as a good selection of local foodstuffs and wine.

BÁV
ANTIQUES

Map p244 (Bizományi Kereskedőház és Záloghitel; ☑1-473 0666; www.bav.hu; XIII Szent István körút 3; ⓞ10am-6pm Mon-Fri, to 2pm Sat; ◪4, 6) This chain of pawn and secondhand shops, with a number of branches around town, is a fun place to comb for trinkets and treasures, especially if you don't have time to get to the Ecseri or City Park flea markets. Check out this branch for china, textiles, artwork and furniture.

ROMANI DESIGN
FASHION, CLOTHING

Map p244 (☑06 30 258 9774, 1-788 1034; www.romani.hu; ⓥ Szent István tér 3, 2nd & 3rd fls; ⓞ10am-6pm Mon-Fri; ⓜM3 Arany János utca, ◪4, 6) At once stylish and theatrical, the Roma-designed ready-to-wear, with its bright colours and extravagant pleating, would literally stop traffic. Designer Erika Varga is a jeweller and many of her pieces in silver and textile bear good-luck motifs: horseshoe, four-leaf clover and lentils (it's a local thing).

PINTÉR ANTIK
ANTIQUES

Map p244 (☑1-311 3030; www.pinterantik.hu; ⓥ Falk Miksa utca 10; ⓞ10am-6pm Mon-Fri, to 2pm Sat; ◪2, 4, 6) With a positively enormous antique showroom (some 2000 sq metres) in a series of cellars near the Parliament building, Pintér has everything – from furniture and chandeliers to oil paintings and china – and is the best outfit on Falk Miksa utca for browsing.

DÁRIUS ANTIQUES
ANTIQUES

Map p244 (☑1-311 2603; www.dariusantiques.com; ⓥ Falk Miksa utca 24-26; ⓞ10am-6pm Mon-Fri, to 1pm Sat; ◪2, 4, 6) This shop handles antique furniture, paintings, glass, porcelain, clocks and weapons; it's another good option on V Falk Miksa utca and the owner is particularly knowledgeable and helpful.

ANNA ANTIKVITÁS
ANTIQUES

Map p244 (☑1-302 5461; www.annaantikvitas.eu; ⓥ Falk Miksa utca 18-20; ⓞ10am-6pm Mon-Fri, to 1pm Sat; ◪2, 4, 6) Anna is the place to go if you're in the market for embroidered antique tablecloths and bed linen. They're stacked up all over the shop and of very good quality.

SZŐNYI ANTIKVÁRIUMA
BOOKS

Map p244 (☑1-311 6431; www.szonyi.hu; ⓥ Szent István körút 3; ⓞ10am-6pm Mon-Fri, 9am-1pm Sat; ◪2, 4, 6) This long-established antiquarian bookshop has, in addition to old tomes, an excellent selection of antique prints and maps. Just open the drawers in the chests at the back and have a peek.

CEU BOOKSHOP
BOOKS

Map p244 (☑1-327 3096; www.facebook.com/pages/CEU-Bookshop/162951417153756; ⓥ Zrínyi utca 12; ⓞ10am-7pm Mon-Fri, 11am-3pm Sat; ◪15, ⓜM1/2/3 Deák Ferenc tér) The bookshop at Budapest's renowned Central European University has an excellent selection of academic and business titles with a regional focus. The Hungarian literary fiction in translation section is among the best in town.

CARTOGRAPHIA
MAPS

Map p244 (☑1-312 6001; www.cartographia.hu; VI Bajcsy-Zsilinszky út 37; ⓞ10am-6pm Mon-Fri; ⓜM3 Arany János utca) This outlet of the national map-making company stocks the full range of maps, including the best folding ones of Budapest at scales of 1:22,000 (990Ft) and 1:30,000 (790Ft). If you plan to explore the city more thoroughly, its 1:20,000 *Budapest Atlas* (small/large format 2750/3990Ft) is indispensable. There's also a 1:25,000 pocket atlas available for 1690Ft.

TÉRKÉPKIRÁLY — MAPS

Map p244 (✑1-221 9707; www.mapking.hu; VI Bajcsy-Zsilinszky út 21; ☺10am-6.30pm Mon-Fri; ⓂM3 Arany János utca) The 'Map King' stocks a wide variety of maps and its staff are particularly helpful and knowledgeable.

MANIER — FASHION

Map p244 (✑1-354 1878; www.manier.hu; VI Hajós utca 12; ☺11am-7pm Mon-Sat; ⓂM1 Opera) Just behind the Opera House, Anikó Németh's new outlet shows her luxury ready-to-wear and designer streetwear to dramatic effect backed by a planted wall.

NÁRAY TAMÁS ATELIER — FASHION

Map p244 (✑1-266 2473; www.naraytamas.hu; VI Hajós utca 17; ☺11.30am-6pm Mon-Fri; ⓂM1 Opera) The principal outlet for one of Hungary's most celebrated and controversial designers, Paris-trained Tamás Náray, stocks elegant ready-to-wear fashion for women and accepts tailoring orders. Ball gowns are a speciality.

MALATINSZKY WINE STORE — WINE

Map p238 (✑1-317 5919; www.malatinszky.hu; V József Attila utca 12; ☺10am-6pm Mon-Sat; ⓂM1/2/3 Deák Ferenc tér, 🚊2) Owned and operated by a one-time sommelier at the Gundel restaurant, this shop has an excellent selection of high-end Hungarian wines. Ask the staff to recommend a bottle.

NÁDORTEX — HOMEWARES

Map p238 (✑1-317 0030; V József nádor tér 12; ☺10am-5pm Mon-Fri; ⓂM1/2/3 Deák Ferenc tér, 🚊2) Goose-feather or down products such as pillows or duvets (comforters) are of excellent quality in Hungary and a highly recommended purchase. Nádortex, small and

monolingual but reliable, has some of the best prices.

HEREND — PORCELAIN

Map p238 (✑1-317 2622; www.herend.com; V József nádor tér 11; ☺10am-6pm Mon-Fri, to 2pm Sat; ⓂM1/2/3 Deák Ferenc tér, 🚊2) A central branch of the iconic Hungarian brand. Herend makes an excellent – though pricey – souvenir or gift.

HAAS & CZJZEK — PORCELAIN, GLASSWARE

Map p244 (✑1-311 4094; www.porcelan.hu; VI Bajcsy-Zsilinszky út 23; ☺10am-7pm Mon-Fri, 10am-3pm Sat; ⓂM3 Arany János utca) Not far from the basilica, this chinaware and crystal shop, in situ since 1879, sells Herend and Zsolnay pieces as well as more affordable Hungarian-made Hollóháza and Alföldi porcelain.

AJKA KRISTÁLY — CRYSTAL

Map p238 (✑1-317 8133; www.ajka-crystal.hu; V József Attila utca 7; ☺10am-6pm Mon-Fri, to 1pm Sat; ⓂM1/2/3/Deák Ferenc tér, 🚊2) Established in 1878, Ajka has Hungarian-made lead-crystal pieces and stemware. A lot of it is very old-fashioned and ornate, but there are some more contemporary pieces worth a second look.

JÁTÉKSZEREK ANNO — TOYS

Map p244 (✑1-302 6234; www.jatekanno.hu; VI Teréz körút 54; ☺10am-6pm Mon-Fri, to 2pm Sat; ⓂM3 Nyugati pályaudvar, 🚊4, 6) The tiny but exceptional 'Anno Playthings' shop sells finely made reproductions of antique wind-up and other old-fashioned toys.

WAVE MUSIC — MUSIC

Map p244 (✑1-331 0718; www.wave.hu; VI Révay köz 1; ☺11am-7pm Mon-Fri, to 3pm Sat; ⓂM1 Bajcsy-Zsilinszky út) Wave is an excellent outlet for both Hungarian and international indie guitar music, as well as underground dance music. Great T-shirts too.

Margaret Island & Northern Pest

MARGARET ISLAND | ÚJLIPÓTVÁROS

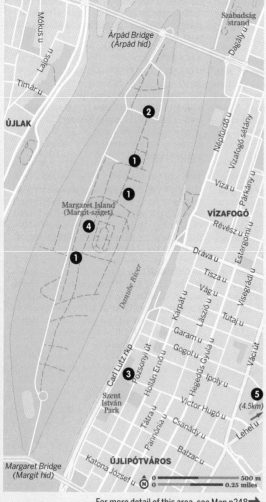

Neighbourhood Top Five

1 Revisiting Budapest's medieval past on Margaret Island by strolling from the ruins of the **Franciscan church and monastery** (p110), past the one-time **Dominican convent** (p110) where St Margaret is buried and on to the Romanesque **Premonstratensian church** (p110).

2 Pampering yourself at the **Danubius Health Spa Margitsziget** (p110), one of the most modern spas in town.

3 Paying homage to the heroic Raoul Wallenberg at his statue in **Szent István Park** (p111).

4 Exploring the length and breadth of Margaret Island on two or four wheels with a **rental bicycle** or **pedal coach** (see Top Tip, opposite page).

5 Getting behind the wheel of one of the big locomotives at the **Hungarian Railway History Park** (p111).

For more detail of this area, see Map p248 ➡

Explore: Margaret Island & Northern Pest

Neither Buda nor Pest, though part of district XIII, 2.5km-long Margaret Island (Margit-sziget) in the middle of the Danube was always the domain of one religious order or another until the Turks arrived and turned what was then called the Island of Rabbits into – appropriately enough – a harem, from which all 'infidels' were barred. It's been a public park open to everyone since the mid-19th century.

The island is not overly endowed with important sights and landmarks. But boasting a couple of large swimming complexes, a thermal spa, gardens and shaded walkways, it is a lovely place to head on a hot afternoon. Cars are allowed on Margaret Island from Árpád Bridge only as far as the two big hotels at the northern end; the rest is reserved for pedestrians and cyclists.

Szent István körút, the northernmost stretch of the Big Ring Rd (Nagykörút) in Pest, runs from Margaret Bridge to Nyugati tér. The area north of Szent István körút is known as Újlipótváros (New Leopold Town) to distinguish it from Lipótváros (Leopold Town) to the south of the boulevard. A wonderful neighbourhood with tree-lined streets, boutiques, restaurants and cafes, it's best seen on foot.

Local Life

➡ **Music** The incomparable Budapest Jazz Club (p113) is now wowing Újlipótváros with its big international and local talent gigs.

➡ **Eating** Outside the hotels catering is limited on Margaret Island, so visit Gasztró Hús-Hentesáru (p76) opposite the tram stop (4 or 6) on the Buda side of Margaret Bridge to stock up on edibles.

➡ **Sport** The Alfréd Hajós swimming complex (p111) is a good spot to catch some of the 'almost national' game of water polo.

Getting There & Away

➡ **Tram** Both districts served by trams 4 and 6. Tram 2 to XIII Jászai Mari tér from the Inner Town.

➡ **Bus** 26 covers the length of Margaret Island running between Nyugati train station and Árpád Bridge. Újlipótváros via bus 15.

➡ **Trolleybus** 75 and especially 76 excellent for Újlipótváros.

➡ **Metro** The eastern end of Újlipótváros best reached by metro (M3 Nyugati pályaudvar).

Lonely Planet's Top Tip

The variety of moving conveyances available on Margaret Island knows no bounds. You can hire a bicycle from one of several stands on the northern end of the athletic stadium as you walk from Margaret Bridge. Long-established **Bringóhintó** (Map p248; ✆1-329 2073; www.bringo-hinto.hu; mountain bike per 30/60min 690/990Ft, pedal coach for 4 people per 30/60 2180/3480Ft; ⊘8am-dusk) rents out all kinds of equipment from the refreshment stand near the Japanese Garden in the northern part of the island.

✖ Best Places to Eat

➡ Firkász (p112)
➡ Pozsonyi Kisvendéglő (p112)
➡ Laci Konyha (p113)

For reviews, see p112➡

🍷 Best Places to Drink

➡ Holdudvar (p113)
➡ Budapest Jazz Club (p113)
➡ Dunapark (p113)

For reviews, see p113➡

🏊 Best Places to Take the Plunge

➡ Danubius Health Spa Margitsziget (p110)
➡ Palatinus Strand (p111)
➡ Aquaworld (p111)

For reviews, see p110➡

◉ SIGHTS

◉ Margaret Island

MARGARET BRIDGE BRIDGE

Map p248 (Margit híd; 🚊2, 4, 6) Margaret Bridge, which has finally emerged from a massive three-year reconstruction, introduces the Big Ring Rd to Buda. It's unique in that it doglegs in order to stand at right angles to the Danube where it converges at the southern tip of Margaret Island. The bridge was originally built by French engineer Ernest Gouin in 1876; the branch leading to the island was added in 1901.

CENTENNIAL MONUMENT MONUMENT

Map p248 (Centenariumi emlékmű; 🚊26, 🚊4, 6) This monument, in the flower-bedded roundabout 350m north of the tram stop on Margaret Bridge, was unveiled in 1973 to mark the 100th anniversary of the union of Buda, Pest and Óbuda. As it was an entirely different era in Budapest more than 40 years ago, the sculptor filled the strange split cone with all sorts of socialist and nationalist symbols. It's like a time capsule.

WATER TOWER & OPEN-AIR THEATRE ARCHITECTURE

Map p248 (Víztorony és Szabadtéri Színpad; 🗹06 20 383 6352; Lookout Gallery adult/child 300/200Ft; ⊙Lookout Gallery 11.30am-7pm May-Oct; 🚊26) Erected in 1911 in the north-central part of Margaret Island, the octagonal water tower rises 66m above the recently renovated **open-air theatre** (szabadtéri színpad), which is used for concerts and plays in summer. The tower contains the **Lookout Gallery** (Kilátó Galéria). Climbing the 153 steps will earn you a stunning 360-degree view of the island, Buda and Pest.

FRANCISCAN CHURCH & MONASTERY RUIN

Map p248 (Ferences templom és kolostor; 🚊26) The ruins – no more than a tower and a wall dating to the late 13th century – are in the centre of the island. Habsburg Archduke Joseph built a summer residence here when he inherited the island in 1867. It was later converted into a hotel, which operated until 1949.

DOMINICAN CONVENT RUIN

Map p248 (Domonkos kolostor; 🚊26) A ruin is all that remains of the 13th-century convent built by Béla IV, where his daughter, St Margaret (1242–71), lived. According to the story, the king promised to commit his daughter to a life of devotion in a nunnery if the Mongols were driven from the land. They were and she was – at nine years of age. A red-marble sepulchre cover surrounded by a wrought-iron grille marks her original resting place.

Canonised in 1943, St Margaret commands something of a cult following in Hungary. A short distance southeast of the sepulchre there's a much-visited brick shrine with ex-votives thanking her for various favours and cures.

PREMONSTRATENSIAN CHURCH CHURCH

Map p248 (Premontre templom; 🚊26) This reconstructed Romanesque Premonstratensian Church dedicated to St Michael by the order of White Canons dates back to the 12th century. Its 15th-century bell mysteriously appeared one night in 1914 under the roots of a walnut tree knocked over in a storm. It was probably buried by monks during the Turkish invasion.

JAPANESE GARDEN GARDENS

Map p248 (Japánkert; 🚊26) This attractive garden at the northwestern end of the island has koi, carp and lily pads in its ponds, as well as bamboo groves, Japanese maples, swamp cypresses, a small wooden bridge and a waterfall. Just north on a raised gazebo is the **Musical Fountain** (Zenélőkút), a replica of one in Transylvania in desperate need of some tender loving care.

DANUBIUS HEALTH SPA MARGITSZIGET SPA

Map p248 (🗹1-889 4737; www.danubius hotels.com; Mon-Fri 4900Ft, Sat & Sun 5900Ft; ⊙6.30am-9.30pm; 🚊26) Among the most modern (but least atmospheric) of all Budapest bathhouses, this thermal spa is in the Danubius Thermal Hotel Margitsziget. The baths are open to men and women in separate sections on weekdays and mixed at the weekend. A daily ticket includes entry to the swimming pools, sauna and steam room, as well as use of the fitness machines.

FUN FOR THE FAMILY

Hungarian Railway History Park

The mostly outdoor **Hungarian Railway History Park** (Magyar Vasúttörténeti Park; ☑1-450 1497; www.vasuttortenetipark.hu; XIV Tatai út 95; adult/child 1400/600Ft; ⊙10am-6pm Tue-Sun Apr-Oct; ☒30, 30A, ☒14) contains some 50 locomotives (a dozen of them still working) and rolling stock and an exhibition on the history of the railroad in Hungary, including a house full of models. For kids there's a wonderful array of hands-on activities – mostly involving getting behind the wheel.

Aquaworld

In northern Pest, **Aquaworld** (☑1-231 3760; www.aqua-world.hu; Íves út 16; 2hr/day Mon-Fri adult 2690/4990Ft, child 1350/2490Ft, Sat & Sun adult 2990/5690Ft, child 1500/2840Ft; ⊙6am-10pm; ☒30) is one of Europe's largest water parks, with an adventure centre covered by a 72m dome, pools with whirlpools and a dozen slides, and an array of saunas to keep the whole family gainfully at play. A free shuttle bus departs from in front of the Museum of Fine Arts in Heroes' Sq (M1 Hősök tere) at 9.30am, 1.30pm, 5.30pm and 7.30pm.

DAGÁLY SWIMMING COMPLEX SWIMMING

Map p248 (☑1-452 4500; www.dagalyfurdo.hu; XIII Népfürdő utca 36; adult weekday/weekend 2400/2600Ft, child 1900Ft; ⊙outdoor pools 6am-7pm May-Sep, indoor pools 6am-8pm; ☒M3 Árpád híd, ☒1) This huge postwar complex has a total of 10 pools, including two thermal ones and a whirlpool. The surrounding park offers plenty of grass and shade.

PALATINUS STRAND SWIMMING

Map p248 (☑1-340 4505; www.en.palatinus strand.hu; XIII Margit-sziget; adult/child weekday 2600/1900Ft, weekend 3000/1900Ft; ⊙9am-7pm May-Aug; ☒26) The largest series of pools in the capital, the 'Palatinus Beach' complex has upwards of a dozen pools (two with thermal water), wave machines, water slides and kids' pools.

DANUBIUS HEALTH SPA HÉLIA SPA

Map p248 (☑1-889 5820; www.danubiushotels.com; XIII Kárpát utca 62-64; before/after 8pm Mon-Fri 4200/2900Ft, Sat & Sun 5300/3300Ft; ⊙7am-10pm; ☒M3 Dózsa György út, ☒75) This ultramodern swimming and spa centre in the four-star Danubius Hélia Hotel boasts three pools, a sauna and steam room and an abundance of therapies.

ALFRÉD HAJÓS SPORTS POOLS SWIMMING

Map p248 (Nemzeti Sportuszoda; ☑1-450 4214; XIII Margit-sziget; adult/child 1800/1100Ft; ⊙outdoor pools 6am-7pm May-Sep, indoor pools 6am-7pm Mon-Fri, to 5pm Sat & Sun Oct-Apr; ☒26, ☒4, 6) The two indoor and two out-door pools at the Alfréd Hajós swimming complex make up the National Sports Pool, where the Olympic swimming and water-polo teams train. You can watch water-polo league at the weekends.

⊙ Újlipótváros

JÁSZAI MARI TÉR SQUARE

Map p248 (☒2, 4, 6) The gateway to both Margaret Island and Újlipótváros, Jászai Mari tér is split in two by the foot of Margaret Bridge. The modern building south of the square, nicknamed the **White House**, was once the headquarters of the Central Committee of the ruling Hungarian Socialist Workers' Party. It now contains offices of the members of Hungary's parliament.

To the north of the square is an elegant apartment block forming part of the **Palatinus Houses**, built in 1912 and facing the Danube. They contain some of the most expensive flats for sale or rent in Budapest.

SZENT ISTVÁN PARK PARK

Map p248 (Szent István körút; ☒15,75) St Stephen Park contains a **statue of Raoul Wallenberg** (p68) doing battle with a snake (evil). Erected in 1999, it is titled *Kígyóölő* (Serpent Slayer) and replaces one created by sculptor Pál Pátzay that was mysteriously removed the night before its unveiling in 1948. Facing the river is a row of Bauhaus apartments, which were the delight of modernists when they were built in the late 1920s.

COMEDY THEATRE NOTABLE BUILDING

Map p248 (Vígszínház; ☏1-329 2340; www.vigsz-inhaz.hu; XIII Szent István körút 14; ☐4, 6) The attractive little building on Szent István körút roughly halfway between the Danube and Nyugati tér is where comedies (including Shakespearean ones in translation) and musicals are staged. When it was built in 1896 it was criticised for being too far out of town.

LEHEL CHURCH CHURCH

Map p248 (Lehel templom; XIII Lehel tér; Ⓜ M3 Lehel tér) If you look north up XIII Váci út from Nyugati tér you'll see the twin spires of this 1933 copy of a celebrated 13th-century Romanesque church (now in ruins) at Zsámbék, 33km west of Budapest. Just beyond it is **Lehel Market** (◷6am-6pm Mon-Fri, to 2pm Sat, to 1pm Sun), a great traditional market housed in a hideous boatlike structure designed by László Rajk, son of the Communist minister of the interior executed for 'Titoism' in 1949. They say this building is his revenge.

 ## EATING

There are not a lot of options on Margaret Island unless you go for hotel fare. The same is not true of Újlipótváros, which contains a tremendous number of eateries in a relatively small area.

POZSONYI KISVENDÉGLŐ HUNGARIAN $

Map p248 (☏1-787 4877;6; XIII Radnóti Miklós utca 38; mains 1100-2500Ft; ◷11am-11pm; ☐2, 4, 6, ☐75, 76) Visit this neighbourhood restaurant on the corner of Pozsonyi út for the ultimate local Budapest experience: gargantuan portions of Hungarian classics (don't expect gourmet), rock-bottom prices and a cast of local characters. There's a bank of tables on the pavement in summer and a weekday set menu for 950Ft.

CAFÉ PANINI SANDWICHES $

Map p248 (☏06 70 946 8072; www.cafepanini.hu; XIII Radnóti Miklós utca 45; sandwiches & salads 890-1400Ft; ◷8am-10pm Mon-Fri, 9am-10pm Sat, 9am-7pm Sun; ☐75, 76) With an enviable location along the Danube, this upbeat and very casual venue is worth a visit for the tasty views of Margaret Island alone. But come for great *panini* and salads, breakfast (1290Ft to 1990Ft) at any time and a two-course set lunch for 1390Ft.

SARKI FŰSZERES CAFE $

Map p248 (Grocery Store on Corner; ☏1-238 0600; www.sarkifuszeres.hu; Pozsonyi út 53-55; breakfast & sandwiches 750-1900Ft; ◷8am-8pm Mon-Fri, to 3pm Sat; ☐76) This delightful retro-tyle cafe on tree-lined Pozsonyi út is the perfect place for brunch, a late breakfast or just a quick sandwich.

DONUT LIBRARY BREAKFAST $

Map p248 (https://www.facebook.com/thedo-nutlibrary; XIII Pozsonyi út 22; doughnuts 290Ft; ◷10am-8pm Mon-Sat, noon-8pm Sun; ☐2, 4, 6, ☐75, 76) Budapest's first bona fide doughnut outlet sells dozens of varieties of both coated and filled fried dough. Great place for a quick breakfast and there's a book exchange here too.

★ FIRKÁSZ HUNGARIAN $$

Map p248 (☏1-450 1118; www.firkasz.hu; Tátra utca 18; mains 2490-5420Ft; ◷noon-midnight; ☐15) Set up by former journalists, this retro-style restaurant called 'Hack', with lovely old mementos on the walls, great homestyle cooking, a good wine list and nightly piano music, has been one of our favourite Hungarian 'nostalgia' eateries for years.

PÁNDZSÁB TANDOORI INDIAN $$

Map p248 (☏1-270 2974; http://pandzsabtan-doori.blog.hu; XIII Pannónia utca 3; mains 1560-3800Ft; ◷noon-11pm; ☏; ☐15, 115) It may not look like much, but get closer and your olfactories will tell you that this little hole-in-the-wall place with upstairs tables serves some of the best home-cooked Indian food in Budapest. The signature tandoori dishes are excellent, and there's also a good choice of vegetarian dishes.

KISKAKUKK HUNGARIAN $$

Map p248 (☏1-450 0829; www.kiskakukk.hu; XIII Pozsonyi út 12; mains 2190-3990Ft; ◷noon-midnight; ☐75, 76, ☐4, 6) This ever-so-traditional Hungarian eatery with the retro shop sign in front has been serving up classic *gulyásleves* (hearty beef soup; 780Ft), bone marrow on toast (1650Ft) and Kaposvár-style stuffed cabbage (2250Ft) for over a century. It's tried and tested and true.

OKAY ITALIA ITALIAN $$

Map p248 (☏1-349 2991; www.okayitalia.hu; XIII Szent István körút 20; pizza & pasta 1390-2590Ft, mains 1990-5490Ft; ◷11am-midnight Mon-Fri, noon-midnight Sat & Sun; ☐4, 6) A perennially popular eatery started by Italians more than 20 years ago, Okay Italia does a full range of dishes, but most people come for the pasta and pizza. The terrace on the Big Ring Rd is a lively place to meet in summer.

TRÓFEA GRILL
BUFFET $$

Map p248 (☑1-270 0366; www.trofeagrill. hu; XIII Visegrádi utca 50/a; lunch weekdays/ weekends 3899/5999Ft, dinner 5499/5999Ft; ☺noon-midnight Mon-Fri, 11.30am-midnight Sat, 11.30am-8.30pm Sun; ☑15, ⓂM3 Lehel tér) This is the place to head when you really could eat a horse (which may or may not be on one of the serving tables). It's an enormous buffet of more than 100 cold and hot dishes over which appreciative diners swarm like bees.

LACI KONYHA
HUNGARIAN $$$

Map p248 (☑06 70 370 7475; http://lacikonyha. com; Hegedűs Gyula utca 56; mains 3400-4500Ft; ☺noon-3pm & 6-10pm Mon-Fri; ☑15, ⓂM3 Lehel tér) One of the most ambitious eateries in Budapest, this self-styled 'boutique restaurant' in the unlikely northern wilds of Újlipótváros is under the watchful gaze of chef Gábor Mogyorósi, who puts an eclectic spin on old favourites (bok choy with guinea fowl, Japanese mushrooms with oxtail). The daily two-course lunch is a snip at 2200Ft. Mogyorósi's five-course tasting menu is 6500Ft.

🍷 DRINKING & NIGHTLIFE

★HOLDUDVAR
CLUB

Map p248 (☑1-236 0155; www.holdudvar.net; XIII Margit-sziget; ☺11am-midnight Sun-Tue, to 2am Wed, to 4am Thu-Sat; ☑4, 6) Trying to be all things to all people – restaurant, bar, gallery, open-air cinema, disco and kert (outdoor garden club) – is not always advisable, but the 'Moon Court', occupying a huge indoor and outdoor space on Margaret Island, does a decent job of juggling all five tasks. Most people, though, come for the pulsating seasonal outdoor club (no noise worries here!), which rocks to different music styles each night.

DUNAPARK
CAFE

Map p248 (☑1-786 1009; www.dunaparkkavehaz. hu; XIII Pozsonyi út 38; ☺8am-11pm Mon-Fri, 10am-11pm Sat, 10am-10pm Sun; ☑75, 76) Built in 1938

as a cinema, this Art Deco place with a lovely upstairs gallery and views of Szent István Park is also a restaurant. But we still think of – and use – it as a cukrászda (cake shop); its cakes (375Ft to 650Ft) are among the best this side of the Danube.

L.A. BODEGITA
COCKTAIL BAR

Map p248 (☑1-789 4019; www.labodegita.hu; XIII Pozsonyi utca 4; cocktails 800-1900Ft; ☺11am-midnight Mon-Thu, to 2am Fri & Sat, to 6pm Sun; ☑2, 4, 6, ☑75, 76) Some people come here for Cuban tapas (from 590Ft). We say leave that to the experts at La Bodeguita del Medio (p127) and taste master mixologist András Lajsz' incomparable American-style (hi, LA!) cocktails. Live Cuban music on Friday night.

BLUE TOMATO
BAR

Map p248 (☑1-339 8099; www.bluetomato. hu; XIII Pannónia utca 5-7; ☺11.30am-midnight Mon & Tue, to 2am Wed & Thu, to 4am Fri & Sat, to 11pm Sun; ☑15, 115) This big boozer is like something out of the old American sitcom Cheers, especially the upstairs bar. It's been a popular feature of the district for a decade and a half and the food – mostly Med-Hungarian, with mains from 1390Ft to 3190Ft – is more than just the usual bar or pub blotter.

KABBALA CUKRÁSZDA
CAFE

Map p248 (☑1-786 6196; Hollán Ernő utca 25; cakes 320-690Ft; ☺10am-7pm Mon-Thu, to 6pm Fri & Sun; ☑75, 76) What is probably the first kosher cake shop–cafe to open in Újlipótváros since WWII serves all the usual favourites, including killer flódni (a substantial three-layer cake with apple, walnut and poppy-seed fillings). Good selection of Judaica on sale, too.

BRIÓS
CAFE

Map p248 (☑1-789 6110; www.brioskavezo.hu; XIII Pozsonyi út 16; ☺7.30am-8pm; ☑75, 76) Kids in tow? This place is for you, with toys and games and other things to keep the ankle-biters at bay while you tuck into breakfast (590Ft to 1290Ft), the set lunch (1200Ft) or just a reviving kávé (coffee).

☆ ENTERTAINMENT

BUDAPEST JAZZ CLUB
JAZZ

Map p248 (☑06 70 413 9837; www.bjc.hu; XIII Hollán Ernő utca 7; ☺10am-midnight; ☑75, 76)

MARGARET ISLAND & NORTHERN PEST DRINKING & NIGHTLIFE

A very sophisticated venue – now pretty much the most serious one in town – for traditional, vocal and Latin jazz by local and international talent. Concerts most nights at 9pm, with jam sessions at 10pm or 11pm on Friday, Saturday and Monday.

 ## SHOPPING

MÉZES KUCKÓ FOOD
Map p248 (Honey Nook; XIII Jászai Mari tér 4; ⊗10am-6pm Mon-Fri, 9am-1pm Sat; ⛟2, 4, 6) This hole-in-the-wall is the place to go if you have the urge for something sweet; its nut-and-honey cookies (240Ft per 10 decagrams) are to die for. A colourfully decorated *mézeskalács* (honey cake; 220Ft to 650Ft) in the shape of a heart makes a lovely gift.

PENDRAGON BOOKS
Map p248 (☎1-340 4426; www.pendragon.hu; XIII Pozsonyi út 21-23; ⊗10am-6pm Mon-Fri, to 2pm Sat; ⛟75,76) This exclusively English-language bookshop, which takes its name from the legend of King Arthur, has an excellent selection of books and guides, including Lonely Planet ones.

BOOK STATION BOOKS
Map p248 (☎1-413 1158; www.bookstation.hu; XIII Katona József utca 13; ⊗10am-7pm Mon-Sat; ⓜM3 Nyugati pályaudvar) A key player in the used-books business, Book Station has thousands of titles in English and a babel of other languages on two floors.

Erzsébetváros & the Jewish Quarter

ERZSÉBETVÁROS | ANDRÁSSY ÚT & TERÉZVÁROS (EAST)

Neighbourhood Top Five

❶ Marvelling at the exotic architecture of the **Great Synagogue** (p117), the largest Jewish house of worship in Europe, and taking a 2000-year tour at the attached **Hungarian Jewish Museum** (p117).

❷ Enjoying a performance at the **Hungarian State Opera House** (p130), the capital's sumptuously appointed temple to classical music.

❸ Strolling along **Andrássy út** (p120), the gracious tree-, shop- and sight-lined boulevard that appears on Unesco's World Heritage list.

❹ Drinking and dancing the night away at any of central Pest's ruin pubs, such as **Szimpla Kert** (p125), **Lokál** (p124) or **Ellátó Kert** (p126).

❺ Tasting something sweet along with something warm on the terrace of a traditional cafe like the **Művész Kávéház** (p129) on Andrássy út.

For more detail of this area, see Map p250 ➡

Lonely Planet's Top Tip

It may not be immediately apparent, but the M1 metro, also known as the Kis Metró (Little Metro), which runs just below Andrássy út from Deák Ferenc tér as far as City Park, sticks to its side of the road underground and there is no interchange down below. So if you are heading north, board the trains on the east side of Andrássy út. For points south, it's the west side. Another possible source of confusion on the M1 is that one station is called Vörösmarty tér and another, five stops away, is Vörösmarty utca.

✖ Best Places to Eat

→ Kádár (p121)
→ Macesz Huszár (p123)
→ Klassz (p124)
→ Zeller Bistro (p123)

For reviews, see p121 ➡

🍷 Best Places to Drink

→ Mika Tivadar Mulató (p124)
→ CoXx Men's Bar (p125)
→ Lokál (p124)
→ Alexandra Book Cafe (p129)

For reviews, see p124 ➡

🛍 Best Places to Shop

→ Gouba (p130)
→ Printa (p130)
→ Massolit (p130)
→ Szimpla Farmers' Market (p130)

For reviews, see p130 ➡

Explore: Erzsébetváros & the Jewish Quarter

The two main areas that visitors will want to focus on here are the densely packed tangle of streets on the western side of Erzsébetváros, and the environs of long and stately Andrássy út. There's plenty to occupy your daytime in the latter, with a simple stroll along the length of the street, ending at Heroes' Sq (Hősök tere), the best way to get the measure of this part of town. On or just nearby you'll find a number of museums and notable buildings, including the House of Terror and the State Opera House. The eastern side of Erzsébetváros is rather run-down, with little of interest to travellers except the Keleti train station on Baross tér.

The western side, bounded by the Little Ring Rd, has always been predominantly Jewish, and this was the ghetto where Jews were forced to live when the Nazis occupied Hungary in 1944. It's also where nocturnal Budapest really comes alive and you'll find most of its famous ruin pubs and garden clubs. It heaves on weekends with tourists and locals jumping from bar to bar. In the day it's an atmospheric place to wander, with plenty of evidence of the large Jewish community here, and some great shops, cafes and restaurants.

Local Life

→ **Jewish heritage** Visit the area's impressive synagogues, lunch at Kádár (p121), munch on gorgeous cakes at Fröhlich Cukrászda (p125), and listen to some *klezmer* at Spinoza Café (p123).

→ **Bar-Hop** Seek out the smaller, backstreet haunts, away from the crowds, where locals hang out to the wee hours (p128).

→ **Market** Join the foodies getting their artisan produce at the Sunday Szimpla Farmers' Market (p130).

Getting There & Away

→ **Metro** Three metro lines converge at Deák Ferenc tér, handy for western Erzsébetváros; Oktogon is on the M1 metro line and Blaha Lujza tér is on the M2 and M4; also useful are the M2 and M4 Astoria and Keleti pályaudvar stations.

→ **Tram** VII Erzsébet körút for tram 4 or 6 to Buda or rest of Big Ring Rd in Pest.

→ **Trolleybus** VII Wesselényi utca and Dohány utca for 74 to Little Ring Rd or City Park.

TOP SIGHT
GREAT SYNAGOGUE

Budapest's stunning Great Synagogue, with its crenellated red-and-yellow glazed brick facade and two enormous Moorish-style towers, is the largest Jewish house of worship in the world outside New York City, seating 3000 worshippers.

Built in 1859 according to the designs of Viennese architect Ludwig Förster, the copper-domed Neolog (strict conservative) synagogue contains both Romantic-style and Moorish architectural elements. Because some elements of it recall Christian churches – including the central **rose window** with an inscription from the second book of Moses – the synagogue is sometimes referred to as the 'Jewish cathedral'. It was renovated in the 1990s largely with private donations, including a cool US$5 million from Estée Lauder, who was born in New York to Hungarian Jewish immigrants. Inside, don't miss the carvings on the **Ark of the Covenant** by Frigyes Feszl and the sumptuous **organ**, dating back to 1902.

The **Hungarian Jewish Museum**, in an annexe of the synagogue, contains objects related to religious and everyday life. Interesting items include 3rd-century Jewish headstones from Roman Pannonia, a vast amount of ritualistic silver, and a handwritten book of the local Burial Society from the late 18th century. The **Holocaust Memorial Room** relates the events of 1944–45.

On the synagogue's north side, the **Holocaust Memorial**, designed by Imre Varga in 1991, stands over the mass graves of those murdered by the Nazis in 1944–45. On the leaves of the metal 'tree of life' are the family names of some of the hundreds of thousands of victims. On the other side of the memorial garden, you'll find the **Jewish Quarter Exhibition**, with interactive displays, video and artefacts documenting what life was like in this area through the eras.

DON'T MISS...

➤ Ark of the Covenant
➤ Rose window
➤ Hungarian Jewish Museum
➤ Holocaust Memorial

PRACTICALITIES

➤ Nagy zsinagóga
➤ Map p250
➤ www.dohanystreet-synagogue.hu
➤ VII Dohány utca 2
➤ incl museum adult/student & child 2850/2000Ft
➤ ⊙10am-5.30pm Sun-Thu, to 3.30pm Fri Mar-Oct, reduced hours Nov-Feb
➤ Ⓜ M2 Astoria

⊙ SIGHTS

⊙ Erzsébetváros

GREAT SYNAGOGUE
SYNAGOGUE

See p117.

LISZT ACADEMY
NOTABLE BUILDING

Map p250 (Liszt Zeneakadémia; www.zeneakademia.hu; VI Liszt Ferenc tér 8; Ⓜ M1 Oktogon) The Art Nouveau Liszt Academy, built in 1907, attracts students from all over the world and is one of the top venues for concerts. Having undergone an extensive renovation to restore much of its interior to its original style and function, it reopened in 2014, with improved access, ventilation and heating. The interior, which has five concert halls and is richly embellished with Zsolnay porcelain and frescoes, is worth a look even if you're not attending a performance.

MIKSA RÓTH MEMORIAL HOUSE
MUSEUM

Map p250 (Róth Miksa Emlékház; www.facebook.com/rothmiksaemlekhaz; VII Nefelejcs utca 26; adult/child 750/375Ft; ☺2-6pm Tue-Sun; Ⓜ M2/4 Keleti pályaudvar) This fabulous museum exhibits the work of the eponymous Art Nouveau stained-glass maker (1865–1944) on two floors of the house and workshop where he lived and worked from 1911 until his death. The master's stunning mosaics are less well known. Róth's dark-brown living quarters stand in sharp contrast to the lively, technicolor creations that emerged from his workshop.

ORTHODOX SYNAGOGUE
SYNAGOGUE

Map p250 (Ortodox zsinagóga; VII Kazinczy utca 29-31; admission 1000Ft; ☺10am-5.30pm Sun-Thu, to 12.30pm Fri; Ⓜ M2 Astoria, 🚊47, 49) Once one of a half-dozen synagogues and prayer houses in the Jewish Quarter, the Orthodox Synagogue was built in 1913 to a very modern – at the time – design. It has late Art Nouveau touches and is decorated in bright colours throughout. The stained-glass windows in the ceiling were designed by Miksa Róth, although what you see today are reconstructions as the originals were bombed during WWII.

NEW THEATRE
NOTABLE BUILDING

Map p250 (Új Színház; www.ujszinhaz.hu; VI Paulay Ede utca 35; Ⓜ M1 Opera) The New Theatre is a Secessionist gem – embellished with monkey

---

⊙ TOP SIGHT
HOUSE OF TERROR

The startling museum called the House of Terror is housed in what was once the headquarters of the dreaded ÁVH secret police. The building has a ghastly (and presumably ghostly) history, for it was here that many activists of every political persuasion that was out of fashion before and after WWII were taken for interrogation and torture. The walls were of double thickness to mute the screams.

The museum focuses on the crimes and atrocities committed by both Hungary's fascist and Stalinist regimes in a permanent exhibition called *Double Occupation*, and visitors are greeted at the entrance by the red Communist star and the black 'arrow cross' of the fascists. But the years after WWII leading up to the 1956 Uprising get the lion's share of the exhibition space. The **tank** in the central courtyard is a jarring introduction and the wall outside displaying many of the victims' photos speaks volumes. Even more harrowing are the reconstructed **prison cells** (collectively called 'the gym') and the final **Perpetrators' Gallery**, featuring photographs of the turncoats, spies, torturers and 'cogs in the wheel' from both sides, many of them still alive, who allowed or caused these atrocities to take place. Never again.

DON'T MISS...
➜ Tank in the central courtyard
➜ Reconstructed prison cells
➜ Perpetrators' Gallery

PRACTICALITIES
➜ Terror Háza
➜ Map p250
➜ www.terrorhaza.hu
➜ VI Andrássy út 60
➜ adult/concession 2000/1000Ft
➜ ☺10am-6pm Tue-Sun
➜ Ⓜ M1 Oktogon

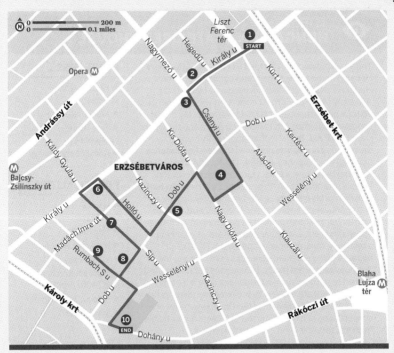

Neighbourhood Walk
Erzsébetváros & the Jewish Quarter

START VI LISZT FERENC TÉR
FINISH VII DOHÁNY UTCA
LENGTH 1KM; ONE TO TWO HOURS

Begin the walk in restaurant- and cafe-packed VI Liszt Ferenc tér, where you should poke your head into the recently renovated **1 Liszt Academy** (p118).

Walking southwest along Király utca you'll pass the **2 Church of St Teresa**, built in 1811 and containing a massive neo-classical altar designed by Mihály Pollack in 1822. At Király utca 47 is an interesting **3 neo-Gothic house** built in 1847.

Turning into Csányi utca, head southeast over Dob utca to the heart of the old Jewish Quarter, **4 Klauzál tér**. The square and surrounding streets retain a feeling of prewar Budapest. A continued Jewish presence is still evident – at a kosher bakery and pizzeria (Kazinczy utca 28), at the Fröhlich Cukrászda cake shop and cafe, and at a butcher just next to the **5 Orthodox Synagogue** (p118).

Walk up Holló utca and turn left. Enter the gate at Király utca 15 – someone will buzz you in should it be locked – and at the rear of the courtyard is a 30m-long piece of the original **6 ghetto wall** rebuilt in 2010. Votive lamps and stones stand before it in tribute to victims of the Holocaust. The next turning on the left is the passageway called **7 Gozsdu udvar**, originally built in 1901 and now emerging as the number-one nightlife destination in the district; it's lined with bars, cafes and restaurants and pulses with music and merrymakers come the evening.

At Dob utca 12 is an unusual antifascist **8 monument to Carl Lutz**, a Swiss consul who, like Raoul Wallenberg, provided Jews with false papers in 1944. It portrays an angel on high sending down a long bolt of cloth to a victim. Just around the corner a 1000-sq-metre **9 mural** painted in 2013 commemorates the 60th anniversary of the footballing victory of Hungary's 'Golden Team', the first time a continental team beat England at Wembley (6–3).

Retrace your steps and you'll find the **10 Great Synagogue** (p117).

TOP SIGHT
HUNGARIAN STATE OPERA HOUSE

The small but perfectly formed Hungarian State Opera House is home to the state opera company and the Hungarian National Ballet. Rivalled only by the Liszt Academy as the city's most important venue for serious cultural performances, it is said to have the third-best acoustics in Europe after Milan's La Scala and the Opéra Garnier in Paris; the latter had apparently inspired architect Miklós Ybl when he designed the neo-Renaissance building, which opened in 1884. The facade is bedecked with statues of opera greats Liszt, Mozart, Verdi and Puccini. Inside, prepare to be dazzled by the **main hall**, with its marble columns, gilded vaulted ceilings, murals and chandeliers. The horseshoe-shaped **auditorium** with its (for the time) innovative proscenium arch stage and magnificent ceiling painted by Károly Lotz holds a relatively small number of spectators (1261), but because of the excellent acoustics even those in the 3rd-floor gallery are happy. Hungarians approach music as the French do wine. Performances here are never stuffy and you are as likely to see people in jeans as more formal dress. If you cannot attend an opera, ballet or concert here, join one of the tours. Tickets are available from the souvenir shop inside to the left.

DON'T MISS...

➡ Facade with statues
➡ Main hall
➡ Two-tonne chandelier
➡ Károly Lotz ceiling

PRACTICALITIES

➡ Magyar Állami Operaház
➡ Map p250
➡ www.operavisit.hu
➡ VI Andrássy út 22
➡ tours adult/concession 2900/1900Ft
➡ ⊙tours 3pm & 4pm
➡ Ⓜ M1 Opera

faces, globes and geometric designs – which opened as the Parisiana music hall in 1909. It's worth having a peek inside too.

⊙ Andrássy út & Terézváros (East)

ANDRÁSSY ÚT   STREET

Map p250 (Ⓜ M1 Opera) Andrássy út starts a short distance northeast of Deák Ferenc tér and stretches for 2.5km, ending at Heroes' Sq (Hősök tere) and the sprawling City Park (Városliget). On Unesco's World Heritage list, it is a tree-lined parade of knock-out architecture and is best enjoyed as a long stroll from the Opera House (p120) out to the park. On the way, don't miss the New Theatre (p118), Művész Kávéház (p129), the House of Terror (p118) and the beautiful Kodály körönd, a square (or more accurately a circus) just over halfway along.

GYÖRGY RÁTH MUSEUM   MUSEUM

Map p250 (Ráth György Múzeum; www.imm. hu/rath; VI Városligeti fasor 12; adult/child 1000/500Ft; ⊙10am-6pm Tue-Sun; Ⓜ M1 Kodály körönd) An overspill of Ferenc Hopp Museum exhibits are shown at the György Ráth Museum, in an Art Nouveau residence a few minutes' walk south down Bajza utca.

FERENC HOPP MUSEUM OF EAST ASIAN ART   MUSEUM

Map p250 (Hopp Ferenc Kelet-Ázsiai Művészeti Múzeum; www.hoppmuzeum.hu; VI Andrássy út 103; adult/child 1000/500Ft; ⊙10am-6pm Tue-Sun; Ⓜ M1 Bajza utca) The Ferenc Hopp Museum of East Asian Art is housed in the former villa of its benefactor and namesake. Founded in 1919, the museum shows temporary exhibitions from its collection of Chinese and Japanese ceramics, porcelain, textiles and sculpture, Indonesian wayang puppets and Indian statuary as well as lamaist sculpture and scroll paintings from Tibet.

ISTVÁN ZELNIK SOUTHEAST ASIAN GOLD MUSEUM   MUSEUM

Map p250 (Zelnik István Délkelet-Ázsia Arany Múzeum; www.thegoldmuseum.eu; VI Andrássy út 110; adult/child 3400/1700Ft; ⊙11am-5pm Tue-Sun; Ⓜ M1 Bajza utca) Inside the reconstructed 19th-century Rausch Villa, you'll find the collection of Dr István Zelnik, a former diplomat who started his career in

Southeast Asia and became a zealous collector of the art and culture of the region. It's an immaculately presented set of glistering masks, statues and religious objects. There's a lovely Asian-style garden and teahouse here too.

FRANZ LISZT MEMORIAL MUSEUM MUSEUM
Map p250 (Liszt Ferenc Emlékmúzeum; www.lisztmuseum.hu; VI Vörösmarty utca 35; adult/child 1300/600Ft; ⊙10am-6pm Mon-Fri, 9am-5pm Sat; M̄M1 Vörösmarty utca) This wonderful little museum is housed in the Old Music Academy, where the great composer lived in a 1st-floor apartment for five years until his death in 1886. The four rooms are filled with his pianos (including a tiny glass one), portraits and personal effects. Concerts (included in the entry fee) are usually held here on Saturday at 11am.

EATING

This large area captures a tremendous number of eateries – from kosher and Jewish *étkezdék* (canteens serving simple Hungarian dishes) to Indian, Italian and Middle Eastern. There's something here to suit everyone, from swish dining and homestyle restaurants to street food and burger bars.

Erzsébetváros

KÁDÁR HUNGARIAN $
Map p250 (☑1-321 3622; X Klauzál tér 9; mains 1250-2500Ft; ⊙11.30am-3.30pm Tue-Sat; 🚎4, 6) Located in the heart of the Jewish district, Kádár is probably the most popular and authentic *étkezde* you'll find in town and attracts the hungry with its ever-changing menu. It usually closes for most of the month of July.

BORS GASZTRO BÁR SANDWICHES $
Map p250 (www.facebook.com/BorsGasztroBar; VII Kazinczy utca 10; baguettes 540-780Ft, soup 540Ft; ⊙11.30am-midnight; 🖊; M̄M2 Astoria) We love this thimble-sized place, not just for its hearty, imaginative soups (how about sweet potato with coconut?) but for equally good grilled baguettes: try 'Bors Dog' (spicy sausage and cheese) or 'Brain Dead' (pig's brains are the main ingredient here). It's not really a sit-down kind of place; most people loiter by the doorway.

SZIMPLA FARMERS' CAFE CAFE $
Map p250 (www.szimpla.hu/szimpla-farm-shop; VII Kazinczy utca 7; daily menu 1100Ft, sandwiches 490Ft; ⊙8am-10pm; 🖳🖊; M̄M2 Astoria) Sourcing its ingredients from the farmers selling their wares at the Sunday market (p130) across the road, this lovely, rustic cafe has a daily menu using seasonal ingredients (soup and a main course), sandwiches , pastries, fresh fruit juices and Has Bean coffee.

ERDÉLYI-MAGYAR ÉTKEZDE ÉTKEZDE $
Map p250 (www.erdelyimagyar.lapunk.hu; VII Dohány utca 36; daily menu 750-950Ft; ⊙11am-4pm Mon-Fri; M̄M2 Blaha Lujza tér, 🚎4, 6) This little *étkezde* serves Transylvanian and Hungarian specialities to appreciative diners but, alas, keeps bankers' hours. But if you can do any better than this for the price, let us know.

KIS PARÁZS THAI $
Map p250 (☑06 70 517 4550; www.parazspresszo.com; VII Kazinczy utca 7; soup 680-1350Ft, wok dishes 1580-1980Ft; ⊙noon-10pm; 🖳; M̄M2 Astoria) The sister eatery of Parázs Presszó (p103), with simpler dishes, has become a pre-club chow-down venue of choice in central Pest.

MONTENEGRÓI GURMAN SOUTH SLAV $
Map p250 (☑06 70 434 9898; www.mnggurman.com; VII Rákóczi út 54; dishes 1290-3990Ft; ⊙24hr; 🚎7, M̄M2 Blaha Lujza tér) When we're famished, broke and it's well past the witching hour, we head for this South Slav eatery and join all the taxi drivers chomping on grills like *csevapcsicsa* (spicy meatballs), *pljeskavica* (spicy meat patties) or *razsnyics* (shish kebab). You can also take away.

BANGLA BÜFÉ BANGLADESHI $
Map p250 (☑1-266 3674; www.banglabufe.com; VII Akácfa utca 40; mains 950-1390Ft; ⊙noon-11pm Sat-Thu, from 2.30pm Fri; 🖊; 🚎4 or 6) This place, started up by a Bangladeshi expat, has as authentic samosas, chicken and lamb *biryani* and dhal as you'll find. Simple but tasty.

FRICI PAPA KIFŐZDÉJE ÉTKEZDE $
Map p250 (☑1-351 0197; www.fricipapa.hu; VI Király utca 55; mains 699-749Ft; ⊙11am-11pm Mon-Sat; M̄M1 Oktogon, 🚎4, 6) 'Papa Frank's Canteen' is larger and more modern than most *étkezde* in Budapest. Excellent *főzelék* (traditionally prepared vegetable) dishes are around 400Ft. We love the funny old murals of Pest in the days of yore.

THE JEWS OF BUDAPEST

Jews have lived in Hungary since the 9th century AD; Budapest's large Jewish community in particular steadily contributed to Hungary's scholarly, artistic and commercial progress. After WWI, from which Hungary emerged the loser, Jews were blamed for the economic depression that followed and the territories lost. In 1920 the notorious Numerus Clausus legislation came into play, limiting to 5% the number of Jewish students admitted to universities. Jews fared better in Hungary in the lead-up to WWII than in other eastern European countries, despite Hungary being Germany's ally, but pressure was put on the Hungarian government to adopt Jewish laws (based on the Nazi Nuremberg laws) in 1938, 1940 and 1941, which progressively stripped Jews of property rights, the right to belong to various professions and even to have sexual intercourse with non-Jews.

Following Hungary's occupation by German forces in March 1944, Jews were forced to wear a yellow star of David and their movement within the city was severely restricted. In July 1944 about 200,000 Jews were moved into 2000 homes within Erzsébetváros, which became the main ghetto. Though more than 15,000 Budapest Jews had already died before the German occupation – worked to death in labour camps or as service personnel accompanying Hungarian troops – they had managed to avoid mass deportation. Then, just 10 months before the end of the war, about half of Budapest's Jewish population was sent to Auschwitz and other camps. At the same time, agents of neutral states were working to save Jews by moving them into protected houses within Budapest. Nevertheless, the gangs of the fascist Arrow Cross Party, in power from mid-October 1944, roamed the city in search of Jews, killing them indiscriminately.

Soviet troops liberated the two ghettos in Budapest on 16 January 1945. When other Jews returned from labour camps and came out of hiding, it transpired that the prewar Jewish population of Hungary (about 750,000) had been reduced by about two thirds. Still, Budapest Jews fared better than their brethren in the provinces, who were almost all deported to the camps. The Jewish population further dwindled after the war, due to emigration, but there has been a renaissance of Jewish culture and music in Budapest since the fall of the Iron Curtain. The **Jewish Summer Festival** (www.zsidonyarifesztival.hu) is a week of music, exhibitions, cuisine and more, with a number of events held at the Great Synagogue (p117). Other important Jewish sites include the Holocaust Memorial Center (p117) and the traditional Jewish businesses that survive in Erzsébetváros, where you can also find a number of kosher restaurants.

But while there has been a revival of Jewish culture in Budapest, there has also been a resurgence of openly expressed anti-Semitism. In November 2012, Márton Gyöngyösi, an MP for the far-right Jobbik party, called for the government to compile a national list of Hungarian Jews, especially Jewish government members, whom he described as a 'national security risk' for alleged solidarity with Israel. The outrage caused by this remark led the leaders of the right-wing, centre and left-wing parties to address a demonstration against anti-Semitism in front of the Parliament building, pledging their support for the Jewish community. Viktor Orbán, the prime minister, stated that the remark was 'unworthy of Hungary'. The party's stances remain popular with voters, though: Jobbik polled 20% of the vote in the April 2014 parliamentary election.

FALAFEL FALODA VEGETARIAN, MIDDLE EASTERN **$**
Map p250 (⌨1-351 1243; VI Paulay Ede utca 53; salad bowls 830-1080Ft, felafel 910Ft; ⊙10am-8pm Mon-Fri, to 6pm Sat; ⌨; Ⓜ️M1 Oktogon) This inexpensive place just south of Budapest's theatre district has Israeli-style nosh. You pay a fixed price to stuff a piece of pita bread or fill a plastic container from a great assortment of salads. It also has a good variety of soups. Loft seating above.

CARIMAMA KOSHER, PIZZERIA **$**
Map p250 (www.carimama.hu; VI Kazinczy utca 28; pizzas 2000-3000Ft; ⊙8am-8pm Sun-Thu, 7am-2hr before Shabbat Fri; Ⓜ️M2 Astoria) A lit-

tle cafe that will ply you with kosher pizza, baked goods and also breakfast.

★MACESZ HUSZÁR
JEWISH, HUNGARIAN $$

Map p250 (⌕1-787 6164; www.maceszhuszar.hu; VII Dob utca 26; mains 1990-5190Ft; ⊙11.30am-midnight; M1/2/2 Deák Ferenc tér) A wonderful marriage of modern and traditional, the Macesz Huszár serves up Hungarian Jewish dishes in a swish bistro-style dining room, handsomely dressed up with lace tablecloths, flock wallpaper and rocking horses. The Jewish-style eggs and matzo-ball soup are standout starters, and goose and duck feature heavily on the list of excellent mains.

★ZELLER BISTRO
HUNGARIAN $$

Map p250 (⌕06 30 651 0880; www.facebook.com/pages/Zeller-Bistro/486188564780604; VII Izabella utca 38; mains 2000-4900Ft; ⊙noon-3pm & 6-11pm Tue-Sat; 🖥; M1 Vörösmarty utca, ⛢4,6) You'll receive a very warm welcome at this gorgeous candle-lit cellar where the attentive staff serves food sourced largely from the owner's family and friends in the area around Lake Balaton. The Hungarian home cooking includes some first-rate dishes such as grey beef, duck leg and beef cheeks. Popular with an international crowd; reservations essential.

M RESTAURANT
HUNGARIAN $$

Map p250 (⌕1-322 3108; metterem.hu; VII Kertész utca 48; mains 2100-3400Ft; ⊙6pm-midnight; 🖥; M1 Oktogon, ⛢4, 6) Small, romantic spot with laid-back vibe and a short menu of Hungarian dishes with a French twist.

KŐLEVES
INTERNATIONAL $$

Map p250 (⌕06 20 213 5999; www.koleves vendeglo.hu; VII Kazinczy utca 37-41; mains 1750-3600Ft; ⊙8am-1am Mon-Fri, from 9am Sat & Sun; 🖥; M1/2/3 Deák Ferenc tér) Always buzzy and lots of fun, the 'Stone Soup' attracts a young crowd with its international menu, lively decor and reasonable prices. Great vegetarian choices. Breakfast (790Ft to 1090Ft) is served from 8am to 11.30am.

SPINOZA CAFÉ
HUNGARIAN $$

Map p250 (⌕1-413 7488; www.spinozacafe.hu; VII Dob utca 15; mains 1850-4350Ft; ⊙8am-midnight; 🖥🍴; M2 Astoria) This attractive cafe-restaurant includes an art gallery and theatre, where *klezmer* (traditional Jewish music) concerts are staged at 7pm on Friday, along with a coffee house and restaurant where there's live piano music nightly.

The food is mostly Hungarian/Jewish comfort food, not kosher, but no pork. The €5 breakfast is a steal.

NAPFÉNYES ÍZEK
VEGETARIAN $$

Map p250 (⌕06 20 313 5555; www.napfenyeset-terem.hu; VII Rózsa utca 39; mains 1700-3800Ft; ⊙noon-10.30pm; 🖥🍴; M1 Kodály körönd) 'Sunny Tastes' is a titch out of the way (though not if you're staying on or near Andrássy út), but the friendly welcome, cute cellar space and wholesome vegan foods are worth the trip. There is an organic shop where you can stock up on both packaged and baked goods, including excellent cakes.

CARMEL PINCE
KOSHER $$

Map p250 (⌕1-322 1834; www.carmel.hu; VII Kazinczy utca 31; mains 3800-6600Ft; ⊙noon-11pm Sun-Thu, to 2pm Fri, noon-2pm & 6-11pm Sat; 🖥🍴; M2 Astoria, ⛢47, 49) Carmel, a glatt kosher eatery, offers authentic Ashkenazi specialities such as gefilte fish, matzo-ball soup and a *cholent* (hearty brisket and bean casserole) that's almost as good as the one Aunt Goldie used to make. Pre-paid Shabbat dinner service is available Friday evening and Saturday lunch.

HANNA
JEWISH, KOSHER $$

Map p250 (⌕1-342 1072; VII Dob utca 35; mains 2800-3300Ft; ⊙8am-10pm Sun-Fri, 11am-2pm Sat; ⛢4, 6) Housed upstairs in an old school in the Orthodox Synagogue complex, this eatery is pretty basic, but if you answer to a Higher Authority on matters culinary it is another option for kosher food. On Shabbat you order and pay for meals in advance. Set three-course menu is 5300Ft.

BOCK BISZTRÓ
HUNGARIAN $$$

Map p250 (⌕1-321 0340; www.bockbisztropest.hu; VII Erzsébet körút 43-49; mains 3700-7400Ft; ⊙noon-midnight Mon-Sat; 🖥; M1 Oktogon, ⛢4, 6) An elegant and upmarket place to try a good range of traditional Hungarian delicacies and wines from around the country. It's formal but not stuffy, with helpful, friendly service and well-prepared dishes. Reservations recommended. There's also a branch (p80) in the Buda Hills.

FAUSTO'S
ITALIAN $$$

Map p250 (⌕1-269 6806; www.fausto.hu; VII Dohány utca 3; mains osteria 2400-4800Ft, restaurant 3600-15,200Ft; ⊙noon-11pm Mon-Sat; 🖥; M2 Astoria) Elegant Fausto's offers a top-class dining room and a cheaper osteria just around the corner from the Great Synagogue. It does brilliant pasta dishes, daily specials and desserts. There's also a well-chosen selection of Italian and Hungarian wine. Two-course lunches in the osteria (2900Ft) or three-course in the restaurant (5000Ft) are a better-value way to dine here.

✗ Andrássy út & Terézváros (East)

RING CAFE   BURGERS $
Map p244 (☏1-331 5790; www.ringcafe.hu; VI Andrássy út 38; burgers 1650-2790Ft; ◷10am-midnight Mon-Sat, to 10pm Sun; ☏; ⓜM1 Oktogon) Excellent burgers, with lots of different varieties, in this small, modern joint that also does snacks, salads, sandwiches, and breakfast till 1pm.

MENZA   HUNGARIAN $$
Map p250 (☏1-413 1482; www.menzaetterem.hu; VI Liszt Ferenc tér 2; mains 2390-4690Ft; ☏; ⓜM1 Oktogon) This stylish restaurant on one of Budapest's more lively squares takes its name from the Hungarian for a drab school canteen – something it is anything but. It's always packed with diners, who come for its simple but well-prepared Hungarian classics with a modern twist, in trendy, mid-century-styled dining rooms. Weekday two-course set lunches are 1090Ft; reservations recommended.

BIGFISH   FISH $$
Map p244 (☏1-269 0693; www.facebook.com/thebigfish.hu; VI Andrássy út 44; fish market prices, sides 570Ft, other mains 890-3890Ft; ◷noon-10pm; ☏; ⓜM1 Oktogon) Select your type and cooking method at the glass counter, choose a side, and then sit back and wait for super-fresh fish and shellfish to be delivered to your table. This simply decorated restaurant has plenty of tables inside, as well as along busy Andrássy út. And there are bibs for you messy eaters. Pasta and rice dishes also available.

CIRCUS   HUNGARIAN $$
Map p250 (☏1-413 6764; www.facebook.com/circusbarbp; VI Liszt Ferenc tér 11; mains 1890-3800Ft; ◷11am-midnight; ☏; ⓜM1 Oktogon) One of the more interesting choices on Liszt Ferenc tér, colourful Circus, decorated appropriately with big game, serves traditional Hungarian dishes with some inter-national touches. It also serves cocktails and coffee and is a fun option on the sunny side of this square.

KLASSZ   INTERNATIONAL $$
Map p250 (www.klasszetterem.hu; VI Andrássy út 41; mains 1890-5490Ft; ◷11.30am-11pm; ☏; ⓜM1 Oktogon) Owned by the local wine society, Klassz is mostly about wine – Hungarian, to be precise – and here you can order by the 0.1L measure from an ever-changing list of up to four dozen wines to sip and compare. The food is of a very high standard. Reservations are not accepted; just show up and wait. Permanent fixtures on the menu include foie gras in its various avatars and native *mangalica* (a breed of pig) pork, and there are also more unusual (and fleeting) dishes like *blanquette de veau* (veal stew) and lamb and vegetable ragout.

🍺 DRINKING & NIGHTLIFE

🍷 Erzsébetváros

MIKA TIVADAR MULATÓ   GARDEN CLUB
Map p250 (www.mikativadarmulato.hu; VII Kazinczy utca 47; ◷5pm-midnight Sun-Wed, to 6am Thu-Sat; ☏; ⓜM1/2/3 Deák Ferenc tér) This grand, erstwhile copper factory dating from 1907 now sports a chilled ground-floor bar, a small venue downstairs and a fantastic garden, complete with a rowing boat. DJs and live music (all sorts, including jazz, swing, punk and funk) run most nights. And that's glass in the loos, not a mirror.

LOKÁL   RUIN PUB
Map p250 (www.lokalbar.hu; VII Dob utca 18; ◷5pm-midnight Mon-Wed, to 4am Thu-Sat; ☏; ⓜM1/2/3 Deák Ferenc tér) A convivial ruin pub offering a variety of distractions – from the escape game in the basement to the upstairs swing bar and, dangerously, a tattoo parlour. The less adventurous can rifle through its fancy-dress shop or enjoy a drink in the garden or ground-floor bar.

DOBLO   WINE BAR
Map p250 (www.budapestwine.com; VII Dob utca 20; ◷10am-2am Mon-Fri, 5pm-3am Sat, 5pm-1am Sun; ☏; ⓜM1/2/3 Deák Ferenc tér) Brick lined and candlelit, Doblo is where you go to

ANDRÁS TÖRÖK'S TOP SPOTS

András Török is the author of the cult *Budapest: A Critical Guide*, still going strong after eight editions. We asked him to share some of his favourite eateries.

I love **Olimpia** (p150) – a tiny place, only for 20 people or so, always packed – and the chef is always coming up with something creative. **Klassz** (p124) is one of my favourite wine restaurants, but I also like the newly opened **Bordó Bisztró** (p105). I love **Café Zsivagó** (p129), a cafe with a Russian slant, as you would expect. But to really get away from the hustle and bustle of the city I head for **Művész Kávéház** (p129) early, at 9am when it has just opened and there's no one else there.

taste Hungarian wines, with scores available by the 1.5cL glass for 800Ft to 1650Ft. There's food too, such as salads, sandwiches and mixed platters of meat or cheese.

COXX MEN'S BAR
GAY

Map p250 (www.coxx.hu; VII Dohány utca 38; ☺9pm-4am Sun-Thu, to 5am Fri & Sat; ☎; Ⓜ M2 Blaha Lujza tér, 🚊4, 6) Probably the cruisiest gayme in town, this place with the in-your-face name has 400 sq metres of hunting ground, three bars and some significant play areas in back. Don't bring sunglasses.

KISÜZEM
BAR

Map p250 (www.facebook.com/Kisuzem; VII Kis Diófa utca 2; ☺noon-2am Mon-Wed & Sun, to 3am Thu-Sat; ☎; 🚊4, 6) Plants adorn the bare-brick interior of this relaxed corner bar with a bohemian vibe. A mixed-age crowd mingles at the bar or on the pavement outside, or chats at the tables ranged around the interior. It hosts sporadic live music such as jazz, folk and experimental, and serves bar food and locally roasted coffee.

BOUTIQ' BAR
COCKTAIL BAR

Map p250 (☏06 30 229 1821; www.boutiqbar.hu; V Paulay Ede utca 5; ☺6pm-2am Tue-Sat; Ⓜ M1 Bajcsy-Zsilinszky utca) Low-lit 'speakeasy' serving expertly mixed cocktails using fresh juices and an educated selection of craft spirits. For something specifically Hungarian, try a creation that includes Tokaji wine or *pálinka* (fruit brandy). Charming service; reservations advised.

FEKETE KUTYA
BAR

Map p250 (Black Dog; www.facebook.com/feketekutja; VII Dob utca 31; ☺5pm-2am Mon-Sat, to midnight Sun; ☎; Ⓜ M1/2/3 Deák Ferenc tér) A small bar, popular with a loyal, local crowd who come to play chess, chat and drink craft beer in a casual setting.

GMK
CLUB

Map p250 (Gozsdu Manó Klub; www.gozsdu-mano.hu; cnr Madách Imre út & Gozdu udvar; ☺4pm-2am Mon-Wed & Sun, to 5am Thu-Sat; ☎; Ⓜ M1/2/3 Deák Ferenc tér) There's an upstairs bar and restaurant here, but the real draw is the basement club, which puts on excellent live music and DJs in a cavernous space with a quality sound system, an unpretentious vibe and a devoted local following.

SZIMPLA KERT
RUIN PUB

Map p250 (www.szimpla.hu; VII Kazinczy utca 14; ☺noon-3am; ☎; Ⓜ M2 Astoria) Budapest's first *romkocsma* (ruin pub), Szimpla Kert is firmly on the drinking-tourists' trail (you can even buy a T-shirt) but remains a landmark place for a drink. It's a huge building with nooks filled with bric-a-brac, grafitti, art and all manner of unexpected items. Sit in an old Trabant, watch open-air cinema, down shots or join in an acoustic jam session.

VITTULA
BAR

Map p250 (www.vittula.hu; VII Kertész utca 4; ☺6pm-whenever; ☎; Ⓜ M2 Blaha Lujza tér, 🚊4, 6) Great studenty cellar bar covered in graffiti, where hedonistic folk and bearded men drink late into the night accompanied by alternative music and plenty of fun.

MOZAIK
TEAHOUSE

Map p250 (mozaikteahaz.hu; VI Király utca 18; ☺10am-10.30pm; ☎; Ⓜ M1/2/3 Deák Ferenc tér) A calm little teahouse on a busy street, with a lovely upper level where you can grab a piece of chalk and leave your mark while you sup on the 120 types of tea on offer. Booze and cakes available too.

FRÖHLICH CUKRÁSZDA
CAFE

Map p250 (www.frohlich.hu; VII Dob utca 22; ☺9am-6pm Mon-Thu, to 2pm Fri, 10am-6pm Sun; Ⓜ M1/2/3 Deák Ferenc tér) This kosher cake shop and cafe in the former ghetto, dating back to 1953, makes and sells old Jewish favourites (230Ft to 450Ft) such as *flódni* (a scrumptious three-layer cake with apple, walnut and poppy-seed fillings) as well as holiday sweets. For Purim there is *kindli* (cookies with nuts or poppy seeds) and *hamentaschen* ('pocket' biscuits filled with nuts and poppy seeds or apricot jam) and for Rosh Hashanah, *lekach* (honey and nut pastry).

SZIMPLA
BAR

Map p250 (www.szimpla.hu; VII Kertész utca 48; ☉10am-2am Mon-Fri, from noon Sat, 4pm-midnight Sun; 🖥; ⓂM1 Oktogon, 🚋4, 6) Part of the Szimpla family of establishments, this small, relaxed cafe serves cocktails, craft beer and coffee, as well as food, to a low-key, boho crowd.

ELLÁTÓ KERT
RUIN PUB

Map p250 (www.facebook.com/ellato.kert; VII Kazinczy utca 48; ☉5pm-4am; 🖥; ⓂM1/2/3 Deák Ferenc tér) A perenially popular, huge ruin pub, ranged over a number of rooms full of plants and paper lanterns. Ping-pong, billiards, darts, table football and Mexican munchies keep everyone amused.

CSAK A JÓ SÖR
BAR

Map p250 (www.csakajosor.hu; VII Kertész utca 42-44; ☉2-9pm Mon-Sat; ⓂM1 Oktogon, 🚋4, 6) True to its name (which translates as 'only good beer'), the shelves of this tiny shop are stacked high with brown bottles containing an extensive selection of international bottled craft beer. About six beers are usually also available on draught, including the owner's own quality brews.

GIERO
BAR

Map p250 (VI Paulay Ede utca 58; ☉10am-late; ⓂM1 Oktogon) This basement bar (mind your head on the way in) is the place to come to listen to Gypsy music, as Roma musicians play it here when they're off duty from playing saccharine junk at top-end hotels. Expect a warm welcome but no frills.

MY LITTLE MELBOURNE
CAFE

Map p250 (www.facebook.com/MyLittleMelbourneEspressoBar; Madách Imre út 3; ☉7am-7pm Mon-Fri, 9am-6pm Sat & Sun; 🖥; ⓂM1/2/3 Deák Ferenc tér) A Budapest couple who fell in love with Melbourne have come home to re-create a little slice of Australia in Erzsébetváros. With carefully chosen coffee from London (Workshop) and Italy (dansi), they

serve a mean flat white, as well as pastries and other goodies – including, appropriately, lamingtons (Australian cakes) – in this tiny space over two floors.

KADARKA
WINE BAR

Map p250 (www.facebook.com/kadarkabar; VII Király utca 42; ☉4pm-midnight; 🖥; ⓂM1 Opera) A buzzy, modern wine bar that serves a dizzying array of varieties, in a range of volumes, to suit all appetites and tastes. The staff are on hand to advise on the list, as well as the great selection of *pálinka*.

ANKER'T
RUIN PUB

Map p250 (www.ankert.hu; VI Paulay Ede utca 33; ☉4pm-2am Mon-Wed & Sun, to 4am Thu-Sat; 🖥; ⓂM1 Opera) Sister bar to the Anker Klub (p127), this achingly cool, grown-up ruin pub has a monochrome decor and lighting that sets off the impressive surrounds to great effect. There's a vast garden, numerous bars, food, a long drinks list, DJs and live music.

TELEP
BAR

Map p250 (www.facebook.com/TelepGaleria; VII Madách Imre út 8; ☉noon-2am Mon-Fri, from 4pm Sat; 🖥; ⓂM1/2/3 Deák Ferenc tér) A small art gallery and exhibition space that also holds gigs and hosts DJs, this hipster haunt is steps away from busy Gozsdu udvar on a pedestrian street, where drinkers hang out late into the evening.

CASTRO BISZTRÓ
CAFE, BAR

Map p250 (www.castrobistro.tumblr.com; VII Madách Imre tér 3; ☉11am-midnight Sun-Thu, noon-1am Fri & Sat; 🖥; ⓂM1/2/3 Deák Ferenc tér) This eclectic place just off the Little Ring Rd has a mixed clientele, Serbian finger food like *ćevapčiči* (spicy meatballs; 1100Ft to 2400Ft) and tasty *pljeskavica* (spicy meat patties; 1390Ft), and a chilled vibe.

KUPLUNG
RUIN PUB

Map p250 (kuplungbp.tumblr.com; VI Király utca 46; ☉5pm-4am Mon-Sat, 6pm-4am Sun; 🖥; ⓂM1 Opera) Grease monkeys, ahoy! The 'Klutch' is a former garage, gritty and grimy on the outside and one of the most happening places in town. Expect DJs, live acts and, for the more dextrous among the audience, table tennis and table football.

FOGAS HÁZ
RUIN PUB

Map p250 (www.fogashaz.hu; VII Akácfa utca 51; ☉4pm-4am; 🖥; 🚋4, 6) This huge tree-filled complex hides a warren of good times, including art, film clubs, workshops, live music and nightly DJs. There is plenty of indoor space for inclement weather and you can always climb the stairs to club Lärm for something harder.

LÄRM
CLUB

Map p250 (www.larmbudapest.tumblr.com; VII Akácfa utca 51; ☺11pm-6am Fri & Sat Sep-Mar; ☎; ⌂4, 6) Intimate club, with two small bars, overlooking the courtyard of Fogas Ház (p126), dedicated to quality electronic music.

KŐLEVES KERT
GARDEN CLUB

Map p250 (www.kolevesvendeglo.hu; VII Kazinczy utca 37-41; ☺noon-1am Sun-Wed, to 2am Thu-Sat May-Sep; ☎; MM1/2/3 Deák Ferenc tér) Lie back in a hammock at this large, brightly decorated garden club, popular with diners from parent restaurant Kőleves (p123) next door.

NEW YORK CAFÉ
CAFE

Map p250 (www.newyorkcafe.hu; VII Erzsébet körút 9-11; ☺9am-midnight; ☎; MM2 Blaha Lujza tér, ⌂4, 6) Considered the most beautiful in the world when it opened in 1894, this Renaissance-style place has been the scene of many a literary gathering. It has now been extensively renovated but lacks the warmth and erudite crowd of most traditional cafes. Still, the opulence and the history will impress and it's a great place for breakfast (2300Ft to 10,500Ft; 9am to 11am).

400 BAR
BAR

Map p250 (www.400bar.hu; VII Kazinczy utca 52; ☺11am-2am Sun-Wed, to 4am Thu-Sat; ☎; MM1/2/3 Deák Ferenc tér) One of the most popular cafe-bars in Pest, the 'Négyszáz' is a big space, with outside seating in a no-car zone. Come just to relax over a drink, or try the daily lunch menu (890Ft).

LÉHŰTŐ
BAR

Map p250 (www.facebook.com/lehuto.kezmuvessorozo; VII Holló utca 12-14; ☺4pm-midnight Mon, Tue & Sun, to 2am Wed-Thu, to 4am Fri & Sat; ☎; MM1/2/3 Deák Ferenc tér) Drop into this friendly basement bar if you fancy a craft beer, of which it does a large Hungarian and international range, with staff willing to advise and let you try before you buy. There's also above-ground seating amid an often-buzzing crowd that gathers at this crossroads on warm nights.

LA BODEGUITA DEL MEDIO
BAR

Map p250 (www.labodeguitadelmedio.hu; VII Dob utca 55; ☺11am-1am Mon-Thu & Sun, to 3am Fri & Sat; ☎; ⌂4, 6) Anchor tenant of the Fészek Club, meeting place of artists and intellectuals since 1901, La Bodeguita del Medio is a Cuban restaurant whose major draw is the city's most beautiful courtyard, filled with trees and surrounded by tiled galleries – a wonderful place to sit and sip a cocktail.

ANKER KLUB
CLUB

Map p250 (www.ankerklub.hu; VI Anker köz 1-3; ☺11am-4am; ☎; MM1/2/3 Deák Ferenc tér) A cafe that turns into hipster hang-out in the evening, the Anker is spacious and minimalist and about as central as you'll find.

GRANDIO
GARDEN CLUB

Map p250 (www.grandiopartyhostel.com; VII Nagy Diófa utca 8; ☺midnight-3am; ☎; MM2 Blaha Lujza tér, ⌂4, 6) Large *kert* (outdoor garden club) in a courtyard below a party hostel. What sets Grandio apart are the hearty urban weeds that have taken back their share of space and created not a 'garden' but a 'forest club'. The big, long bar dispenses copious drinks to enthusiastic punters.

BLUE BIRD CAFE
CAFE

Map p250 (www.facebook.com/bluebirdcafehungary; VII Gozsdu udvar, Dob utca 16; ☺9am-10pm Mon-Thu, to midnight Fri-Sun; ☎; MM1/2/3 Deák Ferenc tér) Warmly decorated cafe on busy Gozsdu udvar with a small terrace, serving own-roast coffee, cakes and simple breakfasts, including crêpes, from 9.30am to 11am.

SPÍLER
CAFE, BAR

Map p250 (www.spilerbp.hu; VII Gozsdu udvar, Király utca 13; ☺8am-midnight Sun-Wed, to 2am Thu-Sat; ☎; MM1/2/3 Deák Ferenc tér) Big, bold and bustling bar on nightlife-central Gozsdu udvar, Spíler serves craft beer, wine and cocktails to an up-for-it crowd. Sit under the awnings on the jam-packed street or at one of the bars inside. Nightly DJs and a street-food menu too. Hop across the road for Asian-inspired food and drinks at sister branch **Spíler Shanghai** (Map p250; VII Gozsdu udvar, Király utca 13; ☎; MM1/2/3 Deák Ferenc tér).

ERZSÉBETVÁROS & THE JEWISH QUARTER DRINKING & NIGHTLIFE

ERZSÉBETVÁROS & THE JEWISH QUARTER

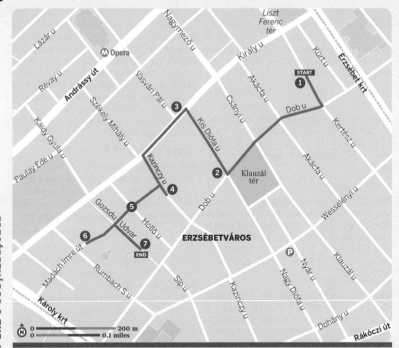

Local Life
A Night Out in Erzsébetváros

Wander along Király utca or down Gozsdu udvar on a Friday night and it can feel like the whole world is here. Jostling with wide-eyed tourists and hen and stag parties may leave you wondering whether the locals have deserted this area altogether. They haven't – you just need to know where to find them.

❶ Sample a Hungarian Craft Brew

Small but excellent Csak a jó sör (p126) closes early, so it's a good place to start your evening. Perch by the tiny bar and sample one of owner Armando Otchoa's most recent draught beers. There are usually about six on tap, or go for one of the many Hungarian or international craft beers stocked here (such as Brewdog, Mikkeller, Duvel) – shelves and shelves of bottles line the walls.

❷ Check Out a Little Local Bar

With your appetite whet, it's just a short hop to Kisüzem (p125), where relaxed drinkers hang out on the corner, chatting on the bar's little outside benches. Head inside for another beer or perhaps a shot of *pálinka* (fruit brandy), grab a table if you can and check out what live music is on the agenda.

❸ Taste Some Hungarian Wine

On bustling Király utca, Kadarka (p126) offers a huge list of Hungarian wines in a modern, sociable bar. Take a table on the street for a spot of people-watching, or settle on a tall bar stool inside and ask for some advice from the ever-helpful experts who'll serve you.

❹ Hang Out in a Garden Club

Just around the corner, the grand facade of Mika Tivadar Mulató (p124) stands out from a strip of garden clubs. Inside this former copper factory you'll find a purple-and-gold ground-floor bar and live music in the small downstairs venue. In the fairy-lit garden, take a seat in the boat and enjoy a drink.

❺ Stroll a Nightlife Street

Just across the road, Madách Imre út is usually packed with drinkers and street-food

Vittula (p124)

fans. Numerous bars line the pedestrian alley, but locals favour 400 Bar (p127), where you can grab a bite to eat if you're starting to get peckish. Further along, Léhűtő (p127) is another great spot for a craft beer or two. Just up from here, packed Gozsdu udvar heaves at night with locals and tourists alike.

❻ Listen to Some Live Music

If you cross Gozsdu udvar and keep on Madách Imre út, you'll emerge at a more low-key hang-out, where local 20-somethings make for Telep (p126), an exhibition space and art gallery, wall-papered with stickers and hosting nightly live music or DJs. If the weather's warm, the street will be filled with folk hanging out on the pavement with a beer.

❼ Head to a Club

If you're ready to ramp things up a bit, head back towards Gozsdu udvar, where the basement club at GMK (p125) has an excellent sound system and a good reputation for quality DJs and live music. For something more retro, skip down the passage to Lokál (p124), nip upstairs and throw yourself into a swing session. If you really want to make it a trip to remember, you could always get inked in its on-site tattoo parlour.

🍷 Andrássy út & Terézváros (East)

ALEXANDRA BOOK CAFE
CAFE

Map p250 (www.parisi.hu; VI Andrassy út 39; ⊙10am-10pm; 🛜; M M1 Opera, 🚌4, 6) Inside one of Budapest's best bookshops, this glitzy cafe in the revamped Ceremonial Hall shows off Károly Lotz frescoes and other wonderful touches of opulence. Great spot for a light lunch or coffee pre- or post-browse.

CAFÉ ZSIVÁGÓ
CAFE, BAR

Map p250 (www.cafezsivago.hu; VI Paulay Ede utca 55; ⊙10am-midnight Mon-Fri, from noon Sat, 2-10pm Sun; 🛜; M M1 Oktogon, 🚌4, 6) A little Russian living room with lace tablecloths, wooden dressers, mismatched tea sets, hat stands and vintage lamps provides a relaxing daytime coffee stop that morphs into a jumping bar at night offering cocktails, champagne and vodka. If you can, bag the little alcove upstairs.

MŰVÉSZ KÁVÉHÁZ
CAFE

Map p250 (Artist Coffeehouse; www.muvesz-kavehaz.hu; VI Andrássy út 29; cakes 690-890Ft; ⊙9am-10pm Mon-Sat, 10am-10pm Sun; 🛜; M M1 Opera) Almost opposite the Hungarian State Opera House, the Artist Coffeehouse is an interesting place to people-watch (especially from the shady terrace), though some say its cakes (690Ft to 890Ft) are not what they used to be (though presumably they're not thinking as far back as 1898, when the cafe opened).

ECOCAFE
CAFE

Map p250 (www.ecocafe.hu; VI Andrássy út 68; ⊙7am-8pm Mon-Fri, from 8am Sat & Sun; 🛜; M M1 Vörösmaty utca) A welcome stop along Andrássy út, this simple cafe serves great coffee alongside smoothies, juices, teas, sandwiches and cakes, which are almost all organic. There's also a salad bar (1090Ft), and tables on the pavement outside.

☆ ENTERTAINMENT

LISZT ACADEMY
CLASSICAL MUSIC

Map p250 (Liszt Zeneakadémia; 📞1-321 0690; www.zeneakademia.hu; VI Liszt Ferenc tér 8; ⊙ticket office 11am-6pm; M M1 Oktogon) Budapest's most important concert hall has recently emerged from extensive renovations and is looking more fantastic than ever. Performances are usually booked up at least a week in advance, but (expensive) last-minute tickets can sometimes be available – it's always worth checking.

HUNGARIAN STATE OPERA HOUSE OPERA
Map p244 (Magyar Állami Operaház; ✍box office 1-353 0170; www.opera.hu; VI Andrássy út 22; ⊙box office 11am-5pm Mon-Sat, from 4pm Sun; Ⓜ M1 Opera) The gorgeous neo-Renaissance opera house is worth a visit as much to admire the incredibly rich decoration inside as to view a performance and hear the perfect acoustics.

GÖDÖR LIVE MUSIC
Map p250 (www.godorklub.hu; VII Király utca 8-10; ☎; Ⓜ M1/2/3 Deák Ferenc tér) Having moved to a new location, Gödör has maintained its reputation for scheduling an excellent variety of indie, rock, jazz, electronic and experimental music, as well as hosting quality club nights in its spare, industrial space.

BETHLEN SQUARE THEATRE DANCE
Map p250 (Bethlen Téri Színház; ✍1-342 7163; www.bethlenszinhaz.hu; VII Bethlen Gábor tér 3; tickets from 500Ft; Ⓜ M2/4 Keleti pályaudvar) This small and atmospheric theatre puts on drama, dance and puppet shows, as well as stand-up comedy (if your Hungarian's up to it). Also has a cafe and gallery. Enter from VII István út 4.

LADÓ CAFÉ LIVE MUSIC, DANCE
Map p250 (www.ladocafe.hu; VII Dohány utca 50; ⊙8am-11.30pm; ☎; Ⓜ M2 Blaha Lujza tér) An unassuming place by day with decent food and excellent service, the Ladó comes into its own at night when it hosts live entertainment – everything from folk music and jazz to opera and tango.

OLD MAN'S MUSIC PUB LIVE MUSIC
Map p250 (✍1-322 7645; www.oldmans.hu; VII Akácfa utca 13; ⊙4.30pm-4am; ☎; Ⓜ M2 Blaha Lujza tér) Jazz and blues, plus swing, folk-rock and acoustic – this fab basement venue has live music nightly. DJs then take over and dancing continues till dawn.

ÖRÖKMOZGÓ CINEMA
Map p250 (✍1-342 2167; www.filmarchive.hu/ orokmozgo/program; VII Erzsébet körút 39; ☐4, 6) Part of the Hungarian Film Institute, this cinema (whose mouthful of a name vaguely translates as 'moving picture') screens an excellent assortment of foreign classic films in their original languages.

BUDAPEST PUPPET THEATRE THEATRE
Map p250 (Budapest Bábszínház; ✍bookings 1-342 2702; www.budapest-babszinhaz.hu; VI Andrássy út 69; ♿; Ⓜ M1 Vörösmarty utca) The city's puppet theatre, which usually doesn't require fluency in Hungarian, presents a variety of shows for children.

SHOPPING

🔒 Erzsébetváros

MASSOLIT BOOKS
Map p250 (www.facebook.com/MassolitBudapest; VII Nagy Diófa utca 30; ⊙10am-8pm Mon-Sat, from noon Sun; ☎; Ⓜ M2 Astoria) Branch of the celebrated bookshop in Kraków, Poland, Massolit is one of Budapest's best, with new and secondhand English-language fiction and nonfiction, including Hungarian history and literature in translation. It has a beautiful shady garden and tables set among the shelves, so you can enjoy coffee, sandwiches, cakes and bagels as you browse the volumes.

PRINTA CRAFT, CLOTHING
Map p250 (www.printa.hu; VII Rumbach Sebestyén utca 10; ⊙11am-7pm Mon-Fri, noon-6pm Sat; Ⓜ M1/2/3 Deák Ferenc tér) This wonderful, hip silkscreen studio, design shop and gallery focuses on local talent: bags, leather goods, prints, T-shirts, stationery and jewellery. Also serves great (Has Bean) coffee.

GOUBA MARKET
Map p250 (www.gouba.hu; VII Gozsdu udvar; ⊙10am-7pm Sun; Ⓜ M1/2/3 Deák Ferenc tér) Weekly arts and crafts market lining Gozsdu udvar, where you can pick up some interesting pieces from local artists and designers. A great place to shop for souvenirs.

SZIMPLA FARMERS' MARKET MARKET
Map p250 (www.szimpla.hu/szimpla-market; VII Kazinczy utca 14; ⊙9am-2pm Sun; ☎; Ⓜ M2 Astoria) Every Sunday, Szimpla Kert (p125) holds a charming farmers' market where you can buy all manner of locally produced jam, honey, yoghurt, cheese and bread. Also

available are paprika, vegetables, fruit, cured meat and fruit juice. Grab a coffee from the courtyard while you browse.

TISZA CIPŐ
SHOES

Map p250 (www.tiszacipo.hu; VII Károly körút 1; ☺10am-7pm Mon-Fri, to 4pm Sat; Ⓜ M2 Astoria) 'What goes around comes around', the old saying tells us, and that's certainly true of Tisza Shoes, which has metamorphosed from Communist-era producer of forgettable footwear ('since 1971') to trendy trainer manufacturer.

LUDOVIKA
FASHION, ACCESSORIES

Map p250 (www.facebook.com/ludovikashop; VII Rumbach Sebestyén utca 15; ☺noon-8pm Mon-Fri, to 6pm Sat; Ⓜ M1/2/3 Deák Ferenc tér) Small vintage clothes shop stocking carefully selected pieces for women from a range of eras over two floors. Great handbags.

RETROCK
FASHION, ACCESSORIES

Map p250 (www.retrock.com; VI Anker köz 2; ☺11am-9pm Mon-Fri, to 8pm Sat & Sun; Ⓜ M1/2/3 Deák Ferenc tér) Large, hip store with a vast collection of vintage clothing, bags, jewellery and shoes, and a small line in Hungarian streetwear designers.

SZPUTNYIK
FASHION

Map p250 (www.szputnyikshop.hu; VII Dohány utca 20; ☺11am-8pm Mon-Fri, to 6pm Sat; Ⓜ M2 Astoria) A bright, open space, stuffed with vintage fashion (such as US college jackets and Converse trainers), plus a selection of new alternative lines from international designers.

LÁTOMÁS
FASHION, ACCESSORIES

Map p250 (www.latomas.hu; VII Dohány utca 16-18; ☺11am-7.30pm Mon-Fri, to 6pm Sat; Ⓜ M2 Astoria) One of a trio of shops selling fashionable ready-to-wear, jewellery, bags and shoes.

BILLERBECK
HOMEWARES

Map p250 (www.billerbeck.hu; VII Dob utca 49; ☺10am-7pm Mon-Fri, to 3pm Sat; 🚇4, 6) With several branches around town, Billerbeck has a large selection of feather- and goose-down duvets and other bedding sold by helpful staff. Enter from Akácfa utca. There's a **Király utca branch** (Map p250; VII Király utca 3; Ⓜ M1/2/3 Deák Ferenc tér) with the same hours.

🏛 Andrássy út & Terézváros (East)

ÍRÓK BOLTJA
BOOKS

Map p250 (Writers' Bookshop; www.irokboltja.hu; VI Andrássy út 45; ☺10am-7pm Mon-Fri, to 1pm Sat; Ⓜ M1 Oktogon) For Hungarian authors in translation the Writers' Bookshop is the place to go.

ALEXANDRA
BOOKS, WINE

Map p250 (www.alexandra.hu; VI Andrássy út 39; ☺10am-10pm; Ⓜ M1 Opera, 🚇4, 6) In what was originally opened as the Grande Parisienne department store in 1911, you'll now find a branch of the Alexandra bookstore chain. The foreign-language section is on the 1st floor, and there's a range of souvenirs and wine on the ground floor. Don't leave before checking out the fantastic cafe (p129).

LISZT FERENC ZENEMŰBOLT
MUSIC, BOOKS

Map p250 (Ferenc Liszt Music Shop; www.lisztbolt.hu; VI Andrássy út 45; ☺10am-7pm Mon-Fri, from 11am Sat; Ⓜ M1 Oktogon) The Ferenc Liszt Music Shop has mostly classical CDs as well as sheet music and books of local interest.

🏃 SPORTS & ACTIVITIES

CLAUSTROPHILIA
ESCAPE GAME

Map p250 (www.claustrophilia.hu; VII Erzsébet körút 8; per team 6000-10,000Ft; ☺10am-10pm; Ⓜ M2 Blaha Lujza tér, 🚇4, 6) Skillfully choreographed escape game that begins the moment you step through the entrance of this intricate set of puzzle rooms. Search through the treasures from Lord Wicklewood's travels to reveal the riddles required to unlock the final door. A second location offers the chance to save a voodoo priestess, and the world, from an evil sorcerer.

MINDQUEST
ESCAPE GAME

Map p250 (www.mindquest.hu; VII Klauzál utca 19; per team 6000-10,000Ft; ☺1pm-midnight; Ⓜ M2 Blaha Lujza tér, 🚇4, 6) Set above a ruin pub, MindQuest currently offers three escape rooms: a Cold War bomb to diffuse, a diamond to steal and a matrix to outwit, with more rooms in the works. Drop-ins are possible, although it's usually fully booked Friday to Sunday.

PETER ERIK FORSBERG / MARKETS / ALAMY ©

1. Rákóczi tér market (p143) **2.** Nagycsarnok (p143) **3.** Escéri Piac (p142) **4.** Art market in Gozsdu udvar

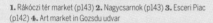

THEPURPLEDOOR / GETTY IMAGES ©

Budapest's Markets

From grand 19th-century food halls bursting with a rainbow of fruit and veg, rows of dangling cured meats and fresh-from-the-farm jams and honey, to Communist-era flea and cutting-edge design, Budapest's markets provide the perfect opportunity to see a slice of local life and bag some great souvenirs into the bargain.

Food Markets

The best place to soak up the sights, smells and sounds of a Budapest produce market is at the granddaddy of them all, **Nagycsarnok** (p143). This is the place to pick up some potted foie gras or paprika, or head upstairs for a whole world of Hungarian souvenirs. For something more low-key, try **Rákóczi tér** (p143) or the **Szimpla Farmers' Market** (p130), held in a ruin pub every Sunday.

Flea Markets

Jostling with locals shopping for bargains at **Ecseri Piac** (p142), one of Central Europe's largest flea markets, is a fabulous way to spend a Saturday morning. Lose yourself amid a cornucopia of gramophones, rocking horses, uniforms, violins and even suits of armour. If you can't make it here, the smaller **Pecsa Bolhapiac** (p153) offers a less impressive jumble of vintage knickknacks.

Design Markets

A regular fair that takes place roughly once a month, **WAMP** (p102; held in various locations throughout the city) showcases the latest of Hungary's hippest designers. Clothes, bags and jewellery are hung alongside artworks, prints and photos, and coffee and cakes sweeten the shopping. It's a great place to buy one-of-a-kind souvenirs you may not find in stores. More frequent **Gouba** (p130) offers a smaller selection of local arts and crafts.

Southern Pest

JÓZSEFVÁROS | FERENCVÁROS

Neighbourhood Top Five

1 Taking a trip through the near and distant past by wandering the corridors of the **Hungarian National Museum** (p136), the nation's treasure trove of historical artefacts.

2 Strolling through the **Nagycsarnok** (p143), southern Pest's well-endowed Great Market.

3 Admiring the art and architecture of the Art Nouveau **Museum of Applied Arts** (p138).

4 Testing your problem-solving skills at the city's first escape game, **Parapark** (p144).

5 Paying your respects to the permanent residents of **Kerepesi Cemetery** (p137).

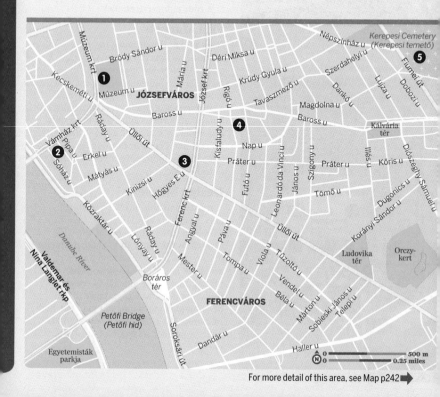

For more detail of this area, see Map p242

Explore: Southern Pest

From Blaha Lujza tér, named after a leading 19th-century stage actress and sheltering one of the liveliest subways in the city (with hustlers, beggars, peasants selling their wares, musicians and, of course, pickpockets), the Big Ring Rd runs through district VIII, also known as Józsefváros (Joseph Town). The western side of Józsefváros transforms itself from a neighbourhood of lovely 19th-century town houses and villas around the Little Ring Rd to a large student quarter. East of the boulevard is the once rough-and-tumble district so poignantly described in the Pressburger brothers' *Homage to the Eighth District,* and where much of the fighting in October 1956 took place. The neighbourhood south of Üllői út is Ferencváros (Francis Town), home to the city's most popular football team, Ferencvárosi Torna Club (FTC), and many of its tough, green-and-white-clad supporters.

Both are ever-changing and developing areas of the city, with new shops, bars and restaurants popping up constantly. Some quarters feel less salubrious than other places in the city, but it's full of interesting and alternative spots – try Mikszáth Kálmán tér, Tűzoltó utca or Ráday utca.

Local Life

➡ **Market** It might attract tourists in droves, but the Nagycsarnok (p143) is always a hive of activity and a great place for one-stop shopping.

➡ **Museum** The cutting-edge Ludwig Museum of Contemporary Art (p138) hosts excellent temporary exhibitions.

➡ **Classical Music** The Béla Bartók National Concert Hall (p142) at the Palace of Arts is reputed to have the best acoustics in Budapest.

➡ **Alfresco clubs** Two excellent venues here allow for some serious time with your hands in the (open) air.

Getting There & Away

➡**Metro** The red M2 line runs along the northern border of Józsefváros, while the blue M3 line serves points in Ferencváros. The green M4 line now handily connects Fővám tér with Keleti pályaudvar. Key stops include Blaha Lujza tér and Keleti pályaudvar on the M2, Corvin-negyed on the M3, Rákóczi tér on the M4, and Kálvin tér, where the M3 and M4 intersect.

➡**Tram** Both districts are served by trams 47 and 49, and further east by trams 4 and 6.

Lonely Planet's Top Tip

Southern Pest is made up of two fascinating, traditionally working-class districts – Józsefváros and Ferencváros. A good way to tackle this vast area is to pick a major sight and then spend some time wandering in the nearby streets. Start with the Hungarian National Museum (p136) and then mosey round Gutenberg, Rákóczi and Mikszáth Kálmán térs, or head to the Museum of Applied Arts (p138) and then take in the streets that stretch out to the Danube.

✖ Best Places to Eat

➡ Múzeum (p140)
➡ Rosenstein (p140)
➡ Építész Pince (p139)
➡ Petrus (p141)

For reviews, see p139

🍷 Best Places to Drink

➡ Élesztő (p141)
➡ Lumen (p141)
➡ Corvintető (p141)

For reviews, see p141

🔒 Best Places to Shop

➡ Nagycsarnok (p143)
➡ Portéka (p143)
➡ Magyar Pálinka Ház (p143)

For reviews, see p143

SOUTHERN PEST

TOP SIGHT
HUNGARIAN NATIONAL MUSEUM

The Hungarian National Museum houses the nation's most important collection of historical relics. Founded in 1802, when Count Ferenc Széchényi donated his personal collection of more than 20,000 prints, maps, manuscripts, coins and archaeological finds to the state, it is now housed in an impressive neoclassical edifice, purpose built by Mihály Pollack in 1847.

A year after its move, the museum was the scene of a momentous event (though, as is often the case, not recognised as such at the time). On 15 March a crowd gathered to hear the poet Sándor Petőfi recite 'Nemzeti Dal' (National Song), a prelude to the 1848–49 revolution.

Exhibits on the 1st floor trace the history of the Carpathian Basin and its peoples from earliest times to the end of the Avar period in the early 9th century; move upstairs for the ongoing story of the Magyar people and their nation from the conquest of the basin to the end of communism.

In its own room on the 1st floor, you'll find King Stephen's beautiful crimson silk **coronation mantle**, stitched by nuns in 1031. Also on this level, in the Between East and West gallery, keep an eye out for the Celtic gold and silver **jewellery**. On the 2nd floor, don't miss the **Broadwood piano** used by both Beethoven and Liszt, and **memorabilia from socialist times**.

On the ground floor, among finds from Roman, medieval and early modern times, there's a stunning 2nd-century **Roman mosaic** from Balácapuszta, near Veszprém.

DON'T MISS...

➡ Coronation mantle
➡ Celtic gold and silver jewellery
➡ Socialist memorabilia
➡ 2nd-century Roman mosaic

PRACTICALITIES

➡ Magyar Nemzeti Múzeum
➡ Map p242
➡ www.hnm.hu
➡ VIII Múzeum körút 14-16
➡ adult/concession 1600/800Ft
➡ ⏱10am-6pm Tue-Sun
➡ 🚊47, 49, Ⓜ M3/4 Kálvin tér

◉ SIGHTS

◉ Józsefváros

HUNGARIAN NATIONAL MUSEUM MUSEUM
See p136.

ERVIN SZABÓ CENTRAL LIBRARY LIBRARY
Map p242 (Fővárosi Szabó Ervin Könyvtár; www.fszek.hu; VIII Reviczky utca 1; ⊙10am-8pm Mon-Fri, to 4pm Sat; Ⓜ M3/4 Kálvin tér) FREE Southeast of the national museum is the main repository of Budapest's public library system, with access to 930,000 books, 1000 periodicals and 66,000 audiovisual and digital items. Completed in 1889 and exquisitely renovated, the public reading room has gypsum ornaments, gold tracery and enormous chandeliers. It's worth quickly registering (with photo ID) to gain access, but you can just visit the ground-floor cafe to get a sense of the building.

TELEPHONE EXCHANGE BUILDING BUILDING
Map p242 (VIII Horváth Mihály tér 18; Ⓜ M4 Rákóczi tér, 🚋 4, 6) Built in 1910, the old Telephone Exchange Building is an impressive yet decaying structure adorned with reliefs of classical figures tracing communications through the ages: Mercury, homing pigeons and that newfangled invention, the telephone.

HUNGARIAN NATURAL HISTORY MUSEUM MUSEUM
Map p242 (Magyar Természettudományi Múzeum; www.nhmus.hu; VIII Ludovika tér 2-6; adult/child 1600/800Ft; ⊙10am-5pm Wed-Mon; Ⓜ M3 Klinikák) A fin-whale skeleton greets you at Budapest's Natural History Museum, which houses a raft of interactive displays over three floors. Interesting exhibits focus on the biodiversity of coral reefs and the natural resources of the Carpathian Basin. Noah's Ark, part of the new *Variety of Life* exhibit on the 3rd floor, and the outdoor Dinosaur Garden are particularly fun. It also hosts a range of temporary exhibitions, and admission is free for under-26s on the first Sunday of the month.

◉ Ferencváros

HOLOCAUST MEMORIAL CENTER JEWISH
Map p242 (Holokauszt Emlékközpont; www.hdke.hu; IX Páva utca 39; adult/child 1400/700Ft;

◉ TOP SIGHT
KEREPESI CEMETERY

Established in 1847, Kerepesi Cemetery is Budapest's answer to London's Highgate or Paris' Père Lachaise. Some of the 3000 gravestones and mausoleums in this 56-hectare necropolis, which is also called the National Graveyard (Nemzeti Sírkert), are worthy of a pharaoh. Maps indicating the location of noteworthy graves are available free from the conservation office at the entrance, which is about 500m southeast of Keleti station. Head right from here and you'll find the **Piety Museum** (⊙9am-5pm Mon-Fri, to 2pm Sat), which looks at the approach to death through history in Hungary and Hungarian-speaking regions. From the museum continue to the huge Workers' Movement Pantheon for party honchos, topped with the words 'I lived for Communism, for the people'. Just off to the left is the simple grave of Communist leader János Kádár (1912–89). Sitting just behind the Pantheon, plot 21 contains the graves of many who died in the 1956 Uprising. Also worth seeking out are the resting spots of statesmen and national heroes Lajos Kossuth, Ferenc Deák and Lajos Batthyány.

DON'T MISS...

➡ Workers' Movement Pantheon
➡ Lajos Kossuth mausoleum
➡ Piety Museum

PRACTICALITIES

➡ Kerepesi temető
➡ Map p242
➡ www.nemzetisirkert.hu
➡ VIII Fiumei út 16
➡ admission free
➡ ⊙7.30am-5pm, to 8pm May-Jul, to 7pm Apr & Aug
➡ Ⓜ M2/4 Keleti pályaudvar, 🚋 24

⊙10am-6pm Tue-Sun; Ⓜ M3 Corvin-negyed) Part interactive museum, part educational foundation and housed in a striking, fortress-like building, the superb Holocaust Memorial Center opened in 2004 on the 60th anniversary of the start of the Holocaust in Hungary. The thematic permanent exhibition traces the rise of anti-Semitism in Hungary and follows the path to genocide of Hungary's Jewish and Roma communities, from the initial deprivation of rights through the increasing removal of freedom and dignity and, finally, mass deportations to German death camps in 1944–45.

The exhibits consist of a series of maps, graphic videos, photographs, personal effects and interactive displays. The music is festive to begin with, but the final exhibits are accompanied by the pounding heartbeat of the doomed communities. The videos of the death camps, taken by the liberators, are particularly harrowing, featuring piles of corpses and emaciated survivors. A sublimely restored synagogue in the central courtyard, designed by Leopold Baumhorn and completed in 1924, hosts temporary exhibitions, while an 8m wall outside features the names of Hungarian victims of the Holocaust. A combined ticket with the Zwack Unicum Heritage Visitors' Centre costs 2800Ft.

ZWACK UNICUM HERITAGE VISITORS' CENTRE   MUSEUM

Map p242 (Zwack Múzeum és Látogatóközpont; www.zwack.hu; IX Dandár utca 1; adult/under 18yr 1800/800Ft; ⊙10am-5pm Mon-Fri; 🚌2, 24) Unicum, the thick medicinal-tasting aperitif made from 40 herbs and spices, is one of Hungary's favourite drinks and bitter as a loser's tears. To delve into its history head to this small museum, which starts with a rather schmaltzy video, has an enormous collection of miniatures from across the globe and concludes with an educated tasting session. A combined ticket with the Holocaust Memorial Center costs 2800Ft.

LUDWIG MUSEUM OF CONTEMPORARY ART   MUSEUM

Map p242 (Ludwig Kortárs Művészeti Múzeum; www.ludwigmuseum.hu; IX Komor Marcell utca 1; adult/student & child 1300/650Ft; ⊙10am-8pm Tue-Sun; 🚌2, 24, 🚋HÉV7 Közvágóhíd) Housed in the architecturally controversial Palace of Arts opposite the National

TOP SIGHT
MUSEUM OF APPLIED ARTS

The Museum of Applied Arts has two fascinating permanent collections. One features Hungarian furniture dating from the 18th and 19th centuries, Art Nouveau and Secessionist artefacts, and objects related to the history of trades and crafts (glassmaking, bookbinding, goldsmithing, leatherwork etc). The other displays Islamic textiles, weaponry and ceramics covering a broad geographical sweep from North Africa to Asia, and dating from the 9th to the 19th centuries. On the ground and 1st floors, you'll also find a number of ever-changing temporary exhibitions. Most recent additions to the collection include ceramic pieces donated by collector Magda Bácsi, a Hungarian violinist whose treasures date across five millennia. The beautiful museum building, designed by Ödön Lechner and decorated with Zsolnay ceramic tiles, was completed for the Millenary Exhibition in 1896 but was badly damaged during WWII and again in 1956. It was said to have been inspired by the Victoria & Albert Museum in London. The white-on-white main hall was modelled on the Alhambra in Spain; check out the stunning stained-glass skylight.

DON'T MISS...

➜ Moorish main hall
➜ Zsolnay roof tiles
➜ Collection of Herend and other porcelain
➜ Islamic Art

PRACTICALITIES

➜ Iparművészeti Múzeum
➜ Map p242
➜ www.imm.hu
➜ IX Üllői út 33-37
➜ adult/student 2000/1000Ft
➜ ⊙10am-6pm Tue-Sun
➜ Ⓜ M3 Corvin-negyed, 🚌4, 6

WORTH A DETOUR

NEW MUNICIPAL CEMETERY

This huge **cemetery** (Új Köztemető; X Kozma utca 8-10; ⊙7.30am-5pm, to 8pm May-Jul; 🚌28, 37), easily reached by tram from Blaha Lujza tér, is where Imre Nagy, prime minister during the 1956 Uprising, and 2000 others were buried in unmarked graves (plots 298–301) after executions in the late 1940s and 1950s. The area has been turned into a moving National Pantheon and is about a 30-minute walk from the entrance; follow the signs pointing the way to '298, 300, 301 parcela'.

At peak periods you can take a microbus marked '*temető járat*' around the cemetery or hire a taxi at the gate.

Theatre, the Ludwig Museum holds Hungary's most important collection of international contemporary art. Works by American, Russian, German and French artists span the past 50 years, while Hungarian, Czech, Slovakian, Romanian, Polish and Slovenian works date from the 1990s. The museum also holds frequent and very well received temporary exhibitions. Note that the permanent collection closes at 6pm.

NATIONAL THEATRE THEATRE

Map p242 (Nemzeti Színház; www.nemzetiszinhaz.hu; IX Bajor Gizi Park 1; 🚌2, 🚈HÉV7 Közvágóhíd) Hard by the Danube in southwestern Ferencváros, the National Theatre opened in 2002 to much controversy. The design, by architect Mária Siklós, is supposedly 'Eclectic' to mirror other great Budapest buildings (Parliament, Opera House). The overall effect, however, is a pick-and-mix of classical and folk motifs, porticoes, balconies and columns. An interesting feature is the prow-shaped terrace by the main entrance that appears to be sailing into the Danube. The ziggurat-like structure outside offers good views of the river and maze.

NEW BUDAPEST GALLERY GALLERY

Map p242 (Új Budapest Galéria; www.budapestgaleria.hu; IX Fővám tér 11-12; adult/child 1000/500Ft; ⊙10am-6pm Tue-Sun; MM4 Fővám tér) Inside Bálna (p144), the whale-shaped complex beached by the Danube, the New Budapest Gallery is a spare, modern space in a restored warehouse hosting changing exhibitions that aim to encompass a broad range of works by artists from the city. It focuses on those with ties to the international community and the contemporary art scene.

 EATING

Ráday utca, a long strip whose pavement tables fill with diners on warm summer days, is a lively place to head to in this district. The area east of the Hungarian National Museum, particularly VIII Krúdy Gyula utca in Józsefváros, is another happy hunting ground for restaurants and cafes. If you fancy a bite by the water, check out the range of riverside cafes at Bálna (p144).

✗ Józsefváros

MACSKA VEGETARIAN $

Map p242 (www.facebook.com/macska23; VIII Bérkocsis utca 23; dishes 1000-2100Ft; ⊙6pm-1am Mon-Thu, 4pm-2am Fri & Sat; 🛜🍴; MM4 Rákóczi tér, 🚌4, 6) 'Cat' is a peculiar little cafe-bar, with veggie and vegan dishes on the menu and, as befitting its name, felines in various guises as part of its eclectic decor. Chilled atmosphere, occasional DJ appearances and good beer.

AFRICAN BUFFET AFRICAN $

Map p242 (VIII Bérkocsis utca 21; dishes from 700Ft; ⊙10am-11pm Mon-Sat; MM4 Rákóczi tér, 🚌4, 6) We love the food and the warm welcome at this little African oasis just round the corner from the Rákóczi tér market. It's family run and the food's homemade; try the spicy goat soup and the Zanzibar rice studded with good things.

ÉPÍTÉSZ PINCE HUNGARIAN $$

Map p242 (📞1-266 4799; www.epiteszpince.hu; VIII Ötpacsirta utca 2; mains 1990-3790Ft; ⊙11am-10pm Mon-Thu, to midnight Fri & Sat; 🛜; MM3/4 Kálvin tér) This basement restaurant behind the Hungarian National Museum is stunningly designed and why wouldn't it be? It's in the neoclassical headquarters of the

Magyar Építész Kamara (Chamber of Hungarian Architects). The food is mostly enlightened Hungarian favourites; come here for the decor, artsy crowd and the gorgeous paved courtyard that's candlelit come dusk.

FÜLEMÜLE
HUNGARIAN, JEWISH $$

Map p242 (☑1-266 7947; www.fulemule.hu; VIII Kőfaragó utca 5; mains 2600-5200Ft; ☺noon-10pm Sun-Thu, to 11pm Fri & Sat; ☎; Ⓜ M4 Rákóczi tér, ☒4, 6) This quaint Hungarian restaurant with long wooden tables and old photos on the wall is quite a find in deepest Józsefváros and well worth the search. Dishes mingle Hungarian and international tastes with some old-style Jewish favourites.

PADRÓN
TAPAS $$

Map p242 (☑06 30 900 1204; www.facebook.com/padrontapas; VIII Horánsky utca 10; tapas 490-1190Ft; ☺noon-11pm Wed-Sat, from 5pm Mon & Tue; ☎; Ⓜ M4 Rákóczi tér) An authentic slice of Spain in the backstreets of Budapest, Padrón is passionately run by well-informed staff and expertly trained chefs. There's a great range of tapas staples such as tortilla, *jamón iberico* (cured ham), *gambas pil-pil* (garlic prawns) and its signature *pimientos de padrón* (Padrón peppers), as well as delicious seasonal options. Grab a seat at the bar or looking out of the floor-to-ceiling windows.

CURRY HOUSE
INDIAN $$

Map p242 (☑1-264 0297; www.curryhouse.hu; VIII Horánszky utca 1; mains 1800-3100Ft; ☺11am-11pm Tue-Sun; ☎☑; Ⓜ M4 Rákóczi tér) This richly decorated and well-run Indian restaurant offers a warm welcome, attentive service and a wide range of dishes. There are lots of options for vegetarians, as well as lunchtime thalis (trays with a variety of tasting-size dishes), succulent tandoori and accomplished curries.

MATRJOSKA BISZTRÓ
RUSSIAN $$

Map p242 (☑1-796 8496; www.matrjoskabisztro.com; VIII Lőrinc pap tér 3; mains 1800-2900Ft; ☺noon-midnight Tue-Sat; ☎; Ⓜ M3/4 Kálvin tér, ☒4, 6) Set on a cute little square, this Russian-influenced bistro, with high ceilings, a contemporary forest theme and waiters buzzing between tables, does great caviar, borscht, *pelmeny* (dumplings) and of course a wide selection of vodka. Book ahead at weekends or perch on a stool at the enormous shared barrel.

STEX HÁZ
HUNGARIAN $$

Map p242 (☑1-318 5716; www.stexhaz.hu; VIII József körút 55-57; mains 2790-4990Ft; ☺8am-4am Mon-Sat, 9am-2am Sun; ☎; Ⓜ M3 Corvin-negyed, ☒4, 6) A big, noisy place that's open *almost* round the clock, the Stex is north of the Museum of Applied Arts. The menu offers soups, sandwiches, pasta, fish and meat dishes. It transforms into a lively bar at night and there's breakfast (500Ft to 1850Ft) too.

★ MÚZEUM
HUNGARIAN $$$

Map p242 (☑1-267 0375; www.muzeumkavehaz.hu; VIII Múzeum körút 12; mains 3600-7200Ft; ☺6pm-midnight Mon-Sat; ☎; Ⓜ M3/4 Kálvin tér) This cafe-restaurant is the place to come if you like to dine in old-world style with a piano softly tinkling in the background. It's still going strong after 130 years at the same location near the Hungarian National Museum. The goose-liver parfait (3400Ft) is to die for, the goose leg and cabbage (3900Ft) iconic, plus good selection of Hungarian wines.

★ ROSENSTEIN
HUNGARIAN, JEWISH $$$

Map p242 (☑1-333 3492; www.rosenstein.hu; VIII Mosonyi utca 3; mains 2500-9950Ft; ☺noon-11pm Mon-Sat; ☎; Ⓜ M2/4 Keleti pályaudvar, ☒24) A top-notch Hungarian restaurant in an unlikely location, with Jewish tastes and aromas and super service. Family run, it's been here for years, so expect everyone to know each other. The extensive menu features some interesting game dishes as well as daily lunch specials that are a steal at as little as 2200Ft.

✕ Ferencváros

DANG MUOI
VIETNAMESE $

Map p242 (www.vietnamietterem.hu; IX Ernő utca 30-34; mains 800-2500Ft; ☺10.30am-11pm; ☎; Ⓜ M3 Nagyvárad tér) A little out of the way, but handy for the Hungarian Natural History Museum, this spacious, functional-looking restaurant has an extensive, excellent-value and authentic menu of *pho* (noodle soup), *bún* (rice noodles), *bánh mì* (sandwiches) and other Vietnamese favourites, and attracts a loyal local following.

PATA NEGRA
SPANISH $

Map p242 (☑1-215 5616; www.patanegra.hu; IX Kálvin tér 8; tapas 520-2450Ft, plates 840-2200Ft; ☎☑; Ⓜ M3/4 Kálvin tér, ☒47, 49) Centrally located branch of a popular tapas restaurant in Óbuda (p78).

PETRUS
FRENCH, HUNGARIAN $$

Map p242 (☑1-951 2597; www.petrusrestaurant. hu; IX Ferenc tér 2-3; mains 2690-3590Ft; ⊘noon-11pm Tue-Sat; 🕾; Ⓜ M3 Klinikák, 🚋4, 6) Owned by prominent Hungarian chef Zoltán Feke, Petrus offers a sumptous combination of classic Hungarian and home-style French cooking using high-quality produce. The restaurant artfully balances modern and traditional decor, with views onto peaceful Ferenc tér outside. Daily specials showcase locally sourced, seasonal ingredients, and the wine list and service are excellent.

BORBÍRÓSÁG
HUNGARIAN $$

Map p242 (Wine Court; ☑1-219 0902; www.borbirosag.com; IX Csarnok tér 5; mains 2250-4450Ft; ⊘noon-11.30pm Mon-Sat; 🕾; Ⓜ M4 Fővám tér, 🚋47, 49) The simple, classy Wine Court, where almost 100 Hungarian wines are available by the glass and the food – especially duck – is taken pretty seriously, is just by Nagycsarnok market (p143). The large terrace is a delight in the warmer months.

SOUL CAFÉ
INTERNATIONAL $$

Map p242 (☑1-217 6986; www.soulcafe.hu; IX Ráday utca 11-13; mains 2490-5990Ft; ⊘noon-midnight; 🕾; Ⓜ M3/4 Kálvin tér) One of the better choices along a street heaving with so-so restaurants and cafes with attitude, the Soul has inventive continental food and decor, and a great terrace on both sides of the street. Three-course daily menu is 1490Ft.

COSTES
HUNGARIAN, FUSION $$$

Map p242 (☑1-219 0696; www.costes.hu; IX Ráday utca 4; mains €28-38; ⊘6.30pm-midnight Wed-Sun; 🕾; Ⓜ M3/4 Kálvin tér) The first Hungarian restaurant to gain a Michelin star, Costes is the carefully orchestrated high-end dining experience you might expect. The service is scrupulous yet friendly, the setting is sleek, and the food is expertly created using top-quality ingredients and beautifully presented with some innovative touches. The menu changes regularly to reflect what's in season. Book ahead.

🍷 DRINKING & NIGHTLIFE

LUMEN
CAFE

Map p242 (www.facebook.com/lumen.kavezo; VIII Mikszáth Kálmán tér 2-3; ⊘8am-midnight Mon-Fri, from 10am Sat & Sun; 🕾; Ⓜ M3/4 Kálvin tér, 🚋4, 6) A relaxed gallery, cafe and bar with a little terrace on Mikszáth Kálmán tér, this plant-bedecked joint roasts its own coffee and serves Hungarian and international craft beer and wine. In the evenings it fills with an arty crowd who come for the eclectic program of live music and DJ nights.

★ CORVINTETŐ
CLUB

Map p242 (www.corvinteto.com; VIII Blaha Lujza tér 1; cover 300-1200ft; ⊘10pm-6am Wed-Sat; Ⓜ M2 Blaha Lujza tér) On the top of the former Corvin department store, this excellent club, with stunning views from its open-air dance floor, holds a variety of nights from techno to rooftop cinema. If you can't face the stairs head next door (once you've paid) to bar Villa Negra and take a seat in the goods lift for a ride to the roof.

ÉLESZTŐ
RUIN PUB

Map p242 (www.facebook.com/elesztohaz; IX Tűzoltó utca 22; ⊘3pm-3am; 🕾; Ⓜ M3 Corvin-negyed, 🚋4, 6) This ruin pub, set in a former glass-blowing workshop, is appropriately named – *élesztő* means yeast – given its unrivalled selection of craft beer. With a brewery onsite, 20 brews on draught, beer cocktails and brewing courses, it's a hophead's dream.

BUDAPEST PARK
CLUB

Map p242 (budapestpark.hu; IX Soroksári út 60; ⊘5pm-dawn days vary Apr-Sep; 🚋2, 24, 🚈HÉV7 Közvágóhíd, 🚋923, 979) Vast outdoor club and venue hosting Hungarian, international and big-name rock, metal, pop, indie and electronic artists, as well as mini festivals.

RENGETEG ROMKAFÉ
CAFE

Map p242 (www.facebook.com/Rengeteg; IX Tűzoltó utca 22; ⊘10am-10pm; Ⓜ M3 Corvin-negyed, 🚋4, 6) Children and adults alike are treated to a warm welcome at this little rabbit warren, endearingly cluttered with teddy bears, old sewing machines, books, games and assorted bric-a-brac. As well as tea, coffee, homemade syrups and cake, if you're lucky the owner will rustle you up one of his chocolate concoctions, which taste like heaven in a cup.

TAMP & PULL
CAFE

Map p242 (www.tamppull.hu; IX Czuczor utca 3; ⊘7am-7pm Mon-Fri, Sat 9am-6pm, noon-4pm Sun; Ⓜ M4 Fővám tér) The original venture of Attila Molnár, four times Hungarian National Barista Champion, Tamp & Pull is a small,

SOUTHERN PEST DRINKING & NIGHTLIFE

WORTH A DETOUR

ECSERI PIAC

One of the biggest flea markets in Central Europe, and often just called the *piac* (market), **Ecseri Piac** (www.piaconline.hu; XIX Nagykőrösi út 156; ☺8am-4pm Mon-Fri, 5am-3pm Sat, 8am-1pm Sun) sells everything from antique jewellery and Soviet army watches to Fred Astaire–style top hats. Saturday is the best day to go; dealers get here early to search for those proverbial diamonds in the rough. Take bus 54 from Boráros tér in Pest or, for a quicker journey, express bus 84E, 89E or 94E from the Határ út stop on the M3 metro line further afield in Pest and get off at the Fiume utca stop. Follow the crowds over the pedestrian bridge.

bare-brick cafe with a few tables inside and out, and coffee-related art on the walls. It serves the UK's Has Bean coffee, delicious cakes and biscuits, juices and sandwiches.

CAFÉ CSIGA
CAFE

Map p242 (www.facebook.com/cafecsiga; VIII Vásár utca 2; ☺10am-midnight; ☎; MM4 Rákóczi tér, ⬚4, 6) The Snail is a very popular, welcoming place just opposite the Rákóczi tér market. The relaxed space, with battered wooden floorboards, copious plants and wide-open doors on sunny days attracts a boho crowd. It does food, too, including lots of veggie options, breakfast and an excellent set lunch for 1090Ft.

GONDOZÓ
RUIN PUB

Map p242 (www.facebook.com/Gondozokert; VIII Vajdahunyad utca 4; ☺3pm-1am Wed-Sun, to 3am Fri & Sat; ☎; ⬚4, 6) Laid-back ruin pub in what was once a social-care home, with an ivy-clad garden, an ad-hoc live-music line-up, and the city's first escape game, Parapark (p144), in the basement.

VOSTRO
CAFE

Map p242 (www.vostrobudapest.hu; VIII Krúdy Gyula utca 2; ☺8am-8pm Mon-Fri, from 9am Sat & Sun; ☎; MM3/4 Kálvin tér, ⬚4, 6) Tiny cafe over two levels with additional pavement seating, serving excellent coffee, cakes, milkshakes and a simple weekend brunch.

JELEN
BAR

Map p242 (www.mostjelen.hu; VIII Blaha Lujza tér 1-2; ☺10am-2am; ☎; ⬚5, 7, MM2 Blaha Lujza tér) From the guys behind Most Kortárs Bisztró (p103) comes this equally enthusiastic, spacious and bohemian cafe-bar tucked down a backstreet off Rákóczi út. Food is available from breakfast to evening grills, and it also hosts local live music.

ZAPPA CAFFE
CAFE

Map p242 (www.zappacaffe.hu; VIII Mikszáth Kálmán tér 2; ☺10am-4am Mon-Fri, from noon Sat & Sun; ☎; MM3/4 Kálvin tér, ⬚4, 6) An anchor tenant in a car-free square loaded with students and locals, this laid-back, large cafe (and bar and restaurant) has one of the largest terraces in the area. Good music.

☆ ENTERTAINMENT

★PALACE OF ARTS
CONCERT VENUE, CLASSICAL MUSIC

Map p242 (Művészetek Palotája; ☎1-555 3300; www.mupa.hu; IX Komor Marcell utca 1; ☺box office 10am-6pm; ☎; ⬚2, ⬚HÉV7 Közvágóhíd) The main concert halls at this palatial arts centre by the Danube and just opposite the National Theatre are the 1700-seat **Béla Bartók National Concert Hall** (Bartók Béla Nemzeti Hangversenyterem) and the smaller **Festival Theatre** (Fesztivál Színház), accommodating up to 450 people. Both are purported to have near-perfect acoustics. Students pay 500Ft for a standing-only ticket one hour before all performances.

TRAFÓ HOUSE OF CONTEMPORARY ARTS
DANCE

Map p242 (Trafó Kortárs Művészetek Háza; ☎bookings 1-215 1600; www.trafo.hu; IX Liliom utca 41; ☺bookings 4-8pm; ☎; MM3 Corvin-negyed, ⬚4, 6) This hip stage in Ferencváros presents a mixture of music, theatre and especially the cream of the crop of dance, including a good pull of international acts. Also has a gallery and club.

URÁNIA NATIONAL CINEMA
CINEMA

Map p242 (Uránia Nemzeti Filmszínház; ☎1-486 3400; www.urania-nf.hu; VIII Rákóczi út 21; ⬚7) This Art Deco/neo-Moorish extravaganza is a tarted-up film palace. It has an excellent cafe on the 1st floor overlooking Rákóczi út.

NATIONAL THEATRE
THEATRE

Map p242 (Nemzeti Színház; ☑bookings 1-476 6868; www.nemzetiszinhaz.hu; IX Bajor Gizi Park 1; tickets 1300-3800Ft; ☺bookings 10am-6pm Mon-Fri, 2-6pm Sat; 🚃2, 🚊HÉV7 Közvágóhíd) This rather eclectic venue is the place to go if you want to brave a play in Hungarian or just check out the theatre's bizarre and very controversial architecture.

CORVIN CINEMA
CINEMA

Map p242 (Corvin Mozi; ☑1-459 5050; www.corvin.hu; VIII Corvin köz 1; Ⓜ M3 Corvin-negyed, 🚃4, 6) A restored Art Deco building, the Corvin sits in the middle of a square flanked by Regency-like houses. Note the two wonderful reliefs outside the main entrance to the cinema and the monument to the *Pesti srácok,* the heroic 'kids from Pest' who fought and died in the neighbourhood during the 1956 Uprising. Heart-wrenching stuff.

JEDERMANN
LIVE MUSIC

Map p242 (www.jedermannkavezo.blogspot.com; XI Ráday utca 58; ☺8am-1am; 🕾; 🚃4, 6) This uber-chilled cafe and restaurant, at the southern end of Ráday utca, turns into a great venue at night, focusing mainly on jazz. Gigs are at 9pm Monday and Wednesday, and on Saturday during winter. There's an eclectic, changing menu – from breakfast and grilled meats to salads and cake.

BUDAPEST MUSIC CENTER
CONCERT VENUE

Map p242 (BMC; www.bmc.hu; IX Mátyás utca 8; tickets 1000-2500Ft; ☺library 9am-4.30pm Mon-Fri; 🕾; Ⓜ M4 Fővám tér) Hosting a fantastic line-up of mainly Hungarian jazz and classical performances, the recently opened Budapest Music Center comprises a classy 350-capacity concert hall, the Opus Jazz Club and restaurant, and a library and recording studios. Head here on Wednesday, when there are free concerts.

NOTHIN' BUT THE BLUES
BLUES, JAZZ

Map p242 (www.facebook.com/bluespubbudapest; VIII Krúdy Gyula utca 6; ☺9am-midnight; Ⓜ M3/4 Kálvin tér, 🚃4, 6) The oldest blues venue in town, NBB has been wailing for over two decades now and the Jim Morrison and Blues Brothers paintings let you know that. Almost every night from November to April you'll find someone strumming downstairs.

FLÓRIÁN ALBERT STADIUM
FOOTBALL

Map p242 (FTC Stadion Albert Flórián; www.fradi.hu; IX Üllői út 129; Ⓜ M3 Népliget) No other club has dominated Budapest football over the years like Ferencvárosi Torna Club (FTC), the country's loudest, brashest and most popular team. You either love the Fradi boys in green and white or you hate 'em. Watch them play at the recently rebuilt Flórián Albert Stadium opposite Népliget bus station, with space for 22,600 raucous spectators.

🛍 SHOPPING

★NAGYCSARNOK
MARKET

Map p242 (Great Market; www.piaconline.hu; IX Vámház körút 1-3; ☺6am-5pm Mon-Fri, to 3pm Sat; Ⓜ M4 Fővám tér) This is Budapest's biggest market, though it has become a tourist magnet since its renovation for the millecentenary celebrations in 1996. Still, plenty of locals come here for the fruit, vegetables, deli items, fish and meat. Head up to the 1st floor for Hungarian folk costumes, dolls, painted eggs, embroidered tablecloths, carved hunting knives and other souvenirs.

Gourmets will appreciate the Hungarian and other treats available at a fraction of what they'd cost on nearby Váci utca.

PORTÉKA
GIFTS

Map p242 (www.portekabolt.hu; Horánszky utca 27; ☺10am-6pm Mon-Fri, to 2pm Sat; Ⓜ M3/4 Kálvin tér, 🚃4, 6) Just off Krúdy Gyula utca, Portéka is a little treasure chest of national delicacies and design. It has a good selection of honey, jam, syrups, spices and organic wine, as well as jewellery, bags, notebooks and postcards. Best of all is the fine range of Szántó Tibor's bean-to-bar chocolate.

MAGYAR PÁLINKA HÁZA
DRINK

Map p242 (Hungarian Pálinka House; www.magyarpalinkahaza.hu; VIII Rákóczi út 17; ☺9am-7pm Mon-Sat; 🚃7) This large shop stocks hundreds of varieties of *pálinka* (fruit brandy). Szicsek is a premium choice.

RÁKÓCZI TÉR MARKET
MARKET

Map p242 (www.piaconline.hu; VIII Rákóczi tér 7-9; ☺6am-4pm Mon, to 6pm Tue-Fri, to 1pm Sat; Ⓜ M4 Rákóczi tér, 🚃4, 6) Recently revamped Rákóczi tér has sported this handsome blue-and-yellow market hall since 1897. Renovated in the early 1990s after a fire, inside you'll find all the usual staples – fruit, veg, cured meats, pasta, cheese and baked goods, as well as branches of chains Spar (supermarket) and Rossman (beauty products).

A RACE AGAINST THE CLOCK: BUDAPEST'S LIVE ESCAPE GAMES

In the last few years, Budapest has seen the emergence of a new, quirky and justifiably popular activity: live escape games, in which teams of between two and six willingly lock themselves in a set of rooms in order to spend 60 minutes working through numerous riddles that will eventually unlock the door back to freedom.

Similar to the city's ruin pubs, the games are often set in empty and disused apartment blocks, especially their dank and atmospheric basements. Each game has a distinct theme and story – from Ancient Egypt and medieval to Cold War and sci-fi – and involves not only the solving of puzzles but, crucially, the ability to identify the puzzles in the first place.

Inspired by escape-the-room video games, some claim the game is unique to the city, although a similar idea was actually developed in Japan in 2007. Mentally challenging – teams frequently get 'locked in' – the games are incredibly addictive and popular with tourists and locals alike; it's estimated that Budapest now has as many as 100 of them, with more appearing all the time.

Some of the first to open their doors are still the best: Parapark (p144), Claustrophilia (p131), TRAP (p144) and MindQuest (p131) all offer testing challenges, while newer ventures such as **Trap Factory** (trapfactory.hu) take things to a grander level. No Hungarian is required and it's best to book in advance, although you may get lucky if you just show up. For solo travellers, TRAP offers a helpful find-a-teammate option when booking.

Tips for First-Timers

Failing is half the fun, but if you want a head start, game creators suggest the following:

➡ Don't waste time; don't hesitate; try all of your ideas

➡ Search everywhere – look up, under and behind, and go back and forward between spaces

➡ Share your findings with your team – cooperate and listen to each other

➡ Don't be ashamed to ask for help – your captors will happily give you clues along the way

➡ Don't think too hard – make sure you enjoy it!

IGUANA FASHION, HOMEWARES

Map p242 (VIII Krúdy Gyula utca 9; ⊙10am-6pm Mon-Fri, to 2pm Sat; ⓂM3/4 Kálvin tér, ☒4, 6) Gloriously cluttered little store selling vintage clothes of all kinds, plus homewares, electricals, lamps, signs and bikes.

BÁLNA MALL

Map p242 (www.balnabudapest.hu; IX Fővám tér 11-12; ⊙10am-8pm; ⓂM4 Fővám tér) Best appreciated from the opposite side of the Danube, the 'Whale', a striking glass structure, was designed by Dutchman Kas Oosterhuis and built around two existing warehouses on the riverbank. It houses the New Budapest Gallery (p139), hosts events and has a range of shops, restaurants and cafes.

BABAHÁZ ARTS & CRAFTS

Map p242 (Dollhouse; www.dollhouse.uw.hu; IX Ráday utca 14; ⊙11am-7pm Mon-Sat; ⓂM3/4 Kálvin tér) Dolls and their fabulous period outfits are made in-house. The owner does a nice line of teddy bears and fabric flowers too.

SPORTS & ACTIVITIES

PARAPARK ESCAPE GAME

Map p242 (☎06 20 626 2471; www.parapark.hu; VIII Vajdahunyad utca 4; per team 9000Ft; ☒4, 6) The city's first escape game, now with three different themes, set in the basement of Gondozó (p142) ruin pub. Teams of two to six can test their puzzling skills on scenarios that will have you riding an elevator, summoning spirits or picking through a crime scene.

TRAP ESCAPE GAME

Map p242 (www.trap.hu; VIII Mária utca 19; per team 12,000Ft; ⊙11am-10pm; ⓂM4 Rákóczi tér, ☒4, 6) The third escape game to open in the city, TRAP (Team Race Against Puzzles) offers two basement rooms in which teams of two to five players race against the clock to defuse a time bomb or search for a secret urn. Great for solo travellers, who can use the find-a-teammate function on the website. Cash only.

City Park & Beyond

Neighbourhood Top Five

1 Taking the waters at the 'wedding-cake' **Széchenyi Baths** (p148) in Budapest's sprawling City Park, which boasts some of the hottest thermal water of all the city's spas and arguably its most waterlogged chess players.

2 Enjoying the stunning architecture and the friendly residents of the Elephant House at the **Budapest Zoo** (p149).

3 Having a close call with one Great Master after another at the rich **Museum of Fine Arts** (p147).

4 Strolling City Park and then relaxing with an alfresco beer at **Pántlika** (p151) or **Kertem** (p152).

5 Reaching City Park on the toy-like **M1 metro**, Continental Europe's first underground train.

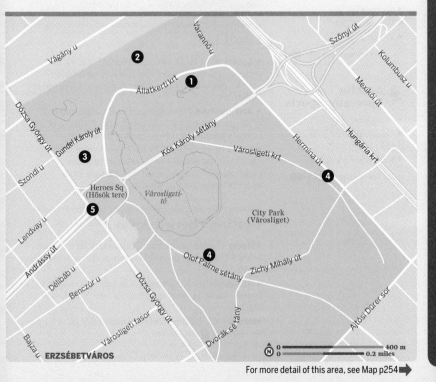

For more detail of this area, see Map p254

Lonely Planet's Top Tip

When the sun's out, a peaceful option for whiling away an hour in City Park is to rent a rowing boat on the lake. Just beyond Heroes' Sq, landlubbers take to the water for 1200Ft for half an hour of rowing, 1800Ft for an hour.

◉ Best Buildings

➡ Palace of Art (p149)

➡ National Institute for the Blind (p150)

➡ Vajdahunyad Castle (p150)

For reviews, see p149 ➡

✖ Best Places to Eat

➡ Olimpia (p150)

➡ Gundel (p151)

➡ Wang (p151)

For reviews, see p150 ➡

✦ Best for Spectator Sports

➡ Hungaroring (p152)

➡ Ferenc Puskás Stadium (p153)

➡ Kincsem Park (p152)

For reviews, see p153 ➡

Explore: City Park & Beyond

Stately Andrássy út ends at Heroes' Sq (Hősök tere), which more or less forms the entrance to City Park (Városliget). City Park is Pest's green lung, an open space measuring almost exactly a square kilometre that hosted most of the events during Hungary's 1000th-anniversary celebrations in 1896. And while it may not compete with the Buda Hills as an escapist's destination, there are more than enough activities and attractions to keep everyone happy and entertained.

The park area was originally marshland and served for a time as a royal hunting ground. Leopold I (Lipót; r 1658–1705) gave it to the city of Pest, but it was not drained and planted for another half-century. The arrangement you see today dates from the late 19th century, when the *angol park* (English park), an idealised view of controlled nature, was all the rage throughout Europe. The park's green spaces contain a large number of both exotic and local trees (largely maple, oak and beech), which attract up to 100 bird species.

Most of the museums, galleries and important statues and monuments lie to the south of XIV Kós Károly sétány, the path that runs east–west just below the top third of the park. Activities and attractions of a less cerebral nature – the Capital Circus of Budapest, Budapest Zoo and Széchenyi Baths – are to the north.

Local Life

➡ **Eating** Most locals wouldn't consider dining in the evening at pricey Gundel (p151), but come Sunday and the punters arrive in droves for its excellent-value buffet.

➡ **Architecture** The neighbourhoods south and east of the park are happy hunting grounds for some of the capital's grandest Art Nouveau buildings (p192).

➡ **Sport** In winter the City Park Ice-Skating Rink (p153) attracts not just casual skaters but also aficionados of bandy, a sport with its own rules alternatively known as Russian hockey.

Getting There & Away

➡**Metro** The M1 metro from Vörösmarty tér and then below VI Andrássy út to Hősök tere and Széchenyi fürdő.

➡**Trolleybus** No 70 to/from V Kossuth Lajos tér, 72 to/from V Arany János utca and 75 to/from XIII Jászai Mari tér.

➡**Bus** No 105 linking points in Buda and V Deák Ferenc tér in Pest with Hősök tere.

TOP SIGHT
MUSEUM OF FINE ARTS

The Museum of Fine Arts houses the city's most outstanding collection of foreign works of art dating from antiquity to the 21st century. The nucleus of the collection dates back to 1870, when the state purchased the private collection of Count Miklós Esterházy. It moved into its present home, a neoclassical building on the northern side of Heroes' Sq, in 1906.

The enormous collection is spread over four levels. Egyptian artefacts and temporary exhibitions are in the basement, where you'll also find 20th-century and contemporary arts. Classical antiquities are on the ground floor, along with further temporary exhibition space. The bulk of the rest of the works are hung on the 1st floor. A small section of the 2nd floor is reserved for Dutch paintings dating from about 1600 to 1800, and European sculpture.

The Old Masters collection is the most complete, with some 3000 works from the Dutch and Flemish, Spanish, Italian, German, French and British schools between the 13th and 18th centuries. Importantly, the museum owns seven paintings by El Greco. Among the most famous of all the works on display is the so-called **Esterházy Madonna**, painted by Raphael, the supreme High Renaissance painter, around 1508. It is unfinished but still manages to achieve the beauty and harmony for which the paragon of classicism is acclaimed. It was among the 700-odd works that formed the original Esterházy collection.

Other sections include 19th-century paintings, watercolours, graphics and sculpture, including some important impressionist works. The museum's collection of prints and drawings is among the largest in Europe, with upwards of 10,000 prints and 10 times as many drawings. At the very top of the building, the **European sculpture** room holds some wonderful pieces, including the fascinating work of Franz Xaver Messerschmidt.

Especially fine – and a real hit with children because of a program that allows them to handle original artefacts and works of art from the period – is the collection of **Egyptian artefacts**, including decorated sarcophagi and mummy portraits. Up a level on the ground floor, the **classical section** contains Greek, Etruscan and Roman works. The collection of Greek vases and urns ranks among the finest and most complete in Europe.

There's usually a couple of excellent temporary exhibitions going on at any given time; a combined ticket will get you into everything. Free English-language tours of permanent collections depart at 11am Tuesday to Saturday, 1pm Tuesday to Thursday and 2pm Tuesday to Friday. Kids' sessions are held on Wednesday and Sunday between 10.15am and 1.15pm and on Saturday between 2.15pm and 5.15pm.

DON'T MISS...

➡ Mummy sarcophagus of Dihoriaut

➡ *Esterházy Madonna* by Raphael

➡ *The Penance of St Mary Magdalene* by El Greco

➡ *Water Carrier* by Goya

➡ Messerschmidt sculptures

PRACTICALITIES

➡ Szépmüvészeti Múzeum

➡ Map p254

➡ www.mfab.hu

➡ XIV Dózsa György út 41

➡ adult/concession 1800/900Ft, temporary exhibitions 3800/2000Ft

➡ ⊙10am-6pm Tue-Sun

➡ Ⓜ M1 Hősök tere

TOP SIGHT
SZÉCHENYI BATHS

The gigantic 'wedding cake' of a building in City Park dates from just before the outbreak of WWI and houses the Széchenyi Baths, whose hot-water spring was discovered while a well was being drilled in the late 19th century. The water here is the hottest in the city, reaching the surface at a scalding 76°C. It also stands out for its immensity (it is the largest medicinal bath extant in Europe and has 15 indoor pools and three outdoor); the bright, clean atmosphere; and the high temperatures of the water (up to 38°C), which really are what the wall plaques say they are.

It's open to both men and women at all times in mixed areas, so bathing suits (available for hire at 1100Ft) must be worn. Use of the three outdoor thermal pools at the Széchenyi is included in the general admission fee. Because the pools contain hot mineral water they're open all year, and it's quite a sight to watch men and women playing chess on floating boards while snow dusts the treetops in City Park. The water, high in calcium, magnesium and hydrogen carbonate, is good for pains in the joints, arthritis, blood circulation and disorders of the nervous system. The whirlpool and Jacuzzi jets in the outdoor pool are also enormous fun. The baths host club nights, appropriately named Sparties (p152), every Saturday.

DON'T MISS...

➡ Budapest's hottest spa water (up to 38°C)

➡ Chess players in the outdoor thermal pools

➡ A go in the outdoor whirlpool

PRACTICALITIES

➡ Széchenyi Gyógyfürdő

➡ Map p254

➡ www.szechenyibath.hu

➡ XIV Állatkerti körút 9-11

➡ ticket incl locker/cabin Mon-Fri 4100/4600Ft, Sat & Sun 4300/4800Ft

➡ ⊗6am-10pm

➡ Ⓜ M1 Széchenyi fürdő

 SIGHTS

MUSEUM OF FINE ARTS   MUSEUM
See p147.

PALACE OF ART   MUSEUM
Map p254 (Műcsarnok; www.mucsarnok.
hu; XIV Dózsa György út 37; adult/concession
1800/900Ft; ☉10am-6pm Tue, Wed & Fri-Sun,
noon-8pm Thu; Ⓜ M1 Hősök tere) The Palace
of Art, reminiscent of a Greek temple, is
among the city's largest exhibition spaces
and now focuses on contemporary visual
arts, with some three to four major exhibitions staged annually. Go for the scrumptious venue and excellent museum shop.
Concerts are sometimes staged here as well.

BUDAPEST ZOO   ZOO
Map p254 (Budapesti Állatkert; www.zoobuda-
pest.com; XIV Állatkerti körút 6-12; adult/child/
family 2500/1800/7300Ft; ☉9am-6.30pm Mon-
Thu, to 7pm Fri-Sun May-Aug, reduced hours Sep-
Apr; ♿; Ⓜ M1 Széchenyi fürdő, ⬚72) This huge
zoo, which opened with 500 animals in
1866, has an excellent collection of big cats,
hippopotamuses, polar bears and giraffes,
and some of the themed houses (eg Mada-
gascar, wetlands, nocturnal Australia) are
world class. Away from our furred and
feathered friends, have a look at the Secessionist animal houses built in the early part
of the 20th century, such as the **Elephant
House** with Zsolnay ceramics, and the
Palm House with an aquarium erected by
the Eiffel Company of Paris.

The zoo's newest attraction, the Varázsh-
egy (Magic Mountain), is an interactive
exhibition inside the Great Rock, covering
earth's evolution and diversity through 3D
film, live animal demonstrations, games
and all manner of simple and fun educational tools.

HOLNEMVOLT PARK   AMUSEMENT PARK
Map p254 (www.zoobudapest.com/pannonpark;
XIV Állatkerti körút 6-12; ☉admission 500Ft, with
zoo admission free; ♿; Ⓜ M1 Széchenyi fürdő,
⬚72) A great place for kids to get up close
and personal with a whole range of animals, 'Once Upon a Time' Park, an extension of the Budapest Zoo, offers a veritable
menagerie that can be petted, fed and rid-
den on. Added amusement is provided by a
set of rather tame (but very child-friendly)
rides including a carousel, a roller-coaster
and a fairy-tale boat.

TOP SIGHT **HEROES' SQUARE & MILLENARY MONUMENT**

Heroes' Sq is the largest and most symbolic square in
Budapest. Flanked by the two most important – and
luxurious – spaces for art in Pest (the Museum of Fine
Arts and the Palace of Art), the square contains the **Millenary Monument** (Ezeréves emlékmű), a 36m-high
pillar backed by colonnades to the right and left. It was
designed in 1896 to mark the 1000th anniversary of the
Magyar conquest of the Carpathian Basin.

Seemingly about to take off from the top of the pillar is the Archangel Gabriel, who is offering Vajk – the
future King Stephen – the Hungarian crown. At the base
of the column is a stone cenotaph called the **Heroes
Monument**, dedicated to those 'who gave their lives
for the freedom of our people and our national independence'. Surrounding the column are Árpád and six
other Magyar chieftains – Előd, Ond, Kond, Tas, Huba
and Töhötöm (Tétény) – who occupied the Carpathian
Basin in the late 9th century (and even most Hungarians
can't name them). The 14 statues in the colonnades are
of **rulers and statesmen**. The four allegorical figures
atop are (from left to right): Work and Prosperity; War;
Peace; and Knowledge and Glory.

DON'T MISS...

➔ Archangel Gabriel
statue

➔ Magyar chieftains

➔ View down
Andrássy út

➔ God of War statue

PRACTICALITIES

➔ Hősök tere

➔ Map p254

➔ ⬚105, Ⓜ M1 Hősök
tere

Among the four-legged creatures you'll spot here are camels, goats, horses, sheep, deer, llamas and wild boars, while the winged variety includes emus, ostriches and flamingos. There are sandpits, wooden play houses and climbing frames too.

HUNGARIAN AGRICULTURAL MUSEUM
MUSEUM

Map p254 (Magyar Mezőgazdasági Múzeum; www.mmgm.hu; Vajdahunyad Castle, XIV Vajdahunyadvár; adult/child 1100/550Ft; ⊙10am-5pm Tue-Sun Apr-Oct, to 4pm Tue-Fri, to 5pm Sat & Sun Nov-Mar; ⓂM1 Hősök tere) This rather esoteric museum is housed in the stunning baroque wing of **Vajdahunyad Castle**. Built for the 1896 millenary celebrations on the little island in the park's lake, the castle was modelled after a fortress in Transylvania – but with Gothic, Romanesque and baroque wings and additions to reflect architectural styles from all over Hungary. Spread over 5200 sq metres of floor space, it has Europe's largest collection of things agricultural (fruit production, cereals, wool, poultry, pig slaughtering, viticulture etc).

JÁK CHAPEL
CHURCH

Map p254 (Jáki kápolna; XIV Vajdahunyadvár; admission 100Ft; ⓂM1 Hősök tere) The little church with the cloister opposite Vajdnahunyad Castle is called Ják Chapel because its intricate portal was copied from the 13th-century Abbey Church in Ják in western Hungary.

TRANSPORTATION MUSEUM
MUSEUM

Map p254 (Közlekedési Múzeum; www.mmkm.hu; XIV Városligeti körút 11; adult/child 1600/800Ft; ⊙10am-5pm Tue-Fri, to 6pm Sat & Sun May-Sep, reduced hours Oct-Apr; 🚶; ☐74, 75) The Transportation Museum has one of the most enjoyable collections in Budapest and is a great place for kids. In old and new wings there are scale models of ancient trains (some of which run), classic late 19th-century automobiles, sailing boats and lots of those old wooden bicycles called 'boneshakers'. There are a few hands-on exhibits. Outside are pieces from the original Danube bridges that were retrieved after the bombings of WWII, and a cafe in an old MÁV coach.

ART NOUVEAU BUILDINGS
NOTABLE BUILDINGS

Two of the most extravagant Art Nouveau/Secessionist buildings in Budapest are within easy walking distance of City Park.

To the southeast is Sándor Baumgarten's **National Institute for the Blind** (Map p254; XIV Ajtósi Dürer sor 39; ⓂM1 Bajza utca), dating from 1904, and to the south is the **Institute of Geology** (XIV Stefánia út 14), designed by Ödön Lechner in 1899 and probably his best-preserved work. Check out the three figures bent under the weight of a globe atop the stunning blue Zsolnay-tiled roof.

✕ EATING

City Park offers some wonderful options for dining outdoors in the warmer months. Its environs are a little limited, but there are some places that are worth making the effort to seek out.

TÓPART
CAFE, HUNGARIAN $

Map p254 (📱06 30 740 8758; www.topartbudapest.hu; XIV Olof Palme sétány 5; ⊙10am-4am May-Sep; ⓂM1 Hősök tere) A series of cafes, restaurants and bars strung out along the edge of the lake in City Park, this seasonal strip offers coffee, traditional Hungarian food, pasta, ice cream and even a pub specialising in *szaft* (stew-like gravy). It's a great place to relax and watch rowers on the lake.

OLIMPIA
HUNGARIAN $$

Map p254 (📱1-321 0680; www.alparutca5. hu; VII Alpár utca 5; 2/3-course lunches 1950/2250Ft, 4/5/6/7-course dinners 5900/7000/7900/8500Ft; ⊙noon-3pm & 7-10pm Mon-Fri, 7-10pm Sat; 🚇; ☐79, ⓂM2 Keleti pályaudvar) Traditional Hungarian with a twist is on offer at this brilliant restaurant that offers a table d'hôte set-lunch menu of one to three courses and a dinner menu of up to seven. Book ahead.

BAGOLYVÁR
HUNGARIAN $$

Map p254 (📱1-468 3110; www.bagolyvar.com; XIV Gundel Károly út 4; mains 3500-5900Ft; ⊙noon-11pm; 🚇🖉; ⓂM1 Hősök tere) With reworked Hungarian classics that make it a winner, the 'Owl's Castle' attracts the Budapest cognoscenti, who leave its sister restaurant, Gundel, next door, to the expense-account brigade. There are three-course set menus for 4700Ft (3100Ft for vegetarians) and 2500Ft mains at lunch on weekends, all served in a pleasantly old-fashioned dining room.

WANG
CHINESE $$

Map p254 (📞1-251 2959; www.kinaikonyha.hu; XIV Gizella út 46/a; dishes 2490-9900Ft; ⊘noon-11pm; 🛜📶; 🚇5, 7) A short walk from the northeastern corner of City Park, this upscale restaurant uses good-quality ingredients to create a long menu of dishes from across China. Stone floors, brick walls and heavy furniture make for an elegant atmosphere, backed by a counter kitchen where the chefs chop, prep and fry furiously. Waiters are friendly and efficient.

GUNDEL
HUNGARIAN $$$

Map p254 (📞1-889 8100; www.gundel.hu; XIV Gundel Károly út 4; mains 3600-25,000Ft; ⊘noon-midnight; Ⓜ M1 Hősök tere) Gundel, next to the zoo and directly behind the Museum of Fine Arts, is the city's fanciest (and most famous) restaurant, with a tradition dating back to 1894. Sunday brunch (11.30am to 3pm; 6800/3400Ft per adult/child), a multicourse themed gobble-fest of cold and warm dishes and desserts that changes every week, is heartily recommended.

At other times we've always found Gundel to be vastly overpriced, offering little value for money. Apparently it still feeds the Habsburgs (or what's left of them) when they're in town.

ROBINSON
INTERNATIONAL $$$

Map p254 (📞1-422 0222; www.robinsonrestaurant.hu; XIV Városligeti tó; mains 3200-13,700Ft; ⊘11am-5pm & 6-11pm; 🛜; Ⓜ M1 Hősök tere) Located within the leafy park, Robinson is the place to secure a table on the lakeside terrace on a warm summer's evening. Starters include goose-liver terrine (3700Ft) and beef-tenderloin carpaccio (2900Ft), and mains feature grilled *fogas* (Balaton pike-perch; 4800Ft) and various meats cooked over charcoal (4500Ft to 13,900Ft). It's pricey, but – as ever – it's all about location, location, location.

🍷 DRINKING & NIGHTLIFE

PÁNTLIKA
BAR, CLUB

Map p254 (www.pantlika.hu; XIV Városligeti körút; ⊘11.30am-midnight Sun-Thu, to 2am Fri & Sat; 🚋1, 1A, 🚌72, 74) For a place housed in a Communist-era kiosk dating back to the 1970s with a bizarre flyaway roof, this DJ bar and cafe is very hip and has a great terrace. Food – soups, stews and hamburgers from 950Ft – emerges from a tiny kitchen, and the selection of *pálinka* (fruit brandy) is extensive. It's opposite XIV Hermina út 47.

CITY PARK STATUES & MONUMENTS

City Park boasts a number of notable statues and monuments. Americans (and collectors of greenbacks) might be surprised to see a familiar face in the park south of the lake. The **statue of George Washington** on XIV Washington György sétány was funded by Hungarian-Americans and erected in 1906.

The statue of the hooded figure opposite Vajdahunyad Castle is that of **Anonymous**, the unknown chronicler at the court of King Béla III who wrote a history of the early Magyars. Note the pen with the shiny tip in his hand; writers (both real and aspirant) stroke it for inspiration.

The **Timewheel** (Időkerék) in XIV Felvonulási tér (Procession Sq), on the park's western edge and directly behind the Palace of Art, is the world's largest hourglass, standing 8m high and weighing in at 60 tonnes. Unfortunately, it no longer functions; when it did the 'sand' (actually glass granules) flowed from the upper to the lower chamber for one year, finishing exactly at midnight on New Year's Eve, when the wheel was reset to begin its annual flow. Unveiled on 1 May 2004 to commemorate Hungary's entry into the EU, it provocatively stands a short distance from the parade grounds of Dózsa György út, where Communist honchos once stood to watch May Day processions and where the 25m-tall statue of Joseph Stalin was pulled down by demonstrators on the first night of the 1956 Uprising. This spot has now been filled by the **1956 Revolution Monument**, a monolithic assembly of rusting (and controversial) steel columns erected in 2006 to mark the 50th anniversary of the abortive uprising.

WORTH A DETOUR

HUGARORING

Reintroduced in 1986 after a break of half a century, the Formula 1 Hungarian Grand Prix, Hungary's prime sporting event, is part of the World Championship Series that takes place at the **Hungaroring** (www.hungaroring.hu) in Mogyoród, 24km northeast of Budapest, in late July. Practice is on the Friday, the qualifying warm-up on Saturday and the race begins after morning practice at 2pm on Sunday. The seats with the best views of the starting grid are Super Gold ones (and are covered) and cost €498 for the weekend; cheaper are Gold (€298 to €330) and Silver (€199 to €250) tickets. Standing room costs €90 for the weekend, €80 for Sunday.

KERTEM
BAR, CLUB

Map p254 (www.kertemfesztival.hu; XIV Olof Palme sétány 3; ◷11am-4am; MM1 Hősök tere) Right in the middle of City Park, Kertem is a wonderful beer garden, filled with multicoloured chairs and trees strung with fairy lights. By day it's an easygoing oasis full of families, by night it's a great place to grab a beer and a burger and listen to live music (hosted on weekend evenings).

DÜRER KERT
GARDEN CLUB

Map p254 (www.durerkert.com; XIV Ajtósi Dürer sor 19-21; ◷5pm-5am; ☎; 🚉1, 🚍74, 75) A very relaxed open space and club on the southern edge of City Park, Dürer Kert boasts some of the best DJs on the 'garden' circuit. Concerts, too, from indie to jazz.

SPARTY
CLUB

Map p254 (www.spartybooking.com; XIV Állatkerti út 1; admission from €25; ◷10.30pm-3am Sat; MM1 Széchenyi fürdő) Sparty (see what they did there?) organises a variety of weekly club nights in the Széchenyi Baths (p148) combining drinking, house and funk DJs, VJs, acrobatics and bathing with a very up-for-it and underdressed crowd. Don't forget your goggles.

 ENTERTAINMENT

PETŐFI CSARNOK
CONCERT VENUE

Map p254 (☎1-848 0206; www.petofirendezve-nykozpont.hu; XIV Zichy Mihály út 14; ◷ticket office 10am-4pm Mon-Fri; 🚍72, 74, MM1 Széchenyi fürdő) In the southeastern corner of City Park is Budapest's main youth leisure centre, with an outside stage for up to 4500 spectators and the indoor Nagyterem (Great Hall) with space for up to 2500 people.

KINCSEM PARK
HORSE RACING

(☎1-433 0520; www.kincsempark.com; X Albertirsai út 2-4; MM2 Pillangó utca) Kincsem Park, named after a 19th-century horse called 'My Treasure', is the place to go for both *ügető* (trotting) and *galopp* (flat racing). Schedules can change, but in general three trotting meetings of 10 or 11 races take place from 2pm to 9pm on Saturday year-round and flat racing from 2pm on Sunday between April and late November.

The biggest event of the year is Ügetőszilveszter, a vastly popular extraordinary trotting meeting that attracts all ages on the afternoon of New Year's Eve.

It's about 2.5km southeast of City Park close to Ferenc Puskás Stadium.

LÁSZLÓ PAPP BUDAPEST SPORTARÉNA
LIVE MUSIC

Map p254 (☎1-422 2600; www.budapestarena. hu; XIV Stefánia út 2; ◷box office 9am-5pm Mon-Fri; MM2 Puskás Ferenc Stadion) This purpose-built 15,000-seat arena named after a local boxing great is where big local and international acts (eg George Michael, Britney Spears, Rihanna) perform.

CAPITAL CIRCUS OF BUDAPEST
CIRCUS

Map p254 (Fővárosi Nagycirkusz; ☎1-343 8300; www.circus.hu; XIV Állatkerti körút 12/a; adult 1900-3900Ft, senior 1700-2900Ft, child 1500-2700Ft; MM1 Széchenyi fürdő) Europe's only permanent big top has everything one would expect from a circus, including acrobats, big cats and daredevils on horseback. Performances are usually at 3pm Wednesday to Sunday, with additional shows at 11am and 7pm on Saturday and at 11am on Sunday, but call ahead or check the website.

FERENC PUSKÁS STADIUM FOOTBALL
Map p254 (Stadion Puskás Ferenc; ☎1-471 4221; XIV Istvánmezei út 1-3; Ⓜ M2 Puskás Ferenc Stadion) Hungary's national football team plays at the erstwhile 'People's Stadium', at full capacity capable of accommodating almost 70,000 fans. But don't expect any miracles.

SHOPPING

PECSA BOLHAPIAC MARKET
Map p254 (www.bolhapiac.com; XIV Zichy Mihály utca 14; admission 150Ft; ◷8am-2pm Sat & Sun; 🚊1, 🚌72, 74) If you don't have the time for Ecseri Piac, the next best thing is this Hungarian flea market held next to the Petőfi Csarnok concert venue. There's everything from old records and draperies to candles and honey on offer. Sunday is the better day.

SPORTS & ACTIVITIES

SZÉCHENYI BATHS BATHHOUSE
See p148.

CITY PARK ICE-SKATING RINK ICE-SKATING
Map p254 (Városligeti Műjégpálya; www.mujegpalya.hu; XIV Olof Palme sétány 5; ◷9am-1pm & 4-8pm Mon-Fri, 10am-2pm & 4-8pm Sat & Sun mid-Nov–Feb; Ⓜ M1 Hősök tere) In winter Europe's largest outdoor skating rink operates on the western edge of the lake in City Park in the shadow of Vajdahunyad Castle. Skates can be rented. If you want to avoid the crowds, visit on a weekday morning.

Day Trips from Budapest

Gödöllő Royal Palace p155
Hungary's most painstakingly restored aristocratic residence, the Royal Palace at Gödöllő is within easy striking distance of the capital and an easy 'walk' through Hungarian history.

Szentendre p156
A town on the scenic Danube Bend that has changed little since the 18th century, Szentendre is well worth the easy trip from Budapest for its museums, galleries, architecture and shops.

Eger p158
Provincial Hungary's prettiest city contains a plenitude of museums and important architecture, a castle that helped save the nation and a valley awash in wine.

Balatonfüred p161
Arguably the most stylish of all the towns along Lake Balaton, Balatonfüred was once the preserve of the well-heeled infirm but now attracts both fun- and sun-seekers in equal measure.

TOP SIGHT
GÖDÖLLŐ ROYAL PALACE

The Royal Palace at Gödöllő (roughly pronounced 'good-duh-luh'), 30km northeast of Budapest and easily accessible on the HÉV suburban train, rivalled aristocratic residences throughout the Habsburg empire when it was completed in the 1760s and is the largest baroque manor house in Hungary. The town itself, full of lovely baroque buildings and monuments, is also worth exploring.

The palace was designed in 1741 by Antal Mayerhoffer for Count Antal Grassalkovich (1694–1771), confidante of Empress Maria Theresa. After the formation of the Dual Monarchy over a century later, it was enlarged as a summer retreat for and gifted to Emperor Franz Joseph and soon became the favoured residence of his consort, the much-loved Habsburg empress and Hungarian queen Elizabeth (1837–98), affectionately known as Sissi (or Sisi). Between the two world wars the regent, Admiral Miklós Horthy, also used it as a summer residence, but after the Communists came to power part of the mansion was used as a barracks for Soviet and Hungarian troops and as an old people's home. The rest was left to decay.

Partial renovation of the mansion began in the mid-1980s, and today almost three dozen rooms are open to the public on the ground and 1st floors. They have been restored to the period when the imperial couple was in residence, and Franz Joseph's suites (done up in manly deep red) and Sissi's lavender-coloured private apartments on the 1st floor are impressive. Check out the **Ornamental Hall**, all gold tracery, stucco and chandeliers, where chamber-music concerts are held throughout the year. Also see the **Queen's Reception Room**, with a Secessionist-style oil painting of Sissi patriotically repairing the coronation robe of King Stephen with needle and thread; the **Queen Elizabeth Memorial Exhibit**, which looks at the queen's assassination by Italian anarchist Luigi Lucheni, who stabbed her to death with a needle file; and the **Grassalkovich Era Exhibition**, which offers a glance at the palace during its first century.

You can also visit the splendid **Baroque Theatre** (adult/student 1400/800Ft; ⊙Sat & Sun) and the WWII-vintage **Horthy's Bunker** (adult/student 800/500Ft) with a guide; be aware that the permanent exhibition is also by guided tour (three to five departures) during the week in winter. Audioguides cost 800Ft. There's a helpful **tourist office** (☑28-415 402; www.gkrte.hu; ⊙10am-6pm Tue-Sun Apr-Oct, to 5pm Tue-Sun Nov-Mar) just inside the palace's main entrance.

There's a cafe in the palace with drinks and snacks. In town, **Pizza Palazzo** (☑28-420 688; www.pizzapalazzo.hu; Szabadság tér 2; pizza & pasta 1020-1590Ft; ⊙11am-10pm Sun-Thu, to 11pm Fri & Sat) is a popular pizzeria that also has more substantial pasta dishes; it's attached to Szabadság tér HÉV station. **Solier Cafe** (☑06-20 396 5512; www.solier.hu; Dózsa György utca 13; mains 1500-2450Ft, set lunch 1150Ft; ⊙8am-10pm), next to the post office, has a wonderful *cukrászda* (cake shop) on the ground floor and an upbeat restaurant above. About 500m north of the Szabadság tér HÉV stop, **Szélkakas** (Weathervane; ☑28-423 119; www.godolloisze-lkakas.hu; Bajcsy-Zsilinszky utca 27; mains 1650-2650Ft; ⊙11.30am-8pm Sun & Mon, to 10pm Tue-Thu, noon-11pm Fri & Sat) is a charming eatery with a covered garden; it's great for Sunday lunch.

DON'T MISS...

➡ Ornamental Hall
➡ Queen Elizabeth Memorial Exhibit
➡ Baroque Theatre
➡ Horthy's Bunker

PRACTICALITIES

➡ Gödöllői Királyi Kastély
➡ ☑28-410 124
➡ www.kiralyikastely.hu
➡ Szabadság tér 1
➡ adult/child 2200/1100Ft
➡ ⊙10am-6pm Apr-Oct, to 5pm Tue-Sun Nov-Mar
➡ ⊟ hourly from Stadion bus station (560Ft, 40min), ⊟ frequent HÉV services from Örs vezér tere to Gödöllő's Szabadság tér station (720Ft, 45min)

DAY TRIPS FROM BUDAPEST GÖDÖLLŐ ROYAL PALACE

Szentendre

Explore

Szentendre, Hungarian for 'St Andrew', is the gateway to the Danube Bend, the S-shaped curve in Hungary's mightiest river that begins just below Esztergom and twists and turns for 20km before reaching Budapest. As an art colony turned lucrative tourist centre, Szentendre strikes many as a little too 'cute', and the town can get pretty crowded in high season. Still, the many art museums, galleries and Orthodox churches (built largely by Serbians fleeing unrest in the 18th century), which give the town its unique Balkan feel, make the easy trip worthwhile.

The Best...

➡ **Sight** Margit Kovács Ceramic Collection (p156)

➡ **Place to Eat** Promenade (p157)

➡ **Place to Drink** Adria (p157)

Top Tip

Szentendre is best avoided on weekends in summer when hordes of tourists descend and between November and mid-March when much of the town shuts on weekdays.

Getting There & Away

➡ **Bus** Buses from Pest's Újpest-Városkapu train station, which is on the M3 blue metro line, run to Szentendre at least once an hour (370Ft, 25 minutes).

➡ **HÉV** Trains depart from Batthyány tér in Buda (640Ft, 40 minutes) every 10 to 20 minutes throughout the day. Note that a yellow city bus/metro ticket (350Ft) is good only as far as the Békásmegyer stop on the way; you'll have to pay 370Ft extra to get to Szentendre. Many HÉV trains run only as far as Békásmegyer, where you must cross the platform to board the train for Szentendre. The last train returns to Budapest several minutes after 11pm.

Need to Know

➡ **Area Code** 26

➡ **Location** 24km north of Budapest

➡ **Tourist Office** (✆26-317 965; www.szentendreprogram.hu; Bercsényi utca 4; ⊙10am-5.30pm Mon-Thu, to 6pm Fri-Sun)

◉ SIGHTS

FŐ TÉR SQUARE

(Main Square) The colourful heart of Szentendre is surrounded by 18th- and 19th-century burghers' houses, with the **Memorial Cross** (1763), an iron cross decorated with faded icons on a marble base, in the centre. To the northeast is the Serbian Orthodox **Blagoveštenska Church** (Blagoveštenska templom; ✆26-310 554; admission 350Ft; ⊙10am-5pm Tue-Sun), built in 1754. With fine baroque and rococo elements, it hardly looks 'eastern' from the outside. But the ornate iconostasis and elaborate 18th-century furnishings inside immediately give the game away.

MARGIT KOVÁCS CERAMIC COLLECTION MUSEUM

(Kovács Margit Kerámiagyüjtemény; ✆26-1310 244; www.pmmi.hu/hu/museum/6/intro; Vastagh György utca 1; adult/concession 1000/500Ft; ⊙10am-6pm) Established in an 18th-century salt house, this museum is devoted to the work of Szentendre's most famous artist. Margit Kovács (1902–77) was a ceramicist who combined Hungarian folk, religious and modern themes to create Gothic-like figures. Some of her works are overly sentimental, but many others are very powerful, especially the later ones in which mortality is a central theme.

BELGRADE CATHEDRAL CHURCH

(Belgrád Székesegyház; ✆26-312 399; Pátriárka utca 5; admission incl art collection 600Ft; ⊙10am-6pm Tue-Sun May-Sep, to 5pm Tue-Sun Oct-Apr) The seat of the Serbian Orthodox bishop in Hungary, built in 1764, rises from within a walled courtyard to the north of Fő tér. One of the cathedral's outbuildings contains the excellent **Serbian Ecclesiastical Art Collection** (Szerb Egyházművészeti Gyüjtemény; ✆26-312 399; Pátriárka utca 5; admission 600Ft; ⊙10am-6pm Tue-Sun May-Sep, to 5pm Tue-Sun Oct-Apr), a treasure trove of icons, vestments and gold church plate.

HUNGARIAN OPEN-AIR ETHNOGRAPHICAL MUSEUM MUSEUM

(Magyar Szabadtéri Néprajzi Múzeum; ✆26-502 500; www.skanzen.hu; Sztaravodai út; adult/student 1500/750Ft, on festival days 1600/800Ft; ⊙9am-5pm Tue-Sun Apr-Oct, 10am-4pm Sat & Sun Nov–early Dec & Feb-Mar) Just 5km northwest of Szentendre and accessible by bus 230 from the local station is Hungary's most ambitious *skanzen* (open-air folk museum), with farmhouses, churches, bell towers, mills and so on set up in eight regional divisions, as well as the walls of a Roman villa excavated in the area. Craftspeople and artisans do their thing on random days (generally at the weekend) from Easter to early December, and the museum hosts festivals throughout the season.

✖ EATING & DRINKING

ERM'S   HUNGARIAN $$
(☏26-303 388; www.etterem.hu/6928; Kossuth Lajos utca 22; mains 1590-3700Ft; ⊙11am-11pm Mon-Wed, Fri & Sat, to 10pm Sun) Subtitled 'Csülök & Jazz', retro-style Erm's, with its walls festooned with early 20th-century memorabilia and simple wooden tables, is where to go for Hungarian-style pork knuckle in all its guises, and live music at the weekend. Burgers now too.

PALAPA   MEXICAN $$
(☏26-302 418; www.palapa.hu; Dumtsa Jenő utca 14/a; mains 1680-4560Ft; ⊙noon-10pm Sun-Thu, to midnight Fri & Sat) The Mexican food – from tacos to fajitas – at this colourful restaurant (with live music at the weekend) makes it the perfect place for a change from Hungarian fare. The garden fills up quickly in warm weather.

★PROMENADE   INTERNATIONAL $$$
(☏26-312 626; www.promenade-szentendre.hu; Futó utca 4; mains 1850-4450Ft; ⊙11am-11pm Tue-Sun) Vaulted ceilings, whitewashed walls, a huge cellar for tasting wine and a wonderful terrace overlooking the Danube are all highlights at the Promenade, one of Szentendre's best restaurants, serving 'enlightened' Hungarian and international dishes.

ADRIA   CAFE
(☏06 20 448 8993; www.szeresdszentendret. hu/emblemasok_2010_05_11_adria_kavezo. html; Kossuth Lajos utca 4; ⊙noon-10pm) This funky little spot by the canal has a cosy interior bedecked in bright colours and a tree-shaded terrace. Expect soulful music served alongside your choice of coffee or tea and cake. It does Balkan grilled dishes (from 800Ft), too.

DAY TRIPS FROM BUDAPEST SZENTENDRE

CRUISING THE DANUBE

The Danube Bend is pint-sized compared to Hungary's other regions, but what it lacks in size it makes up for with an overabundance of natural beauty and a venerable wealth of human endeavour. The river itself is a perfect highway, and regular boats ferry tourists to four delightful towns from Budapest over the summer months.

The closest, of course, is Szentendre, for centuries a community open to new settlers, unorthodox religions, and artists, and now a tourist hot spot with cobbled streets and a profusion of church spires. Further round the bend is tiny Visegrád, once the seat of Hungary's kings and queens and today home to Renaissance-palace ruins and a forbidding hilltop castle. Esztergom, for so many years the Pope's 'eyes and ears' in Hungary, is now a sleepy town with the biggest basilica this side of the Balkans. Vác, on the east bank of the Danube, is a lovely spot with a laid-back attitude, another fine cathedral and a macabre crypt of mummies.

➡ **Szentendre** From May to September, a Mahart ferry plies the Danube to/ from Vigadó tér in Pest and Batthyány tér in Buda, departing at 10am daily except Monday and arriving in Szentendre at 11.30am (one way/return 2000/2500Ft, 1½ hours). The return boat leaves at 5pm and takes one hour. The service usually reduces to weekends only in April.

➡ **Vác, Visegrád and Esztergom** Between May and late August there's a ferry from Vigadó tér pier in Pest at 9am, calling in at Vác (11am, one way/return 1500/2250Ft) and Visegrád (noon, 2000/3000Ft) before carrying on to Esztergom (1.45pm, 2500/3750Ft). It returns from Esztergom/Visegrád/Vác at 4.45/6/6.30pm, reaching Budapest at 8pm. The service is reduced to Saturday only in September. Hydrofoils travel from Budapest to Visegrád (one way/return 4000/6000Ft, one hour) and Esztergom (one way/return 5000/7500Ft, 1½ hours) on Saturday and Sunday from early May to September; boats leave at 9.30am and return at 5pm from Esztergom and 5.30pm from Visegrád.

JOVIALIS
CAFE

(📞06 30 939 4779; www.jovialis.hu; Görög utca 2; ⊙10am-6pm) Our favourite recent addition in Szentendre is an ultramodern but very comfortable little cafe attached to the Margit Kovács Ceramic Collection. The welcoming staff are fonts of information.

AVAKUMICA KÁVÉHÁZ
BAR

(📞06 20 537 4900; www.avakumica.hu; Alkotmány utca 14; ⊙8am-10pm Mon-Thu, to midnight Fri, 10am-midnight Sat, to 10pm Sun) Slither into this place, a cellar bar and cafe near Castle Hill named after a kind of zither, to escape the tourist hordes and rehydrate.

Eger

Explore

Everyone loves Eger and it's immediately apparent why. Lavished with beautifully preserved baroque architecture, Eger is a jewellery box of a town with loads to see and do. Explore the bloody history of Turkish occupation and defeat at the hilltop castle, climb an original minaret or hear an organ performance at the colossal basilica. Then spend time traipsing from cellar to cellar in the Valley of the Beautiful Women, tasting the celebrated Eger Bull's Blood (Egri Bikavér) and other local wines from the cask, and the following morning take the cure in a superbly renovated Turkish bath. Eger could easily become a 'days trip' from Budapest.

The Best...

→ **Sight** Eger Castle (p158)
→ **Place to Stay** Hotel Senator-Ház (p160)
→ **Place to Eat** Macok Bistro & Winebar (p160)

Top Tip

Even though Eger Castle is closed to the public on Monday, you can still visit the castle grounds, Heroes' Hall and the casemates at a reduced price of 1100/550Ft per adult/child.

Getting There & Away

→**Bus** Hourly buses link Eger with Stadion bus station in Pest (2830Ft, two hours).

→**Train** There are eight direct daily trains to/from Pest's Keleti train station (2725Ft, two hours).

Need to Know
→ **Area Code** 36
→ **Location** 132km northeast of Budapest
→ **Tourist Office** (📞36-517 715; www.eger.hu; Bajcsy-Zsilinszky utca 9; ⊙9am-6pm Mon-Fri, to 1pm Sat & Sun mid-Jun–mid-Sep, to 5pm Mon-Fri, to 1pm Sat mid-Sep–mid-Jun)

◉ SIGHTS

EGER CASTLE
FORTRESS

(Egri Vár; 📞36-312 744; www.egrivar.hu; Vár köz 1; castle grounds adult/child 800/400Ft, incl museum 1400/700Ft; ⊙exhibits 10am-5pm Tue-Sun Mar-Oct, 10am-4pm Tue-Sun Nov-Feb, castle grounds 8am-8pm May-Aug, to 7pm Apr & Sep, to 6pm Mar & Oct, to 5pm Nov-Feb) Erected in the 13th century after the Mongol invasion, Eger Castle is largely a modern reconstruction, but you can still see the foundations of 12th-century **St John's Cathedral** on the eastern side of the complex. Models and drawings in the **István Dobó Museum**, housed in the former Bishop's Palace (1470), painlessly explain the history of the castle. On the ground floor, a statue of Dobó takes pride of place in the **Heroes' Hall**.

The 19th-century building to the northwest houses the Eger Art Gallery, which includes works by Canaletto and Ceruti. The terrace of the renovated 1549 **Dobó Bastion**, which collapsed in 1976, offers stunning views of the town; it now hosts temporary exhibits. Beneath the castle are **casemates** hewn from solid rock, which you may tour with a Hungarian-speaking guide. (The tour is included in the admission price, but a foreign-language guide costs 800Ft extra.) Other attractions, including the **Panoptikum** and **3D film**, bear an additional charge. Alternatively, you can just wander the castle grounds, which are also open Monday, when most exhibits are closed. The best view of the city can be had by climbing up cobblestone Vár köz from Dózsa György tér.

EGER BASILICA
CHURCH

(Egri Főszékesegyhá; 📞36-515 725; www.eger-bazilika.plebania.hu; Pyrker János tér 1; ⊙7.30am-6pm Mon-Sat, from 1pm Sun) FREE A highlight

THE SIEGE OF EGER

The story of the Turkish attempt to take Eger Castle is the stuff of legend. Under the command of István Dobó, a mixed bag of 2000 soldiers held out against more than 100,000 Turks for a month in 1552. As every Hungarian kid in short trousers can tell you, the women of Eger played a crucial role in the battle, pouring boiling oil and pitch and hot sand on the invaders from the ramparts and 'murder holes'.

Also making a star appearance was Eger's wine – if we are to believe the legend. Apparently Dobó sustained his soldiers with the popular ruby-red local vintage. When they fought on with increased vigour – and stained beards – rumours began to circulate among the Turks that the defenders were gaining strength by drinking the blood of bulls. Egri Bikavér (Eger Bull's Blood) was born.

Géza Gárdonyi's *Egri Csillagok* (1901), which can be found in English translation in many Budapest bookshops as *Eclipse of the Crescent Moon*, describes the siege in thrilling detail.

of the town's amazing architecture is the neoclassical basilica designed in 1836 by József Hild. A good time to visit is when the ornate altars and a soaring dome create interesting acoustics for the half-hour **organ concert** (adult/child 800/400Ft; ☉11.30am Mon-Sat, 12.45pm Sun mid-May–mid-Oct).

LYCEUM HISTORIC BUILDING
(Líceum; ☑36-325 211; www.mheger.hu; Eszterházy tér 1; library adult/student 800/500Ft; ☉9.30am-3.30pm Tue-Sun Apr–mid-Oct, 9.30am-1pm Sat & Sun mid-Oct–mid-Dec, 9.30am-1.30pm Tue-Sun Feb & Mar) The 60,000-volume library on the 1st floor of the renovated Zopf-style Lyceum's south wing contains hundreds of priceless manuscripts and codices. The *trompe l'oeil* ceiling fresco (1778) depicts the Counter-Reformation's Council of Trent (1545–63), with a lightning bolt setting heretical manuscripts ablaze. The **Astronomy Museum** (Csillagászati Múzeum; ☑36-520 400; www.varazstorony.ektf.hu; adult/student Ft800/1000) on the 6th floor of the east wing contains 18th-century astronomical equipment, an observatory and a planetarium with regularly scheduled star shows. Climb up three more floors to the so-called Magic Tower (Varász Torony) observation deck to try out the camera obscura, the 'eye of Eger', designed in 1776 to entertain townspeople.

DOBÓ ISTVÁN TÉR SQUARE
On the southern side of Eger's main square below the castle stands the **Minorite Church of St Anthony of Padua** (Páduai Szent Antal Minorita Templom; Dobó István tér 6; ☉9am-5pm Tue-Sun), built in 1771 and, to our collective mind, probably the most beautiful baroque building in the world. Statues

of István Dobó and his comrades-in-arms routing the Turks fill the square in front of the church. Just north of and visible from the square is the 40m-tall **minaret** (☑06-70 202 4353; Knézich Károly utca; admission 250Ft; ☉10am-6pm Apr-Oct), which can be climbed via 97 narrow spiral steps.

COUNTY HALL NOTABLE BUILDING
(Megyeháza; Kossuth Lajos utca 9) The tree-lined street of Kossuth Lajos utca boasts dozens of architectural gems, including the delightful County Hall, the main door of which is crowned by a wrought-iron representation of Faith, Hope and Charity by Henrik Fazola, a Rhinelander who settled in Eger in the mid-18th century. Walk down the passageway, and you'll see more of his magnificent work – two baroque wrought-iron gates that have superseded the minaret as the symbol of Eger.

✖ EATING & DRINKING

PALACSINTAVÁR CREPERIE $
(Pancake Castle; ☑36-413 980; www.palacsintavar.hu; Dobó István utca 9, enter from Fazola Henrik utca; mains 1590-1960Ft; ☉noon-11pm Tue-Sat, to 10pm Sun) Pop art and groovy music fill the space of this eclectic eatery. Savoury meat *palacsinták* – Hungarian crêpes, for lack of a better word – are served with an abundance of fresh vegetables and range in flavour from Asian to Italian. There's a large choice of sweet ones too.

SZÁNTÓFER VENDÉGLŐ HUNGARIAN $$
(Plough; ☑36-1517 298; www.szantofer.hu; Bródy Sándor utca 3; mains 1300-2500Ft) Choose the

'Plough' for hearty, home-style Hungarian fare. Farming equipment and cooking utensils hang like prize trophies on the walls, and a covered courtyard out back is perfect for escaping the summer heat. Two-course weekday lunches are a snip at 890Ft.

MACOK BISTRO & WINEBAR HUNGARIAN $$

(Macok Bisztró és Borbár; [phone]36-516 180; www.imolaudvarhaz.hu; Dósza György tér 4; mains 1490-2950Ft; noon-10pm Mon-Thu, to 11pm Fri & Sat, to 4pm Sun) This very stylish bistro in the Imola Udvarház Hotel at the foot of the castle, with its inventive menu and excellent wine card, gets consistently rave reviews. We'll come back in particular for the budget-enhancing two-/three-course lunch (1000/1300Ft) and the four-/six-course *degusztációs* (tasting) menus (4900/7500Ft), which change every two months.

SENATOR HÁZ ÉTTEREM INTERNATIONAL $$

([phone]36-320 466; www.senatorhaz.hu; Dobó István tér 11; mains 1900-3200Ft; noon-11pm) Seats in the antique-filled dining room of this charming hotel are coveted, but the outdoor ones in summer are the hot seat of Eger's main square. Try the cream of pumpkin soup served with duck liver (950Ft) and the *borjúpaprikás* (veal stew; 2300Ft).

BIKAVÉR BORHÁZ WINE BAR

([phone]36-413 262; Dobó István tér 10; 9am-10pm) Try one or two of the region's best wines at this central wine bar. The waiters can guide you with the right selection and supply a plate of cheese or grapes to help you cleanse your palate.

MARJÁN CUKRÁSZDA CAFE

([phone]36-312 784; www.marjancukraszda.hu; Kossuth Lajos utca 28; cakes 200-550Ft; 9am-10pm Jun-Sep, to 7pm Oct-May) Linger over coffee and sweets on the big terrace south of Dózsa György tér and directly below the castle.

SPORTS & ACTIVITIES

VALLEY OF THE BEAUTIFUL WOMEN WINE TASTING

(Szépasszony-völgy) Don't miss visiting the wine cellars of this evocatively named valley just over 1km southwest of the centre. This is the place to sample Bull's Blood – one of very few reds produced in Eger – or any of the whites: Leányka, Olaszrizling and Hárslevelű from nearby Debrő. The choice of wine cellars can be daunting (there are two dozen), so walk around and have a look yourself. Be careful, though; those 100mL glasses (around 100Ft) go down easily and quickly. The taxi fare back to the centre of Eger costs about 1000Ft. Unmissable.

TURKISH BATH SPA

(Török Fürdő; [phone]36-510 552; www.egertermal.hu; Fürdő utca 3-4; 2½hr session adult/child 2200/1500Ft; 4-9pm Mon & Tue, 3-9pm Wed & Thu, 1-9pm Fri, 9am-9pm Sat & Sun) After a hard day's drinking in the Valley of the Beautiful Women, nothing beats a soak and steam at this historic (and totally renovated) spa, which has a bath dating to 1617 at its core. It boasts five pools, saunas, steam room and hammam (Turkish bath). Various kinds of massage and treatments are also available. Highly recommended.

SLEEPING

AGRIA RETUR PANZIÓ GUESTHOUSE $

([phone]36-416 650; http://agria.returvendeghaz.hu; Knézich Károly utca 18; s/d/tr 3800/6400/9200Ft;) You couldn't find sweeter hosts than the daughter and mother who own this *panzió* (pension) near the minaret. Walking up three flights, you enter a cheery communal kitchen and eating area central to four rooms. Out back is a huge garden with tables and barbecue at your disposal.

HOTEL SENATOR-HÁZ BOUTIQUE HOTEL $$

(Senator House Hotel; [phone]36-411 711; www.senatorhaz.hu; Dobó István tér 11; s/d €50/70;) Eleven warm and cosy rooms occupy the upper two floors of this delightful inn on Eger's main square. Its ground floor is shared between a quality restaurant and a reception area stuffed with antiques and curios. Its sister property **Pátria Panzió** ([phone]36-411 711; www.senatorhaz.hu; Szúnyo köz 3; apt for 2/3/4 €65/95/115;), with three rooms and two huge apartments, is just round the corner.

HOTEL ROMANTIK HOTEL $$

([phone]36-310 456; www.romantikhotel.hu; Csíky Sándor utca 26; s/d €50/65;) This cosy 15-room hotel, with a pretty back garden and a delightful breakfast room, is an easy walk from the city centre, but far enough away to escape any noise in the summer months. Room 20 has its own balcony facing the garden. The friendly owner has bicycles for rent.

Balatonfüred

Explore

Balatonfüred is the oldest and most fashionable resort on Lake Balaton, Hungary's 'inland sea' 130km southwest of Budapest. In its glory days in the 19th century the wealthy and famous built large villas along its tree-lined streets, and their architectural legacy can still be seen today. More recently, the lake frontage received a massive makeover, and it now sports the most stylish marina on Balaton. The town is also known for its thermal water, but it's reserved for patients at the town's world-famous coronary hospital. You'll have to content yourself with swimming in the lake.

The Best...

➡ **Sight** Kisfaludy Strand (p162)
➡ **Place to Eat** Stefánia Vitorlás (p162)
➡ **Place to Drink** Karolina (p162)

Top Tip

High season in Lake Balaton is July and August; crowds descend and prices skyrocket. If you're keen to enjoy the water activities but don't want the crowds, try to time your visit in June or September, when the water is warm, everything is still open and it feels summery – without the intense humidity.

Getting There & Away

➡ **Bus** Six direct buses link Népliget station in Pest (2520Ft, 2½ hours) with Balatonfüred every day. Otherwise, you'll have to change in Veszprém.

➡ **Train** Three daily trains not requiring a change connect Déli train station in Buda with Balatonfüred (2725Ft, 2¼ hours). Dozens more go via Székesfehérvár.

Need to Know

➡ **Area Code** 87
➡ **Location** 130km southwest of Budapest
➡ **Tourist Office** (☑87-580 480; http://balatonfured.info.hu/oldal/tourinform; Blaha Lujza utca 5; ☺9am-7pm Mon-Sat, 10am-4pm Sun mid-Jun–Aug, 9am-5pm Mon-Fri, to 3pm Sat Sep–mid-Jun)

 SIGHTS

GYÓGY TÉR   SQUARE
(Cure Sq) This leafy square is home to the **State Hospital of Cardiology** (Országos Szívkórház; Gyógy tér 2), which put Balatonfüred on the map. In the centre you'll encounter the **Kossuth Pump House** (1853), a natural spring that dispenses slightly sulphuric, but drinkable, thermal water. If you can ignore the water's pale-yellow hue, join the locals lining up to fill their water bottles. On the northern side of the square is the **Balaton Pantheon**, with memorial plaques from those who took the cure here.

JÓKAI MEMORIAL MUSEUM   MUSEUM
(Jókai emlékmúzeum; ☑87-343 426; www.furedkult.hu; Honvéd utca 1; adult/concession 900/450Ft; ☺10am-5pm Tue-Sun) This museum is housed in the summer villa of the prolific writer Mór Jókai, north of Vitorlás tér. In his study, Jókai churned out many of his 200 novels under the stern gaze of wife, actress Róza Laborfalvi. The museum is filled with family memorabilia and period furniture.

WORTH A DETOUR

TIHANY

While in Balatonfüred, don't miss the chance to visit Tihany, a small peninsula 14km to the southwest and the place with the greatest historical significance on Lake Balaton. Activity here is centred on the tiny settlement of the same name, which is home to the celebrated **Benedictine Abbey Church** (Bencés Apátság Templom; ☑87-538-200; http://tihany.osb.hu; András tér 1; adult/child incl museum 1000/500Ft; ☺9am-6pm May-Sep, 10am-4.30pm Apr, 10am-5pm Oct, 10am-4pm Nov-Mar), filled with fantastic altars, pulpits and screens carved in the mid-18th century by an Austrian lay brother; all are baroque-rococo masterpieces in their own right. The church attracts a lot of tourists, but the peninsula itself has an isolated, almost wild feel to it. Hiking is one of Tihany's main attractions; there's a good map outlining the trails near the front of the church. Buses bound for Tihany depart Balatonfüred's bus/train station (310Ft, 30 minutes) at least hourly.

ROUND CHURCH
CHURCH

(Kerek templom; ☑87-343 029; Blaha Lujza utca 1; ☉services only) **FREE** Inspired by the Pantheon in Rome, the tiny neoclassical Round Church was completed in 1846. The *Crucifixion* (1891) by János Vaszary sits above the altar on the western wall.

VASZARY VILLA
GALLERY

(☑87-950 876; www.vaszaryvilla.hu; Honvéd utca 2-4; adult/child 1700/850Ft; ☉10am-5pm Wed-Sun) This beautifully restored villa (1892), once the residence of the Vaszarys, exhibits some works of the best-known family member, the painter János Vaszary, as well as a wonderful collection of arts and crafts from the 18th century.

🍴 EATING & DRINKING

BALATON
HUNGARIAN $$

(☑87-481 319; www.balatonetterem.hu; Kisfaludy utca 5; mains 1890-4700Ft; ☉11am-11pm) This cool, leafy oasis amid all the hubbub is set back from the lake in the shaded park area. Generous portions and decent fish selection.

ARANY CSILLAG PIZZÉRIA
PIZZA $$

(☑87-482 116; www.aranycsillagpizzeria.hu; Zsigmond utca 1; pizza & pasta dishes 1280-2880Ft; ☉noon-11pm Sun-Thu, to midnight Fri & Sat) A convivial pizzeria away from the flashy waterfront, Arany Csillag is a local favourite that attracts a mix of people. Its small shaded terrace fills quickly in summer, so either come early (6pm-ish) or book ahead.

STEFÁNIA VITORLÁS
HUNGARIAN $$$

(☑87-343 407; www.vitorlasetterem.hu; Tagore sétány 1; mains 1990-3950Ft; ☉9am-midnight) This enormous wooden villa sits right on the lake's edge at the foot of the town's pier. It's a prime spot to watch the yachts sail in and out of the harbour from the terrace while munching on Hungarian cuisine and sipping local wine.

KAROLINA
CAFE, BAR

(☑87-583 098; http://karolina.hu; Zákonyi Ferenc utca 4; ☉noon-9pm) Hands down the most popular gathering spot in town, Karolina is a sophisticated cafe-bar that does an excellent job of serving fresh coffee, aromatic teas and quality local wines. The Art Nouveau interior has a decadent air about it, while the terrace area with sofas couldn't be more laid-back.

KREDENC BORBISZTRÓ
WINE BAR

(☑06 20 518 9960; www.boraszportal.hu/kredencborbisztro-galeria; Blaha Lujza utca 7; ☉10am-11pm Tue-Sat, to 5pm Sun Apr-Oct, 10am-11pm Wed-Sat Nov-Mar) This family-run wine bar-bistro is a peaceful retreat only steps from the lakefront. The menu features oodles of local wines and the lovely menu also makes this an excellent choice for a light meal. The bar moonlights as a retail wine shop.

🏃 SPORTS & ACTIVITIES

ESZTERHÁZY & KISFALUDY STRANDS
BEACHES

Balatonfüred's most accessible grassy beaches, measuring about 1km in length, are **Eszterházy Strand** (www.balatonfuredistrandok.hu; Tagore sétány; adult/child 950/570Ft; ☉8.30am-7pm mid-Jun–mid-Aug, 9am-6pm mid-May–mid-Jun & mid-Aug–mid-Sep), with a water park right in town, and the more attractive **Kisfaludy Strand** (www.balatonfuredistrandok.hu; Aranyhíd sétány; adult/child 660/410Ft; ☉8.30am-7pm mid-Jun–mid-Aug, 8am-6pm mid-May–mid-Jun & mid-Aug–mid-Sep) further east.

🛏 SLEEPING

BALATON VILLA
HOTEL $$

(☑87-788 290; www.balatonvilla.hu; Deák Ferenc utca 38; s/d €25/50; ❈🕙) There are nine large rooms upstairs in this pastel-yellow and brick-red villa uphill from the lake. Each has its own balcony overlooking a sunny garden and grape vines, and guests can use the well-equipped kitchen and grill area.

HOTEL BLAHA LUJZA
HOTEL $$

(☑87-581 219; www.hotelblaha.hu; Blaha Lujza utca 4; s €38-45, d €54-75; ❈🕙) This was the summer home of the much-loved 19th-century actress-singer Lujza Blaha from 1893 to 1916. Its 22 rooms are a little snug but very comfy. Close to the lake.

★ANNA GRAND HOTEL
HOTEL $$$

(☑87-342 044; www.annagrandhotel.eu; Gyógy tér 1; s/d from 24,000/33,000Ft; ❈@🕙🏊) In a former life, the Anna Grand was the town's sanatorium, but it is now a luxury hotel with 100 rooms. Choose ones with either period antiques or modern furnishings, and views of the hotel's peaceful inner courtyard or tree-shaded Gyógy tér.

 # Sleeping

Accommodation in Budapest runs the gamut from hostels in converted flats and private rooms in far-flung housing estates to luxury guesthouses in the Buda Hills and five-star properties charging upwards of €300 a night. In general, accommodation in the Buda neighbourhoods is more limited than on the other side of the Danube River in Pest.

Hotels

Hotels – *szállók* or *szállodák* in Hungarian – can be anything from (rapidly disappearing) run-down socialist-era hovels to luxurious five-star palaces.

A cheap hotel is generally more expensive than a private room but may be the answer if you are only staying one night or arrive too late to get a room through an agency. Two-star hotels usually have rooms with a private bathroom; bathrooms are almost always in the hall in one-star places. Three- and four-star hotels can be excellent value compared with those in other European cities.

Because of the changing value of the forint, many midrange and top-end hotels quote their rates in euros, as we have here.

Serviced Apartments

Budapest is chock-a-block with serviced apartments and apartment (or suite) hotels. All have private bathrooms and usually kitchens – at the very least. Some are positively luxurious, while others are bare bones.

Guesthouses

There are scores of *panziók* (pensions) and *vendégházak* (guesthouses), but many are in the outskirts of Pest or the Buda Hills and not very convenient unless you have your own transport. They offer a homey atmosphere and (usually) great breakfasts. Pensions can cost as much as a moderate hotel, although there are some notable exceptions.

Hostels

Ifjúsági szállók (youth hostels) are open year-round, with the number of options increasing substantially during the university summer holidays (from mid-June or July to late August), when private outfits rent vacant dormitories and turn them into hostels.

You don't need to belong to Hostelling International or an associated organisation to stay at any of Budapest's hostels, but membership will sometimes get you a 10% discount or an extra night's accommodation. For information, check out the **Hungarian Youth Hostel Association** (MISZSZ; www.miszsz.hu), affiliated with Hostelling International.

Private Rooms

Fizetővendég szolgálat (paying-guest service) in Budapest is a great deal and still relatively cheap, but with the advent of stylish and affordable guesthouses it's not as widespread as it was a decade or so ago.

Private rooms generally cost from 7500Ft for a single, 8500Ft for a double and 12,000Ft to 16,000Ft for a small apartment. To get a room in the centre of town you may have to try several agencies. Individuals on the streets outside the main train stations may offer you a private room, but prices are usually higher and there is no quality control.

Budapest Info (p211) does not arrange private accommodation, but will send you to a travel agency such as **To-Ma** (Map p244; ☎1-353 0819; www.tomatour.hu; V Nádor utca 20; ⊙9am-7pm; Ⓜ M3 Arany János utca, 🚊2). Among the best agencies for private rooms are Ibusz (p211) and Vista (p211).

NEED TO KNOW

Price Ranges
The following price indicators represent the cost per night of a standard double room in high season.

€ under 15,000Ft (€50)

€€ 15,000Ft to 33,500Ft (€50 to €110)

€€€ over 33,500Ft (€110)

Extra Costs
➡ Travel agencies levy a surcharge (at least for the first night) if you stay fewer than three nights in a private room.

➡ Budapest levies a 4% local tourist tax on those aged 18 to 70.

➡ Some top-end hotels in Budapest do not include the whopping 18% ÁFA (value-added tax; VAT) on accommodation in their listed rack rates; make sure you read the bottom line.

Seasons
The low season for hotels runs roughly from mid-October or November to March (not including the Christmas and New Year holidays). The high season is the rest of the year, when prices can increase substantially.

Breakfast
The rate quoted for hostel and hotel accommodation usually includes breakfast, but check.

Lonely Planet's Top Choices

Four Seasons Gresham Palace Hotel (p170) Still the city's most luxurious hotel, risen phoenixlike from a derelict Art Nouveau palace.

Gerlóczy Rooms deLux (p168) Tastefully designed, homey accommodation above a popular cafe-restaurant in a quiet central square.

Zara Continental Hotel (p172) Stunning spa hotel recreated from an old-time city bath, with a rooftop swimming pool and panoramic garden.

Brody House (p173) Old and new meeting and greeting in what was once the residence of Hungary's prime minister.

Lánchíd 19 (p166) Award-winning boutique hotel with stunning design both inside and out.

Best by Budget

€

Maverick City Lodge (p171) Modern, warehouse-style hostel with great facilities.

Shantee House (p167) Budapest's first hostel grows (up) in size and design.

Aventura Boutique Hostel (p170) Colourful number that shuns bunk beds and curfews.

Hotel Császár (p167) Small but perfectly formed, with an Olympic pool attached.

Maria & István (p173) B&B that feels like you're staying with old friends.

€€

Baltazár (p166) Midrange hotel with a high-end Castle District location.

Casati (p172) An artful conversion of a beautiful building with sustainable credentials.

Budapest Rooms (p174) Well-run, good-looking B&B and a very helpful host.

Hotel Papillon (p168) Delightful 'country-style' hotel in the Buda Hills.

€€€

Buddha Bar Hotel (p169) Opulent makeover of one of the towering Klotild Palaces.

Art'otel Budapest (p166) Uber-designed caravanserai hard by the Danube.

Kempinski Hotel Corvinus (p169) Probably the best-run hotel in town.

Hotel Palazzo Zichy (p174) Impressive palace hotel on a lovely little square.

Best Boutique Hotels

Lánchíd 19 (p166) Award-winning boutique hotel with changing facade.

Zara Boutique Hotel (p168) Charming boutique style in the Belváros, steps from the Danube.

Soho Hotel (p173) Striking decor in the heart of the nightlife district.

Bohem Art (p168) A must for art lovers – you choose your room by what hangs on its walls.

Best Cool Hostels

Wombat's (p171) Huge, colourful and award-winning hostel in the heart of Erzsébetváros.

11th Hour Hostel (p168) Film buffs will want to lay their heads here.

Shantee House (p167) Colourful and cool hostel reinvents itself.

Penthouse Privates (p171) Quiet hostel with fun, couple-themed rooms.

Where to Stay

Neighbourhood	For	Against
Castle District	In the thick of historic Buda with million-dollar views of the Danube and Pest	Not particularly good value for money; relatively limited entertainment and somewhat isolated
Gellért Hill & Tabán	Great views of the city and river; very green and tranquil	Away from it all in a negative sense, though transport links are good
Óbuda & Buda Hills	Excellent choice if you're looking for the countryside in the city	Terrible choice if you're not looking for the countryside in the city
Belváros	Close to just about everything, especially eating, drinking and entertainment options	Noisy all day and night; more expensive than most other parts of the city
Parliament & Around	Very central to things that matter; lots of important sights nearby	Not always a great selection of places to eat and things to do after dark
Margaret Island & Northern Pest	Excellent mix of built-up areas and parkland	Not much in the way of sights; transport gaps (unless you count trolleybuses)
Erzsébetváros & the Jewish Quarter	Entertainment central – the district for the party animal you know you are	In-your-face and touristy; can be very noisy at night
Southern Pest	Full of 'real' neighbourhoods with far fewer tourists than other districts	Red-light districts and dodgy bars – the only area in the city where your should keep your eyes open at all times
City Park & Beyond	Budapest's biggest park, with lots and lots of things to see and do	Very far away from real life, despite relatively good transport links

SLEEPING

🛏 Castle District

BALTAZÁR
BOUTIQUE HOTEL **$$**

Map p230 (🖉1-300 7051; http://baltazarbu-dapest.com/; I Országház utca 31; r from €95; ✳@🛜; 🚌16, 16A, 116) This family-run boutique hotel at the northern end of the Castle District has 11 colourful rooms decorated with vintage furniture. Nods to more recent times include street art on the walls and a rain shower in the bathrooms. One of the rooms has a lovely little balcony with views to the castle. Excellent value. The in-house restaurant is particularly known for its wine card.

HOTEL VICTORIA
HOTEL **$$**

Map p230 (🖉1-457 8080; www.victoria.hu; I Bem rakpart 11; s €82-119, d €90-124; 🅿✳🛜; 🚌86, 🚋19, 41) This rather elegant hotel has 27 comfortable and spacious rooms with million-dollar views of Parliament and the Danube. Despite its small size it gets special mention for its friendly service and facilities, including the renovated rooms of the 19th-century Jenő Hubay Music Hall (p63), attached to the hotel, which now serves as a small concert venue and theatre.

BURG HOTEL
HOTEL **$$**

Map p230 (🖉1-212 0269; www.burghotelbuda pest.com; I Szentháromság tér 7-8; s/d/ste from €85/99/109; 🅿✳🛜; 🚌16, 16A, 116) This small hotel with all the mod cons has 26 rooms that have been freshened up but are not much more than just ordinary. But, as they say, location is everything. It's just opposite Matthias Church.

BIBI PANZIÓ
PENSION **$$**

Map p230 (🖉1-786 0955; www.bibipanzio.hu; II Dékán utca 3; s €45-55, d €55-65; 🅿✳🛜; 🚇M2 Széll Kálmán tér) Just a block off the northern side of Széll Kálmán tér, this pension under new management may look ordinary from the outside but has 10 comfortable, though small, rooms. Decor is the basic 'just off the assembly line' look. We love the wall map with pins indicating where all the guests hail from.

★ LÁNCHÍD 19
BOUTIQUE HOTEL **$$$**

Map p230 (🖉1-419 1900; www.lanchid19hotel. hu; I Lánchíd utca 19; r €110-325; ✳@🛜; 🚋19, 41) This award-winning boutique number facing the Danube has the wow factor in spades. Each of the 45 rooms and three 'panoramic' suites is different, with distinctive artwork and a unique chair ('Can you actually *sit* on that?') designed by art-college students. You can't lose with the views: to the front is the Danube and to the back Buda Castle.

Stand outside and watch the front elevation form pictures as special sensors reflect the movements of the Danube. Cool or what?

ART'OTEL BUDAPEST
HOTEL **$$$**

Map p230 (🖉1-487 9487; www.artotels.com/bu dapest; I Bem rakpart 16-19; s/d/ste €99/109/149, with Danube view €174/190/254; 🅿✳🛜; 🚌86, 🚋19, 41) The Art'otel is a minimalist establishment that would not look out of place in London or New York. But what makes this 165-room place unique is that it cobbles together a seven-storey modern building (views of the castle and the Danube) and an 18th-century baroque building, linking them with a leafy courtyard-atrium. We love the gaming theme throughout.

HILTON BUDAPEST
HOTEL **$$$**

Map p230 (🖉1-488 6600; www.budapest.hilton. com; I Hess András tér 1-3; r €130-200; 🅿✳🛜; 🚌16, 16A, 116) Perched above the Danube on Castle Hill, the Hilton was built carefully in and around a 14th-century church and baroque college (though it still has its hard-core preservationist detractors). It has 322 somewhat sombre rooms, with dark carpeting and low lighting, but you can't beat the views. Guests pay for wi-fi.

BUDA CASTLE
FASHION HOTEL
BOUTIQUE HOTEL **$$$**

Map p230 (🖉1 224 7900; www.budacastlehotel budapest.com; I Úri utca 39; r €110-150; ✳🛜; 🚌16, 16A, 116) The Mellow Mood Group's flagship top-end hotel is housed in a 15th-century town house, but apart from a bit of vaulted brick ceiling in the lobby you'd never know that. The 25 rooms and suites, done up in warm shades of brown, tan and beige, look on to a cobbled street or face a relaxing courtyard planted with grass and trees.

ST GEORGE RESIDENCE
BOUTIQUE HOTEL **$$$**

Map p230 (🖉1-393 5700; www.stgeorgehotel. hu; I Fortuna utca 4; ste from €119-300; 🛜; 🚌16, 16A, 116) Housed in a venerable 700-year-old building right in the heart of the Castle District, this somewhat over-the-top boutique hotel is all period grandeur, its four classes of suites featuring such touches as green marble in the decor, imported Italian furniture and Jacuzzis (which are a welcome anachronism).

🛏 Gellért Hill & Tabán

★SHANTEE HOUSE
HOSTEL $

(📞1-385 8946; www.backpackbudapest.hu; XI Takács Menyhért utca 33; beds in yurt €10, dm large/small €13/16, d €38; ❊ @ 🛜; 🚌7, 7A, 🚋19, 49) Budapest's first hostel, the Back Pack Guesthouse, has added two floors to its colourfully painted suburban 'villa' in south Buda and been reborn as Shantee House. It's all good and the fun (and sleeping bodies in high season) still spills out into a lovely landscaped garden, with hammocks, a yurt and a gazebo. Two of the five doubles are en suite. The upbeat attitude of friendly, much-travelled owner-manager Attila seems to permeate the place, and the welcome is always warm. Ask about excursions to the Pilis Mountains and other activities.

CHARLES HOTEL & APARTMENTS
APARTMENT $

(📞1-212 9169; www.charleshotel.hu; I Hegyalja út 23; studios €45-80, apt €75-155; ❊ @ 🛜; 🚌8, 112, 178) On the Buda side and somewhat on the beaten track (a train line runs right past it), the Charles has 70 'studios' (larger-than-average rooms) with kitchens, as well as good-sized two-room apartments. Rental bikes cost 2000Ft a day.

KISGELLÉRT VENDÉGHÁZ
GUESTHOUSE $

(📞1-279 0346; www.kisgellert.hu; XI Otthon utca 14; s/d/tr 6000/8000/11,500Ft; ❊ @; 🚌8, 112, 🚋61) This cute little guesthouse with 11 rooms is named after the 'Little Gellért' hill to the west of the more famous larger one and sits dreamily in 'At Home St'. It's away from the action but leafy and quiet and easily reached by bus.

CITADELLA HOTEL
HOSTEL $

Map p236 (📞1-466 5794; www.citadella.hu; XI Citadella sétány; dm 3200Ft, s & d with shared shower/shower/bathtub 10,500/11,500/12,500Ft; @; 🚌27) This hotel in the fortress atop Gellért Hill is pretty threadbare, though the dozen guestrooms are extra large, retain some of their original features and have their own shower or bath (toilets are on the circular corridor). The two dorm rooms have six and 12 beds and shared facilities.

ORION HOTEL
HOTEL $$

Map p236 (📞1-356 8583; www.bestwestern-ce.com/orion; I Döbrentei utca 13; s/d from €70/90; ❊ @ 🛜; 🚌18, 19, 41) Hidden away in the Tabán district, the Orion is a cosy place with a relaxed atmosphere and within easy walking distance of the Castle District. The 30 rooms are bright and of a good size, and there's a small sauna for guest use.

DANUBIUS HOTEL GELLÉRT
LUXURY HOTEL $$$

Map p236 (📞1-889 5500; www.danubiusgroup.com/gellert; XI Szent Gellért tér 1; s/d/ste from €85/170/268; ❊ P ❊ @ 🛜; Ⓜ M4 Szent Gellért tér, 🚌18, 19, 47, 49) Buda's *grande dame* is a 234-room four-star hotel with loads of character. Completed in 1918, the hotel contains examples of late Art Nouveau, notably the thermal spa's entrance hall and Zsolnay ceramic fountains. Prices depend on which way your room faces and what sort of bathroom it has. Use of the thermal baths is free for hotel guests.

The Gellért was the inspiration (but not the actual film location) for the hotel in Wes Anderson's *The Grand Budapest Hotel*, which opened in early 2014.

🛏 Óbuda & Buda Hills

HOTEL CSÁSZÁR
HOTEL $

Map p234 (📞1-336 2640; www.csaszarhotel.hu; II Frankel Leó utca 35; s €39-49, d €48-59, ste €99-120; ❊ 🛜 🛜; 🚌86, 🚋17) The huge yellow building in which the 'Emperor' is located was built in the 1850s as a convent, which might explain the size of the 45 cell-like rooms. Request one of the superior rooms, which are larger and look onto the nearby outdoor Olympic-size pools of the huge Császár-Komjádi swimming complex.

GRAND HOSTEL BUDAPEST
HOSTEL $

Map p233 (📞1-274 1111; www.grandhostel.hu; XII Hüvösvölgyi utca 69; dm €10-17, s/d from €24/32; P @ 🛜) 'Grand' might be overstating things a titch, but this colourful hostel does come pretty close, with its cavern-like cocktail bar, tiled rooms, communal barbecues and DJ nights, to being 'great'. There's a sociable feel and the staff are happy to help arrange all manner of excursions. To get here, take tram 61 to the Kelemen Laszlo utca stop.

SLEEPING GELLÉRT HILL & TABÁN

★HOTEL PAPILLON HOTEL **$$**

Map p234 (📞1-212 4750; www.hotelpapillon.
hu; Il Rózsahegy utca 3/b; s/d/tr €44/54/69, apt
€78-90; P ✴@📶❄; 🚍4, 6) One of Buda's
best-kept accommodation secrets, this
cosy hotel in Rózsadomb (Rose Hill) has a
delightful back garden with a small swim-
ming pool, and some of the 20 rooms have
balconies. There are also four apartments
available in the same building, one boast-
ing a lovely roof terrace.

BEATRIX PANZIÓ HOTEL GUESTHOUSE **$$**

Map p233 (📞1-275 0550; www.beatrixhotel.
hu; Il Széher út 3; s €45-55, d €50-60, apt €55-
80; P @📶; 🚍5, 🚍61) On the way up to the
Buda Hills, but still easily accessible by frequent public transport, this is an attractive,
award-winning pension with 15 rooms and
four apartments. Surrounding the property
is a lovely garden with a fish pond, sun terraces and a grill; a barbecue might even be
organised during your stay.

🛏 Belváros

11TH HOUR HOSTEL HOSTEL **$**

Map p238 (📞1-266 2153; www.11thhourcinema
hostel.com; V Magyar utca 11; dm €21-27, apt
€66-90; @📶; Ⓜ️M2 Astoria) A must for film
fans, this excellent hostel is set in its very
own three-storey townhouse, with en-suite
dorms sleeping four to 13 as well as private
apartments. Three hundred movies are
available in its projection room, and there
are relaxed communal areas as well as table
football.

MAVERICK HOSTEL HOSTEL **$**

Map p238 (📞1-267 3166; www.mavericklodges.
com; V Ferenciek tere 2; dm €10-20, d €35-60;
@📶; Ⓜ️M3 Ferenciek tere) A clean, well-run
hostel with 19 rooms over three floors in a
splendid old building, the Maverick has a
kitchen on each floor, a comfortable common room, private doubles and four- to 10-
bed dorms (no bunks). Two dorms and one
double share bathrooms. It attracts a range
of travellers, including families, and hosts relaxed evening events such as wine tastings.

GINGKO HOSTEL HOSTEL **$**

Map p238 (📞1-266 6107; www.gingko.hu; V Szép
utca 5; dm/d/tr 3500/11,000/15,000Ft; @📶;
Ⓜ️M2 Astoria) In an old apartment block, this
homely hostel has six rooms, with two doubles and seven-bed dorms, all sharing bath-

rooms. It has a relaxed atmosphere, with the
feel of a big, friendly shared house.

RED BUS HOSTEL HOSTEL **$**

Map p238 (📞1-266 0136; www.redbusbudapest.
hu; V Semmelweiss utca 14; dm €8.75-16, s €25;
@📶; Ⓜ️M2 Astoria) One of the very first independent hostels for travellers in Pest, Red
Bus is a quiet, sociable and well-managed
place, with five large and airy rooms. There
are two- to five-bed dorms and a great single. Two-night minimum stay.

★GERLÓCZY ROOMS
DELUX BOUTIQUE HOTEL **$$**

Map p238 (📞1-501 4000; www.gerloczy.hu; V
Gerlóczy utca 1; r €80-95; ✴📶; Ⓜ️M2 Astoria)
A standout choice in the city, Gerlóczy hits
the mark with an excellent combination of
good value, decor, atmosphere and profes-
sional service. Set over four floors of an
1890s building on an attractive square, the
individually designed and well-proportioned
rooms all have king-size beds. The winding
wrought-iron staircase, domed stained-glass
skylight and etched glass are wonderful
touches. Of the 19 rooms, two have balconies
overlooking the square and four are in the
attic with exposed wooden beams.

KATONA APARTMENTS APARTMENT **$$**

Map p238 (📞06 70 221 1797; www.kartik.hu; V
Petőfi Sándor utca 6; apt for 2/4 €49/69, 2-room
apt for 4/6/8 €99/119/139; ✴📶; Ⓜ️M3 Ferenciek tere) Simply furnished and cleverly
arranged apartments in a quiet old block,
set right in the heart of the Belváros. Additional twin beds pull out from under each
double, making these fantastic for families.
Each is equipped with kitchen, TV, fan or
air-con, washing machine, hairdryer and
iron. The owners are helpful and a font of
knowledge on the latest city news.

ZARA BOUTIQUE HOTEL BOUTIQUE HOTEL **$$**

Map p238 (📞1-577 0700; www.boutiquehotelbu-
dapest.com; V Só utca 6; r €84-104, ste €200-
300; ♿✴📶; Ⓜ️M4 Fővám tér) This boutique
hotel with 74 smallish but well-designed
rooms on seven floors has been created
from two buildings linked by an open-air
corridor. Make sure you ask for a room fac-
ing Só utca (eg no 37) as half of the rooms
look down onto an uninspiring courtyard.

BOHEM ART HOTEL BOUTIQUE HOTEL **$$**

Map p238 (📞1-327 9020; www.bohemarthotel.
hu; V Molnár utca 35; r €90-160, ste €159-200;

P ✱ @ 🛜; MM4 Fővám tér) Though the rooms at this delightful small hotel are a little on the compact side, each one is decorated in its own individual style, with giant prints, bold touches of colour amidst monochrome decor and ultra-modern furnishings present throughout. An indulgent buffet breakfast is included in the price.

HOTEL ART   HOTEL $$
Map p238 (☑1-266 2166; www.threecorners.com; V Király Pál utca 12; s €44-89, d €69-99; ✱🛜; MM3/4 Kálvin tér) Part of a small chain, this orderly corner hotel has Art Deco touches (including a pink facade) in the public areas, a small fitness centre and sauna, and 36 clean and well-kept guestrooms, including four apartments with separate sitting and sleeping areas.

BUTTERFLY HOME   HOTEL $$
Map p238 (☑06 30 964 7287; www.butterflyhome.hu; V Képíró utca 3; s €58, d €75-104, ste €112; ✱🛜; MM3/4 Kálvin tér) In a quiet little backstreet close to Kálvin tér, this small and welcoming hotel has a large, sweeping staircase leading to spacious, plainly decorated rooms. It's professionally run, with lots of friendly advice from the cheerful owner, and breakfast is included.

LA PRIMA FASHION HOTEL   HOTEL $$
Map p238 (☑1-799 0088; www.laprimahotel.hu; V Piarista utca 6; d €80-120; P ⊖ @ 🛜; MM3 Ferenciek tere) Although the turquoise-and-brown colour theme is a little overpowering, this bright hotel is in a great location close to both the Danube and Váci utca. There are 80 rooms and one suite; bathrooms are attractive and some have tubs.

LEO PANZIÓ   PENSION $$
Map p238 (☑1-266 9041; www.leopanzio.hu; V Kossuth Lajos utca 2/a; s/d/tr €65/75/104; ⊖✱🛜; MM3 Ferenciek tere) At this very centrally located place, a dozen of the 14 immaculate rooms look down on busy Kossuth Lajos utca, but they all have double glazing and are quiet. Two rooms face an internal courtyard. It's well run, well kept and traditionally furnished.

KEMPINSKI HOTEL
CORVINUS   LUXURY HOTEL $$$
Map p238 (☑1-429 3777; www.kempinski-budapest.com; V Erzsébet tér 7-8; r from €300; P ⊖ ✱ @ 🛜 ✱✱; MM1/2/3 Deák Ferenc tér) The public areas, guestrooms and suites (of which there are 340) at this high-end hotel remain among the classiest in town, even with the advent of so many five-star and boutique hotels. The two restaurants offer excellent traditional Central European cuisine or world-class Japanese in modern surrounds. There's a spa on the 2nd floor.

BUDDHA BAR HOTEL   HOTEL $$$
Map p238 (☑1-799 7300; www.buddhabarhotel budapest.com; V Váci utca 34; d €150-300; ✱ @ 🛜; MM3 Ferenciek tere) This glamorous five-star hotel inhabits one of the impressive neo-baroque Klotild Palaces that tower over Szabad sajtó út. The hotel has retained some of its period features, such as the original staircase, but is kitted out throughout in a modern, oriental style (in keeping with this international chain's theme). Rooms are opulently dressed, and there's a restaurant and bar, where you can listen to the hotel's signature Buddha Bar DJs while supping cocktails. The wellness centre is beautifully designed.

MILLENNIUM COURT MARRIOTT
EXECUTIVE APARTMENTS   APARTMENT $$$
Map p238 (☑1-235 1800; www.marriott.com/buder; V Piarista utca 4; studio/1-bed apt €165, 2-bed apt €190; P ⊖ ✱ 🛜; MM3 Ferenciek tere) This upmarket, well-run establishment offers 108 traditionally furnished, well-equipped studios and one- and two-bed apartments, and has laundry facilities on each of its nine floors. Studios measure 61 sq metres, one-beds 50 sq metres, and two-beds 75 sq metres.

🛏 Parliament & Around

HOME-MADE HOSTEL   HOSTEL $
Map p244 (☑1-302 2103; www.homemade hostel.com; VI Teréz körút 22; dm €11-17, d €40-50; @🛜; MM1 Oktogon, 🚋4, 6) This homey, extremely welcoming hostel with 20 beds in four rooms has recycled tables hanging upside down from the ceiling and old valises under the beds serving as lockers. The whole idea was to use forgotten objects from old Budapest homes in a new way. The old-style kitchen is museum-quality. You may want to stay forever.

CENTRAL BACKPACK
KING HOSTEL   HOSTEL $
Map p244 (☑06 30 667 9669; www.centralbackpackking.hostel.com; V Október 6 utca 15; dm €12-18, d €45-52; @🛜; 🚋15, 115, MM3 Arany János

utca) This upbeat place in the heart of the Inner Town has dorm rooms with seven or eight beds on one floor and doubles, triples and quads on another. There's a small, scrupulously clean kitchen, a large, bright common room, and views across Október 6 utca.

TRENDY BUDAPEST B&B HOSTEL   HOSTEL $

Map p244 (⏎06 30 611 9541, 06 70 513 2200; www.trendybudapesthostel.com; V Oktober 6 utca 19; d/q from €29/39; @☎; 🚌15, 115, MM3 Arany János utca) Bright, stylish and spacious, the half-dozen rooms at this apartment B&B live up to the name. Each room is individually decorated, with designer wallpaper and pinks, reds and creams predominating. Its ideal location in the centre of Pest is paired with the owner's excellent knowledge of the city's hot spots. Two of the rooms share facilities.

GARIBALDI GUESTHOUSE & APARTMENTS   B&B $

Map p244 (⏎1-302 3457; www.garibaldiguesthouse.hu; V Garibaldi utca 5; s €28-36, d €44-68, 2-/4-person apt €54/116; @☎; MM2 Kossuth Lajos tér, 🚌2) This guesthouse has five rooms with shared bathroom and kitchen in a flat just around the corner from Parliament. In the same building, there are a half-dozen apartments available on four floors; one large one has a balcony overlooking Garibaldi utca. Central and comfortable.

HOTEL PARLAMENT   HOTEL $$

Map p244 (⏎1-374 6000; www.parlament-hotel.hu; V Kálmán Imre utca 19; r €70-150; P✳@☎; 🚌15, 115, MM2 Kossuth Lajos tér) This minimalist delight in Lipótváros has 65 recently renovated rooms. The nonallergenic white pine floors are a plus, as is the self-service bar off the lobby, the dedicated ironing room, the adorable wellness centre with its own private dressing room, and the free tea and coffee at 5pm daily. Test your knowledge on the unique 'design wall' in the lobby with photographs and the names of famous Magyars etched in the glass.

MEDOSZ HOTEL   HOTEL $$

Map p244 (⏎1-374 3000; www.medoszhotel.hu; VI Jókai tér 9; s €49-59, d €59-69, ste €99-109; P☎; MM1 Oktogon) One of the most central cheaper hotels in Pest, the Medosz is just opposite the restaurants and bars of Liszt Ferenc tér. All of the 74 rooms have now been refitted and boast parquet floors, double glazing and small but up-to-the-minute

bathrooms. Choose a room with a balcony (eg 903, 1001 or 1003).

COTTON HOUSE HOTEL   PENSION $$

Map p244 (⏎1-354 2600; www.cotton-house-hotel-budapest.com; Jókai utca 26; r €40-80; ✳@☎; 🚌4, 6) This 23-room place has a jazz/speakeasy theme that gets a bit tired after a while (though the old radios and vintage telephones do actually work). Prices vary widely depending on the season and rooms have shower, tub or Jacuzzi. Enter from Weiner Leó utca 19.

★FOUR SEASONS GRESHAM PALACE HOTEL   LUXURY HOTEL $$$

Map p244 (⏎1-268 6000; www.fourseasons.com/budapest; V Széchenyi István tér 5-6; r/ste from €310/1000; P✳@☎♨; 🚌16, 🚌2) This magnificent 179-room hotel was created out of the long-derelict Art Nouveau Gresham Palace (1906) and a lot of blood, sweat and tears. No expense was spared to piece back together the palace's Zsolnay tiles, mosaics and celebrated wrought-iron Peacock Gates leading north and south from the enormous lobby, and the hotel is truly worthy of its name. The spa on the 5th floor, with a smallish infinity lap pool and iced towels at the ready, is among the most beautiful in the city.

🛏 Margaret Island & Northern Pest

AVENTURA BOUTIQUE HOSTEL   HOSTEL $

Map p248 (⏎1-239 0782; www.aventurahostel.com; XIII Visegrádi utca 12; dm €9-19, d €29-56, apt €38-66; @☎; MM3 Nyugati pályaudvar, 🚌4, 6) This has got to be the most chilled hostel in Budapest. Run by two affable ladies, it has four themed rooms (India, Africa, Japan and – our favourite – Space). We love the colours and fabrics, the in-house massage, and the dorms with loft sleeping for four to eight. There are a couple of nearby apartments available as well.

BOAT HOTEL FORTUNA   HOTEL $$

Map p248 (⏎1-288 8100; www.fortunahajo.hu; XIII Szent István Park, Carl Lutz rakpart; with bathroom s €55-80, d €65-100, with washbasin s €20-25, d €30-35; ✳@☎; 🚌76) Sleeping on a former river ferry anchored in the Danube may not be everyone's idea of a good time, but it's a unique experience. This 'boatel' has 42 single and double air-conditioned rooms with shower and toilet at water level.

Below deck, an additional 14 rooms with one, two or three beds and washbasin are not unlike old-fashioned hostel accommodation. There's a popular restaurant serving Balkan grills on deck.

PETER'S APARTMENTS APARTMENT $$

Map p248 (☎06 30 520 0400; www.peters.hu; XIII Victor Hugó utca 25-27; s/d/tr from €42/52/62; ❄@📶; 🚌15, 115, 🚌76) This budget to midrange place in Pest offers 15 studio apartments of approximately 20 sq metres with kitchenettes in a basic but clean building at some rock-bottom prices. The more expensive units have air-con and balconies; all have TV. Prices are negotiable, especially during the low season (November to mid-March) and at weekends.

DANUBIUS GRAND HOTEL MARGITSZIGET HOTEL $$$

Map p248 (☎1 -889 4700; www.danubiushotels.com; XIII Margit-sziget; s €146-226, d €160-240, ste €206-300; P❄≋; 🚌26) Constructed in the late 19th century, this comfortable (but not grand) and tranquil hotel has 164 rooms that boast all the mod cons. It's connected to the Danubius Health Spa Margitsziget (p111) via a heated underground corridor, and the cost of taking the waters is included in the hotel rate. Guests pay for wi-fi in their rooms.

NH BUDAPEST HOTEL $$$

Map p248 (☎1-814 0000; www.nh-hotels.com; XIII Vígszínház utca 3; r €99-159; P❄@📶; 🚋4, 6) There are 160 rooms spread out over this eight-floor purpose-built hotel, and two or three rooms on each floor have a balcony. We especially like the hotel's location behind the Comedy Theatre, the minimalist but welcoming and very bright atrium lobby, and the flash fitness centre on the 8th floor.

ADINA APARTMENT HOTEL APARTMENT $$$

Map p248 (☎1-236 8888; www.adina.hu; XIII Hegedüs Gyula utca 52-54; studio €160-246, 1-bedroom apt €191-320, 2-bedroom apt €271-442; ❄@📶≋; 🚌15, 76, Ⓜ M3 Lehel tér) This lovely property close to Váci út and the West End City Centre mall has 97 tastefully furnished units of between 45 and 110 sq metres in three wings, a gorgeous courtyard garden, marble finishings throughout, classical music in the lobby and an indoor swimming pool and fitness centre. Discounted rates are available at the weekend.

Erzsébetváros & the Jewish Quarter

MAVERICK CITY LODGE HOSTEL $

Map p250 (☎1-793 1605; www.mavericklodges.com; Kazinczy utca 24-26; dm from €10, d €40; @📶; Ⓜ M2 Astoria) Sister to Maverick Hostel (p168), recently opened Maverick City Lodge has three floors of dorms and private rooms, decorated in a modern, warehouse style with white wood, bold colours and bean bags. Each bed has locker, curtain and reading light; private rooms with mezzanines are good for families. Common areas, including the kitchen, are all well thought out and equipped.

BIG FISH HOSTEL HOTEL $

Map p250 (☎06 70 302 2432; www.bigfishhostel.com; VII Erzsébet körút 33; dm €12-18, d €22; @📶; Ⓜ M2 Blaha Lujza tér, 🚋4, 6) If you like your music, you'll want to stay in this not-so-small pond where visiting bands lay their heads and the sound-engineer owner is a nightlife encyclopedia. There are five rooms – two dorms with eight to 10 beds, one with four, and two private doubles – plus a separate apartment available in summer.

PENTHOUSE PRIVATES HOSTEL $

Map p250 (☎06 70 671 2723; www.facebook.com/penthouseprivates; VI Király utca 56; s 5500-6500Ft, d 12,000-15,000Ft; 📶; Ⓜ M1 Oktogon, 🚋4, 6) Although nominally a hostel, Penthouse Privates offers just that – six double rooms, one en suite and three with balcony, high above Király utca. Each of the six rooms has a couple theme – be it Sid & Nancy or Bert & Ernie – and the whole set-up is bright, clean and convivial.

WOMBAT'S HOSTEL $

Map p250 (☎1-883 5005; www.wombats-hostels.com; Király utca 20; dm €16-20, d €29; 📶; Ⓜ M1/2/3 Deák Ferenc tér) Well located for Erzsébetváros nightlife – it's directly opposite buzzing Gozsdu udvar – this slick and well-equipped hostel can accommodate a whopping 465 guests in its 120 rooms. Choose from four- to eight-bed dorms or doubles, all of which are en suite. There's a clean, cool design throughout and a large common area set in a colourful glass-roofed atrium. It's part of a Central European award-winning chain of hostels.

LOFT HOSTEL
HOSTEL $

Map p238 (☑1-328 0916; www.lofthostel.hu; V Veres Pálné utca 19; dm 4400-5600Ft, apt 14,000Ft; @ 🛜; ☐5, 7, Ⓜ M3/4 Kálvin tér) This hostel may well succeed in its loft-y aspirations to be the hottest backpacker magnet in town. Travellers end up lingering longer than expected, seduced by the wonderful atmosphere; it feels like staying at a friend's house. Private apartment also available.

CARPE NOCTEM
HOSTEL $

Map p244 (☑06 70 670 0384; www.carpenoctem original.com; VI Szobi utca 5; dm 5400Ft; @ 🛜; Ⓜ M3 Nyugati pályaudvar, ☐4, 6) Part of the Budapest Party Hostels chain, this relaxed place offers a smaller, more laid-back option than its sister establishments. With just three rooms of six- to eight-bed dorms, it has an intimate, easygoing atmosphere. It's right at the top of an apartment block – so expect quite a hike with your bags.

UNITY HOSTEL
HOSTEL $

Map p250 (☑1-413 7377; www.unityhostel. com; VI Király utca 60, 3rd fl; dm €15, d €30-40; ✳ @ 🛜; Ⓜ M1 Oktogon, ☐4, 6) This hostel's location in the heart of party town would be draw enough, but add to that a roof terrace with breathtaking views of the Ferenc Liszt Music Academy and the amiable, relaxed atmosphere and you have a winner. It sleeps 54 people over two levels and offers both air-con and fans.

BLUE DANUBE HOSTEL
HOSTEL $

Map p250 (☑06 30 299 0870; huqwerty@ya-hoo.com; VII Kazinczy utca 5; dm/s/tw €15/25/36; 🛜; Ⓜ M2 Astoria, ☐47, 49) This place gets top marks for the sheer effort the super-knowledgeable host, Sándor, puts into making guests feel welcome, equipping them with maps and advice and even picking them up at ungodly hours. The hostel consists of several rooms in a self-contained apartment – shared bathroom and en suites available.

MARCO POLO HOSTEL
HOSTEL $

Map p250 (☑1-413 2555; www.marcopolohos-tel.com; VII Nyár utca 6; dm/tw €10/40; @ 🛜; Ⓜ M2 Blaha Lujza tér, ☐4, 6) The Mellow Mood Group's very central flagship hostel is a long-established, pastel-painted 47-room place with TVs in all the rooms (except the dorms) and a lovely courtyard. Even the five spotless 12-bed dorms are 'private', with the dozen beds separated by lockers and curtains. There's also a basement bar. Efficiently run.

GRANDIO
HOSTEL $

Map p250 (☑06 70 670 0390; www.grandiopar-tyhostel.com; VII Nagy Diófa utca 8; dm 3300-4700Ft; 🛜; Ⓜ M2 Blaha Lujza tér, ☐4, 6) Above the ruin bar (p127) of the same name, this hostel's rooms are ranged around the 2nd floor of the pub's central, tree-filled courtyard. Laidback, sociable and pretty basic, it's all about the good times here, so don't expect to sleep much.

★ KAPITAL INN
B&B $$

Map p250 (☑06 30 915 2029; www.kapita-linn.com; VI Aradi utca 30, 4th fl; r €89-125, ste €199; ✳ @ 🛜; Ⓜ M1 Vörösmaty utca) Stylishly decorated and well-run B&B with just four luxurious rooms and a two-bed suite on the 4th floor of a beautiful 1893 building. The sleek, recently revamped breakfast room has a fridge stocked with goodies that can be raided at any time, and the 56-sq-metre terrace is a great place to take breakfast or just relax in the sun. Guests can also use a little office with its own laptop. The cheaper rooms share a bathroom and there's no lift.

★ ZARA CONTINENTAL HOTEL
HOTEL $$

Map p250 (☑1-815 1000; www.continentalhotel-budapest.com; VII Dohány utca 42-44; r/ste from €90/150; P ✳ @ 🛜 ✳; Ⓜ M2 Blaha Lujza tér, ☐4, 6) A sympathetic renovation of the glorious Hungária Fürdő (Hungária Bath), the Zara Continental has atmosphere and style in spades. With 272 large and beautifully furnished rooms and a huge atrium lobby retaining some of the original 19th-century building's features, the major draw here is the wellness centre on the top floor and the panoramic garden with swimming pool.

CASATI
HOTEL $$

Map p250 (☑1-343 1198; www.casatibuda-pesthotel.com; VI Paulay Ede utca 31; r €90-130; P ✳ 🛜; Ⓜ M1 Opera) 🏾 The ground-floor gallery and art-adorned reception set the tone at this classy hotel, set in a made-over 18th-centurybuilding that has tastefully retained a number of original features. Rooms come in a variety of cool and contemporary styles and breakfast is served in a funky covered courtyard. There's a gym and sauna. It's won awards for sustainable practices.

ANDRÁSSY HOTEL
HOTEL $$

Map p250 (☑1-462 2100; www.mamaison.com; Andrássy út 111; r/ste from €105/190; P ✳ @ 🛜; Ⓜ M1 Bajza utca) Just off leafy Andrássy út (enter from Munkácsy Mihály utca 5-7), this hotel has 68 tastefully decorated rooms (most with balconies) in a heritage-listed Bauhaus building dating from 1937.

CONNECTION
GUEST HOUSE
GUESTHOUSE **$$**

Map p250 (☑1-267 7104; www.connectionguest-house.com; VII Király utca 41; s €30, d €50-90; ❀🛜; Ⓜ M1 Opera, 🚊4, 6) Very central gay-friendly guesthouse above a leafy courtyard with nine bedrooms, two of which share a bathroom. Attracts all ages and has super-helpful owners. Larger rooms have sofas and mezzanine levels. Breakfast is available.

HOTEL BAROSS
HOTEL **$$**

Map p250 (☑1-461 3010; www.barosshotel.hu; VII Baross tér 15; s/d/tr/q/apt €60/70/90/110/160; ❀@🛜; Ⓜ M2/4 Keleti pályaudvar) Part of the Mellow Mood group, the Baross is an old-school, comfortable caravanserai conveniently located directly opposite Keleti train station. Rooms are simply and uniformly furnished, and reception, on the 5th floor, is clean and bright. The large, two-room apartments sleeping up to six are good for families or sharers. Also has a lift.

CORINTHIA HOTEL
BUDAPEST
LUXURY HOTEL **$$$**

Map p250 (☑1-479 4000; www.corinthia.hu; VII Erzsébet körút 43-49; r/ste from €135/340; P❀@🛜❄; Ⓜ M1 Oktogon, 🚊4, 6) Decades in the remaking, the one-time Royal Hotel is now a very grand 434-room five-star hotel. Its lobby – a double atrium with massive marble staircase – is among the most impressive in the capital, while the restored Royal Spa dating back to 1886 is now as modern as tomorrow with a 15m-long pool and a dozen treatment rooms.

RESIDENCE IZABELLA
APARTMENT **$$$**

Map p250 (☑1-475 5900; www.residence-izabella.com; VI Izabella utca 61; 1-bed €110-150, 2-bed €240-280, 3-bed €350-380; P❀@🛜; Ⓜ M1 Vörösmarty utca) This fabulous conversion of a 19th-century Eclectic building has 38 apartments measuring between 45 and 97 sq metres just off swanky Andrássy út. The apartments surround a delightful and very tranquil central courtyard garden and are set off by terracotta-toned decor.

SOHO HOTEL
BOUTIQUE HOTEL **$$$**

Map p250 (☑1-872 8292; www.sohohotel.hu; VII Dohány utca 64; s/d/ste €189/199/249; P❀@🛜; Ⓜ M2 Blaha Lujza tér, 🚊4, 6) This delightfully stylish boutique hotel with 68 rooms and six suites stands opposite the New York Palace, and we know which one feels more like the Big Apple. We adore the lobby bar in eye-popping reds, blues and lime greens, nonallergenic rooms with bamboo matting on the walls and parquet floors, and a music/film theme throughout.

🛏 Southern Pest

⭐KM SAGA GUEST
RESIDENCE
GUESTHOUSE **$**

Map p242 (☑1-217 1934; www.km-saga.hu; IX Lónyay utca 17, 3rd fl; s €30-40, d €35-55; ❀@❀; Ⓜ M4 Fővám tér) This unique place has five themed rooms, an eclectic mix of 19th-century furnishings, and hospitable, multilingual Hungarian-American owner Shandor. It's essentially a gay B&B, but everyone is welcome. Two rooms share a bathroom.

⭐MARIA & ISTVÁN
B&B **$**

Map p242 (☑06 20 931 2223, 1-216 0768; www.mariaistvan.hu; IX Ferenc körút 39, 4th fl; s €18-22, d €30-34, tr €36-42; P❀🛜; Ⓜ M3 Corvin-negyed, 🚊4, 6) This Italian-Hungarian couple must be doing something right, they've been welcoming guests to their bright and spotless flat for decades and no one has a bad word to say about it. There's a kitchen, too, for guests' use. It's like staying with friends.

CASA DE LA MUSICA
HOSTEL **$**

Map p242 (☑06 70 373 7330; www.casadelamusicahostel.com; VIII Vas utca 16; dm €9-12, d €28-32; ❀@🛜❀; Ⓜ M4 Rákóczi tér, 🚊4, 6) This colourful place has 100 beds, including dorms with four to 16 beds (two are for women only) and twins and doubles. There's a great kitchen and common room, as well as a terrace with bar, a summer kitchen and a pool if you fancy a splash about. (It's small and plastic but full of water. It's a pool, trust us.) The hostel is located above a Latin American cultural centre.

⭐BRODY HOUSE
BOUTIQUE HOTEL **$$**

Map p242 (☑1-266 1211; www.brodyhouse.com; VIII Bródy Sándor utca 10; r €70-130; ❀@🛜; Ⓜ M3 Kálvin tér, 🚊47, 49) Offering retro chic at its hippest, this erstwhile residence of the prime minister when Parliament sat at No 8 (as seen on the 20,000Ft note) has been refurbished but not substantially, with antique furnishings and modern art blending seamlessly in its eight unique guestrooms dedicated to local and international artists. A minor drawback is the lack of a lift. The public rooms are light, breezy and enormous; one even has a piano. The hotel also offers apartments for long and short let.

KÁLVIN HOUSE   HOTEL $$
Map p242 (☑1-216 4365; www.kalvinhouse.hu; IX Gönczy Pál utca 6; s/d/tr/ste from €49/59/79/79; @☎; ⓂM3/4 Kálvin tér, ☑47, 49) Rooms in this atmospheric old apartment block range over four storeys and have original wooden floors, enormously high ceilings (particularly no 109), plants, and vintage furniture dating to the early 20th century. Some of the 36 rooms have balconies and bathtubs. The rooms facing the inner courtyard are cooler in summer, and happily there's a lift. Breakfast is included.

BUDAPEST ROOMS   B&B $$
Map p242 (☑1-630 4743; www.budapestrooms. eu; VII Szentkirályi utca 15; s/d €48/62; ☎; ⓂM2 Astoria, M3/4 Kálvin tér, ☑47, 49) This small and very clean B&B consists of just five tranquil rooms with high ceilings and great showers, each individually decorated in soothing colours and presided over by one of the nicest, most helpful hosts in town. The fully equipped kitchen is a boon for self-caterers.

BO18 HOTEL   HOTEL $$
Map p242 (☑1-468 3526; www.bo18hotelbudapest.com; Vajdahunyad utca 18; d €60-100; P☎; ⓂM3 Corvin-negyed, ☑4, 6) An independent hotel on a quiet street, Bo18 has 50 simply yet stylishly decorated rooms, a small sauna and gym, super-clean tiled bathrooms and a tiny garden area. Buffet breakfast included.

FRASER RESIDENCE   APARTMENT $$
Map p242 (☑1-872 5900; http://budapest.frasershospitality.com; Nagytemplom utca 31; apt studio €65-75, 1-bed €85-100, 2-bed €130-140; ✳@☎; ⓂM3 Corvin-negyed) Part of an international chain, the 51 apartments here attract both long- and short-staying guests. Half of the huge, clean flats come with balconies and all have kitchens, washer/dryers, large beds and Occitane toileries. There's also a little sun terrace.

HOTEL SISSI   HOTEL $$
Map p242 (☑1-215 0082; www.hotelsissi-budapest.com; IX Angyal utca 33; s/d from €64/69; P☺✳@☎; ⓂM3 Corvin-negyed, ☑4, 6) Named in honour of Elizabeth, the Habsburg empress, Hungarian queen and consort of

Franz Joseph much beloved by Hungarians, the Hotel Sissi is decorated in a minimalist-elegant sort of style, and the 44 guestrooms spread over six floors are of a good size. Some rooms look onto a back garden.

CORVIN HOTEL   HOTEL $$
Map p242 (☑1-218 6566; www.corvinhotel-budapest.hu; IX Angyal utca 31; s/d/apt from €50/60/73; P☺✳@☎; ⓂM3 Corvin-negyed, ☑4, 6) This purpose-built hotel in Ferencváros has 42 very comfortable rooms with all mod cons on a quiet street. There are five apartments with small kitchens, some with balconies overlooking a little garden. The bright and airy breakfast room is a bonus.

THOMAS HOTEL   HOTEL $$
Map p242 (☑1-218 5505; www.hotelthomas.eu; IX Liliom utca 44; s/d €43/65; P☺✳@☎✖; ⓂM3 Corvin-negyed) A brightly coloured place, the Thomas has 43 rooms that are a real bargain for its central location. Some rooms have balconies looking onto an inner courtyard. The goofy-looking kid in the logo is the owner as a young 'un.

★HOTEL PALAZZO ZICHY   HISTORIC HOTEL $$$
Map p242 (☑1-235 4000; www.hotel-palazzo-zichy.hu; VII Lőrinc pap tér 2; r/ste from €125/150; P☺✳@☎✖; ⓂM3 Corvin-negyed, M3/4 Kálvin tér, ☑4, 6) Once the sumptuous 19th-century residence of the aristocratic Zichy family, the 'palace' has been transformed into a lovely hotel, with its original features, such as wrought-iron banisters, blending seamlessly with the ultramodern decor. The 80 rooms, all charcoals and creams, are enlivened by red-glass-topped desks, the showers are terrific, and there's a sauna and fitness room in the cellar crypt.

🛏 City Park & Beyond

MIRAGE FASHION HOTEL   HOTEL $$
Map p254 (☑1-462 7070; www.miragehotelbudapest.com; Dózsa György út 88; d €80-120; ☎; ⓂM1 Hősök tere) The location couldn't be grander – mere steps from Heroes' Sq and City Park – at this recently renovated hotel boasting 37 well-kitted-out rooms over three floors, plus a suite. The building dates from the 1820s and four front rooms come with access to impressive stone balconies, with views over the square.

Understand Budapest

Budapest Today

There have been some good, some bad and some ugly happenings in Budapest in recent years. The city has welcomed all sorts of innovations, from modes of transport to a whole new world of fun and games. The economy coughs and wheezes, but it still breathes. And a national election has returned the old guard with more power than ever.

Best on Film

Kontroll (2003) A dark, high-speed comic thriller set almost entirely in the Budapest metro in which assorted outcasts, lovers and dreamers commune.
Moszkva tér (Moscow Square; 2001) Comic tale of Buda teenage boys in 1989 oblivious to the life-changing events taking place around them.
Children of Glory (Szabadság, Szerelem; 2006) The 1956 Uprising in Budapest through the eyes of a player on the Olympic water-polo team.
The Grand Budapest Hotel (2014) 'Budapest' in name only (it was filmed in Germany), but the setting for this quirky film was inspired by the Danubius Hotel Gellért.

Best in Print

Prague (Arthur Phillips; 2002) Young expat American who wants to live in bohemian Prague focuses on life in Budapest just after the changes in 1989.
Under the Frog (Tibor Fischer; 2001) Amusing account of two members of Hungary's elite national basketball team in Budapest from WWII to 1956.
The Paul Street Boys (Ferenc Molnár; 1906) Satirical turn-of-the-century novel about boys growing up in the tough Józsefváros district.

Capital of Nightlife

They say that good things come to those who wait. Long in its gestation but quick in its delivery, Budapest is now the crowned king (or would that be queen?) of nightlife in Europe. Clubs – especially the outdoor 'garden' ones – heave throughout the week in summer, 'ruin pubs' (a Budapest phenomenon that has been imitated elsewhere but never feels quite the same) are filled to the brim and everyone wants just one last shot of *pálinka* (fruit brandy).

Along with all the bopping and grooving, there's a new pursuit in town: the city is now the undisputed nerve centre of live escape games, innovative pastimes in which teams of players are locked into a set of rooms – often in disused apartment blocks – and attempt to set themselves free by working through a series of complex riddles. The choice of venues is amazing and there's a wealth of different games on offer.

Old Guard, New Guard

In the current political environment, naysayers and whingers (and there are plenty of both here – Hungarians are said to 'take their pleasure sadly'; the fact that there's a phrase for it says it all) might be forgiven for conjuring up images of a fiddling Nero with a burning Rome as backdrop.

Prime Minister Viktor Orbán was returned to power in April 2014 with just 45% of the vote. But a series of changes in the election laws – including halving the number of MPs and allowing gerrymandering – transformed this into a two-thirds parliamentary mandate. 'Viktator' (as he is sometimes called in the opposition press) has been accused at home and abroad – often by EU officials – of too much nationalism, of politicising the judiciary and the central bank, and of stirring up ethnic tensions and suppressing media freedom.

Media reports show an increase in attacks on ethnic Roma people in recent years. In a survey conducted by the EU's Fundamental Rights Agency, some 48% of Jews questioned in Hungary said that they had considered emigrating because of safety concerns.

At the same time a controversial tax imposed on media advertising revenues just weeks after the election had some newspapers printing blank front pages and TV stations suspending evening broadcasting for up to 15 minutes.

Economic Ups & Downs

And then there's the economy, stupid. Though the number has almost halved in five years, about 15% of all outstanding mortgages remain in foreign currencies (largely Swiss francs), costing a fortune in forint to repay. And unemployment, though lower in the capital, averages 10% of the workforce nationwide. Encouragingly, GDP growth has accelerated, but the experts tell us that the key driver is public-sector activities – job schemes, public works etc. As we all know, these usually don't last forever.

On the Move

The city's transport options are definitely improving. The Bubi bike-sharing scheme was launched in 2014, and taxis no longer cost an arm and a leg (and the threat of a broken nose). Though it was expensive to build – it cost €1.5 billion, roughly 1.5% of Hungary's annual GDP – the long-awaited M4 metro line has opened at last.

The city also looks great, with newly pedestrianised streets planted with lime trees and a made-over Kossuth Lajos tér providing a dramatic new stage for the beloved Parliament building.

It may not be the Garden of Eden (yet), but it's getting there. Just don't tell Budapesters. A lot of them wouldn't be able to handle the good news.

if Budapest were 100 people

92 would be Magyar (Hungarian)
3 would be Roma
5 would be other

belief systems
(% of population)

52 Roman Catholic
16 Calvinist
3 Lutheran
3 Greek Catholic
26 other

population per sq km

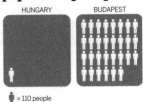

HUNGARY   BUDAPEST

≈ 110 people

History

Strictly speaking, the story of 'Budapest' only begins in 1873, when hilly, residential Buda and historic Óbuda on the western bank of the Danube River merged with flat, industrial Pest on the eastern side to form what at first was called Pest-Buda. But, like everything here, it's not that simple: a lot more took place here before the late 19th century.

The Magyars were so skilled at riding and shooting that a common Christian prayer in the Middle Ages was 'Save us, o Lord, from the arrows of the Hungarians'.

Early Inhabitants

The Carpathian Basin, in which Hungary lies, has been populated for at least half a million years. But the first *permanent* settlement in this area – on the Buda side near the Danube – dates from between 4600 and 3900 BC. Remains from that culture include bone utensils, fishing nets and even a primitive loom.

In about 2000 BC fierce Indo-European tribes from the Balkan Peninsula reached as far as the Carpathian Basin in horse-drawn carts, bringing bows and arrows and copper and bronze tools. Over the next millennium, invaders from the west (Illyrians and Thracians) and the east (Scythians) brought iron, but that metal was not in common use until the Celts arrived in the early 3rd century BC.

The Roman Conquest

In about 35 BC Romans conquered the area of today's Budapest that lies west and south of the Danube. By AD 10 they had established Pannonia province, which was later divided into Upper (Superior) and Lower (Inferior). The Romans brought writing, viticulture, stone architecture and Christianity. At the end of the 1st century AD the Romans established Aquincum, a key military garrison and trading settlement along the Danube in today's Óbuda that would become the administrative seat of Pannonia Inferior in AD 106. A fortress, whose remains are still visible, was built at Contra Aquincum in what is now V Március 15 tér in Pest.

TIMELINE	4600–3900 BC	AD 106	Late 430s
	The first permanent settlement is established on the Buda side of the Danube; household items are uncovered in the area.	Roman Aquincum in today's Óbuda becomes the administrative seat of the province of Pannonia Inferior and a fully fledged colony less than a century later.	Aquincum offers little protection to the civilian population when Huns burn the colony to the ground, forcing the Romans and other settlers to flee.

GET-READY READING

Tony Láng, doyen of Budapest booksellers and owner of Bestsellers (p106), recommends the following five books as reading in preparation for your visit to Budapest:

Budapest 1900: A Historical Portrait of a City and Its Culture (John Lukacs; 1994) Still a classic, this illustrated social history is indispensable for understanding Budapest today.

The Invisible Bridge (Julie Orringer; 2010) Epic saga of a Hungarian Jewish family during WWII.

The Will to Survive: A History of Hungary (Bryan Cartledge; 2011) The best all-round general history of Hungary by a former British diplomat.

Ballad of the Whiskey Robber (Julian Rubinstein; 2005) Unbelievable but true story of one Attila Ambrus, who took up bank robbing when not playing professional ice hockey – a portrait of what was the 'Wild East' of Budapest in the early 1990s.

Twelve Days: The Story of the 1956 Hungarian Revolution (Victor Sebestyen; 2007) Meticulously researched and comprehensive day-by-day account of the 12 days between the outbreak of the popular revolt and its brutal suppression by the Soviets.

The Great Migrations

The first of the so-called Great Migrations of nomadic peoples from Asia reached the eastern outposts of the Roman Empire in Dacia (now Romania) early in the 3rd century AD. Within two centuries the Romans were forced by the Huns, whose short-lived empire was established by Attila, to flee Aquincum.

After the death of Attila in 453, other Germanic tribes occupied the region for the next century and a half until the Avars, a powerful Turkic people, gained control of the Carpathian Basin in the late 6th century and established their main base at the northern end of Csepel Island. They in turn were subdued by Charlemagne in the early 8th century, and the area around Budapest and the Danube Bend was incorporated into the Frankish empire.

The Magyars & the Conquest of the Carpathian Basin

The origin of the Magyars is a complicated subject, not helped by the similarity (in English) of the words 'Hun' and 'Hungary', which are *not* related. The Magyars belong to the Finno-Ugric group of peoples, who

The mystery surrounding the origins of the Magyars have led to some unusual theories. When asked whether he believed extraterrestrial beings existed, the Italian-American Nobel Prize–winning physicist Enrico Fermi (1901–54) replied: 'Of course they do (and) they are already here among us. They are called Hungarians'.

Early 8th century	896–98	955	1000
Charlemagne subdues the Turkic Avars, who had occupied the Carpathian Basin since the late 6th century; the Budapest area is incorporated into the Frankish empire.	Nomadic Magyar tribes set up camp in the Carpathian Basin, with five of the seven original tribes settling in the area that is now Budapest.	Hungarian raids outside the Carpathian Basin as far as Germany, Italy and Spain are stopped for good by German king Otto I at the Battle of Augsburg.	Stephen (István in Hungarian) is crowned 'Christian King' of Hungary on Christmas Day with a crown sent from Rome by Pope Sylvester II.

inhabited the forests somewhere between the middle Volga River and the Ural Mountains in western Siberia as early as 4000 BC.

By about 2000 BC, population growth forced the Finnish-Estonian branch to move west, ultimately reaching the Baltic Sea. The Ugrians moved from the southeastern slopes of the Urals into the region's valleys, and switched from hunting and fishing to farming and raising livestock, especially horses. Their equestrian skills proved useful half a millennium later when drought forced them north onto the steppes.

On the plains, the Ugrians turned to nomadic herding. After about 500 BC, a group moved west to the Bashkiria area in Central Asia. Here, living among Persians and Bulgars, they began referring to themselves as Magyars (from the Finno-Ugric words *mon*, to speak, and *er*, man).

After several centuries, another group split away and moved south to the Don River under the control of the Turkic Khazars. Here they lived under a tribal alliance called *onogur* ('10 peoples'), thought to be the origin of the word 'Hungary'. The Magyars' last migration before the so-called conquest *(honfoglalás)* of the Carpathian Basin brought them to what modern Hungarians call the Etelköz, the region between the Dnieper and lower Danube rivers and north of the Black Sea.

In about 895 seven Magyar tribes under the leadership of Árpád, the chief military commander *(gyula)*, struck out for the Carpathian Basin while under attack. They crossed the Verecke Pass in today's Ukraine some three years later.

Being highly skilled at riding and shooting, the Magyars plundered and pillaged in all directions, taking slaves and amassing booty. Their raids took them as far as Germany, Italy and Spain, but in 955 they were stopped in their tracks by the German king Otto I at the Battle of Augsburg.

This and subsequent defeats forced them to form an alliance with the Holy Roman Empire. In 973 Prince Géza, Árpád's great-grandson, asked the Emperor Otto II to send Christian missionaries to Hungary. Géza was baptised in his capital city, Esztergom, 46km upriver from Budapest, as was his son Vajk, who took the Christian name István (Stephen). When Géza died, Stephen ruled as prince, but on Christmas Day in the year 1000 he was crowned 'Christian King' Stephen I.

King Stephen I & the House of Árpád

Stephen set about consolidating royal authority by expropriating the land of the clan chieftains and establishing a system of counties *(megyék)* protected by castles *(várak)*. Shrewdly, he transferred much land to loyal (mostly German) knights. He also sought the support of the Church and established 10 episcopates. By the time of his death in

If you'd like to learn more about the nomadic Magyars, their history, civilisation and art, go to http://ancient-magyarworld.tripod.com, which also offers a number of useful links.

1083	1220	1222	1241–42
King Stephen is canonised as St Stephen by Pope Victor III in Rome; 20 August is declared his feast day.	The Gothic style of architecture extends into Hungary from northern France, superseding the heavier Romanesque style.	King Andrew II signs the Golden Bull, according the nobility increased rights and powers; it is renewed nine years later in 1231.	Mongols sweep across Hungary, killing some 100,000 people in Pest and Óbuda alone and reducing the national population by up to a half.

THE CROWN OF ST STEPHEN

Legend has it that a bishop called Asztrik presented a crown to Stephen as a gift from Pope Sylvester II around AD 1000. In fact, the two-part crown, with its characteristic bent cross, pendants hanging on either side and enamelled plaques of the Apostles, dates from the 12th century. It is the very symbol of the Hungarian nation and is on display in the Parliament. After WWII American forces in Europe transferred the crown to Fort Knox in Kentucky for safekeeping; it was returned in 1978 to the nation's great relief. Because legal judgments in Hungary had always been handed down 'in the name of St Stephen's Crown', it was considered a living symbol and had thus been 'kidnapped'.

1038, Hungary was a nascent Christian nation, increasingly westward-looking and multiethnic.

The next two and a half centuries – the lifespan of the Árpád dynasty – would test the new kingdom to the limit. The period was marked by dynastic intrigues and relentless struggles among pretenders to the throne, which weakened the young nation's defences against its more powerful neighbours. In the mid-13th century the Mongols, who had raced through the country, attacked the city from every direction. By January 1242 Pest and Óbuda had been burned to the ground and some 100,000 people killed. The Árpád line died out in 1301 with the death of Andrew III, who left no heir.

Medieval Budapest

The struggle for the Hungarian throne after the fall of the House of Árpád involved several European dynasties, with the crown first going to Charles Robert (Károly Róbert) of the French House of Anjou in 1307.

In the following century an alliance between Poland and Hungary gave the former the Hungarian crown. When Vladislav I (Úlászló), son of the Polish Jagiellonian king, was killed fighting the Ottoman Turks at Varna (in today's Bulgaria) in 1444, János Hunyadi, a Transylvanian general, was made regent. His decisive victory over the Turks at Belgrade (Hungarian: Nándorfehérvár) in 1456 checked the Ottoman advance into Hungary for 70 years and assured the coronation of his son Matthias (Mátyás), the greatest ruler of medieval Hungary.

Through his daring military exploits Matthias (r 1458–90), nicknamed 'the Raven' (Corvinus) from his coat of arms, made Hungary one of Central Europe's leading powers. Under his rule Buda enjoyed a golden age and for the first time became the true focus of the nation. His wife, Queen Beatrix, the daughter of the king of Naples, brought

In 1046 a Venice-born bishop named Gerard (Gellért), who had been brought to Hungary by King Stephen himself, was hurled to his death from a Buda hilltop in a spiked barrel by pagan Magyars resisting conversion. Gellért Hill now bears the bishop's name.

1301	1458–90	1514	1526
The line of the House of Árpád ends with the death of Andrew III, who leaves no male heir; a period of great turmoil follows.	Medieval Hungary enjoys a golden age under the enlightened reign of King Matthias Corvinus and Queen Beatrix, daughter of the king of Naples.	A widespread uprising by peasants is crushed; 70,000 people are executed, including the leader, György Dózsa, who dies on a red-hot iron throne wearing a scalding crown.	Hungary is soundly defeated by the Ottomans at the Battle of Mohács, with young King Louis being killed; the ensuing Turkish occupation lasts more than a century and a half.

BUDAN: BUDA ALATURKA

The Turks did little building in what they called Budan, apart from several bathhouses still extant (Király, Rudas), dervish monasteries, and tombs, city walls and bastions; for the most part, they used existing civic buildings for administration and converted churches into mosques. Matthias Church on Castle Hill, for example, was hastily turned into the Büyük Cami (Great Mosque), and the heart of the Royal Palace became a gunpowder store and magazine.

Contemporary accounts suggest that Buda began to look like a Balkan city, with copperware shops lining Kasandzhilar yolu – a transliteration of Kazancilar yolu (Earners St) – which is today's l Szentháromság utca on Castle Hill, for example. The nearby church of St Mary Magdalene, of which only the tower still stands, was shared by Catholics and Protestants, who fought bitterly for every square centimetre of space. Apparently, it was the Muslim Turks who had to keep the peace among the Christians.

artisans from Italy who completely rebuilt, extended and fortified the Royal Palace in the Renaissance style.

Under Matthias' successor Vladislav II (Úlászló; r 1490–1516), what had begun as a crusade in 1514 turned into an uprising against the landlords by peasants, who rallied near Pest under their leader, György Dózsa. The revolt was repressed by Transylvanian leader John Szapolyai (Zápolyai János) and some 70,000 peasants were tortured and executed, including Dózsa himself. The retrograde Tripartitum Law that followed codified the rights and privileges of the barons and nobles and reduced the peasants to perpetual serfdom.

A Hungarian expression recalls the Turkish occupation: *Hátravan még a feketeleves* ('Still to come is the black soup'), suggesting something painful or difficult is on the cards. After a meal the Turks would serve their Hungarian guests an unknown beverage – coffee – which meant it was time to talk about taxes.

The Battle of Mohács

The defeat of the ragtag Hungarian army by the Ottoman Turks at Mohács in 1526 is a watershed in the nation's history. On the battlefield near this small town in Southern Transdanubia, some 195km south of Budapest, a relatively prosperous and independent Hungary died, sending the nation into a tailspin of partition and foreign domination that would last for centuries.

It would be unfair to put all the blame on the weak and indecisive teenage king Louis. Bickering among the nobility and the brutal crackdown on the Dózsa uprising had severely weakened Hungary's military power, and there was virtually nothing left in the royal coffers. By 1526 Ottoman sultan Suleiman the Magnificent (r 1520–66) had taken much of the Balkans, including Belgrade, and was poised to march on Buda and Vienna.

1541	1566	1686	1699
Buda Castle falls to the Ottomans; Hungary is partitioned and shared by three separate groups: the Turks, the Habsburgs and the Transylvanian princes.	Miklós Zrínyi and his 2500 soldiers make their heroic sally at Szigetvár Castle in southern Hungary; Sultan Suleiman I dies in battle.	Austrian and Hungarian forces backed by the Polish army liberate Buda from the Turks, though little of the castle is left standing.	Austria, Poland, Venice and Russia sign a peace treaty with the Turks; Austria receives large accessions of territory in Hungary and Transylvania.

Unwilling to wait for reinforcements from Transylvania under the command of his rival John Szapolyai, Louis rushed from Buda with a motley army of just over 25,000 men to battle the Turks and was soundly thrashed. Among the estimated 18,000 dead was the king himself – crushed by his horse while trying to retreat across a stream.

Turkish Occupation

The Ottoman Turks marched on and occupied Buda in 1541. Hungary was then divided into three parts. The central section, with Buda as the provincial seat, went to the Ottomans, while parts of Transdanubia and what is now Slovakia were governed by the Austrian House of Habsburg, assisted by the Hungarian nobility based at Bratislava (Hungarian: Pozsony). The principality of Transylvania prospered as a vassal state of the Ottoman Empire. This arrangement would remain in place for almost a century and a half.

Turkish power began to wane in the 17th century, especially after the Turkish attempt to take Vienna was soundly defeated. Buda was liberated in 1686 and an imperial army under Eugene of Savoy wiped out the last Turkish army in Hungary at the Battle of Zenta (now Senta in Serbia) 11 years later.

The Habsburgs

The expulsion of the Turks from Hungary at the end of the 17th century did lead to the nation's independence. Buda and the rest of the country were under military occupation, and the policies of the Catholic Habsburgs' Counter-Reformation and heavy taxation further alienated the nobility. In 1703, Transylvanian prince Ferenc Rákóczi II raised an army of Hungarian mercenaries *(kuruc)* against the Habsburgs. The war dragged on for eight years, but superior imperial forces and lack of funds forced the *kuruc* to negotiate a separate peace with Vienna behind Rákóczi's back. The 1703–11 War of Independence had failed, but Rákóczi was the first leader to unite Hungarians against the Habsburgs.

Hungary was now a mere province of the Habsburg empire. Under Maria Theresa (r 1740–80) and her son, Joseph II (r 1780–90), Hungary took great steps forward economically, culturally and politically. But Joseph's attempts to modernise society by dissolving the all-powerful (and corrupt) monastic orders, abolishing serfdom and replacing 'neutral' Latin with German as the official language of state administration were opposed by the Hungarian nobility, and the king rescinded some of the reforms on his deathbed.

Liberalism and social reform found their greatest supporters among certain members of the aristocracy in Pest, including Count István

Joseph II, who ruled as Habsburg emperor from 1780 to 1790, was nicknamed the 'hatted king' because he was never actually crowned in Hungary.

For Count István Széchenyi's many accomplishments, his contemporary and fellow reformer Lajos Kossuth called him 'the greatest Hungarian'. For many of his compatriots, this dynamic but troubled visionary retains that accolade today.

HISTORY TURKISH OCCUPATION

1703–11	1795	1825	1848–49
Ferenc Rákóczi II fights and loses a war of independence against the Habsburgs; he is given asylum in Thrace by the Turkish sultan Ahmet III.	Seven pro-republican Jacobites, including the group's leader, Ignác Martonovics, are beheaded at Vérmező in Buda for plotting against the Habsburg throne.	The so-called Reform Era is in full swing; Pest becomes the cultural and economic centre of the country; first National Theatre is built along with first Hungarian National Museum.	During the War of Independence, Sándor Petőfi dies fighting, Lajos Batthyány and 13 of his generals are executed for their roles, and leader Lajos Kossuth goes into exile.

Széchenyi (1791–1860), a true Renaissance man, who advocated the abolition of serfdom and returned much of his own land to the peasantry, proposed the first permanent link between Buda and Pest (Chain Bridge) and oversaw the regulation of the Danube as much for commerce and irrigation as for safety. But the radicals, dominated by the dynamic lawyer and journalist Lajos Kossuth (1802–94), demanded more immediate action.

The 1848–49 War of Independence

The Habsburg empire began to weaken as Hungarian nationalism increased early in the 19th century and certain reforms were introduced, including a law allowing serfs alternative means of discharging their feudal obligations of service and increased Hungarian representation in the Council of State in Vienna.

But the reforms were too limited and too late. On 15 March a group calling itself the Youth of March, led by the poet Sándor Petőfi, who read out his poem 'Nemzeti Dal' (National Song) on the steps of the Hungarian National Museum, took to the streets of Pest with hastily printed copies of their *Twelve Points* to press for radical reforms and even revolution. Habsburg patience began to wear thin.

In September 1848 Habsburg forces launched an attack. The Hungarians hastily formed a national defence commission and moved the government seat to Debrecen in the east, where Lajos Kossuth was elected leader. In April 1849 the Parliament declared Hungary's full independence.

The new Habsburg emperor Franz Joseph (r 1848–1916) quickly took action, defeating the rebel troops by August. Martial law was declared and a series of brutal reprisals and executions ensued. Kossuth went into exile.

The Dual Monarchy

Following the War of Independence, Hungary was again merged into the Habsburg empire as a conquered province. But disastrous military defeats for the Habsburgs by the French in 1859 and the Prussians in 1866 pushed Franz Joseph to the negotiating table under the leadership of liberal reformer Ferenc Deák.

The result was the Compromise of 1867, which fundamentally restructured the Habsburg monarchy and created the Dual Monarchy of Austria (the empire) and Hungary (the kingdom) – a federated state with two parliaments and two capitals: Vienna and Budapest. This 'Age of Dualism' would carry on until 1918 and spark an economic, cultural and intellectual rebirth in Budapest, culminating with the momentous

1867	1873	1896	1900
The Act of Compromise creates the Dual Monarchy of Austria (the empire), based in Vienna, and Hungary (the kingdom), with its seat at Budapest.	Hilly, residential Buda and historic Óbuda on the western bank of the Danube merge with flat, industrial Pest on the eastern side to form what is at first called Pest-Buda.	Millennium of the Magyar conquest of the Carpathian Basin is marked by a major exhibition in City Park that attracts four million people over six months.	The population of Budapest increases to 750,00 by the turn of the century, up from 280,000 just 50 years before.

THE DESPISED TREATY OF TRIANON

In June 1920 the victorious Allies drew up a postwar settlement under the Treaty of Trianon at Versailles, near Paris, that enlarged some countries, truncated others and created several 'successor states'. As one of the defeated enemy nations and with large numbers of minorities clamouring for independence within its borders, Hungary stood to lose more than most. It was reduced to 40% of its historical size and, while now a largely uniform, homogeneous state, millions of ethnic Hungarians in Romania, Yugoslavia and Czechoslovakia were now the minority.

'Trianon' became the singularly most hated word in Hungary, and *'Nem, Nem, Soha!'* (No, No, Never!) the rallying cry during the interwar years. Many of the problems the so-called *diktátum* created remained in place for decades, and it has coloured Hungary's relations with its neighbours for almost a century.

six-month exhibition in 1896 celebrating the millennium of the Magyar arrival in the Carpathian Basin.

But all was not well in the kingdom. The working class, based almost entirely in Budapest, had almost no rights and the situation in the countryside was almost as dire as it had been in the Middle Ages. Despite a new law enacted in 1868 to protect their rights, minorities under Hungarian control (Czechs, Slovaks, Croats and Romanians) were under increased pressure to 'Magyarise' and many viewed their new rulers as oppressors.

WWI & the Republic of Councils

On 28 July 1914 Austria-Hungary declared war on Serbia and entered WWI allied with the German Empire. The result of this action was disastrous, with widespread destruction and hundreds of thousands killed on the Russian and Italian fronts. At the armistice in 1918, the fate of the Dual Monarchy – and Hungary as a multinational kingdom – was decided and the terms spelled out by the Treaty of Trianon less than two years later.

A new republic was set up in Budapest five days after the armistice was signed, but it would not last long. Rampant inflation, mass unemployment, the occupation and dismemberment of 'Greater Hungary' and the victory of the Bolshevik Revolution in Russia all combined to radicalise much of the Budapest working class.

In March 1919 a group of Hungarian Communists led by a Transylvanian former journalist called Béla Kun seized power. The so-called Republic of Councils (Tanácsköztársaság) set out to nationalise industry and private property and build a fairer society, but Kun's failure to

One of the founders of the actors' union in Budapest during Béla Kun's short-lived Republic of Councils was one Béla Lugosi, who fled to Vienna in 1919 and eventually made his way to Hollywood, where he achieved fame as the lead in the original Dracula films.

1918	1920	1931	1939
Austria-Hungary loses WWI in November and the political system collapses; Hungary declares itself a republic under the leadership of Count Mihály Károlyi.	Treaty of Trianon carves up much of Central Europe, reducing Hungary by almost two-thirds and enlarging the ethnic Hungarian populations in Romania, Yugoslavia and Czechoslovakia.	Strongman Miklós Horthy declares martial law in the face of economic unrest; suspected communists are rounded up, imprisoned and, in some cases, executed.	Nazi Germany invades Poland; Britain and France declare war on Germany two days later, but Hungary remains neutral for the time being.

regain the 'lost territories' brought mass opposition and the government unleashed a reign of 'red terror' around the country. In August Romanian troops occupied the capital, and Kun fled to Vienna.

The Horthy Years & WWII

In March 1920, Hungary's Parliament chose a kingdom as the form of state and – lacking a king – elected as its regent Admiral Horthy. He launched a 'white terror' – every bit as brutal as Béla Kun's red one – that attacked social democrats, Jews and communists for their roles in supporting the Republic of Councils. As the regime was consolidated, it showed itself to be extremely rightist and conservative, advocating the status quo and 'traditional values'.

It was generally agreed that the return of the territories lost through the Treaty of Trianon was essential for national development. Hungary obviously could not count on the victors – France, Britain and the US – to help recoup its land; instead, it would have to seek help from the fascist governments of Germany and Italy.

Hungary's move to the right intensified throughout the 1930s, though it remained silent when WWII broke out in September 1939. Horthy hoped an alliance would not mean actually having to enter the war but joined the German- and Italian-led Axis in June 1941. The war was just as disastrous for Hungary as the 1914–18 one had been and Horthy began secret discussions with the Allies.

When Hitler caught wind of this in March 1944 he sent his army in. Ferenc Szálasi, the deranged leader of the pro-Nazi Arrow Cross Party, was installed as prime minister and Horthy was deported to Germany.

The Arrow Cross Party arrested thousands of the country's liberal politicians and labour leaders. The puppet government introduced anti-Jewish legislation similar to that in Germany, and Jews, who lived in fear but were still alive under Horthy, were rounded up into ghettos by Hungarian pro-Nazis. From May to July of 1944, just 10 months before the end of the war, 450,000 Hungarian Jewish men, women and children – 60% of Hungarian Jewry – were deported to Auschwitz and other labour camps, where they starved to death, succumbed to disease or were brutally murdered. Many of the Jews who did survive owed their lives to heroic men like Raoul Wallenberg, a Budapest-based Swedish diplomat, Swiss consul Carl Lutz and Scottish missionary Jane Haining. All of them are remembered with monuments and/or street names in the capital.

Budapest now became an international battleground for the first time since the Turkish occupation, and bombs began falling everywhere. By Christmas 1944 the Soviet army had surrounded Budapest.

Hungary under Admiral Horthy confused even US President Franklin D Roosevelt. After being briefed by an aide on the country's government and leadership, he reportedly said: 'Let me see if I understand you right. Hungary is a kingdom without a king run by a regent who's an admiral without a navy?'

1941	1944	1945	1946
Hungary joins the Axis led by Germany and Italy against the Allies in WWII, largely in order to recover territories lost under the terms of the Treaty of Trianon.	Germany invades and occupies Hungary; most Hungarian Jews, who had largely been able to avoid persecution under Horthy, are deported to Nazi concentration camps.	Budapest is liberated by the Soviet army in April, a month before full victory in Europe, with three-quarters of its buildings and all of its bridges in ruins.	Hungary experiences the world's worst hyperinflation, with notes of up to 10,000 trillion pengő issued; Liberty Bridge, the first of the spans over the Danube to be rebuilt, reopens.

CARDINAL MINDSZENTY

Born József Pehm in the village of Csehimindszent near Szombathely in western Hungary in 1892, Mindszenty was politically active from the time of his ordination in 1915. Imprisoned by Communist leader Béla Kun in 1919 and again by the fascist Arrow Cross Party in 1944, Mindszenty was made archbishop of Esztergom (and thus primate of Hungary) in 1945, and cardinal in 1946.

In 1948, when he refused to secularise Hungary's Roman Catholic schools under the new Communist regime, Mindszenty was arrested, tortured and sentenced to life imprisonment for treason. Released during the 1956 Uprising, the cardinal took refuge in the US Embassy when the Communists returned to power. He remained there until 1971.

As relations between the Kádár regime and the Holy See began to improve in the late 1960s, the Vatican made several requests for Mindszenty to leave Hungary, which he refused to do. Following the intervention of US president Richard Nixon, Mindszenty left for Vienna, where he continued to criticise the Vatican's relations with Hungary. He retired in 1974 and died the following year. Mindszenty had vowed not to return to Hungary until the last Russian soldier had left Hungarian soil, but his remains were returned in May 1991, several weeks before that pivotal date.

By the time Germany surrendered in April 1945, three-quarters of the city's homes, historical buildings and churches had been severely damaged or destroyed. Some 20,000 Hungarian soldiers and 25,000 civilians of Budapest had been killed. As they retreated the Germans blew up Buda Castle and knocked out every bridge that spanned the Danube.

The People's Republic

When the first postwar parliamentary elections were held in Hungary in November 1945, the Independent Smallholders' Party received 57% of the vote. But Soviet political officers, backed by the occupying army, forced three other parties – the Communists, Social Democrats and National Peasants – into a coalition. Two years later, in a disputed election held under a complicated new electoral law, the Communists declared their candidate, Mátyás Rákosi, the winner. The following year the Social Democrats merged with the Communists to form the Hungarian Workers' Party.

Rákosi, a big fan of Stalin, began a process of nationalisation and unrealistically fast industrialisation at the expense of agriculture. Peasants were forced into collective farms and a network of spies and informers exposed 'class enemies' such as Cardinal József Mindszenty to the secret police – the ÁVO (ÁVH after 1949) – who interrogated

Hungarians sometimes refer to the four decades from 1949 to the change in regime in 1989 as *'az átkos 40 év'* (the damned 40 years).

1949	1956	1957	1958
The Communists, in complete control, form the 'People's Republic of Hungary'; Stalinist show trials of 'Titoists' and other 'enemies of the people' begin in Budapest.	Budapest is in flames after October riots; Hungary briefly withdraws from the Warsaw Pact as a neutral state; the status quo is restored and János Kádár is installed as leader.	Rock-and-roll legend Elvis Presley performs a spiritual song called 'Peace in the Valley' on US TV to express his 'preoccupation with Hungary's plight' after the Uprising.	Imre Nagy and others are executed by the Communist regime for their role in the Uprising and buried in unmarked graves in Budapest's New Municipal Cemetery.

them at their headquarters at VI Andrássy út 60 (now the House of Terror) in Pest and sent them to trial at the then Military Court of Justice in Buda. Some were executed; many more were sent into internal exile or condemned to labour camps. Stalinist show trials became the order of the day and in August 1949 the nation was proclaimed the 'People's Republic of Hungary'.

After Khrushchev's denunciation of Stalin in 1956, Rákosi's tenure was up and the terror began to abate. The reputations of executed apparatchiks were rehabilitated and people like former minister of agriculture Imre Nagy, who had been expelled from the party a year earlier for suggesting reforms, were readmitted. By October 1956 murmured calls for a real reform of the system – 'socialism with a human face' – were being heard.

The 1956 Uprising

Hungary's greatest tragedy – an event that for a while shook the world, rocked international communism and pitted Hungarian against Hungarian – began in Budapest on 23 October 1956, when some 50,000 university students assembled at II Bem József tér in Buda, shouting anti-Soviet slogans and demanding that reformist Imre Nagy be named prime minister. That night a crowd pulled down and sawed into pieces the colossal statue of Stalin on Dózsa György út on the edge of City Park, and shots were fired by ÁVH agents on another group gathering outside the headquarters of Hungarian Radio at VIII Bródy Sándor utca 5-7 in Pest. Budapest was in revolution.

The following day Nagy formed a government, while János Kádár was named president of the Central Committee of the Hungarian Workers' Party. Over the next few days the government offered an amnesty to those involved in the violence, promised to abolish the ÁVH and announced that Hungary would leave the Warsaw Pact and declare its neutrality.

At this, Soviet tanks and troops crossed into Hungary and within 72 hours attacked Budapest and other cities. Kádár had slipped away from Budapest to join the Russian invaders; he was installed as leader.

Fierce street fighting continued for several days, encouraged by Radio Free Europe broadcasts and disingenuous promises of support from the West, which was embroiled in the Suez Canal crisis at the time. When the fighting was over, 25,000 people were dead. Then the reprisals began. An estimated 20,000 people were arrested and 2000 – including Imre Nagy and his associates – were executed. Another 250,000 refugees fled to Austria.

The award-winning website of the Institute for the History of the 1956 Hungarian Revolution (www.rev.hu) will walk you through the build-up to and outbreak and aftermath of Hungary's greatest modern tragedy through photographs, essays and timelines.

1968	1978	1988	1989
Plans for a liberalised economy are introduced in an attempt to overcome the inefficiencies of central planning but are rejected as too extreme by conservatives.	The Crown of St Stephen is returned to Hungary from the USA, where it had been held at Fort Knox in Kentucky since the end of WWII.	János Kádár is forced to retire in May after more than three decades in power; he dies and is buried in Budapest's Kerepesi Cemetery the following year.	Communist monopoly on power is relinquished and the national borders are opened; Imre Nagy is reburied in Budapest; the Republic of Hungary is reborn.

Hungary Under Kádár

After the 1956 Uprising, the ruling party was reorganised as the Hungarian Socialist Workers' Party, and Kádár began a program to liberalise the social and economic structure based on compromise. He introduced market socialism and encouraged greater consumerism; by the mid-1970s Hungary was light years ahead of any other Soviet-bloc country in its standard of living, freedom of movement and opportunities to criticise the government. This 'Hungarian model' attracted Western attention and investment.

But the Kádár system of 'goulash socialism' was incapable of dealing with such 'unsocialist' problems in the 1980s as unemployment, soaring inflation and the largest per-capita foreign debt in the region. Kádár and the 'old guard' refused to hear talk about party reforms. In June 1987 Károly Grósz took over as premier and Kádár retired less than a year later.

In 2007 the grave of the late Communist leader János Kádár in the Kerepesi Cemetery was broken into and his skull and assorted bones removed. The only clue was a note that read: 'Murderers and traitors may not rest in holy ground 1956–2006'. The remains have yet to be recovered despite a substantial reward for information as to their whereabouts.

Renewal & Change

Throughout the summer and autumn of 1988, new political parties formed and old ones were resurrected. In January 1989 Hungary, second-guessing what was to come as Mikhail Gorbachev launched sweeping reforms in the Soviet Union, announced that the events of 1956 had been a 'popular insurrection' and not the 'counter-revolution' that the regime had always dubbed it. In June 1989 some 250,000 people attended ceremonies marking the reburial of Imre Nagy and other victims of 1956 in Budapest's New Municipal Cemetery.

The next month, Hungary began to demolish the electrified wire fence separating it from Austria. The move released a wave of East Germans holidaying in Hungary into the West and the opening attracted thousands more. The collapse of the communist regimes around the region was now unstoppable.

The Republic of Hungary Reborn

At its party congress in February 1989, the ruling Hungarian Socialist Workers' Party changed its name to the Hungarian Socialist Party (MSZP) and later in the year agreed to surrender its monopoly on power, paving the way for free elections in the spring of 1990. On 23 October 1989, the 33rd anniversary of the 1956 Uprising, the nation once again became the Republic of Hungary.

The 1990 election was won by the centrist Hungarian Democratic Forum (MDF), which advocated a gradual transition to capitalism and was led by softly spoken former museum curator József Antall. The social-democratic Alliance of Free Democrats (SZDSZ), which

1990	1991	1994	1995
The centrist MDF wins the first free elections in 43 years in April; Árpád Göncz is chosen as the republic's first president in August.	Last Soviet troops leave Hungary in June, two weeks ahead of schedule; Parliament passes the first act dealing with the return of property seized under Communist rule since 1949.	Socialists win a decisive victory in the general election and form a government under Gyula Horn for the first time since the changes of 1989.	Árpád Göncz of the SZDSZ, arguably the most popular politician in Hungary, is elected for a second (and, by law, final) five-year term as president of the republic.

had called for much faster change, came in a distant second. Hungary had changed political systems with scarcely a murmur. The last Soviet troops left Hungarian soil in June 1991, streets and squares like Lenin körút and Marx tér were renamed, and monuments to 'glorious workers' and 'esteemed leaders' were packed off to a socialist-realist theme park called Memento Park.

In coalition with two smaller parties, the MDF governed Hungary soundly during its difficult transition to a full market economy. But despite initial successes in curbing inflation and lowering interest rates, economic problems slowed development; the government's laissez-faire policies did not help. In a poll taken in mid-1993, 76% of respondents were 'very disappointed' with the way things had worked out.

Perhaps not surprisingly, in the May 1994 elections the MSZP, led by Gyula Horn, won an absolute majority in Parliament. This in no way implied a return to the past, and Horn was quick to point out that his party had initiated the whole reform process in the first place.

The Corvinus Library of Hungarian History (www.hungarianhistory.com) is a font of all knowledge and an excellent first step in exploring the nation's past; the links to related topics – from language to painting – are endless.

The Road to Europe

After its dire showing in the 1994 elections, the Federation of Young Democrats (Fidesz) – which until 1993 had limited membership to those under 35 to emphasise a past untainted by communism, privilege and corruption – moved to the right and added the extension 'MPP' (Hungarian Civic Party) to its name to attract the support of the burgeoning middle class. In 1998 it campaigned for integration with Europe; Fidesz-MPP won the vote by forming a coalition with the MDF and the agrarian conservative FKgP. The party's youthful leader, Viktor Orbán, was named prime minister. Hungary became a fully fledged NATO member the following year.

The electorate grew increasingly hostile to Fidesz-MPP's (and Orbán's) nationalistic rhetoric and unseated the government in April 2002, returning the MSZP, allied with the SZDSZ, to power under Prime Minister Péter Medgyessy, a free-market advocate who had served as finance minister in the Horn government. Hungary was admitted into the EU in May 2004, but three months later Medgyessy resigned when it was revealed that he had served as a counterintelligence officer in the late 1970s and early 1980s while working in the finance ministry. Sports Minister Ferenc Gyurcsány became prime minister.

A Place of Its Own Making

Reappointed prime minister in April 2006 after the electorate gave his coalition 55% of 386 parliamentary seats, Ferenc Gyurcsány immediately began austerity measures to tackle Hungary's budget deficit,

1999	2002	2004	2006
Hungary becomes a fully fledged member of NATO, along with the Czech Republic and Poland; NATO aircraft heading for Kosovo begin using Hungarian airfields.	Budapest, specifically the banks of the Danube, the Castle District and Andrássy út, is included in Unesco's list of World Heritage Sites.	Hungary is admitted to the EU along with nine other new member nations, including neighbouring states Slovakia and Slovenia.	Socialist Ferenc Gyurcsány is re-elected as prime minister; antigovernment riots rock Budapest during the 50th-anniversary celebrations of the 1956 Uprising.

which had reached a staggering 10% of GDP. But in September, just as these unpopular steps were being put into place, an audiotape recorded shortly after the election at a closed-door meeting of the prime minister's cabinet had Gyurcsány confessing that the party had 'lied morning, evening and night' about the state of the economy since coming to power and now had to make amends. Gyurcsány refused to resign, and public outrage led to a series of demonstrations near the Parliament building in Budapest, culminating in widespread rioting that marred the 50th anniversary of the 1956 Uprising.

Since then, demonstrations – sometimes violent – have become a regular feature in Budapest, especially during national holidays. The radical right-wing nationalist party Jobbik Magyarországért Mozgalom (Movement for a Better Hungary), better known as just Jobbik, and its uniformed militia arm, Magyar Gárda (Hungarian Guard), have been at the centre of many of these demonstrations and riots.

Gyurcsány led a feeble minority government until general elections in 2010, when Fidesz-MPP won a majority of 52% in the first round of voting and joined forces with the Christian Democratic People's Party (KDNP) to rule with a two-thirds majority (263 of 386 seats).

Hungary assumed presidency of the EU Council in the first half of 2011. A new constitution that went into effect at the start of 2012 contained an extended preamble (the so-called National Creed) that declares the period from March 1944 (Nazi occupation of Hungary) to May 1990 (first free election since 1945) to be legally nonexistent.

In the April 2014 national elections, the first since constitutional changes reduced voting to a single poll and the number of MPs from 386 to 199, Fidesz took almost 45% of the vote and 133 seats, returning Orbán to the premiership. Next up were Unity, a short-lived coalition of MSZP and four other parties, which took 26% of the vote and 38 seats. Orbán was clearly at the helm once again.

The extreme right-wing nationalist party Jobbik Magyarországért Mozgalom (Movement for a Better Hungary) won just under 17% of the vote nationwide in 2014 and currently holds 23 seats (more than 20% of the total) in parliament.

2008	2011	2012	2014
Government loses key referendum on healthcare reform; SZDSZ quits coalition, leaving the socialists to form a minority government; Hungary is particularly hard hit by the world economic crisis.	In its most high-profile role on the European stage to date, Hungary assumes presidency of the EU Council; a number of key streets and squares in Budapest are renamed.	A new (and controversial) Constitution of Hungary ratified by Parliament that deletes the word 'republic' from the country's official name goes into effect.	Prime Minister Viktor Orbán is returned to power, with his Fidesz party handily winning 133 of 199 parliamentary seats.

Budapest's Art Nouveau Architecture

Art Nouveau architecture (and its Viennese variant, Secessionism) is Budapest's signature style, and examples can be seen throughout the city. Its sinuous curves, flowing, asymmetrical forms, colourful tiles and other decorative elements stand out like beacons in a sea of refined and elegant baroque and mannered, geometric neoclassical buildings. It will have you gasping in surprise.

The Beginning & the End

Above: Primary School (p194)

Art Nouveau was an art form and architectural style that flourished in Europe and the USA from 1890 to around 1910. It began in Britain as the Arts and Crafts Movement founded by William Morris (1834–96), which stressed the importance of manual processes and attempted to create a new organic style in direct opposition to the imitative banalities spawned by the Industrial Revolution.

The style soon spread to Europe, where it took on distinctly local and/or national characteristics. In Vienna a group of artists called the Secessionists lent its name to the more geometric local style of Art Nouveau architecture: Sezessionstil (Hungarian: Szecesszió). In Budapest, the use of traditional facades with allegorical and historical figures and scenes, folk motifs and Zsolnay ceramics and other local materials led to an eclectic style. Though working within an Art Nouveau/Secessionist framework, this style emerged as something that was uniquely Hungarian.

But fashion and styles changed as whimsically and rapidly at the start of the 20th century as they do today, and by the end of the first decade Art Nouveau and its variants were considered limited, passé, even tacky. Fortunately for the good citizens of Budapest and us, the economic and political torpor of the interwar period and the 40-year 'big sleep' after WWII left many Art Nouveau/Secessionist buildings beaten but standing – a lot more, in fact, than remain in such important Art Nouveau centres as Paris, Brussels and Vienna.

Apart from Sezessionstil in Austria and Szecesszió in Hungary, Art Nouveau (from the French 'New Art') is known as Jugendstil in Germany, Modern in Russia, Modernisme in Catalonia and Stile Liberty in Italy.

Budapest Makes Its Mark

The first Hungarian architect to look to Art Nouveau for inspiration was Frigyes Spiegel, who covered traditional facades with exotic and allegorical figures and scenes. At the northern end of VI Izabella utca at No 94 is the restored Lindenbaum apartment block, the first in the city to use Art Nouveau ornamentation, including suns, stars, peacocks, flowers, snakes, foxes and long-tressed nudes.

ÖDÖN LECHNER

Ödön Lechner (1845–1914) has been nicknamed 'the Hungarian Gaudí' because, like the Catalan master, he took an existing style and put his own spin on it, creating something new and unique for his time and place. Hungary has now submitted five of his masterpieces, including three in Budapest (the Museum of Applied Arts, the Royal Postal Savings Bank and the Institute of Geology), for inclusion in Unesco's World Heritage list.

Lechner studied architecture at Budapest's József Trade School, the precursor to the University of Technology and Economics (BME) in Buda, and later at the Schinkel Academy of Architecture in Berlin. At the start of his career, Lechner worked in the prevailing styles and there were few indications that he would leave such an indelible mark on his city and his era. The firm he formed in 1869 received a steady flow of commissions in Pest during the boom years of the 1870s, but, like everyone else, he worked in the popular and all-too-common historicist and neoclassical styles.

Between 1875 and 1878 Lechner worked in France under architect Clément Parent on the renovation and redesign of chateaux. At this time he was also influenced by the emerging style of Art Nouveau.

After his return to Budapest Lechner began to move away from historicism to more modern ideas and trends. A turning point in his career was his commission for Thonet House on Váci utca, his innovative steel structure that he covered with glazed ceramics from the Zsolnay factory in Pécs. ('Birds have eyes too', he explained when asked about the expense.) More ambitious commissions followed, including the Museum of Applied Arts and the Institute of Geology. But not all was right in the world of Hungarian Art Nouveau. Lechner's Royal Postal Savings Bank building, now often seen as the architect's tour de force, was not well received when it was completed in 1901 and Lechner never really worked independently on a commission of that magnitude again.

City Park Calvinist Church

The master of the style, however, was Ödön Lechner: his most ambitious work in Budapest is the Museum of Applied Arts (p138). Purpose-built as a gallery and completed in time for the millenary exhibition in

IN PURSUIT OF THE FINEST

One of the joys of exploring the so-called Queen of the Danube is that you'll find elements of Art Nouveau and Secessionism in the oddest places. A street with a unified image is a rarity in Budapest; keep your eyes open and you'll spot bits and pieces everywhere and at all times. The following are our favourite 'hidden gems':

Bedő House (p98) Emil Vidor, 1903

Elephant House, Budapest Zoo (p149) Kornél Neuschloss-Knüsli, 1912

City Park Calvinist Church (Map p250; VII Városligeti fasor 7) Aladár Arkay, 1913

Egger Villa (Map p250; VII Városligeti fasor 24) Emil Vidor, 1902

Institute of Geology (Map p254) Ödön Lechner, 1899

Léderer Mansion (Map p250; VI Bajza utca 42) Zoltán Bálint and Lajos Jámbor, 1902

National Institute for the Blind (p150) Sándor Baumgarten, 1904

Philanthia (p83) Kálmán Albert Körössy, 1906

Primary school (Map p250; VII Dob utca 85) Ármin Hegedűs, 1906

Sonnenberg Mansion (Map p250; VI Munkácsy Mihály utca 23) Albert Körössy, 1903

Thonet House (p83) Ödön Lechner, 1890

Török Bank House (Map p238; V Szervita tér 3) Henrik Böhm and Ármin Hegedűs, 1906

Vidor Villa (Map p250; VII Városligeti fasor 33) Emil Vidor, 1905

Török Bank House

1896, it was faced and roofed in a variety of colourful Zsolnay ceramic tiles, and its turrets, domes and ornamental figures lend it an Eastern or Mogul feel. His crowning glory (though not seen as such at the time), however, is the sumptuous Royal Postal Savings Bank (p98), a Secessionist extravaganza of floral mosaics, folk motifs and ceramic figures just off Szabadság tér in Lipótváros and dating from 1901.

The Ferenc Liszt Music Academy (p129), completed in 1907, is interesting not so much for its exterior as for its interior decorative elements. There's a dazzling Art Nouveau mosaic called *Art Is the Source of Life* by Aladár Kőrösfői Kriesch, a leader of the seminal Gödöllő Artists' Colony, on the 1st-floor landing and some fine stained glass by master craftsman Miksa Róth, whose home and workshop in central Pest is now a museum (p118). In the music academy take a look at the grid of laurel leaves below the ceiling of the main concert hall, which mimics the ironwork dome of the Secession Building (1897–1908) in Vienna, and the large reflecting sapphire-blue Zsolnay ball finials on the stair balusters.

The Danubius Hotel Gellért (p167), designed by Ármin Hegedűs, Artúr Sebestyén and Izidor Sterk in 1909 but not completed until 1918, contains examples of late Art Nouveau, notably the thermal spa with its enormous arched glass entrance hall and Zsolnay ceramic fountains in the bathing pools. The architects were clearly influenced by Lechner but added other elements, including baroque ones.

Very noteworthy indeed is the arcade near V Ferenciek tere called Párisi Udvar (p83) built in 1909 by Henrik Schmahl. The design contains a myriad influences – from Moorish Islamic and Venetian Gothic architecture to elements of Lechner's own eclectic style.

The Art Nouveau European Route (www.artnouveau. eu) website is among the most comprehensive on the Art Nouveau heritage of Europe.

Music

Hungary's contribution to music – especially the classical variety, called *komolyzene* (serious music) in Hungarian – belies the size of the country and its population; its operas are world class. Of particular note and interest is Hungarian folk music, which has enjoyed something of a renaissance over the past few decades thanks to the *táncház* (dance house) phenomenon.

Classical Music

Ferenc Liszt was born in the Hungarian village of Doborján (now Raiding in Austria) to a Hungarian father and an Austrian mother but never learned to speak Hungarian fluently.

When it comes to Hungarian classical music, one person stands head and shoulders above the rest: Franz (Ferenc) Liszt (1811–86). He established the sublime Ferenc Liszt Music Academy, still the premier performance space in Budapest, and lived in an apartment on VI Vörösmarty utca from 1881 until his death – the apartment is now the Franz Liszt Memorial Museum (p121). Liszt liked to describe himself as 'part Gypsy', and some of his works, notably the *Hungarian Rhapsodies,* do echo the traditional music of the Roma people.

Béla Bartók (1881–1945) and Zoltán Kodály (1882–1967) were both long-term residents of Budapest; Bartók lived at II Csalán út 29 in the Buda Hills (his former residence is also now a museum, p76, while Kodály had an apartment at VI Kodály körönd 1 along Andrássy út for more than four decades. The two made the first systematic study of Hungarian folk music together, travelling and recording throughout the Magyar linguistic regions in 1906. Both integrated some of their findings into their own compositions – Bartók in *Bluebeard's Castle*, for example, and Kodály in his *Peacock Variations.*

The most prestigious orchestras are the Budapest-based Hungarian National Philharmonic Orchestra and the newer Budapest Festival Orchestra.

Opera & Operetta

Ferenc Erkel (1810–93), who taught at the Ferenc Liszt Music Academy from 1879 to 1886 and was the State Opera House's first musical director, is considered the father of Hungarian opera. Two of his works – the stirringly nationalistic *Bánk Bán,* based on József Katona's play of that name and considered *the* national opera of Hungary, and *László Hunyadi* – are standards at the Hungarian State Opera House.

Imre Kálmán (1882–1953) is Hungary's most celebrated composer of operettas. *The Gypsy Princess* and *Countess Mariza* are two of his most popular works and standard fare at the Budapest Operetta. Hungarian by birth but settling in Vienna in his late 20s, Franz (Ferenc) Lehár (1870–1948) is also famous for his operettas, the most successful of which was *The Merry Widow*. It opened at the Magyar Színház (Hungarian Theatre, now the National Theatre) in November 1906 and ran for more than 100 performances.

Folk Music

It is important to understand the differences between the various types of folk music you might hear in Hungary, especially between Hungarian folk music and so-called Gypsy music.

Gypsy Folk Music

Gypsy music as it is known and heard in Hungarian restaurants from Budapest to Boston is urban schmaltz and based on rousing recruitment marching tunes called *verbunkos,* played during the Rákóczi independence wars. For a century the international acclaim afforded the *verbunkos* eclipsed all other forms of traditional Hungarian folk music. At least two fiddles, a bass and a cymbalom (a curious stringed instrument played with sticks) are de rigueur in 'Gypsy' music. You can hear this saccharine music at hotel restaurants throughout Budapest or get hold of a recording by Sándor Déki Lakatos, the sixth band leader from the famous Lakatos musical dynasty.

Hungarian Folk Music

Hungarian folk musicians play violins, zithers, hurdy-gurdies, pipes, bagpipes and lutes on a five-tone diatonic scale; this makes it quite different from the Italian and German music that dominated the rest of Europe and not to everyone's taste (at least at first). Attending a *táncház* (literally 'dance house' though really folk-music and dance workshops) is an excellent way to hear the music and even to learn to dance. It's all good fun and they're easy to find in Budapest, where the dance-house revival began.

Watch out for Muzsikás, Márta Sebestyén, Ghymes (a Hungarian folk band from Slovakia) and the Hungarian group Vujicsics, which mixes elements of South Slav and Hungarian music. Anyone playing the haunting music of the Csángó, an ethnic group of Hungarians living in eastern Transylvania and Moldavia, is a good bet. Another folk musician with eclectic tastes is Beáta Pálya, who combines such sounds as traditional Bulgarian, Persian and Indian music with Hungarian folk.

Roma Folk Music

To confuse matters, real Roma – as opposed to Gypsy – music traditionally does not use instruments but is sung a cappella, though a technique called oral-bassing that vocally imitates the sound of instruments is often used. Some modern Roma music groups – Kalyi Jag (Black Fire), Ando Drom (On the Road) and Romani Rota (Gypsy Wheels) – have added guitars, percussion and electronics to create a whole new sound.

Klezmer Music

Traditional Yiddish music is not as well known as the Gypsy and Roma varieties but is of similar origin, having once been closely associated with Central European folk music. Until WWI, *klezmer* dance bands were led by the violin and cymbalom, but the influence of Yiddish theatre and the first wax recordings inspired the inclusion of the clarinet. *Klezmer* music is going through a renaissance in Budapest, and there are several bands performing, mostly in the Jewish Quarter of Erzsébetváros.

In Anthony Minghella's film *The English Patient* (1996), when László Almásy (Ralph Fiennes) plays a Hungarian folk song on the phonograph for Katharine Clifton (Kristin Scott Thomas), we hear Márta Sebestyén singing 'Szerelem, Szerelem' (Love, Love). Sigh.

Pop Music

Pop music is as popular here as anywhere in the world and covers the full range – from punk (Auróra) and hip-hop (Bëlga) to electronic (Yonderboi). In mid-August Budapest hosts one of Europe's biggest annual pop events, the **Sziget Festival** (http://szigetfestival.com), on Óbuda (Hajógyár) Island north of Margaret Island. It boasts more than 1000 performances over a week and attracts an audience of 400,000 people.

Wines of Hungary

Wine has been made in Hungary since at least the time of the Romans. It is very much a part of Hungarian culture, but only in recent years has it moved on from the local tipple you drank at Sunday lunch with the family or the overwrought and overpriced thimble of rarefied red sipped in a Budapest wine bar to the all-singin', all-dancin', all embracin' obsession that it is today.

The best website for Hungarian wines is www.bortarsasag.hu. It appraises vintners and their vintages and lists prices from the Bortársaság (Budapest Wine Society), Hungary's foremost wine society and wine retail chain.

Choosing Wine

Wine is sold by the glass or bottle everywhere – usually at reasonable prices. Old-fashioned wine bars ladle out plonk by the *deci* (decilitre, or 0.1L), but if you're into more serious wine, you should visit one of Budapest's excellent wine bars such as DiVino Borbár (p103), Doblo (p124) or Innio (p103), a wine restaurant like Klassz (p124), or speciality wine shops like the Malatinszky Wine Store (p107) or Bortársaság (p63) chain.

When choosing a Hungarian wine, look for the words *minőségi bor* (quality wine) or *különleges minőségű bor* (premium quality wine). On a wine label the first word indicates the region, the second the grape variety (eg Villányi Kékfrankos) or the type or brand of wine (eg Tokaji Aszú, Szekszárdi Bikavér). Other important words that you'll see include: *édes* (sweet), *fehér* (white), *félédes* (semisweet), *félszáraz* (semidry or medium), *habzóbor* (sparking), *pezsgő* (champagne), *száraz* (dry) and *vörös* (red).

Wine Regions

Hungary is divided into a half-dozen wine-producing regions, but we're most interested in five of their subdivisions.

Villány

Villány, in Hungary's warm south, is especially noted for its reds: Blauer Portugieser (formerly called Kékoportó), Cabernet Sauvignon and, in particular, Cabernet Franc and Merlot. The region has also been experimenting in Pinot Noir. Red wines here are almost always big-bodied, Bordeaux style and high in tannins.

Among the best vintners in Villány is József Bock, whose Royal Cuvée is a special blend of Cabernet Franc, Pinot Noir and Merlot. Other names to watch out for are Márton Mayer and Alajos Wunderlich. Wines to try from this region include Attila Gere's elegant and complex Cabernet Sauvignon or his Solus Merlot as well as Ede and Zsolt Tiffán's elegant and complex Blauer Portugieser and Cabernet Franc.

Eger

Flanked by two of Northern Hungary's most beautiful ranges of hills, Eger is the home of the celebrated Egri Bikavér (Eger Bull's Blood), a blend of Kékfrankos (Blaufränkisch) mixed with other reds, sometimes

PÉTER LENGYEL'S TOP FIVE

We know what we like, but we're no experts. So we turned to 'he-who-knows-all' – Budapest-based wine translator and maven Péter Lengyel – for his favourite five wines (without regard to vintage and in no particular order):

Ottó Légli's Gesztenyés Rajnai Rizling (South Balaton) Made from fruit harvested ideally ripe in late September from the Gesztenyés vineyard in the village of Gyugy, this fine Riesling is pale in colour and bursts with crisp, fruity flavours.

István Szepsy's Szent Tamás Furmint (Tokaj) With a flavour recalling apples, dry Furmint has the potential to become the best dry white in Hungary; Szepsy's version can hold its own against a top-notch white Burgundy.

Ráspi's Kékfrankos Selection (Sopron) This is an increasingly popular red wine from a varietal known as Blaufränkisch in neighbouring Austria; its pale colour belies its full flavour, finesse and complexity.

Tiffán's Grande Selection (Villány) A Bordeaux-style red blend that plays with the French big ones; profound, concentrated and resonant, with great elegance.

István Szepsy's 6-puttonyos Aszú (Tokaj) Hungary's sweetest 'noble rot' wine from the acknowledged leader of Tokaj vintners; possibly the greatest sweet wine made anywhere in the world.

Kadarka. Bikavér producers to watch out for are Tibor Gál and István Toth; the latter's Bikavér easily compares to any of the 'big' reds from Villány. Look out for Kékfrankos and Merlot from János Bolyki.

Eger's signature grape is Pinot Noir; try Tibor Gál *fils'* version, which is on par with the *premiers crus* from Burgundy. You'll also find several decent whites in Eger, including Leányka (Little Girl), Olaszrizling (Italian Riesling) and Hárslevelű from Debrő.

Szekszárd

Mild winters and warm, dry summers combined with favourable loess soil help Szekszárd in Southern Transdanubia to produce some of the best affordable red wines in Hungary. They are not like the big-bodied reds of Villány, but softer and less complex, with a distinct spiciness. They're easy to drink.

The premier grape here is Kadarka, a late-ripening variety produced in limited quantities. The best Kadarka is made by Ferenc Takler and Pál Mészáros. Kadarka is a traditional ingredient here in making Bikavér, a wine usually associated with Eger. In fact, many wine aficionados in Hungary prefer the Szekszárd 'Bull's Blood'; try Zoltán Heimann's version.

Tamás Dúzsi (Kékfrankos Rosé) is acknowledged to be the finest producer of rosé in Hungary.

Badacsony

Badacsony is named after the 400m-high basalt massif that rises like a bread loaf along the northwestern shore of Lake Balaton. The region's signature Olaszrizling, especially produced by Huba Szeremley and Ambrus Bakó, is among the best dry white wine for everyday drinking available in Hungary. The most reliable Chardonnay is from Ottó Légli on Balaton's southern shore.

The area's volcanic soil gives the unique, once-threatened Kéknyelű (Blue Stalk) wine its distinctive mineral taste; it is a complex tipple of very low yield that ages well. Szeremley's version is the only reliably authentic example.

Two excellent tomes on Hungarian wine are the rather, er, sober *The Wines of Hungary* by Alex Liddell and the much flashier and more colourful *Hungary: Its Fine Wines & Winemakers* by David Copp. Both books look not just at wines but at the whole winemaking process.

VINTAGE ADVANTAGE

Generally speaking, the *évjárat* (vintage) of Hungarian wines has only become important in the past decade or so.

2004 Inferior year throughout, with aggressive whites and thin reds.

2005 The very wet summer was catastrophic for whites, but the quality of reds beat the previous year.

2006 Bad start with a cool summer, but the long, very hot autumn proved excellent for whites and certain reds; good late-harvest sweet whites.

2007 Much hotter summer created more rounded acidity in whites, especially in Tokaj.

2008 Nice quantity of noble rot produced some decent but not outstanding sweet wines.

2009 Favourable weather conditions brought excellent reds and good Tokaj.

2010 Inferior year with incessant rain produced thin and diluted red and white wines.

2011 Balanced weather, with a hot summer and sufficient precipitation, produced wine drinkable after just one year.

2012 Most arid summer in memory produced small quantities of grapes in most regions, but the potential for excellent-quality wine from top growers is great.

2013 Too early to call at press time but seems to have been the third very good year in a row, with many growers rating it eight or nine out of 10.

Tokaj

The volcanic soil, sunny climate and protective mountain barrier of the Tokaj-Hegyalja (Tokaj Uplands) region in northern Hungary make it ideal for growing grapes and making wine. Tokaj wines were exported to Poland and Russia in the Middle Ages and reached the peak of their popularity in Europe in the 17th and 18th centuries.

Louis XIV famously called Tokaj 'the wine of kings and the king of wines', while Voltaire wrote that 'this wine could be only given by the boundlessly good God'!

Tokaj dessert wines are rated according to the number – from three to six – of *puttony* (butts, or baskets for picking) of sweet Aszú grapes added to the base wines. These are grapes infected with 'noble rot', the *Botrytis cinera* mould that almost turns them into raisins on the vine.

For Tokaji Aszú, one name to look out for is István Szepsy; he concentrates on both the upscale six-*puttony* type and the Esszencia – so sweet and low in alcohol it's hardly even wine. His Szepsy Cuvée, aged in stainless-steel barrels for a year or two (against the usual five for Tokaji Aszú), is a complex, elegant blend comparable to Sauternes. Other names to watch out for are Zoltán Demeter, István Hétszőlő, Gróf Degenfeld and Pendits.

Tokaj also produces less sweet wines, including dry Szamorodni (an excellent aperitif) and sweet Szamorodni, which is not unlike an Italian *vin santo;* for the latter try Disznókő's version. Of the four grape varieties grown here, Furmint (try the Oremus and Béres varieties) and Hárslevelű (Linden Leaf) are the driest.

Survival Guide

Transport

ARRIVING IN BUDAPEST

Most people arrive in Budapest by air, but you can also get here from dozens of European cities by bus and train. You can even get to Budapest by Danube hydrofoil from Vienna.

Flights, cars and tours can be booked online at lonelyplanet.com.

Ferenc Liszt International Airport

Budapest's **Ferenc Liszt International Airport** (☎1-296 7000; www.bud.hu) has two modern terminals side by side about 24km southeast of the city centre.

Most international flights land at Terminal 2A. Budget airlines such as **EasyJet** (www.easyjet.com), **Wizz Air** (www.wizzair.com) and **German Wings** (www.germanwings.com) use Terminal 2B, which is next door. There are no scheduled flights within Hungary.

At both terminals you'll also find currency-exchange desks operated by **Interchange** ☺8am-1am) and ATMs. In Terminal 2A there are half a dozen car-rental desks and a **left-luggage office** (per hr from €2; ☺24hr).

Taxi

Fő Taxi (☑1-222 2222; www.fotaxi.hu) has the monopoly on picking up taxi passengers at the airport. Fares to most locations in Pest are about 6000Ft, and in Buda about 7000Ft. Of course you can take any taxi *to* the airport, but the price will be the same.

Bus

The **Airport Shuttle Minibusz** (ASM; ☑1-296 8555; www.airportshuttle.hu; one way/return 3200/5500Ft) carries passengers from both terminals in nine-seat vans directly to their hotel, hostel or residence. Tickets are available at a clearly marked desk in the arrivals halls, though you may have to wait while the van fills up. You need to book your journey back to the airport at least 12 hours in advance.

The cheapest (and most time-consuming) way to get into the city centre from the airport is to take bus 200E (350Ft, on the bus 450Ft; 4am to midnight) – look for the stop on the footpath between terminals 2A and 2B – which terminates at the Kőbánya-Kispest metro station. From there take the M3 metro into the city centre. The total cost is 700Ft to 800Ft. Between midnight and 4am night bus 900 makes the run.

Keleti Pályaudvar

Magyar Államvasutak (MÁV, Hungarian State Railways; ☑06-40 49 49 49, from abroad +36-1 444 4499; www.mav.hu) links up with the European rail network in all directions. Most international trains (and domestic traffic to/from the north and northeast) arrive at **Keleti pályaudvar** (Eastern Train Station; VIII Kerepesi út 2-6; Ⓜ M3, 4 Keleti pályaudvar). The station has left-luggage lockers, a post office and a grocery store that is open late.

Avoid queues by buying your tickets in advance at the **MÁV-Start passenger service centre** (☑1-512 7921; www.mav-start.hu; V József Attila utca 16; ☺ 9am-6pm Mon-Fri).

Metro

Keleti is on two metro lines: the green M4 and the blue M3.

Bus

Night buses serve the station when the metro is closed.

Nyugati Pályaudvar

Trains from some international destinations (eg Romania) and from the Danube Bend and Great Plain arrive at **Nyugati pályaudvar** (Western Train Station; VI Teréz körút 55-57; Ⓜ M3 Nyugati pályaudvar). Amenities are similar to those at Keleti pályaudvar.

Metro

The station is on the blue M3 line.

Bus

Night buses serve the station when the metro is closed.

Déli Pályaudvar

Trains from some destinations in the south, eg Osijek in Croatia and Sarajevo in Bosnia & Hercegovina, arrive at **Déli pályaudvar** (Southern Train Station; I Krisztina körút 37; Ⓜ M2 Déli pályaudvar). Amenities are similar to those at Keleti pályaudvar.

Metro

The station is on the red M2 line.

Bus

Night buses serve the station when the metro is closed.

Népliget Bus Station

All international buses and domestic ones to/from western Hungary arrive at and depart from **Népliget bus station** (Map p242; ☎1-219 8030; IX Üllői út 131; Ⓜ M3 Népliget)in Pest. The **international ticket office**

(☎1-219 8020; ☉6am-6pm Mon-Fri, to 4pm Sat & Sun) is upstairs. **Eurolines** (www. eurolines.com) is represented here, as is its Hungarian associate, **Volánbusz** (☎1-382 0888; www.volanbusz.hu). There's a **left-luggage office** (per piece 350Ft; ☉6am-9pm) downstairs.

Metro

Népliget is on the blue metro M3 (station: Népliget).

Stadion Bus Station

Stadion bus station generally serves cities and towns in eastern Hungary. The **ticket office** (☉6am-6pm Mon-Fri, to 4pm Sat & Sun) and the **left-luggage office** (☉6am-7pm) are on the ground floor.

Metro

Stadion is on the red metro M2 (station: 2 Stadionok).

International Ferry Pier

A hydrofoil service on the Danube River between Budapest and Vienna (5½ to 6½ hours) is run by **Mahart PassNave** (Map p238; ☎1-484 4025; www.mahartpassnave.hu; V Belgrád rakpart; ☉8am-6pm Mon-Fri; ☒2) and operates from late April to late September. Boats leave from Budapest at 9am Tuesday, Thursday and

Saturday; from Vienna they depart at the same time on Wednesday, Friday and Sunday. Adult one-way/return fares are €99/125. (Children between two and 12 years of age travel half-price.) Taking a bicycle costs €25 one way.

In Budapest, hydrofoils arrive at and depart from the **International Ferry Pier** (Nemzetközi hajóállomás; Map p238; ☎1-318 1223; V Belgrád rakpart; ☒2), which is between Elizabeth and Liberty Bridges on the Pest side.

GETTING AROUND BUDAPEST

Budapest is a very easy city to negotiate – the Danube clearly defines east and west and Pest and Buda. There is a safe, efficient and inexpensive public-transport system run by **BKK** (Budapesti Közlekedési Központ; Centre for Budapest Transport; ☎1-258 4636; www.bkk.hu), formerly BKV, that is rapidly being upgraded and will never have you waiting more than five or 10 minutes for any conveyance. Five types of transport are in general use: metro trains on four colour-coded city lines, green HÉV trains on four suburban lines, blue buses, yellow trams and red trolleybuses. But you can also get around under your own steam by bicycle, car or motorcycle.

CLIMATE CHANGE & TRAVEL

Every form of transport that relies on carbon-based fuel generates CO_2, the main cause of human-induced climate change. Modern travel is dependent on aeroplanes, which might use less fuel per kilometre per person than most cars but travel much greater distances. The altitude at which aircraft emit gases (including CO_2) and particles also contributes to their climate change impact. Many websites offer 'carbon calculators' that allow people to estimate the carbon emissions generated by their journey and, for those who wish to do so, to offset the impact of the greenhouse gases emitted with contributions to portfolios of climate-friendly initiatives throughout the world. Lonely Planet offsets the carbon footprint of all staff and author travel.

PUBLIC TRANSPORT FARES & PASSES

➡ To ride the metro, trams, trolleybuses, buses and the HÉV as far as the city limits, you must have a valid ticket, which you can buy at kiosks, newsstands, metro entrances, machines and, in some cases, on the bus for an extra charge. Children aged under six and EU seniors over 65 travel free. Bicycles can only be transported on the HÉV.

➡ The basic fare for all forms of transport is 350Ft (3000Ft for a block of 10), allowing you to travel as far as you like on the same metro, bus, trolleybus or tram line without changing/transferring. A 'transfer ticket' allowing unlimited stations with one change within one hour costs 530Ft. On the metro exclusively, the base fare drops to 300Ft if you are just going three stops within 30 minutes. Tickets bought *on* the bus and all night buses cost 450Ft.

➡ You must always travel in one continuous direction on any ticket; return trips are forbidden. Tickets have to be validated in machines at metro entrances and aboard other vehicles – inspectors will fine you for not doing so.

➡ Life will most likely be simpler if you buy a travel pass. Passes are valid on all trams, buses, trolleybuses, and HÉV (within the city limits) and metro lines, and you don't have to worry about validating your ticket each time you board. The most central place to buy them is the ticket office at the Deák Ferenc tér metro station open from 6am to 11pm daily.

➡ A 24-hour travel card is poor value at 1650Ft, but the 72-hour one for 4150Ft and the seven-day pass for 4950Ft are worthwhile for most people. You'll need a photo for the fortnightly/monthly passes (7000/10,500Ft).

➡ Travelling without a valid ticket or pass is foolhardy; with what seems like constant surveillance (especially in the metro), there's an excellent chance you'll get caught. The on-the-spot fine is 8000Ft, which doubles if you pay it at the **BKK office** (☑ 1-461 6800; VII Akácfa utca 22; ⊙ 6am-8pm Mon-Fri, 8am-1.45pm Sat; Ⓜ M2 Blaha Lujza tér) up to 30 days later. After that date it goes up to 32,500Ft.

➡ If you've left something on any form of public transport, contact the **BKK lost & found office** (Map p250; ☑ 1-258 4636; VII Akácfa utca 18; ⊙ 8am-5pm Mon-Fri; Ⓜ M2 Blaha Lujza tér).

Bicycle

More and more cyclists can be seen on the streets of Budapest, taking advantage of the city's growing network of dedicated bike paths. Some of the main roads might be a bit too busy for enjoyable cycling, but the side streets are fine and there are some areas (eg City Park, Margaret Island) where cycling is positively ideal. You can hire bicycles from:

Bubi Bikes (www.molbubi.hu/; access fee per 24hr/72hr/week 500/1000/2000Ft, hire per 1/2/3/24hr 500/1500/2500/19,500Ft) Budapest's newly launched bicycle-sharing scheme has 1000 bikes available at 76 docking stations across the city. You can collect your bike at any docking station and return it at any of the others. The first 30 minutes are free. Hire is available for a maximum of 24 hours at a time – you must allow five minutes between each access. The scheme is sponsored by oil and gas group MOL.

Bike Base (Map p244; ☑ 06 70 625 8501, 1-269 5983; www.bikebase.hu; VI Podmaniczky utca 19; per 1/2/3 days 2000/2400/2900Ft; ⊙ 9am-7pm; Ⓜ M3 Nyugati pályaudvar) Bike Base has bikes available from April to October.

Budapest Bike (Map p250; ☑ 06 30 944 5533; www.budapestbike.hu; VII Wesselényi utca 13; day/overnight 2500/3500Ft; ⊙ 9am-6pm mid-Mar–mid-Oct, other times by appointment; ⓂM2 Astoria, ☒4, 6) Budapest Bike has bikes available year-round.

Dynamo Bike & Bake (Map p238; ☑ 06 30 868 1107; www.dynamobike.com; V Képíró utca 6; per 24/48/72hr 3500/6000/9000Ft; ⊙8am-7pm Mon & Wed-Fri, 9am-3pm Sat & Sun; ⓂM3 Kálvin tér, ☒47, 49) A fantastic little cake shop–bike rental, Dynamo is run by a keen cycling guide who appreciates the value of good equipment. The hybrid urban bikes and mountain bikes are brand new and meticulously maintained; rental includes safety gear. Cycling tours can be arranged at reasonably short notice.

Yellow Zebra Bikes (Map p250; ☑1-269 3843; www.yellowzebrabikes.com; VI Lázár utca 16; 1hr/full-day hire from 500/2500Ft; ☉9am-8.30pm Apr-Oct, 10am-7pm Nov-Mar; Ⓜ M1 Opera)

Boat

Throughout most of the year passenger ferries run by **BKK** (Budapesti Közlekedési Központ; Centre for Budapest Transport; ☑1-258 4636; www.bkk.hu) depart from alongside the **A38** (Map p236; XI Pázmány Péter sétány 3-11; ☒906, ⛴4, 6) club boat in south Buda up to 10 times a day Monday to Saturday and head for IV Árpád út in northern Pest, a one-hour trip with eight stops along the way. Tickets (adult/child 750/550Ft) are sold on board. The ferry stop closest to the Castle District is I Batthyány tér, and V Petőfi tér is not far from the pier just west of Vörösmarty tér. Transporting a bicycle costs 400Ft.

Bus

An extensive system of buses running on some 260 routes day and night serves greater Budapest. On certain bus lines the same bus may have an 'E' after the number, meaning it is express and makes limited stops.

Buses operate from around 4.15am to between 9pm and 11.30pm, depending on the line. From 11.30pm to just after 4am a network of 40 night buses (always with three digits and beginning with 9) operates every 15 to 60 minutes, again depending on the route.

Following are bus routes (shown with blue lines on most Budapest maps) that you might find useful:

7 Cuts across a large swath of central Pest from XIV Bosnyák tér and down VII Rákóczi út before crossing Elizabeth Bridge to southern Buda. The 7E makes limited stops on the same route.

15 Takes in most of the Inner Town from IX Boráros tér to XIII Lehel tér north of Nyugati train station.

86 Runs the length of Buda from XI Kosztolányi Dezső tér to Óbuda.

105 Goes from V Deák Ferenc tér to XII Apor Vilmos tér in central Buda.

Car & Motorcycle

Driving in Budapest can be a nightmare: ongoing roadworks reduce traffic to a snail's pace; there are more serious accidents than fender-benders; and parking spots are near impossible to find in some neighbourhoods. The public-transport system is good and very inexpensive. Use it.

For information on traffic and road conditions in the capital, check the **Főinform** (☑1-317 1173; www.fovinform.hu; ☉7am-7pm) website.

See p206 for road rules.

Hire

All the international car-rental firms have offices in Budapest, but don't expect many bargains. A Suzuki Swift from **Avis** (☑1-318 4240; www.avis.hu; V Arany János utca 26-28; ☉7am-6pm Mon-Fri, 8am-2pm Sat & Sun; Ⓜ M3 Arany János utca), for example, costs €59/380 per day/week, with unlimited kilometres, collision damage waiver (CDW) and theft protection (TP) insurance. The same car and insurance with 750km costs just €65 for the weekend.

Parking

Parking costs between 175Ft and 450Ft per hour on the streets of Budapest (more on Castle Hill), generally between 8am and 6pm (sometimes 8pm) Monday to Friday and 8am and noon Saturday. Illegally parked cars are usually clamped or booted.

Metro & HÉV

Budapest has four underground metro lines. Three of them converge at Deák Ferenc tér (only): the little yellow (or Millennium) line designated M1 that runs from Vörösmarty tér to Mexikói út in Pest; the red M2 line from Déli train station in Buda to Örs vezér tere in Pest; and the blue M3 line from Újpest-Központ to Kőbánya-Kispest in Pest. The city's long-awaited green M4 metro runs from Kelenföldi train station in southern Buda to Keleti pályaudvar

---

THE RING ROADS

If you look at a map of Budapest you will see that two ring roads – the big one (Nagykörút) and the semi-circular Kiskörút (the 'little ring road') – link three of the bridges across the Danube and essentially define central Pest. The Big Ring Rd consists of Szent István körút, Teréz körút, Erzsébet körút, József körút and Ferenc körút. The Little Ring Rd comprises Károly körút, Múzeum körút and Vámház körút. Important boulevards such as Bajcsy-Zsilinszky út, leafy Andrássy út, Rákóczi út and Üllői út fan out from the ring roads, creating large squares and circles.

ROAD RULES

➡ You must drive on the right-hand side of the road.

➡ Speed limits are 50km/h in built-up areas, 90km/h on secondary and tertiary roads, 110km/h on most highways/dual carriageways and 130km/h on motorways.

➡ The use of seat belts is compulsory.

➡ Motorcyclists must wear helmets at all times.

➡ Drivers must dip their headlights throughout the day outside built-up areas, and motorcyclists at all times.

➡ There is a 100% ban on alcohol when you are driving, which is strictly enforced.

➡ All cars must bear a motorway pass or *matrica* (vignette) to access Hungary's motorways. Passes, which cost 2975/4780Ft for a week/month are available at petrol stations, post offices and some motorway entrances and border crossings. A Hungarian rental car will have one already.

➡ Motorists anywhere in Hungary can call the **Hungarian Automobile Club** (Magyar Autóklub; ☑ 188; www.autoclub.hu) for roadside assistance.

in Pest, where it links with the M2. It links with the M3 at Kálvin tér. All four metro lines run from about 4am and begin their last journey at around 11.15pm.

The HÉV suburban train line, which runs on four lines (north from Batthyány tér in Buda via Óbuda and Aquincum to Szentendre, south to both Csepel and Ráckeve, and east to Gödöllő), is almost like a fifth, aboveground metro line.

Taxi

Taxis in Budapest are cheap by European standards, and are – at long last – fully regulated, with uniform flag-fall (450Ft) and per-kilometre charges (280Ft).

Be careful when hailing a taxi on the street, though. Avoid at all costs 'taxis' with no name on the door and only a removable taxi light on the roof. Never get into a taxi that does not have a yellow license plate and an identification badge displayed on the dashboard (as required by law), the logo of one of the reputable taxi firms on the outside of the side doors and a table of fares clearly visible on the right-side back door.

Reputable taxi firms:

City Taxi (☑1-211 1111; www.citytaxi.hu)

Fő Taxi (☑1-222 2222; www.fotaxi.hu)

Rádió Taxi (☑1-777 7777; www.radiotaxi.hu)

Taxi 4 (☑1-444 4444; www.taxi4.hu)

Tram

BKK (Budapesti Közlekedési Központ; Centre for Budapest Transport; ☑1-258 4636; www.bkk.hu) runs 30 tram lines. Trams are often faster and generally more pleasant for sightseeing than buses.

Important tram lines (always marked with a red line on a Budapest map) are:

2 Scenic tram that travels along the Pest side of the Danube from V Jászai Mari tér to IX Boráros tér and beyond.

4 and 6 Extremely useful trams that start at XI Fehérvári út and XI Móricz Zsigmond körtér in south Buda, respectively, and follow the entire length of the Big Ring Rd in Pest before terminating at II Széll Kálmán tér in Buda. Tram 6 runs every 10 to 15 minutes round the clock.

18 Runs from southern Buda along XI Bartók Béla út through the Tabán to II Széll Kálmán tér before carrying on into the Buda Hills.

19 Covers part of the same route as 18, but then runs along the Buda side of the Danube to I Batthyány tér.

47 and 49 Link V Deák Ferenc tér in Pest with points in southern Buda via the Little Ring Rd.

61 Connects XI Móricz Zsigmond körtér with Déli train station and II Széll Kálmán tér in Buda.

Trolleybus

Trolleybuses on 15 lines go along cross streets in central Pest and so are usually of little use to visitors, with the sole exception of the ones to, from and around City Park (70, 72 and 74) and down to Puskás Ferenc Stadion (75 and 77). A broken red line on a map indicates a trolleybus route.

Directory A–Z

Customs Regulations

Allowances on duty-free goods purchased at airports or on ferries originating *outside* the EU are as follows: 200 cigarettes or 50 cigars or 250g loose tobacco; 4L still wine; 1L spirits. In addition you must declare the import/export of any amount of cash, cheques and securities exceeding the sum of €10,000.

When leaving Hungary, you are not supposed to take out valuable antiques without a special permit, which should be available from the place of purchase.

Discount Cards

Budapest Card (⌨1-438 8080; www.budapestinfo. hu; per 24/48/72hr 4500/7500/8900Ft) Free admission to selected museums and other sights in and around the city; unlimited travel on all forms of public transport; two free guided tours; and discounts for organised tours, car rental, thermal baths and selected shops and restaurants. Available at tourist offfices but cheaper online.

European Youth Card (Euro<26 Card; www.euro26. org; 1yr 2500Ft) Wide range of discounts for under-26s.
International Student

Identity Card (ISIC; www. isic.org; 1yr 2600Ft) Discounts on some transport, and cheap admission to selected museums and other sights for full-time students.
International Teacher Identity Card (ITIC; www. isic.org; 1yr 2050Ft) Similar to ISIC but for full-time teachers.
International Youth Travel Card (IYTC; www. isic.org; 1yr 2050Ft) Similar benefits to the ISIC for nonstudents under 26.

Electricity

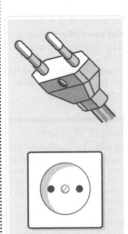

230V/50Hz

Emergency

Any crime must be reported at the police station of the district you are in; if possible, bring along a Hungarian speaker to help.
Ambulance (in English ⌨1-311 1666, 104)
Belváros-Lipótváros Police Station (⌨1-373 1000; V Szalay utca 11; Ⓜ M2 Kossuth Lajos tér) Pest centre.
General Emergency (⌨112) English spoken.
Fire (⌨105)
Police (⌨107)
Roadside Assistance (⌨188; ⊘24hr)

Gay & Lesbian Travellers

Budapest offers just a reasonable gay scene for its size. Most gay people are discreet in public places and displays of affection are rare. Lesbian social life remains very much underground, with a lot of private parties. There have been a couple of violent rightwing demonstrations in response to the Budapest Pride celebrations in the recent past. Attitudes are changing, but society generally remains conservative on this issue.
Budapest Gay Guide (www.budapest.gayguide. net) Good listings and insider advice.

PRACTICALITIES

Newspapers & Magazines Budapest has two English-language newspapers: *Budapest Times* (www.budapesttimes.hu; 750Ft), a thin weekly with straightforward news, opinion pieces and some reviews appearing on Friday, and the fortnightly *Budapest Business Journal* (www.bbj.hu; 1250Ft), an almost archival publication of financial news and business, appearing every other Friday. The monthly *Diplomacy & Trade* (www.dteurope.com; 1710Ft) offers a glimpse into the expat community. The erudite *Hungarian Quarterly* (www.thehungarianquarterly.com; 1500Ft) is a valuable source of current Hungarian thinking in translation, as is the bimonthly *Hungarian Review* (www.hungarianreview.com; 1200Ft). The *Budapest Sun Online* (www.budapestsun.com) has local news and arts and entertainment reviews.

Radio Magyar Radio (www.radio.hu) runs three main stations: MR1-Kossuth (107.8 FM; news, talkback and jazz), MR2-Petőfi (94.8 FM; popular music) and MR3-Bartók (105.3 FM; classical music). Klasszik Radio (92.1 FM; classical music) relays the BBC World Service news at 10pm.

TV & Video Like Australia and most of Europe, Hungary uses PAL, which is incompatible with the North American and Japanese NTSC system or the Secam system used in France.

Weights & Measures Hungary uses the metric system.

Gay Budapest (www.budapest-gay.com) Of some use for accommodation.

Háttér Society (Háttér Társaság; ☎1-329 3380, 06 80 505 605; www.hatter.hu; ☺6-11pm) Advice and help line.

Labrisz Lesbian Association (Labrisz Leszbikus Egyesület; www.labrisz.hu) Info on the city's lesbian scene.

Radio Pink (http://radiopink.hu) Hungary's gay radio, broadcast through web-based live stream.

Internet Access

Almost without exception wireless (wi-fi) access is available at hostels and hotels, though a few of the latter charge a fee for the service. Many restaurants, cafes and bars offer wi-fi, usually free to paying customers.

Most hostels and some hotels have at least one computer terminal available to guests either free or for a nominal sum. If you can't log on where you're staying there's probably an internet cafe nearby, but they open and close at a rapid rate.

Electric Cafe (VII Dohány utca 37; per hr 200Ft; ☺9am-midnight; ⓜM2 Blaha Lujza tér) Large place with attached laundrette.

Fougou (VII Wesselényi utca 57; per hr 200Ft; ☺7am-2am; ⓜM2 Blaha Lujza tér, ⓺4, 6) Internet cafe with call centre.

InternetBuda (II Margit körút 15-17; per hr 200Ft; ☺8am-midnight; ⓺4, 6) Buda-side internet cafe, with photocopying and other services.

Vist@netcafe (XIII Váci út 6; 1st 15min 150Ft, then per 30min 250Ft; ☺24hr; ⓜM3 Nyugati pályaudvar) One of the very few internet cafes open round the clock.

Legal Matters

Penalties for possession, use or trafficking of illegal drugs in Hungary are severe, and convicted offenders can expect long jail sentences and heavy fines.

There's zero tolerance – a 100% ban – on alcohol when driving. Police conduct routine roadside checks with breathalysers and if you're found to have even 0.001%

of alcohol in your blood, you risk having your licence confiscated. If the level is over 0.5% there's a fine up to 100,000Ft and a driving ban of up to a year. In the event of an accident, the drinking party is automatically regarded as guilty.

Medical Services

Foreigners are entitled to first-aid and ambulance services only when they have suffered an accident; follow-up treatment and medicine must be paid for. Treatment at a public outpatient clinic (*rendelő intézet*) is not expensive, but a consultation in a doctor's surgery (*orvosi rendelő*) costs from around 6000Ft (home visits 10,000Ft to 15,000Ft).

Clinics

Consultations and treatment are very expensive in private clinics catering to foreigners. Dental work is usually of a high standard and fairly cheap by European standards.

FirstMed Centers (☎1-224 9090; www.firstmedcenters.com; I Hattyú utca 14, 5th fl;

⊘8am-8pm Mon-Fri, to 2pm Sat, urgent care 24hr; ⓂM2 Széll Kálmán tér) Modern private medical clinic with very expensive round-the-clock emergency treatment (basic consultation 24,500Ft for under 10 minutes).

SOS Dent (☑06-30 383 3333, 1-269 6010; www. sosdent.hu; VI Király utca 14; ⊘8am-9pm) Free dental consultations, with extractions 9000Ft to 12,000Ft, fillings 9000Ft to 18,000Ft and crowns from 32,000Ft.

Pharmacies

Each of Budapest's 23 districts has a rotating all-night pharmacy; a sign on the door of any pharmacy will help you locate the nearest 24-hour place.

Déli Gyógyszertár (☑1-355 4691; XII Alkotás utca 1/b; ⊘7am-8pm Mon-Fri, to 2pm Sat; ⓂM2 Déli pályaudvar)

Teréz Gyógyszertár (☑1-311 4439; VI Teréz körút 41; ⊘8am-8pm Mon-Fri, to 2pm Sat; ⓂM3 Nyugati pályaudvar)

Money

Hungary's currency is the forint (Ft). Notes come in six denominations: 500Ft, 1000Ft, 2000Ft, 5000Ft, 10,000Ft and 20,000Ft. There are coins of 5Ft, 10Ft, 20Ft, 50Ft, 100Ft and 200Ft.

Prices in shops and restaurants are always quoted in forint, but many hotels and guesthouses state their prices in euros. In such cases, we have followed suit and you can usually pay in either euros or forint.

ATMs

ATMs are everywhere in Budapest, including in train and bus stations and at airport terminals.

Credit Cards

Credit cards are widely accepted. Use them at restaurants, shops, hotels, car-rental firms, travel agencies and petrol stations, but don't assume they are accepted at all supermarkets or train and bus stations.

Many banks give cash advances on major credit cards, but they involve both fees and interest.

Moneychangers

Avoid moneychangers (especially those on V Váci utca) in favour of banks if possible. Arrive about an hour before closing time to ensure the *bureau de change* desk is still open.

Tipping

Hungarians are very tip-conscious and nearly everyone in Budapest will routinely hand gratuities to waiters, hairdressers and taxi drivers; doctors and dentists accept 'gratitude money'; even petrol-station attendants, and thermal-spa attendants who walk you to your changing cabin, expect a little something. If you aren't impressed with the service, leave little or nothing at all.

Travellers Cheques

You can change travellers cheques at most banks and post offices, but shops never accept them as payment. *Bureaux de change* generally don't take a commission, but exchange rates can vary; private agencies are always the most expensive. OTP (Országos Takarékpénztár; National Savings Bank) offers among the best rates.

A good option is the **Travelex Cash Passport** (www.travelex.com) – a prepaid travel card that you load up with funds before departure and then use to withdraw cash in local currency as you go along.

Opening Hours

The opening hours of any business are almost always posted on the front door. *Nyitva* means 'open', *zárva* is 'closed'.

In summer, some shops close early on Friday and shut down altogether for at least part of August.

Banks 7.45am to 5pm or 6pm Monday, to 4pm or 5pm Tuesday to Thursday, to 4pm Friday

Bars 11am to midnight Sunday to Thursday, to between 2am and 4am Friday and Saturday

Businesses 9am or 10am to 6pm Monday to Friday, to 1pm Saturday

Clubs Anywhere from between 8pm and 11pm to between 3am and dawn

Grocery stores and supermarkets 6am or 7am to 7pm Monday to Friday, 7.30am to 3pm Saturday, some 7am to noon Sunday

Post offices Main offices 7am or 8am to 7pm or 8pm Monday to Friday, to noon or 2pm Saturday; branches 7am or 8am to 4pm Monday to Friday

Restaurants 10am or 11am to 11pm or midnight

Shops 9am or 10am to 6pm Monday to Friday, to 1pm Saturday, some to 8pm Thursday

Post

The **Hungarian Postal Service** (Magyar Posta; www.posta. hu) has improved greatly in recent years, but the post offices themselves are usually fairly crowded and service can be slow. To beat the crowds, ask at kiosks, newsagents or stationery shops if they sell stamps (*bélyeg*).

Hungarian addresses start with the name of the recipient, followed on the next line by the postal code and city or town and then the street name and number. The

Hungarian postal code consists of four digits. The first indicates the city or town ('1' is Budapest), the second and third the district (kerület) and the last the neighbourhood.

Main post office (Map p244; V Bajcsy-Zsilinsky út 16; ⊗8am-8pm Mon-Fri, to 2pm Sat; Ⓜ M1, 2, 3 Deák Ferenc tér) In the centre of town.

Nyugati train station branch (Map p244; VI Teréz körút 51-53; ⊗7am-8pm Mon-Fri, 8am-6pm Sat; Ⓜ M3 Nyugati pályaudvar) Just south of the station.

Keleti train station branch (Map p242; VIII Baross tér 11/a-11/c; ⊗7am-9pm Mon-Fri, 8am-6pm Sat; Ⓜ M2 Keleti pályaudvar) Most easily reached from platform 6.

Public Holidays

Hungary celebrates 10 ünnep (holidays) each year.

New Year's Day 1 January

National Day 15 March

Easter Monday March/April

Labour Day 1 May

Whit Monday May/June

St Stephen's Day 20 August

1956 Remembrance Day/ Republic Day 23 October

All Saints' Day 1 November

Christmas holidays 25 and 26 December

Taxes & Refunds

ÁFA, a value-added tax of between 5% and 27% (the highest in Europe), covers the purchase of all new goods in Hungary. It's usually included in the quoted price but not always, so it pays to check. Visitors are not exempt, but non-EU residents can claim refunds for total purchases of at least 52,000Ft on one receipt as long as they take the goods out of the country (and the EU) within 90 days.

The ÁFA receipts (available from where you make the purchases) should be stamped by customs at the border, and the claim has to be made within 183 days of exporting the goods. You can collect your refund – minus commission – from the VAT-refund desk at Terminals 2A and 2B at the airport. You can also have it sent to you by bank cheque or deposited into your credit-card account.

Telephone

You can make domestic and international calls from public telephones with both coins and phonecards.

All localities in Hungary have a two-digit area code, except for Budapest, which has just a '1'. To make a local call, pick up the receiver and listen for the neutral and continuous dial tone, then dial the phone number (seven digits in Budapest, six elsewhere).

For an intercity landline call within Hungary and whenever you are calling a mobile phone, dial 06 and wait for the second, more melodious, tone. Then dial the area code and phone number. Cheaper or toll-free blue and green numbers start with the digits 06-40 and 06-80 respectively.

The procedure for making an international call is the same as for a local call, except that you dial 00, wait for the second dial tone, then dial the country code, the area code and the number.

The country code for Hungary is 36.

The following are useful numbers (with English spoken):

Yellow Pages directory assistance (📞197)

Domestic enquiries (📞198)

International enquiries (📞199)

Mobile Phones

You must always dial 06 when ringing mobile (cell) phones, which have specific area codes depending on the company:

T-Mobile (📞06 30)

Telenor (📞06 20; www. telenor.hu)

Vodafone (📞06 70; www. vodafone.hu)

Consider buying a rechargeable SIM chip, which will reduce the cost of making local calls. T-Mobile, for example, sells prepaid vouchers for 4050Ft, with 2700Ft worth of credit. Top-up cards cost from 1500Ft. The following are centrally located offices of mobile-phone providers:

T-Mobile (www.t-mobile.hu; V Petőfi Sándor utca 12; ⊗9am-7pm Mon-Fri, 10am-5pm Sat; Ⓜ M3 Ferenciek tere)

Telenor (www.telenor.hu; II Lövőház utca 2-6, Mammut I, 2nd fl, shop 203; ⊗10am-9pm Mon-Sat, to 6pm Sun; Ⓜ M2 Széll Kálmán tér; 🚋4, 6)

Vodafone (www.vodaphone. hu; VI Váci út 1-3, West End City Centre, 1st fl; ⊗10am-9pm Mon-Wed, Fri & Sat, from 8am Thu, 10am-6pm Sun; Ⓜ Nyugati pályaudvar)

Phonecards

Phonecards issued by outfits like **NeoPhone** (www. neophone.hu) and **No Limits** (www.nolimits.hu) come in values of 1000Ft, 2000Ft and 5000Ft and are available from post offices and newsstands. As elsewhere, public phones are rapidly disappearing with the advent of cheap mobile-phone calls and Skype.

Time

Budapest lies in the Central European time zone. Winter time is GMT plus one hour and in summer it is GMT plus two hours. Clocks are advanced at 2am on the last Sunday in March and set back at 2am on the last Sunday in October.

Hungarians tell the time by making reference to the next hour – not the one before, as we do in English. Thus 7.30am/pm is 'half eight' (*fél nyolc óra*) and the 24-hour system is often used in giving the times of movies, concerts and so on. So a film at 7.30pm could appear on a listing as 'f8', 'f20', '½8' or '½20'. A quarter to the hour has a ¾ in front (thus '¾8' means 7.45) while quarter past is ¼ of the next hour (eg '¼9' means 8.15).

Tourist Information

Budapest Info (☑1-438 8080; www.budapestinfo.hu) has three branches in central Budapest and info desks in the arrivals sections of Ferenc Liszt International Airport's Terminals 2A and 2B.

Main branch (Map p238; V Sütő utca 2; �8am-8pm; Ⓜ M1, 2, 3 Deák Ferenc tér) Best single source of information about Budapest.

Castle Hill branch (Map p230; I Szentháromság tér 6; �9am-7pm Apr-Oct, to 6pm Nov-Mar; ☒16) Small and often very busy in summer.

Oktogon branch (Map p244; VI Liszt Ferenc tér 11; �10am-6pm Mon-Fri; Ⓜ M1 Oktogon, ☒4, 6) Least busy branch.

Travel Agencies

If your query is about private accommodation, flights or international train travel, or you need to change money, you could turn to a commercial travel agency:

Ibusz (☑1-501 4910; www. ibusz.hu; V Aranykéz utca 4-6; �9am-6pm Mon-Fri, to 1pm Sat; Ⓜ M1/2/3 Deák Ferenc tér,

☒2) Books all types of accommodation and sells transport tickets.

Vista (☑1-429 9999; www. vista.hu; VI Andrássy utca 1; �9.30am-6pm Mon-Fri, 10am-4.30pm Sat; Ⓜ M1/2/3 Deák Ferenc tér) Excellent for all your travel needs, both outbound (air tickets, package tours etc) and incoming (room bookings, organised tours etc).

Wasteels (☑1-210 2802; www.wasteels.hu; VIII Kerepesi út 2-6; �8am-8pm Mon-Fri, to 6pm Sat; Ⓜ M2, 4 Keleti pályaudvar) Next to platform 9 at Keleti train station; sells all train tickets, including discounted ones of up to 60% off to those 26 years and under.

Travellers with Disabilities

Budapest has taken great strides in recent years in making public areas and facilities more accessible to the disabled. Wheelchair ramps, toilets fitted for the disabled and inward-opening doors, though not as common as in Western Europe, do exist and audible traffic signals for the blind are becoming commonplace, as are Braille plates in public lifts.

Hungarian Federation of Disabled Persons' Associations (MEOSZ; Map p234; ☑1-250 9013; www. meoszinfo.hu; III San Marco utca 76) Travellers with disabilities who are seeking information can contact this umbrella group.

Visas

Everyone needs a valid passport or, for many EU citizens, a national identification card to enter Hungary.

Citizens of all European countries as well as Australia, Canada, Israel, Japan, New Zealand and the US

do not require visas to visit Hungary for stays of up to 90 days. Nationals of South Africa (among others) still require visas. Check current visa requirements on the website of the **Hungarian Foreign Ministry Consular Service** www.konzuliszolgalat. kormany.hu).

Visas are issued at Hungarian consulates or missions, most international highway border crossings, Ferenc Liszt International Airport and the International Ferry Pier in Budapest. They are rarely issued on international buses and never on trains. Be sure to retain the separate entry and exit forms issued with the visa that is stamped in your passport.

Short-stay visas (€60), which are the best for tourists as they allow stays of up to 90 days, are issued at Hungarian consulates or missions in the applicants' country of residence. They are only extended in emergencies (eg medical ones) and this must be done at the central police station 15 days before the original one expires. As Hungary is part of the Schengen Agreement, if you have a visa valid for entry to other Schengen states, it's also valid here.

Women Travellers

Hungarian men can be sexist in their thinking, but women in Budapest do not suffer any particular form of harassment. Most Hungarian men – even drunks – are effusively polite with women. Women may not be made to feel especially welcome when eating or drinking alone, but it's really no different from most other countries in Europe.

Women for Women Against Violence (NANE; ☑1-267 4900; www.nane.hu)

Women's Line (Nővonal; ☑06-80 505 101; �6-10pm Thu-Tue)

Language

Hungarian (*magyar mo*·dyor) belongs to the Finno-Ugric language family and has more than 14.5 million speakers worldwide. Though distantly related to Finnish, it has no significant similarities to any other language in the world. And while it's very different from English in both vocabulary and structure, it's surprisingly easy to pronounce. If you follow the coloured pronunciation guides that accompany each phrase in this chapter and read them as if they were English, you'll be understood.

A horizontal line over a vowel in written Hungarian (eg *ā*) indicates the vowel is pronounced as a long sound. Double consonants (eg *tt*) are drawn out a little longer than in English.

Note that aw is pronounced as in 'law', eu as in 'nurse', ew as 'ee' with rounded lips, and zh as the 's' in 'pleasure'. Also, r is rolled in Hungarian and the apostrophe (') indicates a slight y sound.

In our pronunciation guides, the syllables are separated by a dot (eg *kawn*·tsert) so you can easily isolate each unit of sound. Accent marks in written Hungarian don't influence word stress which always falls on the first syllable of the word. We've indicated stress with italics.

BASICS

Hungarian has separate polite and informal forms of the personal pronoun 'you', as well as the corresponding verbs forms. The polite *Ön* eun form is generally used with strangers, new acquaintances, older people, officials and service personnel. The informal *te* te form is used with relatives, friends, colleagues, children and sometimes foreigners. The form appropriate for the context is used throughout this chapter. For phrases where either form might be appropriate we've given both, indicated by the abbreviations 'pol' and 'inf'.

Hello.	Szervusz. (sg)	*ser*·vus
	Szervusztok. (pl)	*ser*·vus·tawk
Goodbye.	Viszlát.	*vis*·lat
Excuse me.	Elnézést	*el*·ney·zeysht
	kérek.	*key*·rek
Sorry.	Sajnálom.	*shoy*·na·lawm
Please.	Kérem. (pol)	*key*·rem
	Kérlek. (inf)	*keyr*·lek
Thank you.	Köszönöm.	*keu*·seu·neum
You're welcome.	Szívesen.	*see*·ve·shen
Yes.	Igen.	*i*·gen
No.	Nem.	nem

How are you?
Hogy van/vagy? (pol/inf)   hawj von/voj

Fine. And you?
Jól. És Ön/te? (pol/inf)   yāwl aysh eun/te

What's your name?
Mi a neve/neved? (pol/inf)   mi o *ne*·ve/*ne*·ved

My name is ...
A nevem ...   o *ne*·vem ...

Do you speak English?
Beszél/Beszélsz   be·seyl/be·seyls
angolul? (pol/inf)   *on*·gaw·lul

I don't understand.
Nem értem.   nem *eyr*·tem

ACCOMMODATION

campsite	kemping	*kem*·ping
guesthouse	panzió	*pon*·zi·āw
hotel	szálloda	*sal*·law·do
youth hostel	ifjúsági	*if*·yū·sha·gi
	szálló	*sal*·lāw

WANT MORE?

For in-depth language information and handy phrases, check out Lonely Planet's *Hungarian Phrasebook*. You'll find it at **shop.lonelyplanet.com**, or you can buy Lonely Planet's iPhone phrasebooks at the Apple App Store.

Do you have a ... room?	Van Önnek kiadó egy ... szobája?	von *eun*·nek *ki*·o·däw ed' ... *saw*·ba·yo
single	egyágyas	*ej*·a·dyosh
double	duplaágyas	*dup*·lo·a·dyosh

How much is it per ...?	Mennyibe kerül egy ...?	*men*'·nyi·be *ke*·rewl ej ...
night	éjszakára	*ey*·so·ka·ro
person	főre	*fēū*·re

air-con	légkondicionálás	*layg*·kawn·di·tsi·aw·naa·laash
bathroom	fürdőszoba	*fewr*·dēū·saw·bo
laundry	mosoda	*maw*·shaw·do
window	ablak	*ob*·lok

DIRECTIONS

Where's (the market)?
Hol van (a piac)? hawl von (o *pi*·ots)

What's the address?
Mi a cím? mi o tseem

Could you please write it down?
Leírná, kérem? le·*eer*·naa *kay*·rem

How do I get there?
Hogyan jutok oda? haw·dyon *yu*·tawk aw·do

How far is it?
Milyen messze van? *mi*·yen *mes*·se von

Can you show me (on the map)?
Meg tudja mutatni nekem (a térképen)? meg *tud*·yo *mu*·tot·ni ne·kem (o *tayr*·kay·pen)

Turn ...	Forduljon ...	*fawr*·dul·yawn ...
at the corner	be a saroknál	be o *sho*·rawk·naal
at the traffic lights	be a közlekedési lámpánál	be o *keuz*·le·ke·day·shi *laam*·paa·naal
left	balra	*bol*·ro
right	jobbra	*yawbb*·ro

It's ...	... van.	... von
behind ...	... mögött	... *meu*·geutt
in front of ...	... előtt	... e·*lēūtt*
near ...	... közelében	... *keu*·ze·lay·ben
next to ...	... mellett	... *mel*·lett
on the corner	a sarkon	o *shor*·kawn
opposite ...	...val szemben	...·vol *sem*·ben
straight ahead	egyenesen előttünk	e·*dye*·ne·shen e·*lēūt*·tewnk

EATING & DRINKING

I'd like to reserve a table for ...	Szeretnék asztalt foglalni ...	se·*ret*·nayk *os*·tolt *fawg*·lol·ni ...
(eight) o'clock	(nyolc) órára	(nyawlts) *âw*·raa·ro
(two) people	(két) főre	(kayt) *fēū*·re

I'd like the menu, please.
Az étlapot szeretném. oz *eyt*·lo·pawt se·*ret*·neym

What would you recommend?
Mit ajánlana? mit o·*yan*·lo·no

What's in that dish?
Mit tartalmaz ez a fogás? mit *tor*·tol·moz ez o *faw*·gaash

Do you have vegetarian food?
Vannak Önöknél vegetáriánus ételek? von·nok *eu*·neuk·neyl ve·ge·ta·ri·a·nush *ey*·te·lek

I don't eat ...	Én nem eszem ...	ayn nem e·sem ...
eggs	tojást	*taw*·yaasht
fish	halat	*ho*·lot
pork	disznóhúst	*dis*·nāw·hūsht
poultry	szárnyast	*saar*·nyosht

I'll have ...
... kérek. ... *key*·rek

Cheers! (to one person)
Egészségedre! e·*geys*·shey·ged·re

Cheers! (to more than one person)
Egészségetekre! e·*geys*·shey·ge·tek·re

That was delicious.
Ez nagyon finom volt. ez *no*·dyawn *fi*·nawm vawlt

I'd like the bill, please.
A számlát szeretném. o *sam*·lat se·*ret*·neym

Key Words

bottle	üveg	*ew*·veg
bowl	tál	taal
breakfast	reggeli	*reg*·ge·li

cafe	kávézó	kaa·vay·zāw
cold	hideg	hi·deg
cup	csésze	chey·se
dinner	vacsora	vo·chaw·ro
dish	edény	e·dayn'
drink	ital	i·tol
food	ennivaló	en·ni·vo·lāw
fork	villa	vil·lo
glass	pohár	paw·har
hot (warm)	forró	fawr·rāw
knife	kés	kaysh
lunch	ebéd	e·beyd
menu	étlap	ayt·lop
plate	tányér	taa·nyayr
restaurant	étterem	ayt·te·rem
serviette	szalvéta	sol·vay·to
spoon	kanál	ko·naal
with	-val/-vel	·vol/·vel
without	nélkül	nayl·kewl

Meat & Fish

beef	marhahús	mor·ho·hūsh
chicken	csirkehús	chir·ke·hūsh
duck	kacsa	ko·cho
fish	hal	hol
lamb	bárány	baa·raan'
meat	hús	hūsh
oyster	osztriga	awst·ri·go
pork	disznóhús	dis·nāw·hūsh
prawn	garnélarák	gor·nay·lo·raak
salmon	lazac	lo·zots
tuna	tonhal	tawn·hol
turkey	pulyka	pu·y·ko
veal	borjúhús	bawr·yū·hūsh

Fruit & Vegetables

apple	alma	ol·mo
bean	bab	bob
cabbage	káposzta	kaa·paws·to
capsicum	paprika	pop·ri·ko
carrot	répa	ray·po
cauliflower	karfiol	kor·fi·awl
cucumber	uborka	u·bawr·ko
fruit	gyümölcs	dyew·meulch
grapes	szőlő	sēū·lēū
legume	hüvelyes	hew·ve·yesh

KEY PATTERNS

To get by in Hungarian, mix and match these simple patterns with words of your choice:

Where's (a market)?
Hol van (egy piac)? — hawl von (ej pi·ots)

Where can I (buy a padlock)?
Hol tudok — hawl tu·dawk
(venni egy lakatot)? — (ven·ni ej lo·ko·tawt)

I'm looking for (a hotel).
(Szállodát) keresek. — (saal·law·daat) ke·re·shek

Do you have (a map)?
Van (térképük)? — von (tayr·kay·pewk)

Is there (a toilet)?
Van (vécé)? — von (vay·tsay)

I'd like (the menu).
(Az étlapot) — (oz ayt·lo·pawt)
szeretném. — se·ret·naym

I'd like to (buy a phonecard).
Szeretnék — se·ret·nayk
(telefonkártyát — (te·le·fawn·kaar·tyaat
venni). — ven·ni)

Could you please (write it down)?
(Leírná), kérem? — (le·eer·naa) kay·rem

Do I have to (pay)?
Kell érte (fizetni)? — kell ayr·te (fi·zet·ni)

I need (assistance).
(Segítségre) — (she·geet·shayg·re)
van szükségem. — von sewk·shay·gem

lemon	citrom	tsit·rawm
lentil	lencse	len·che
mushroom	gomba	gawm·bo
nut	dió	di·āw
onion	hagyma	hoj·mo
orange	narancs	no·ronch
pea	borsó	bawr·shāw
peach	őszibarack	ēū·si·bo·rotsk
pear	körte	keur·te
pineapple	ananász	o·no·naas
plum	szilva	sil·vo
potato	krumpli	krump·li
spinach	spenót	shpe·nāwt
tomato	paradicsom	po·ro·di·chawm
vegetable	zöldség	zeuld·shayg

Other

bread	kenyér	ke·nyayr
cheese	sajt	shoyt
egg	tojás	taw·yaash

honey	méz	mayz
ice	jég	yayg
ice cream	fagylalt	foj·lolt
noodles	metélt	me·taylt
oil	olaj	aw·lo·y
pasta	tészta	tays·to
pepper (black)	bors	bawrsh
rice	rizs	rizh
salad	saláta	sho·laa·to
salt	só	shāw
soup	leves	le·vesh
sugar	cukor	tsu·kawr
vinegar	ecet	e·tset

Drinks

beer	sör	sheur
coffee	kávé	ka·vey
juice	gyümölcslé	dyew·meulch·lay
milk	tej	te·y
mineral water	ásványvíz	aash·vaan'·veez
orange juice	narancslé	no·ronch·lay
red wine	vörösbor	veu·reush·bawr
soft drink	üdítőital	ew·dee·tēū·i·tal
sparkling wine	habzóbor	hob·zāw·bawr
tea	tea	te·o
water	víz	veez
white wine	fehérbor	fe·hayr·bawr
wine	bor	bawr

EMERGENCIES

Help!
Segítség! — she·geet·sheyg

Go away!
Menjen innen! — men·yen in·nen

Call a doctor!
Hívjon orvost! — heev·yawn awr·vawsht

Call the police!
Hívja a rendőrséget! — heev·yo o rend·ēūr·shey·get

There's been an accident.
Baleset történt. — bo·le·shet teur·taynt

Question Words

What?	Mi?	mi
When?	Mikor?	mi·kawr
Where?	Hol?	hawl
Which?	Melyik?	me·yik
Who?	Ki?	ki
Why?	Miért?	mi·ayrt

I'm lost.
Eltévedtem. — el·tey·ved·tem

Where are the toilets?
Hol a vécé? — hawl o vey·tsey

Can I use your phone?
Használhatom a telefonját? — hos·naal·ho·tawm o te·le·fawn·yaat

I'm ill.
Rosszul vagyok. — raws·sul vo·dyawk

It hurts here.
Itt fáj. — itt faa·y

I'm allergic to (antibiotics).
Allergiás vagyok (az antibiotikumokra). — ol·ler·gi·aash vo·dyawk (oz on·ti·bi·aw·ti·ku·mawk·ro)

SHOPPING & SERVICES

I'd like to buy (an adaptor plug).
Szeretnék venni (egy adapter dugót). — se·ret·nayk ven·ni (ej o·dop·ter du·gāwt)

I'm just looking.
Csak nézegetek. — chok nay·ze·ge·tek

Can I look at it?
Megnézhetem? — meg·nayz·he·tem

How much is it?
Mennyibe kerül? — men'·nyi·be ke·rewl

That's too expensive.
Ez túl drága. — ez tūl dra·go

Do you have something cheaper?
Van valami olcsóbb? — von vo·lo·mi awl·chāwbb

There's a mistake in the bill.
Valami nem stimmel a számlával. — vo·lo·mi nem shtim·mel o saam·laa·vol

bank	bank	bonk
credit card	hitelkártya	hi·tel·kaar·tyo
internet cafe	Internet kávézó	in·ter·net kaa·vay·zāw
market	piac	pi·ots
mobile phone	mobil telefon	maw·bil te·le·fawn
post office	posta-hivatal	pawsh·to·hi·vo·tol
tourist office	turista-iroda	tu·rish·to·i·raw·do

TIME & DATES

What time is it?
Hány óra? — haan' āw·ra

It's (one) o'clock.
(Egy) óra van. — (ej) āw·ra von

It's (10) o'clock.
(Tíz) óra van. — (teez) āw·ra von

Half past (10).
Fél (tizenegy). — fayl (ti·zen·ej)

morning	reggel	reg·gel
afternoon	délután	dayl·u·taan
evening	este	esh·te
yesterday	tegnap	teg·nop
today	ma	mo
tomorrow	holnap	hawl·nop
Monday	hétfő	hayt·fēū
Tuesday	kedd	kedd
Wednesday	szerda	ser·do
Thursday	csütörtök	chew·teur·teuk
Friday	péntek	payn·tek
Saturday	szombat	sawm·bot
Sunday	vasárnap	vo·shaar·nop
January	január	yo·nu·aar
February	február	feb·ru·aar
March	március	maar·tsi·ush
April	április	aap·ri·lish
May	május	maa·yush
June	június	yū·ni·ush
July	július	yū·li·ush
August	augusztus	o·u·gus·tush
September	szeptember	sep·tem·ber
October	október	awk·tāw·ber
November	november	naw·vem·ber
December	december	de·tsem·ber

Numbers

1	egy	ej
2	kettő	ket·tēū
3	három	ha·rawm
4	négy	neyj
5	öt	eut
6	hat	hot
7	hét	heyt
8	nyolc	nyawlts
9	kilenc	ki·lents
10	tíz	teez
20	húsz	hūs
30	harminc	hor·mints
40	negyven	nej·ven
50	ötven	eut·ven
60	hatvan	hot·von
70	hetven	het·ven
80	nyolcvan	nyawlts·von
90	kilencven	ki·lents·ven
100	száz	saaz
1000	ezer	e·zer

bike path	bicikliút	bi·tsik·li·ūt
bus stop	buszmegálló	bus·meg·aal·lāw
platform	peron	pe·rawn
taxi stand	taxiállomás	tok·si·aal·law·maash
ticket office	jegypénztár	yej·paynz·taar
timetable	menetrend	me·net·rend
train station	vasútállomás	vo·shūt·aal·law·maash

TRANSPORT

When's the ... (bus)?	Mikor megy ... (busz)?	mi·kawr mej ... (bus)
first	az első	oz el·shēū
last	az utolsó	oz u·tawl·shāw
next	a következő	o keu·vet·ke·zēū

Which ... goes to (the parliament)?	Melyik ... megy a Parlament)hez?	me·yik ... mej (o por·lo·ment)·hez
bus	busz	bus
metro line	metró	met·rāw
tram	villamos	vil·lo·mawsh
trolleybus	troli	traw·li

One ... ticket to (Eger), please.	Egy ... jegy (Eger)be.	ej ... yej (e·ger)·be
one-way	csak oda	chok aw·do
return	oda-vissza	aw·do·vís·so

What's the next stop?
Mi a következő megálló? — mi o keu·vet·ke·zēū meg·aal·lāw

Please tell me when we get to (...).
Kérem, szóljon, amikor (...)be érünk. — kay·rem sāwl·yawn o·mi·kawr (...)·be ay·rewnk

Please take me to (this address).
Kérem, vigyen el (erre a címre). — kay·rem vi·dyen el (er·re o tseem·re)

I'd like to get off here.
Le szeretnék szállni itt. — le se·ret·nayk saall·ni itt

I'd like my bicycle repaired.
Szeretném megjavíttatni a biciklimet. — se·ret·naym meg·yo·veet·tot·ni o bi·tsik·li·met

GLOSSARY

ÁFA – value-added tax (VAT)

alagút – tunnel

ÁVO – Rákosi's hated secret police in the early years of communism; later renamed ÁVH

bélyeg – stamps

BKV – Budapest Közlekedési Vallálat (Budapest Transport Company)

bolhapiac – flea market

borozó – wine bar; any place serving wine

Bp – abbreviation for Budapest

búcsú – farewell; also a church patronal festival

büfé – snack bar

centrum – town or city centre

cukrászda – cake shop or patisserie

Eclectic – an art/architectural style popular in Hungary in the Romantic period, drawing from indigenous and foreign sources

eszpresszó – coffee shop, often also selling alcoholic drinks and snacks; strong, black coffee; same as *presszó*

étkezde – canteen that serves simple dishes

étterem – restaurant

fapados – wooden bench; budget (in reference to airlines)

fasor – boulevard, avenue

főkapitányság – main police station

forint (Ft) – Hungary's monetary unit

gyógyfürdő – thermal bath, spa

gyógyszertár – pharmacy

gyűjtemény – collection

hajóállomás – ferry pier, landing

ház – house

hegy – hill, mountain

HÉV – Helyiérdekű Vasút (suburban commuter train)

híd – bridge

HNTO – Hungarian National Tourism Office

ifjúsági szálló – youth hostel

kastély – manor house or mansion (see *vár*)

kávéház – coffee house

képtár – picture gallery

kertek – literally 'gardens', but in Budapest any outdoor spot that has been converted into an entertainment zone

kerület – city district

kincstár – treasury

Kiskörút – 'Little Ring Road'

kocsma – pub or saloon

könyvtár – library

korsó – 0.4L glass

körút – ring road

korzó – embankment, promenade

köz – alley, mews, lane

központ – centre

krt – *körút* (ring road)

labdarúgás – football

lépcső – stairs, steps

Mahart – Hungarian passenger ferry company

Malév – Hungary's national airline

MÁV – Magyar Államvasutak (Hungarian State Railways)

megyék – counties

Nagykörút – 'Big Ring Road'

nyitva – open

nyitvatartás – opening hours

önkiszolgáló – self-service

OTP – Országos Takarékpénztár (National Savings Bank)

pálinka – fruit brandy

palota – palace

pályaudvar – train or railway station

panzió – pension, guesthouse

patyolat – laundry

pénztár – cashier

piac – market

pince – wine cellar

pohár – 0.3L glass

presszó – aka *eszpresszó* (coffee shop; strong, black coffee)

pu – abbreviation for *pályaudvar* (train station)

puttony – the number of 'butts' of sweet *aszú* essence added to base wines in making Tokaj wine

rakpart – quay, embankment

rendőrkapitányság – police station

rendőrség – police

romkocsma – 'ruin bar', temporary bars/entertainment zones set up in disused building or site

Secessionism – art/architectural style similar to Art Nouveau

sedile (pl **sedilia**) – medieval stone niche with seats

sétány – walkway, promenade

skanzen – open-air museum displaying village architecture

söröző – beer bar or pub

szálló or **szálloda** – hotel

székesegyház – cathedral

sziget – island

színház – theatre

táncház – folk music and dance workshop

templom – church

tér – town or market square

tere – genitive form of *tér* as in Hősök tere (Square of the Heroes)

tó – lake

turul – eaglelike totem of the ancient Magyars and now a national symbol

u – abbreviation for *utca* (street)

udvar – court

út – road

utca – street

utcája – genitive form of *utca* as in Ferencesek utcája (Street of the Franciscans)

útja – genitive form of *út* as in Mártíroká útja (Street of the Martyrs)

vár – castle

város – city

városház or **városháza** – town hall

vásárcsarnok – market hall

vendéglő – a type of restaurant

zárva – closed

Behind the Scenes

SEND US YOUR FEEDBACK

We love to hear from travellers – your comments keep us on our toes and help make our books better. Our well-travelled team reads every word on what you loved or loathed about this book. Although we cannot reply individually to your submissions, we always guarantee that your feedback goes straight to the appropriate authors, in time for the next edition. Each person who sends us information is thanked in the next edition – the most useful submissions are rewarded with a selection of digital PDF chapters.

Visit **lonelyplanet.com/contact** to submit your updates and suggestions or to ask for help. Our award-winning website also features inspirational travel stories, news and discussions.

Note: We may edit, reproduce and incorporate your comments in Lonely Planet products such as guidebooks, websites and digital products, so let us know if you don't want your comments reproduced or your name acknowledged. For a copy of our privacy policy visit lonelyplanet.com/privacy.

OUR READERS

Many thanks to the travellers who used the last edition and wrote to us with helpful hints, useful advice and interesting anecdotes: Alex Bregman, Kostas Dalaklidis, Lyndon Dighton, Fred Isler, Bob Kalkman, Jasmine Kerry, Clive Knipe, Peter Lonnerberg, Taly Matiteyahu, Steve McInnes, Kate Nicholls, Christos Pappis, Gregory Pizzio, Torben Retboll, Volker Schwan, Virág Vántora, Natalie Walker, Sean Walker, Yarui Zheng

Juhasz, Vera Szűcs-Balás, Regina Papp, Virág Vántora, Ildikó Dudás, Kriszta Tóth, Viktor Oszvald, Miklós Molnár, Zoltan Kovacs, Attila Gyurkovics, Péter Mátyás, András Török and Nick Robertson. And special thanks to Imogen for eagle eyes, Ed for getting locked in with me, Kate for keeping me sane, and Kevin for keeping me company.

ACKNOWLEDGMENTS

Cover photograph: Fishermen's Bastion, Castle Hill, Rob Tilley/Corbis

AUTHOR THANKS

Steve Fallon

I'd like to thank friends Bea Szirti, Balázs Váradi, Erik D'Amato, Tal Lev and Ildikó Nagy Moran for helpful suggestions, assistance and/or hospitality on the ground. Péter Lengyel showed me the correct wine roads, and Michael Buurman opened up his flat, conveniently located next to the Nagy Zsinagóga. I'd like to dedicate this book to my partner, Michael Rothschild, with love and gratitude.

Sally Schafer

At Lonely Planet, thanks to Dora, Brana and co-author Steve. In London Karin Jones, and in Budapest, Bea Szirti, Judit, Reka, Vilma, Ádám, Liana and Saci at Underguide, Emese

THIS BOOK

This 6th edition of *Budapest* was researched and written by Steve Fallon and Sally Schafer. Steve Fallon also wrote the previous five editions. This guidebook was commissioned in Lonely Planet's London office and produced by the following:

Destination Editors Branislava Vladisavljevic, Dora Whitaker
Coordinating Editor Sarah Bailey
Product Editor Martine Power
Senior Cartographer Anthony Phelan
Book Designer Wibowo Rusli

Assisting Editors Justin Flynn, Elizabeth Jones, Kate Kiely, Gabrielle Stefanos
Cartographer Gabriel Lindquist
Cover Researcher Naomi Parker
Thanks to Sasha Baskett, Elin Berglund, David Kemp, Indra Kilfoyle, Wayne Murphy, Karyn Noble, Dianne Schallmeiner, Angela Tinson, Samantha Tyson

See also separate subindexes for:

⚔ **EATING P223**

🍷 **DRINKING & NIGHTLIFE P224**

☆ **ENTERTAINMENT P225**

🔒 **SHOPPING P225**

🛏 **SLEEPING P226**

Index

☆ **ENTERTAINMENT**

🛍 **SHOPPING**

**SPORTS &
ACTIVITIES**

SLEEPING

INDEX SLEEPING

Budapest Maps

Sights
- Beach
- Bird Sanctuary
- Buddhist
- Castle/Palace
- Christian
- Confucian
- Hindu
- Islamic
- Jain
- Jewish
- Monument
- Museum/Gallery/Historic Building
- Ruin
- Shinto
- Sikh
- Taoist
- Winery/Vineyard
- Zoo/Wildlife Sanctuary
- Other Sight

Activities, Courses & Tours
- Bodysurfing
- Diving
- Canoeing/Kayaking
- Course/Tour
- Sento Hot Baths/Onsen
- Skiing
- Snorkelling
- Surfing
- Swimming/Pool
- Walking
- Windsurfing
- Other Activity

Sleeping
- Sleeping
- Camping

Eating
- Eating

Drinking & Nightlife
- Drinking & Nightlife
- Cafe

Entertainment
- Entertainment

Shopping
- Shopping

Information
- Bank
- Embassy/Consulate
- Hospital/Medical
- Internet
- Police
- Post Office
- Telephone
- Toilet
- Tourist Information
- Other Information

Geographic
- Beach
- Hut/Shelter
- Lighthouse
- Lookout
- Mountain/Volcano
- Oasis
- Park
- Pass
- Picnic Area
- Waterfall

Population
- Capital (National)
- Capital (State/Province)
- City/Large Town
- Town/Village

Transport
- Airport
- Border crossing
- Bus
- Cable car/Funicular
- Cycling
- Ferry
- Metro station
- Monorail
- Parking
- Petrol station
- S-Bahn/Subway station
- Taxi
- T-bane/Tunnelbana station
- Train station/Railway
- Tram
- Tube station
- U-Bahn/Underground station
- Other Transport

Note: Not all symbols displayed above appear on the maps in this book

Routes
- Tollway
- Freeway
- Primary
- Secondary
- Tertiary
- Lane
- Unsealed road
- Road under construction
- Plaza/Mall
- Steps
- Tunnel
- Pedestrian overpass
- Walking Tour
- Walking Tour detour
- Path/Walking Trail

Boundaries
- International
- State/Province
- Disputed
- Regional/Suburb
- Marine Park
- Cliff
- Wall

Hydrography
- River, Creek
- Intermittent River
- Canal
- Water
- Dry/Salt/Intermittent Lake
- Reef

Areas
- Airport/Runway
- Beach/Desert
- Cemetery (Christian)
- Cemetery (Other)
- Glacier
- Mudflat
- Park/Forest
- Sight (Building)
- Sportsground
- Swamp/Mangrove

N 0 _____ 2 km
   0 _____ 1 miles

3

REMETE-
HEGY

ÓBUDA

Óbuda
Island
(Óbudai-
sziget)

8

ANGYALFÖLD

Rákos-patak

MÁTYÁSHEGY

ÚJLAK

Danube River

Margaret
Island
(Margit-
sziget)

VÍZAFOGÓ

ZÖLDMÁL

FELHÉVÍZ

10

VÉRHALOM

RÓZSADOMB

HERMINAMEZŐ

ÚJLIPÓTVÁROS

City Park
(Városliget)

ORSZÁGÚT

7

9

VÍZIVÁROS

TERÉZVÁROS

KRISZTINA-
VÁROS

CASTLE HILL
(VÁRHEGY)

LIPÓTVÁROS

Vérmező

ERZSÉBET
VÁROS

Kerepesi Cemetery
(Kerepesi temető)

1

BELVÁROS

NÉMET-
VÖLGY

2

TABÁN

GELLÉRT
HILL

5

JÓZSEFVÁROS

Jubilee Park

SASHEGY

SASAD

FERENCVÁROS

Népliget

Danube River

4

KELENFÖLD

Bajor
Gizi
Park

LÁGYMÁNYOS

6

MAP INDEX

CASTLE DISTRICT

Key on p232

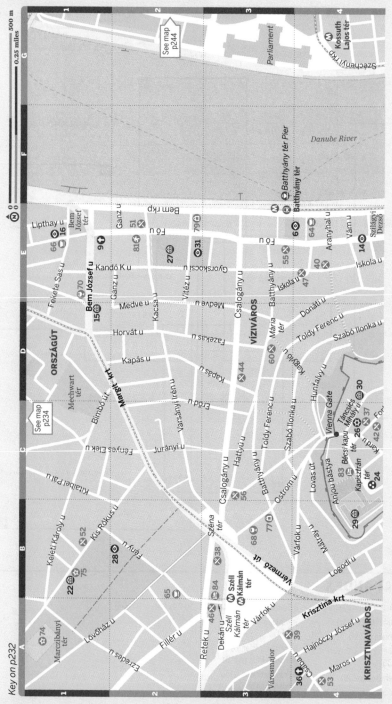

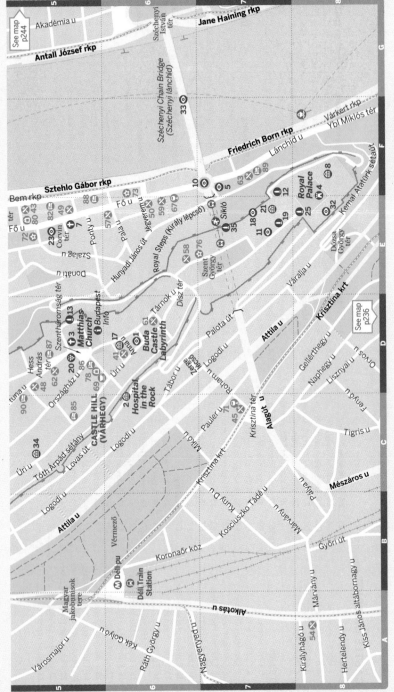

CASTLE DISTRICT *Map on p230*

BUDA HILLS

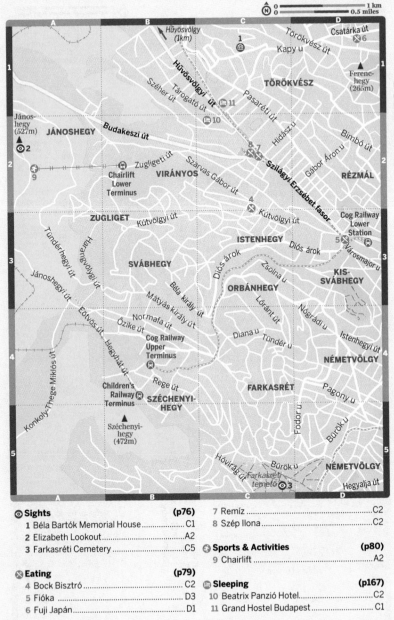

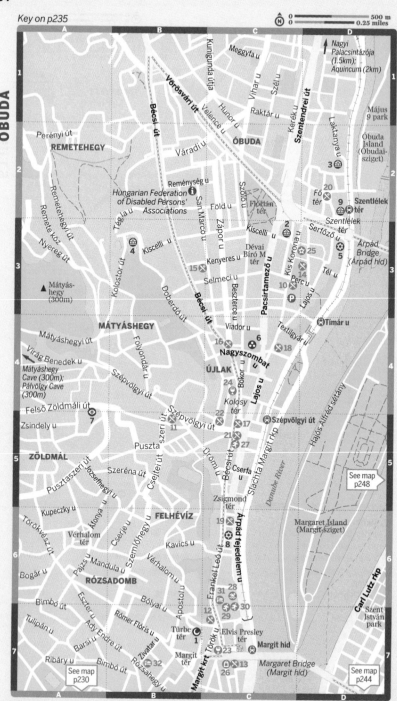

Key on p235

0 — 500 m
0 — 0.25 miles

Nagyi
Palacsintázója
(1.5km);
Aquincum (2km)

Május
9 park

Óbuda
Island
(Óbudai-
sziget)

REMETEHEGY

Perényi út

Váradi u

ÓBUDA

Reménység u

Hungarian Federation
of Disabled Persons'
Associations

Flórián
tér

Fő
tér

20

9

Szentlélek
tér

4

Kiscelli u

2

25

5

Árpád
Bridge
(Árpád híd)

MÁTYÁSHEGY

Mátyás-
hegy
(300m)

15

Dévai
Bíró M
tér

14

10

Perc u

Mátyáshegyi út

Mátyáshegy
Cave (300m);
Pálvölgy Cave
(300m)

16

6

Viador u

Nagyszombat u

18

Timár u

ÚJLAK

24

Kolosy
tér

22

17

Szépvölgyi út

Felső Zöldmáli út

7

11

21

27

Zsindely u

Cserfa
u

ZÖLDMÁL

Szeréna út

Zsigmond
tér

See map
p248

Margaret Island
(Margit-sziget)

Kupeczky u

FELHÉVÍZ

19

Vérhalom
tér

Kavics u

8

Árpád fejedelem u

Törökvész út

Bogár u

RÓZSADOMB

Szent
István
park

Bimbó út

28

Tulipán u

31

30

29

12

Ribáry u

Bimbó út

32

Türbe
tér

1

Elvis Presley
tér

Margit
tér

23

Margit híd

13

26

Margaret Bridge
(Margit híd)

See map
p230

See map
p244

ÓBUDA *Map on p234*

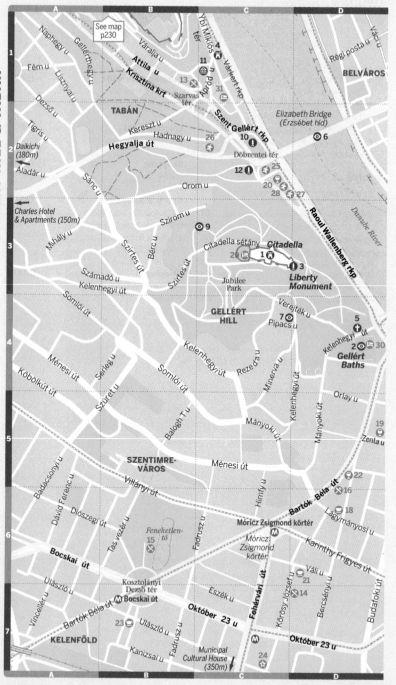

GELLÉRT HILL & TABÁN

▲ 0 ——————— 500 m
Ⓝ 0 ——————— 0.25 miles

See map p238

See map p242

BELVÁROS

Key on p240

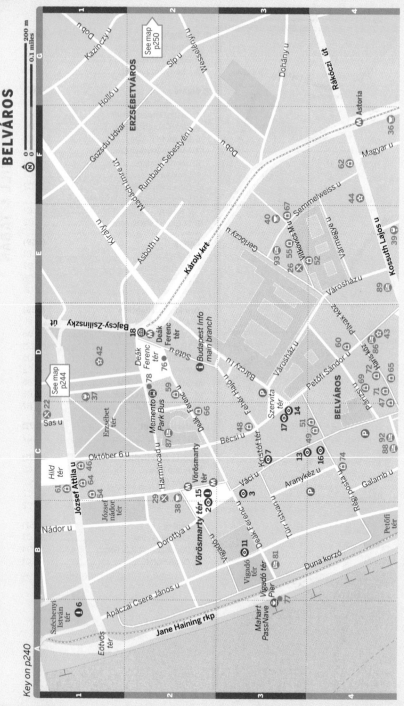

See map p250

See map p244

ERZSÉBETVÁROS

BELVÁROS

Budapest Info main branch

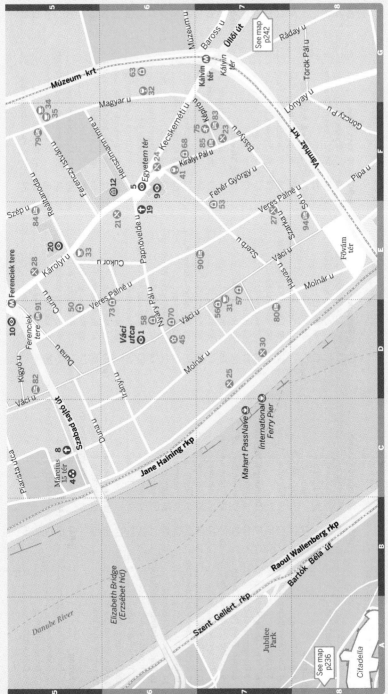

See map p242

See map p36

BELVÁROS

BELVÁROS Map on p238

SOUTHERN PEST *Map on p242*

SOUTHERN PEST

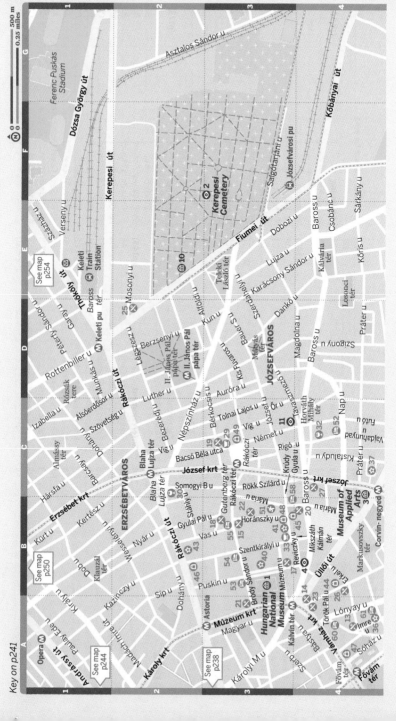

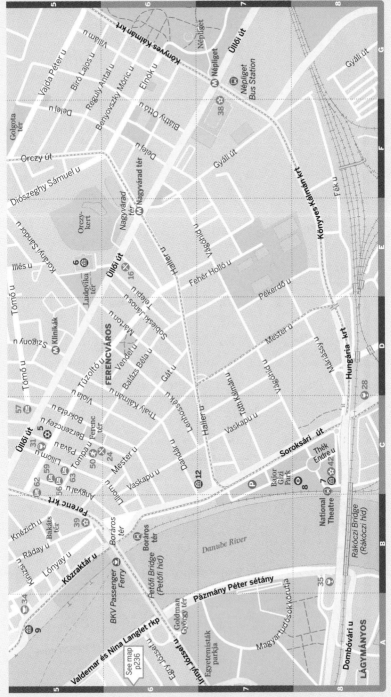

Könyves Kálmán krt

Villám u

Varga Péter u

Biró Lajos u

Reguly Antal u

Benyovszky Móric u

Deléj u

Elnök u

Biróy Ottó u

Golgota tér

Orczy út

Diószeghy Sámuel u

Illés u

Kőbányi Sándor u

Orczy-kert

Nagyvárad tér

Deléj u

Haller u

Gyáli út

Üllői út

Népliget

Üllői út

M Népliget

Népliget Bus Station

Gyáli út

Könyves Kálmán krt

Fék u

Vágóhíd u

Fehér Holló u

Pékerdő u

M Nagyvárad tér

38

Ludovika tér

6

16

Tömő u

M Klinikák

Szigony u

Tömő u

FERENCVÁROS

Tűzoltó u

Márton u

Bokréta u

Sobieski u

Telepi u

Vendel u

Balázs Béla u

Gát u

Lenhossék u

Viola u

Thaly Kálmán u

Haller u

Tóth Kálmán u

Vaskapu u

Mester u

Vágóhíd u

Máriássy u

Mester u

Hungária krt

28

Berzenczey u

Ferenc tér

Pava u

Tompa u

Danube u

Dandár u

Soroksári út

Thék Endre u

57

5

31

Üllői út

Lilliom u

59

62

63

56

Anyai u

Ferenc krt

50

24

Mester u

Lilliom u

Vaskapu u

42

12

8

7

Bajor Gizi Park

National Theatre

Rákóczi Bridge (Rákóczi híd)

Knézich u

Bakáts tér

39

Ráday u

Lónyay u

Kinizsi u

Köztraktár u

Boráros tér

Boráros tér

Petőfi Bridge (Petőfi híd)

BKV Passenger Ferry

Danube River

35

34

9

Valdemar és Nina Langlet rkp

Irinyi József u

Goldman György tér

Pázmány Péter sétány

Egyetemisták parkja

Magyar tudósok körútja

Dombóvári u

LÁGYMÁNYOS

See map p236

PARLIAMENT & AROUND

Key on p246

200 m
0.1 miles

Danube River

ÚJLIPÓTVÁROS

LIPÓTVÁROS

TERÉZVÁROS

Nyugati Train Station

Nyugati pu M

Nyugati tér

Parliament

Kossuth Lajos tér

See map p248

See map p230

See map p250

Váci út

Szent István krt

Balcsy-Zsilinszky út

Teréz krt

Antall József rkp

Széchenyi rkp

Antall József rkp

Izabella u

Vörösmarty u

Csengery u

Eötvös u

Aradi u

Szondi u

Szobi u

Szinyei u

Podmaniczky u

Jókai u

Weiner Leó u

Podmaniczky u

Dessewffy u

Lovag u

Jókai u

Kádár u

Kresz Géza u

Katona József u

Tátra u

Pannónia u

Hegedűs Gyula u

Visegrádi u

Vadász u

Báthory u

Alkotmány u

Kálmán Imre u

Honvéd u

Báthory u

Kozma F u

Vajkay u

Szalay u

Szemere u

Markó u

Nagy Ignác u

Bihari János u

Stollár Béla u

Honvéd tér

Balaton u

Falk Miksa u

Balassi Bálint u

Markó u

59
91
75
93
85
10
36
68
38
87
97
57
55
44
81
73
69
61
79
20
4
2

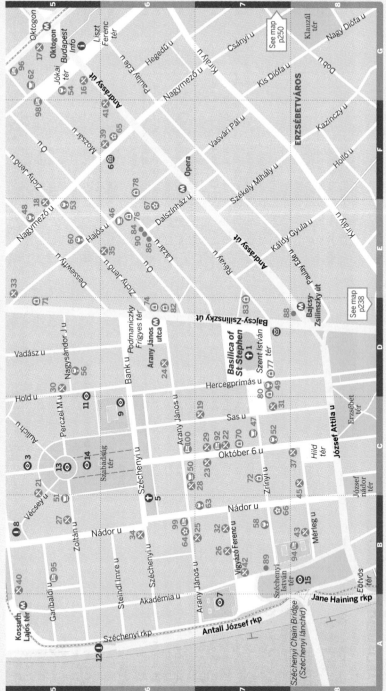

Oktogon
Oktogon
17
96
62
Budapest Info
Liszt Ferenc tér
Jókai tér
54
16
98
Hegedű u
Paulay Ede u
Nagymező u
Király u
Csányi u
Dob u
Klauzál tér
Nagy Diófa u
ERZSÉBETVÁROS
See map p250
Kis Diófa u
41
39
65
Andrássy út
Mozsár u
6
Vasvári Pál u
Székely Mihály u
Kazinczy u
Holló u
Király u
Opera
78
67
Dalszínház u
Székely Mihály u
Andrássy út
33
71
48
18
53
60
35
46
76
84
90
86
Hajós u
Lázár u
Ó u
Révay u
Káldy Gyula u
Paulay Ede u
Nagymező u
Dessewffy u
Zichy Jenő u
Ó u
Zichy Jenő u
83
88
Bajcsy-Zsilinszky út
See map p238
Bajcsy-Zsilinszky
74
73
82
Vadász u
Nagysándor J u
56
Bank u
Podmaniczky Frigyes tér
Arany János utca
24
Basilica of St Stephen
Szent István tér
77 tér
Hercegprímás u
Hold u
30
Perczel M u
11
9
Arany János u
19
Sas u
80
49
31
Aulich u
3
14
13
Szabadság u
Széchenyi u
5
100
29
92
22
70
47
52
Október 6 u
50
28
23
72
Zrínyi u
37
Hild tér
József Attila u
Erzsébet tér
József nádor tér
8
21
51
27
Vécsey u
Zoltán u
Nádor u
34
99
25
64
26
32
58
66
45
Mérleg u
94
43
Vígyázó Ferenc u
89
József nádor tér
Kossuth Lajos tér
40
95
Garibaldi u
Steindl Imre u
Széchenyi u
Arany János u
Nádor u
42
Széchenyi István tér
15
Akadémia u
7
Eötvös tér
Jane Haining rkp
12
2
Széchenyi rkp
Antall József rkp
Széchenyi Chain Bridge (Széchenyi lánchíd)

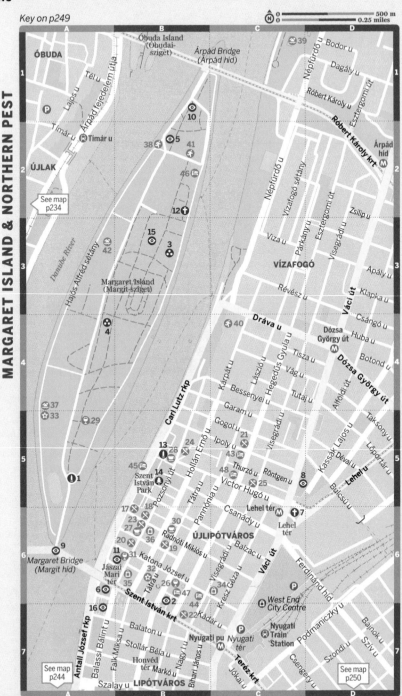

MARGARET ISLAND & NORTHERN PEST

0   500 m
0   0.25 miles

ÓBUDA

Óbuda Island
(Óbudai-sziget)

Árpád Bridge
(Árpád híd)

ÚJLAK

See map
p234

Danube River

Margaret Island
(Margit-sziget)

Róbert Károly krt

Árpád
híd

VÍZAFOGÓ

Váci út

Dózsa
György út

Dózsa György út

Carl Lutz rkp

ÚJLIPÓTVÁROS

Szent
István
Park

Váci út

Lehel tér

Lehel
tér

West End
City Centre

Nyugati
Train
Station

Margaret Bridge
(Margit híd)

Jászai
Mari
tér

Szent István krt

Ferdinánd híd

Nyugati pu

Nyugati
tér

Antal József rkp

LIPÓTVÁROS

Honvéd
tér

Teréz krt

See map
p244

See map
p250

MARGARET ISLAND & NORTHERN PEST

ERZSÉBETVÁROS & THE JEWISH QUARTER

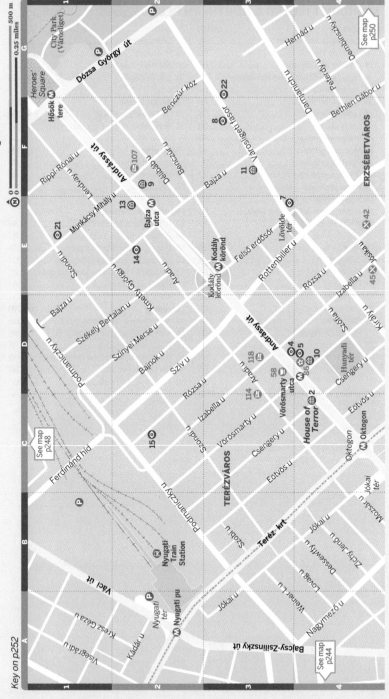

Key on p252

0   0.25 miles
0   500 m

See map p252
See map p248
See map p250
See map p244

City Park (Városliget)
Heroes' Square
Hősök tere

Dózsa György út

Benczúr köz
Benczúr u

Rippl-Rónai u
Lendvay u

Munkácsy Mihály u

Andrássy út

Delibáb u

Bajza u

Városligeti fasor

Hernád u

Damjanich u

Bethlen Gábor u

Pethényi u

Dembinszky u

ERZSÉBETVÁROS

Szondi u

Bajza u

Székely Bertalan u

Szinyei Merse u

Bajnok u

Szív u

Rózsa u

Izabella u

Vörösmarty u

Csengery u

Eötvös u

TERÉZVÁROS

Kmety György u

Aradi u

Felső erdősor u

Lövölde tér

Rottenbiller u

Rózsa u

Izabella u

Király u

Szófia u

Jósika u

Kodály körönd

Andrássy út

Hunyadi tér

Csengery u

Eötvös u

Vörösmarty utca

Andrássy út

House of Terror

Oktogon

Teréz krt

Jókai u

Jókai tér

Mozsár u

Zichy Jenő u

Dessewffy u

Lovag u

Weiner L u

Nagymező u

Jókai u

Szobi u

Podmaniczky u

Vörösmarty u

Ferdinánd híd

Nyugati Train Station

Nyugati pu

Nyugati tér

Váci út

Kresz Géza u

Kádár u

Visegrádi u

Viségrádi u

Balcsy-Zsilinszky út

21
13
14
15
107
9
8
22
11
7
42
45
4
5
10
86
118
58
114
2

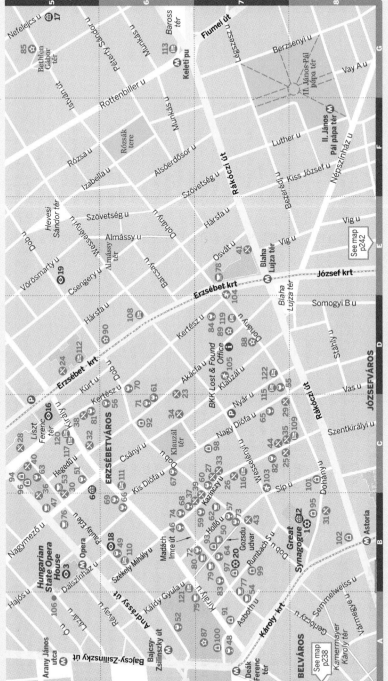

A | B | C | D

1

Lehel u

Jász u

Kerekes u

Rákosrendező

Teleki Blanka u

M3

LŐPORTÁRDŰLŐ

Róbert Károly krt

Szent László u

Dévényi u

BVSC

Szabolcs u

Mohács u

2

Vágány u

Varannó u

Szőnyi út

Mexikói út

Dorozsmai u

Amerikai út

8 27

7

Állatkerti krt

8 Széchenyi Baths

26

Széchenyi fürdő

Hungária krt

Kolumbusz u

Mexikói út

Kős Károly sétány

Hermina út

Gundel Károly út

17 18

20

Museum of Fine Arts

3

Városligeti krt

Liezen-Mayer sétány

Pálma u

3

Heroes' Square

1

2 Millenary Monument

11

6

25

Andrássy út

Hősök tere

13

32

21

9

Városliget-tő

31

30

16

12

Délibáb u

33

P

15

14

City Park (Városliget)

Zichy Mihály út

Benczúr u

Olof Palme sétány

24

Ajtósi Dürer sor

Hermina út

4

P

5

Zichy Géza u

Ajtósi Dürer sor

Dvořák sétány

Stefánia út

22

Városligeti fasor

Dózsa György út

Városligeti krt

23

5

See map p250

Damjanich u

Ajtósi Dürer sor

Abonyi u

Izsó u

Péterdy u

Dembinszky u

Császár András u

Thököly út

ERZSÉBETVÁROS

Marek József u

István út

Cserhát u

Sajó u

10

6

Rottenbiller u

Bethlen Gábor u

Nefelejcs u

Péterfy Sándor u

Hernád u

Murányi u

Garay tér

Alpár u

19

Istvánmezei út

28

Garay u

Thököly út

Százház u

Jobbágy u

7

Munkás u

Munkás u

Keleti pu

Baross tér

Keleti Train Station

Versenyu

See map p242

Kerepesi út

Dózsa György út

A | B | C | D

0 ——————— 500 m
0 ——————— 0.25 miles

CITY PARK & BEYOND

Our Story

A beat-up old car, a few dollars in the pocket and a sense of adventure. In 1972 that's all Tony and Maureen Wheeler needed for the trip of a lifetime – across Europe and Asia overland to Australia. It took several months, and at the end – broke but inspired – they sat at their kitchen table writing and stapling together their first travel guide, *Across Asia on the Cheap*. Within a week they'd sold 1500 copies. Lonely Planet was born.

Today, Lonely Planet has offices in Franklin, London, Melbourne, Oakland, Beijing and Delhi, with more than 600 staff and writers. We share Tony's belief that 'a great guidebook should do three things: inform, educate and amuse'.

Our Writers

Steve Fallon

Coordinating author, Castle District, Gellért Hill & Tabán, Óbuda & Buda Hills, Parliament & Around, Margaret Island & Northern Pest, Day Trips from Budapest Steve, who has worked on every edition of Lonely Planet's *Budapest*, first visited Magyarország in the early 1980s by chance – he'd stopped off on his way to Poland to buy bananas for his friends' children. It was a brief visit but he immediately fell in love with thermal baths, Tokaj wine and *bableves* (bean soup). Unable to survive on the occasional fleeting fix, he moved to Budapest in 1992, where he could enjoy all three in abundance and *magyarul* (in Hungarian). Now based in London, Steve returns to Hungary regularly for all these things and more: *pálinka*, Art Nouveau, the haunting voice of Marta Sebestyén and the best nightlife in Central Europe. Steve also wrote the Plan Your Trip section (with the exception of the Drinking & Nightlife category overview), plus the Understand Budapest section and the Survival Guide, and co-wrote the Sleeping chapter.

Read more about Steve at:
lonelyplanet.com/members/stevefallon

Sally Schafer

Belváros, Erzsébetváros & the Jewish Quarter, Southern Pest, City Park & Beyond Sally first visited Budapest in 2004 when she discovered ruin pubs and danced by the Danube till dawn. This research trip gave her the chance to rediscover old haunts and get locked into some new ones. Sally has worked for Lonely Planet since 2000 in a variety of guises and written about countless global destinations. Sally also wrote the Drinking & Nightlife category overview, and co-wrote the Sleeping chapter.

Published by Lonely Planet Publications Pty Ltd
ABN 36 005 607 983
6th edition – March 2015
ISBN 978 1 74321 003 1
© Lonely Planet 2015   Photographs © as indicated 2015
10 9 8 7 6 5 4 3 2 1
Printed in China

Although the authors and Lonely Planet have taken all reasonable care in preparing this book, we make no warranty about the accuracy or completeness of its content and, to the maximum extent permitted, disclaim all liability arising from its use.